CO[LLECTORS]

Ex[pressions of Self and Other]

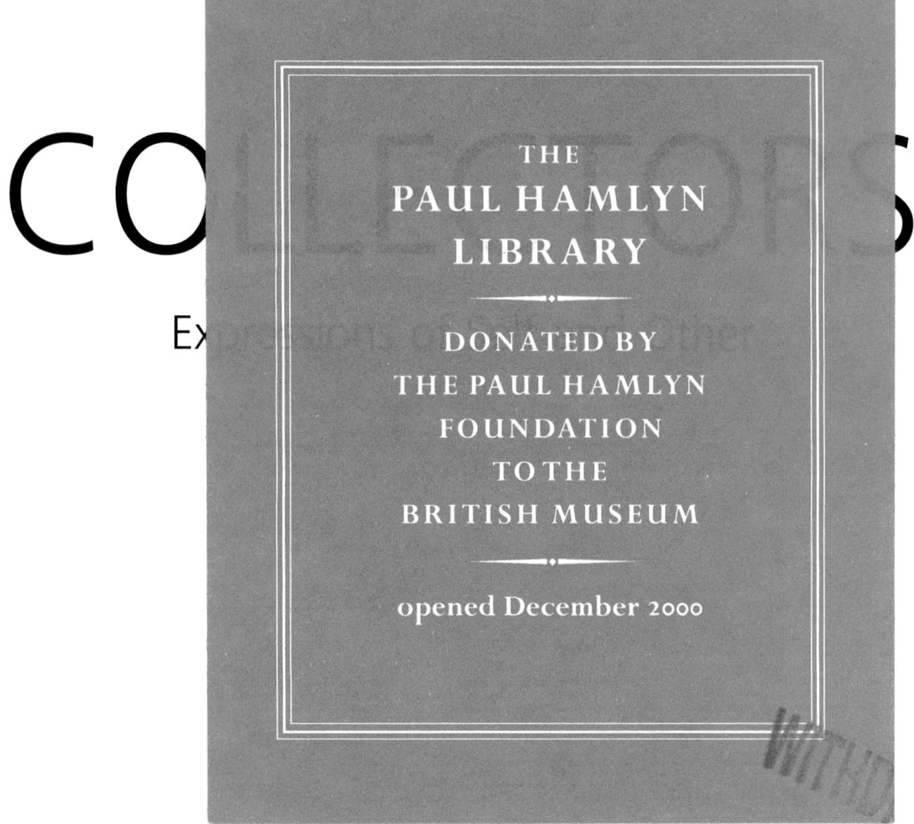

Contributions in Critical Museology and Material Culture

COLLECTORS

Expressions of Self and Other

Edited by

Anthony Shelton

The Horniman Museum and Gardens, London

Museu Antroplógico da Universidade de Coimbra

Contributions in Critical Museology and Material Culture is produced by the Horniman Museum and Gardens, London and The Museu Antropológico da Universidade de Coimbra.

Production
Daria Neklesa

Set in Adobe Garamond 10.5/14.5
Printed in Singapore
The publisher does not accept any responsibility for the opinions expressed by the authors in this book.

ISBN 0-9518141-7-6

Contents

Foreword

There is an academic suspicion that museums are replete with artefacts that are seldom ever seen. These collections may be desired as cultural property and may be the focus of restitution claims, but still we know so little about how they were formed or why they should now command our attention. Scratch the surface and museum practitioners will assert that the purpose of museums is to conserve and study collections. Investigating the paradox between collections and access to them as the justification of the existence of museums and the fact that we know so little about them is the purpose of this volume of essays.

The starting point is that all collections are unique entities and the museums that hold them add a further dimension to their special characters and individual biographies. Working from this premise, every collection has to be taken on its own terms. Researching the collection rather than conducting research on the material elements that constitute the collection, seems to be an interrogative act. In the majority of cases, it is not clear how they were formed or why they have survived. Collectors were instrumental to this in the past but collections escape this constraint and take on a life of their own. But what do we make of them and how do we justify the costs of maintaining them?

The papers in this volume may not provide immediate or easy answers to such interrogation. In some cases, visions of some totalising paradigm are plainly discernible but in others, collections are glosses on fragments unified by name. The fact that collections have histories beyond their collectors further obfuscates their representational value. If museums partially function to gather together and preserve material that would be dispersed or lost to posterity, the bittersweet irony is that they often wilfully or negligently abandon the collector in the midsts of time. Perhaps the individual is not so much lost by the institution but usurped, as the Museum takes on the role of collector. Perhaps museums are a subordinate presence in this collection of essays because this historical misdemeanour is at long last being righted and collectors, rescued from anonymity.

Professor Michael Rowlands
University College London

A distribution map illustrating different styles in the carving of Yoruba Ibejis.
(Photograph: Horniman Museum)

Preface

This volume grew out of the first Horniman Research Conference, *Collections and Innovations*, held in 1997. The conference focused on the means, motivations, and purposes behind collecting and the ability of collections to communicate alternative messages beyond those they were originally intended to illustrate. *Collections and Innovations* was organised at a time when the Museum was preparing to re-display its extensive ethnographic collections and looking forward to a possible large scale re-building project which would provide additional galleries and facilities. One of the core ideas behind the design for the proposed new building, was that it should help re-orientate the Museum away from the busy London Road, towards the extensive gardens which surround it, thereby re-integrating the outside botanical collections with the zoological, ethnographic, and musicology collections displayed in its interior. Faced with such wide ranging potential changes which not only promised additional and larger galleries and the refurbishment of others, but raised questions about what constituted a collection, and the ways collections could be used to communicate meaning, we invited a broad range of museum professionals drawn from natural history, anthropology, musicology, contemporary arts, and public service departments, to debate the nature and uses to which collections had and could be put. When it came to publish the papers, it was decided, for reasons of coherency, to focus solely on those areas most strongly represented at the conference; those of anthropology and musicology.

These core papers were complemented by additional work that over the last few years had been generated by a concerted curatorial research project on the history of the Horniman's own collections, as well as work undertaken in the Art History subject group, and between 1996-1998, in the postgraduate research programme in Critical Museology, taught by Museum staff at the University of Sussex. To those who supported research in collection history at Sussex, I would like to convey my deep appreciation.

The collected papers which constitute this volume have their origin in the kindness, patience, enthusiasm and commitment of many persons. I would like to thank Michael Houlihan, now director of the National Museums of Ulster who supported and provided funding for the first Horniman Research Conference, and Janet Vitmayer, our present director, for making them into an annual event; Professor Roger Silverstone, who as director of the Research Centre in Culture and Communication at the University of Sussex was an erstwhile advocate of the Critical Museology programme and co-operation with the Horniman Museum; Kirsten Walker who organised the first conference, and Claire West who designed and produced publicity material. David Allen and Anne James of the Horniman Library provided extensive bibliographical assistance; Ken Teague and Nicky Levell helped with mailing, registration and the general running of the conference; Margot Granger undertook a thousand kindnesses, and Ms. Daria Neklesa who, as usual, has done an outstanding job in designing and producing the accompanying publication. I would like to thank all the staff of the Horniman Museum for their enthusiasm and help in making this first conference such a success and, nearly four years onwards, for their continued support of the publication which disseminates its proceedings.

Anthony Shelton

Introduction: The Return of the Subject

Anthony Shelton

The work of museums and collectors forms a strange paradox. Though apparently sharing a common set of interests, writers from Walter Benjamin in 1931 (1973: 67) to Nicholas Thomas (1994: 116) have acknowledged different and distinctive motives underlying their actions. Indeed, the intellectual gulf that distinguishes between institutions and individuals sometimes mirrors an attempted physical segregation: one which may lead collectors to feel that their presence is unwanted in some of the museums that have benefited from either their own generosity or that of their forbears. On more than one occasion, I can recall museum personnel taking flight after being informed that a collector had turned-up unannounced for an expected audience; while the sudden appearance of other collectors or dealers was greeted with sighs of weary resignation. Even in 1931 Benjamin noted that the passionate collector was thought of as 'behind the times' and regarded with distrust by the population at large (1973: 66). The time is past, in the United Kingdom at least, when a director or keeper of a national collection could, without any apparent conflict of interest, write for books and magazines supportive of private collecting, serve as a consultant for related commercial interests and still collect for himself/herself, while receiving both academic and curatorial accolades. What historically was a symbiotic relationship, is today, when collecting is more popular than ever before, even more likely to be saturated with ethical ambiguity, distrust over intentions, and ambivalence about the psychological motivations attributed to collectors. After all, what common purposes could possibly relate state or municipal museums with collecting which, as has been argued (Baudrillard 1994: 9), represents nothing less than a regression to the anal stage of childhood?

Differences between museums and private collectors have been determined using varied criteria. Museums portray themselves as economically disinterested, with public and intellectual obligations that far transcend narrow social or financial concerns and commitments. Collectors on the other hand, acknowledge participation in the market to acquire material from auction houses, galleries, dealers, and sometimes associates in foreign lands. They buy, barter, and exchange, sometimes blurring the boundaries between suppliers, sellers and purchasers. They operate in a complex, liminal terrain that museums abhor. Their situation is made even more ambiguous by the rules of discretion, that operate in an art market which relies to a great degree on an oral rather than a written tradition. The art market is regulated, at best, by a code of honour: dates of acquisition, authenticity and provenance of a work are acceded to on the basis of the collector's or dealer's known integrity; good legal title is accepted on their word; the beauty or worth of an object is usually agreed by a consensus of 'tutored' opinion. Unlike the intellectual distance between museum curators and their collections, collectors, or so it is claimed, indulge in an ecstasy and passion that enables them to live through the objects they possess.

Collections, according to Cardinal (this volume) are attempted memory systems. 'Every passion' according to Benjamin, 'borders on the chaotic, but the collector's passion borders on the chaos of memories' (Benjamin 1973: 60). Whether, through word of mouth, taste, or aesthetic consensus the object of the collector's desire becomes the focus of diverse interests, political mediations, economic negotiations and attributed connoisseurial or psychological dispositions - all of which fall outside the carefully regulated written and codified culture to which the museum ascribes. The achievement of acquisitive desire places the collector, alongside his collection, in an interstitial space, between the valuable and the invaluable, between past and present, between the near and the far, between reason and passion, between serial rationality and the fragments of memory, between absence and possession. Such a position is well described in Jeffrey's description of the life of Leon Underwood (this volume), who not only wove together his own art and the visual culture of Africa or pre-Columbian America, but provided an originary point for the twin emergence of British primitivism and the scholarly study of African art history. This attitude is not, in my opinion, not so far removed from the feelings that, sometimes, curators also share (Shelton this volume).

Against this world of human passions and foibles, the museum presents itself as an idealised bureaucratic regime exercising a detached mastery over the legitimating narratives it attaches to its holdings. Its operations have been compared with those of the penitentiary where a disciplinary regime, exercised through the control of vision and signification, constructs and transmits models of exemplary behaviour, gesture and respect which it deems worthy of emulation (Bennett 1995: 61). Theodor Adorno has adopted the term 'museal' to describe objects alienated from the everyday experience of their viewers. Museum objects, stripped of the personal narratives that their previous owners ascribed them, occupy a twilight world, ordered by the rules of an institutionalised knowledge harnessed by the liberal state. For Benjamin, curatorial work - the tracing of the strategies behind acquisitions, the classifications adopted to order material, the museum's history or the uses to which it has been put - are nothing but arbitrary and digressive distractions, '... merely a dam against the spring tide of memories' invested in objects by their former owners (1973: 60).

Despite the museum's attempt to banish the personality of the passionate collector, it nevertheless continues to be dependent on his or her labours and generosity. This seeming paradox has attemptedly been resolved by the formulation of modalities or typologies of collections, based on the dispositions of those that assembled them. Within such typologies, some modes of collecting are more highly valued than others, providing museums with the possibility of selectively identifying themselves with an activity that has become increasingly more ambiguous. Susan Stewart distinguishes between the souvenir, an object redolent with feelings of nostalgia and longing acquired through its ability to interiorise and domesticate external space and condense personal experience (1993: 134-5), and the collection; '... a form of art as play, a form involving the reframing of objects within a world of attention and manipulation of context' (Ibid: 151). The collection expresses classification in place of history, it replaces temporality with order, producing an assemblage of objects whose use value has undergone complete aestheticisation. Within the category of 'collection' Stewart distinguishes the two modalities of antiquarianism and mercantile aesthetics (Ibid: 153); the first devoted to restoration, while the second works to extract and serialise objects into orders and sequences. Elsner and Cardinal, agreeing with Stewart, argue that classification precedes collection.

> *... the plenitude of taxonomy opens up the space for collectibles to be identified, but at the same time the plenitude of that which is to be collected hastens the need to classify.... And if classification is the mirror of collective humanity's thoughts and perceptions, then collection is its material embodiment. Collection is classification lived, experienced in three dimensions. The history of collecting is thus the narrative of how human beings have striven to accommodate, to appropriate and to extend the taxonomies and systems of knowledge they have inherited* (1994: 2).

A more boldly, prescriptive typology distinguishing between systematic, fetishistic and souvenir collections has been proposed by Susan Pearce (1992: 68-9), a past president of the Museums Association. The first of these categories is attributed scientific status, while the other two are determined by the personal predilections of those that have assembled them. Despite its seemingly mechanistic formulation, Pearce nevertheless agrees that most collectors are motivated, to some degree, by all three dispositions.

With few exceptions, museum-based scholarship still prefers collectors who were committed to some systematic form of acquisition, those to whom it can attribute a disinterested motivation and/or a scientific pedigree - Franz Boas, Stewart Cullin, Alfred Cort Haddon, Emil Torday, Alfred Maudslay, Augustus Franks, Pitt Rivers, while the magpies, adventurers, plunderers, and trophy hunters have been incorporated and obscured within the wider histories of the repositories which hold their collections.[1] Non-systematic collections, once institutionalised in museums, may be combined and classified into new and coherent object systems that loose all reference to the conditions surrounding their original acquisition.What distinguishes museum collections from private collections, according to the Museums Association's, *A Manual of Curatorship*, is that objects are '... assembled and maintained within a specific intellectual environment' (Cannon-Brookes 1984: 115). After emphasising '... that museums are storehouses of knowledge as well as storehouses of objects, ...' the manual warns us that 'the whole exercise is liable to be futile unless the accumulation of objects is strictly rational' (Ibid: 116). New acquisitions are recommended on the basis of their ability to throw light on existing objects and bring about a revision in their understanding (Ibid), a view that aids the closure of the hermeneutic circle that the museum creates. Strangely, such a view also implies that the definition of a museum object or collection is always retrospective, an imposition made by the institutional beneficiary itself. This supports Fabian's (1998: 98) provocative contention that the acquisition of ethnographic collections has followed a sequence from commodification, to collection, to interpretation.

Museums not only efface the individual biographies of objects, but also reduce the semiotic relationship between signifiers and signifieds to its classic Saussurian expression. The possibility of different semiotic relationships is excluded as the object is collapsed into merely one representation among others. Museum representations seek to deny that the sign marks only an arbitrary localisation of meaning within an open ended process of signification, confining the epistemological value of all its objects to what Baudrillard has termed the counterfeit simulacra. Other orders of simulacra, production, simulation and the viral (Baudrillard 1984: 61 and Baudrillard 1993: 6) in which the relationship between signs and signifieds may involve a conflation of the two terms, or a replacement of the secondary order of supposedly objectively constituted signifieds by the free, endless and arbitrary self-referentiality and play of signs, are ignored. It is doubtful whether all artefacts from outside the modern western cannon were produced to be viewed as simple representations. Within the western museum context, classical semiotics allows either the signifier or signified, the word or its sensum or object to be privileged, producing what have become termed as aesthetic or ethnographic exhibitionary genres. However, MacGaffey notes that some classes of African artefacts, need to be understood as conflating signifier and signified and might better be regarded as being more like texts than objects. *Minkisi*, consist of medicines combined together to hold a spirit from the realm of the dead. They have been described as 'portable graves' (MacGaffey 1993: 61). The container to hold the medicine, may be a bundle, pot, a stuffed horn or a figurative carving. In all cases however, the importance or relevance of the container is subordinated to that of the particular mixture of earths, organic material, animal parts, etc. which gives it its ability to attract and hold an animating spirit. In this sense it is both signified and signifier. However, MacGaffey further argues that the ingredients from which the medicine is made, are partly chosen on the basis of Kongo word puns based on phonetic similarities between the names of ingredients and the desired powers and qualities expected from them. The original meaning of *minkisi* can better be understood by considering them as texts, instead of objects, even less artistic objects, as they have been represented in museums (MacGaffey 1998: 231).

According to one common professional position, the most important distinction between museums and previously institutionalised or existing private collections, is that between scientific rationalism and individual predilection; objectivity and subjectivity; the institutionally sanctioned representation of knowledge and the subject's individual expression of his or her world. Within the semantic field composed by these binary oppositions, museums are predicated on their ability to convey objective representations which ignore the conditions of their generation, including their localisation within regional and global political, economic, and scientific strategies (Nuno Porto, this volume). Despite the view of history museums attempt to represent, it is already commonly acknowledged that even early historical collections were made under existent or emerging market conditions, which in many cases determined the style and availability of material culture. European collectors of Pacific curiosities, in Fiji for example, operated under market conditions which were well established by the 1870s (Thomas 1991: 170). Similarly, the work of early 20th century collectors in Africa -

Frobenius, Torday and Starr, who endowed Hamburg's Museum für Völkerkunde, the British Museum and the American Museum of Natural History respectively - also took place in an already developed African market (Schildkrout and Keim 1991, 1998). Such historical studies, and others like them on the American Southwest, the Northwest coast (Batkin 1999; Cole 1985) and elsewhere, underline the importance of commodification as a pre-condition for collecting. Collecting, whether conducted by institutions or private individuals, could never be anything but compromised by the milieu in which it occurred (Fabian 1998: 88). Even so-called systematic collections were, therefore, limited by availability and the inter-cultural terms of agreement over what was or wasn't an exchangeable commodity. Given such pre-conditions underlying the collection of ethnographic objects destined for museums and the inevitable effect these could not help but have on any successive museum representation, it is difficult to dispute Bourdieu and Passeron's insistence on the ultimate arbitrary nature of the pedagogic authority which underlie all pedagogic actions (1977: 5).

If museums have instituted certain lacunae in their acknowledgement of some of the collectors that have contributed to their public holdings; collectors, according to Cardinal (this volume), cannot so easily ignore the importance of the catalogue, a device perfected by museums to codify and express their authority, which can also be used to provide the explicit expression of a collector's intentions. Museums, no less than private collectors, exist between the two opposed poles of order and disorder.

The re-focusing of museums on the representation of rational rather than personal knowledge, which has provided the criteria for distinguishing between valid and invalid motives of collectors, and legitimate and illegitimate collecting and collections, had its origin in the Enlightenment ideal of '... the exhibit as a school for instruction through perceptual patterning' (Stafford 1994: 218). Public display was to ensure every specimen, and its relation to similar specimens was to be made immediately obvious to the spectator (Ibid: 263). The advent of rationalism in museum displays also prompted a re-focus, away from the extraordinary to the ordinary, albeit an ordinariness that could no longer be grasped simply through untutored observation, but was unlockable only by the emergent role of the expert curator.

> *Analysis meant that material things were decomposed into their normal or customary elements and then recomposed into a superior system knowable only through intellect, not perception* (Ibid: 266).

These new systems and strategies were applied to the re-organisation of the French *cabinet d' histoire naturelle* from as early as 1745. In England, it was not until after various members of the British Society for the Advancement of Science and, after 1889 when it was founded, the Museums Association, attacked curiosity collections as next to useless, that techniques for constructing orders and seriations became widely adopted for arranging specimens in local museums. Although even Buffon had shied away from the complete re-ordering of specimens according to taxonomic criteria, and retained some of the popular older baroque aesthetic displays, in England, by the end of the 19th century, curiosity or aestheticised displays had fallen victim to the professionalisation of the country's museums. This shift from curiosity to scientific criteria in museum collecting is described in four papers in this volume. Tythacott describes how Liverpool Museum, under the direction of Forbes and Clubb, both natural scientists, intervened to re-direct Ridyard's burgeoning African collections away from exotic Kongo power figures to the more mundane manifestations of 'simple' technology. At the Horniman Museum in London, the collections acquired through the personal taste and predilections of its founder were combined or substituted with others that were required to illustrate the laws of cultural evolution as expounded by Alfred Cort Haddon (Birley, Shelton and Teague, this volume). Elsewhere, however, despite modernising influences, museums like the Powell-Cotton, have retained an inexplicable Edwardian aura (Nicklin, this volume), while others, such as Exeter's Royal Albert Memorial Museum, aspired from its foundation to be nothing other than a scientific and educational institution in the service of rational illustration (Levell, this volume).

Rationalisation has had indelible practical and intellectual consequences not only on collections but more generally on the shape of the European museum movement. Rationalisation in Britain not only meant the visual re-ordering of existing collections, but the widespread displacement of material between museums. The Museums Association had long campaigned for such rationalisation and a Department of Science and Education report of 1973 backed their previous submission to establish key museums as regional centres of excellence. Collections were scrutinised according to what they contained rather than their inimical relationships to local collectors and regional histories. Many regional and local museums lost important specialist collections, particularly ethnographic items which were given to larger museums with a then active focus and curatorial expertise in those areas. Parts of the ethnographic collections of Bethnal Green, the Cuming Museum, Cardiff, Leicester, Canterbury and Reading were absorbed by the Horniman Museum during the 1950-70s; part of the collections once held by Ipswich (1966), Abingdon (1969), Wellcome (1985), and Hampshire Museum Service (1994), were incorporated into the holdings of the Pitt Rivers Museum; the Weston Super Mare collections were transferred to Exeter in 1994; Salford's collections were passed-on to Manchester Museum in 1979, and Truro transferred material to the British Museum in 1986. In some instances, museums happily sold or exchanged ethnographic items for other material which they decided was of greater relevance. A number of collections, it is rumoured, may even have been wilfully destroyed. Some of the smaller, arguably more prudent provincial museums, which did maintain part or all of their holdings, were left with collections derived principally from one or just a few sources - Hastings with the Grey Owl and Brassey collections, or Maidenhead with the Brenchley collection.

Paradoxically, by not deaccessioning some of the larger significant collections made by sole benefactors, museums more clearly exposed the strong nexus they had enjoyed with private individuals and their collections. Left with only very specific or remnant collections, museums significantly narrowed the range of exhibition strategies open to them. Few options existed but to display their remaining material as either art, curiosity, or biographical history. Most chose the latter.

In the few cases where an institution had larger and wider ethnographic holdings, like Exeter, Warrington, Brighton or Ipswich, they attempted geographical displays of the type recommended for the nationals (Coombes 1994: 117). A few larger museums, Glasgow, Bristol, and the British Museum, maintained an active scholarly focus on collectors, but by and large, like the Seligman collection discussed by Levell, collections were usually broken-up, stored according to some extraneous classificatory system (geographical, cultural, chronological or functional), scattered around galleries as part of serial or typological displays or exhibited alone for aesthetic effect.[2] Their donor's histories although preserved, in the institutional memory, was largely erased in their public presentation.

Alongside the effacement of the personalities of the collectors that put museum collections together, reigns a notable silence regarding gender. In the absence of comparative historical case studies on male and female collectors, typological generalisations have flourished. Many of the distinctions made between male and female collectors, based on domestic and scientific acquisition or emotionally invested and disinterested collecting, follow easily recognisable and discredited stereotypes. Three papers in this volume provide specific case studies in which such generalisations have been examined. Levell compares the collections assembled by Brenda Seligman to those of her husband, Charles Seligman; Cheang analyses the motivations behind an apparent serial collection of Dogs of Fo, made by Ellen Stafford and preserved in her former home, Preston Manor in Brighton; while West isolates certain diverse themes, including the predilections of women collectors, which lie behind the Horniman's collection of Naga material culture.

The growth of collections history and critical museology, which have applied insights from anthropology, sociology, psychoanalysis, history, critical theory and other disciplines, provide the basis for a much more sophisticated understanding and appraisal of museums and their collections. Simple and crude oppositions between positive objectification and subjective knowledge are now better acknowledged. Furthermore, exhibitions on ethnographic collectors, like those opened in Brighton (1994), Manchester (1995), Aberdeen (1995) and the Horniman (2001), as well as Walsall's pioneering work on peoples' shows, have demonstrated the public demand and appreciation of exhibitions that look at the subjective motivations underlying collecting.

Studies of collectors and collecting have greatly increased in recent years, stimulated by Impey and MacGregor's pioneering volume, *The Origins of Museums* (1985), and the founding of *The Journal of the History of Collections* (1989). In the main, scholarly studies of collecting fall into one of three approaches; psychological universalising, represented by Werner Muensterberger's *Collecting: An Unruly Passion* (1994), an approach which has long been used by the museum profession to justify accumulative activity and their institution's ancient origins. Second, historical studies, illustrated by Impey and MacGregor's own works, as well as those of Mack (1990, 1997, 1998), McLeod (1977), Bassani and McLeod (1989), Wilson (1984), etc. which focus on the evidential value of collections, and, third, an approach most eloquently exemplified by Stephen Bann (1994), which combines elements from social psychology and history to describes how objects are used to constitute self-identity.

This latter school of enquiry is particularly germane to the proper appreciation of museum collections since, in one of its forms, it looks at objects as signs which are manipulated for creating personal or institutional biographies. Bann demonstrates how a few unremarkable and apparently unrelated objects, assembled together in a 17th century cabinet preserved in Canterbury Cathedral, collectively possess relevance as witnesses to some of the main constituting events of the life of the Kentish traveller, writer and collector, John Bargrave. According to Bann;

> *... the collector is not merely an attribute of the self but also, in a real sense, the model through which the unity of the self is, progressively and retrospectively, achieved. To travel is ... to reinforce identity through a return to the same, which is also an enrichment. To collect is to consolidate identity, through a retrospective specification of fragments, which is also the discursive articulation of those fragments as part of a personal narrative* (1994: 78).

The richest and most pertinent of discourses which sets the person in his or her social and cultural milieu can be extracted from even the smallest of collections, conscientiously and unselfishly preserved and cared for by museums or other institutions.

There is no option between objective and subjective knowledge. All objects, and by extension, collections of objects, carry a double-edged meaning. One system of meaning refers to the circumstances and strategies surrounding acquisition - the field of personal biography mediated by political, social, economic and scientific currents; the unique and unrepeatable act of launching '... individual desire across the intertext of environment and history' (Cardinal 1994: 68); the intimate narrative that makes a 'continuous thread through which selfhood is sewn into the unfolding fabric of a lifetime's experience' (Ibid). The second system of meaning pertains to an object's evidential value, which has been constructed by the particular meta-narrative to which it has been subordinated. However, these two sides of the coin are rarely separable to the extent that public narratives would have us believe. 'When you leave fiction, you re-discover fictions' (Culler 1994: 97); '... collectors are the physiognomists of the world of objects' (Benjamin. Ibid). 'Everything remembered and thought, everything conscious' becomes invested in the object making '... the whole background of an item ... a magic encyclopaedia' (Ibid). Johannes Fabian, emphasising that scientific travel and museum collecting trips ' ... were anything but rational in the sense of being self-controlled, planned, disciplined, and strictly intellectual' (Ibid: 80), even talks of an 'ecstatic ethnography' where the collection of objects and knowledge was not only mediated by science, but also by personal illness and the states induced by medicine and alcohol to alleviate it; by fear and frustration; by sexual fantasies; and by physical brutality and violence. Curators are no less insulated from the allure and excitement that is sometimes generated between a subject and an object than a so-called fetishistic collector (Cardinal, this volume). The diaries and notebooks of curators described as systematic collectors, like Stewart Cullin (Fane 1992) at the Brooklyn Museum or Franz Boas (Jonaitis 1988; 1992) at the American Museum of Natural History, allude to complex economic and social engagements involved in the assembling of collections. Sometimes these attest to competitive motives, disappointment or elation at the quality of individual objects, and the personal circumstances surrounding an acquisition which could sometimes engender complex social networks, long and arduous journeys, hardship, and absence from family and friends. Few can doubt the fascination, enthusiasm and excitement that North-west Coast art kindled for Boas.

My fancy was first struck by the flight of imagination exhibited in the works of art of the British Columbians. ... I divined what a wealth of thought lay hidden behind the grotesque masks and the elaborately decorated utensils of these tribes (Jonaitis 1995: v).

Professional enthusiasm, no less than scientific discipline, is as apparent today as it was a century ago as Malcolm Mcleod's recollections of collecting for the British Museum (1993), or Archer's description of Otto Samson (Shelton this volume) clearly testifies. Indeed, Ronald Berndt, who began his intellectual life as an honorary assistant in ethnology at the South Australian Museum, flatly disputed that he used any systematic criteria whatsoever when he first collected bark paintings and other aboriginal material from the Western Desert and Arnhem Land between 1941-50 (Berndt 1979: 144). However, neither did personal taste or aesthetic criteria determine his choice of material. Rather, his collecting practices were guided by the evidential and illustrative value of the material in shedding light on social relationships. On another occasion, drawings made specially for him, provided a timely, alternative means of making a visual record, after his camera had run out of film (Ibid: 145). Many years later, on reconsidering his collection, he realised its importance as a form of documentation in its own right. Similarly, Torday, rather than putting together systematic collections in the sense that he tried to illustrate an evolutionary sequence or provide the markers for the diffusion of a culture trait from one people to another, was guided by his desire to establish another kind of document on Kuba culture, of equivalent importance to his written texts, photographs and recordings (Mack 1998: 66). Some so-called systematic collectors, Berndt, Boas and Torday among them, on closer inspection, may have been less guided by the exigencies of the narrow dogmas of specific scientific meta-narratives, than by the more general aspiration to create material archives for future anthropological study. The aims and breadth of making collections may not have been so much fixed by pre-existent theories, as has often been thought. Instead, while systematic considerations may have determined the core of a collection, more comprehensive or individual interests might explain its more general elaboration. The implications of this for museums are enormous. With systematic collections, the scientific and public use to which they can be put appears severely limited by the intellectual constraints under which they were made. Their use may even be limited to no more than the illustration of the particular hypothesis or paradigm they were collected to represent. In the more comprehensive view, however, collections become full of untapped potential both for the scientific investigations they can stimulate and the wide possibilities they offer for exhibition. Before we begin to use collections, we need to know the exact conditions of their acquisition to help ascertain their individual nature and epistemological value.

Museums house objects, some of which sometimes once constituted the sum of former personal collections or individual souvenirs. These are sorted and stored according to one system or another, and held as a kind of alphabet, the individual letters of which can be combined and re-combined according to particular recognised grammatical rules to generate easily recognisable narrative meanings. The succession of meta-narratives for which collections have provided visual illustration is itself sufficient to roundly refute any claim that an object or series of objects can prove the truth or untruth of any scientific or aesthetic formulation. The system of objects and the system of narratives have no intrinsic or necessary link between them. Consequently, the supposedly objective basis of systematic collections, and the use of such criteria to distinguish between private and museum-based collections must be seen as having been grounded on wholly fictitious assumptions. The interrogations contained in this volume confront one of the central and most fundamental questions posed by Jean Baudrillard (1994: 24), regarding whether objects can '... ever institute themselves as a viable language? Can they ever be fashioned into a discourse oriented otherwise than to toward oneself?' Although we may still not be able to provide the answer to this taunting question addressed to Museum practitioners, we can using distinct historical case studies, at least, begin to explore it.

Notes

1. T.E Bowditch does not fall into this mould. Though far from disinterested, he was part of the 1817 diplomatic mission to improve Anglo-Asante relations and negotiate trade concessions. The mission is described as becoming 'one of the earliest scientifically planned ventures into the interior of Africa to leave a detailed account of its observations and discoveries' (McLeod 1977: 79). The small collection he made is believed to have been put together in a systematic way (Ibid: 91). Krech's monograph on the Arctic collections assembled by the Fifth Earl of Lonsdale refuses the temptation to impose a retrospective rationalisation on the man's activities. Instead he examines the gulf between Lonsdale and any possible understanding of the cultures from which he purchased material (1989: 95).

2. An exception to this system of classification was the Central African collections made by Emil Torday for the British Museum. So outstanding were their artistic merit, that they were displayed as a single group in galleries that were otherwise arranged by comparative typological criteria (Mack 1994: 70).

Bibliography

BAL, M. 1994. Telling Objectives: A Narrative Perspective on Collecting. In Elsner, J. and Cardinal, R. (eds), *The Cultures of Collecting*. London: Reaktion Books.

BANN, S. 1994. *Under the Sign. John Bargrave as Collector, Traveller, and Witness.* Ann Arbor: The University of Michigan Press.

BAUDRILLARD, J. 1984. The Structural Law of Value and the Order of Simulacra. In Fekete, J. (ed), *The Structural Allegory. Reconstructive Encounters with the New French Thought.* Manchester: Manchester University Press.

BAUDRILLARD, J. 1993. *The Transparency of Evil. Essays on Extreme Phenomena.* London: Verso.

BAUDRILLARD, J. 1994. The System of Collecting. In Elsner, J. and Cardinal, R. (eds), *The Cultures of Collecting*. London: Reaktion Books.

BASSANI, E. and MCLEOD, M. 1989. *Jacob Epstein Collector.* Milan: Associazione Poro.

BATKIN, J. 1999. Tourism is Overrated: Pueblo Pottery and the Early Curio Trade, 1880-1910. In Phillips, R. and Steiner, C. (eds), *Unpacking Culture. Art and Commodity in Colonial and Postcolonial Worlds.* Berkeley and Los Angeles: University of California Press.

BENJAMIN, W. 1973. Unpacking My Library. A Talk about Book Collecting. In *Illuminations.* London: Fontana Books.

BENNETT, T. 1995. *The Birth of the Museum. History, Theory, Politics.* London and New York: Routledge.

BERNDT, R. 1979. Transformation of Persons, Objects and Country: Some Comments. *Occasional Papers in Anthropology* 9. St. Lucia, Anthropology Museum, University of Queensland.

BOURDIEU, P. and PASSERON, J-C. 1977. *Reproduction in Education, Society and Culture.* London and Beverly Hills: Sage.

CANNON-BROOKES, P. 1984. The Nature of Museum Collections. In Thompson, J. et. al. (eds), *Manual of Curatorship. A Guide to Museum Practice.* London: Butterworths.

COLE, D. 1985. *Captured Heritage. The Scramble for Northwest Coast Artifacts.* Seattle and London: University of Washington Press.

COOMBES, A. 1994. *Reinventing Africa. Museums, Material Culture and Popular Imagination.* New Haven and London: Yale University Press.

ELSNER, J. and CARDINAL, R. 1994. Introduction. In Elsner, J. and Cardinal, R. (eds), *The Cultures of Collecting.* London: Reaktion Books.

FABIAN, J. 1998. Curios and curiosity: Notes on reading Torday and Frobenius. In Schildkrout, E. and Keim, C. (eds), *The Scramble for Art in Central Africa.* Cambridge: Cambridge University Press.

FANE, D. 1992. New Questions for 'Old Things': The Brooklyn Museum's Zuni Collection. In Berlo, J. (ed), *The Early Years of Native American Art History.* Seattle and London: University of Washington Press.

IMPEY, O. and MACGREGOR, A. (eds), 1985. *The Origins of Museums: The Cabinet of Curiosities in Sixteenth and Seventeenth Century, Europe.* Oxford and London: Oxford University Press.

JONAITIS, A. 1988. *From the Land of the Totem Poles. The Northwest Coast Indian Art Collection at the American Museum of Natural History.* London: British Museum Publications.

JONAITIS, A. 1992. Franz Boas, John Swanton, and the New Haida Sculpture at the American Museum of Natural History. In Berlo, J. (ed), *The Early Years of Native American Art History.* Seattle and London: University of Washington Press.

JONAITIS, A. (ed), 1995. *A Wealth of Thought. Franz Boas on Native American Art.* Seattle and London, University of Washington Press.

KRECH III, S. 1989. *A Victorian Earl in the Arctic. The Travels and Collections of the Fifth Earl of Lonsdale 1888-89.* Seattle and London: University of Washington Press.

MACGAFFEY, W. 1993. The Eyes of Understanding Kongo Minkisi. In *National Museum of African Art, Astonishment and Power.* Washington and London: Smithsonian Institution Press.

MACGAFFEY, W. 1998. 'Magic, or as we usually say, Art'. A framework for comparing European and African art. In Schildkrout, E. and Keim, C. (eds), *The Scramble for Art in Central Africa.* Cambridge: Cambridge University Press.

MACK, J. 1990. *Emil Torday and the Art of the Congo 1900-1909.* London: British Museum Publications

MACK, J. 1997. Antiquities and the Public: the Expanding Museum 1851-96. In Caygill, M. and Cherry, J. (eds), *A.W. Franks. Nineteenth-Century Collecting and the British.* Museum: London, British Museum Press.

MACK, J. 1998. Kuba Art and the Birth of Ethnography. In Schildkrout, E. and Keim, C. (eds), *The Scramble for Art in Central Africa.* Cambridge: Cambridge University Press.

MCLEOD, M. 1977. T.E. Bowditch; an early collector in West Africa. In *British Museum Yearbook* **2**. Collectors and Collections. London: British Museum Publications.

MCLEOD, M. 1993. Collecting for the British Museum. *Quaderni Poro* **8**.

MUENSTERBERGER, W. 1994. *Collecting. An Unruly Passion. Psychological Perspectives.* Princeton: Princeton University Press.

PEARCE, S. 1992. *Museums, Objects and Collections.* Leicester: Leicester University Press.

SCHILDKROUT, E. 1991. Ambiguous Messages and Ironic Twists: 'Into the Heart of Africa' and the 'Other Museum'. *Museum Anthropology* **15**, 2: 16-23.

SCHILDKROUT, E. and KEIM, C. 1998. Objects and Agendas: Re-collecting the Congo. In Schildkrout, E. and Keim, C. (eds), *The Scramble for Art in Central Africa.* Cambridge: Cambridge University Press.

STAFFORD, B. 1994. *Artful Science. Enlightenment Entertainment and the Eclipse of Visual Education.* Cambridge (Mass.) and London: MIT Press.

STEWART, S. 1993. *On Longing. Narratives of the Miniature, the Gigantic, the Souvenir, the Collection.* Durham and London: Duke University Press.

THOMAS, N. 1991. *Entangled Objects. Exchange, Material Culture, and Colonialism in the Pacific.* Cambridge (Mass.) and London: Harvard University Press.

THOMAS, N. 1994. Licensed Curiosity: Cook's Pacific Voyages. In Elsner, J. and Cardina,l R. (eds), *The Cultures of Collecting.* London: Reaktion Books.

WILSON, D. 1984. *The Forgotten Collector. Augustus Wollaston Franks of the British Museum.* London: Thames and Hudson.

The Eloquence of Objects

1

Roger Cardinal

Anyone who has cleared out a house after a death in the family will have felt themselves wincing at the banality of clutter. Even the most admirable and best-spent lifetime seems to peter out in a residue of old coats and shoes, stacks of faded newspapers, and all kinds of memorabilia lodged in jars, boxes, chests and cupboards, their significance poignantly annulled. Last spring my father died, bequeathing a considerable stock of inconsequentials - a bag of saved-up elastic bands, tins thriftily filled with old nails and screws, a chiming clock without a key, a clutch of obsolete copper coins. I found it hard to trace any continuity in these relics.

It was while I was rummaging through a batch of papers, where I was touched to find a blood donor's card and some documents about my father's service as an auxiliary fireman in the Blitz, that a single London bus-ticket came to light. It bore the date January 1935, and the context of its finding suggested it to be a private souvenir, perhaps of a momentous conversation on the top deck with my mother during their courtship. The ticket was faded and partly torn, yet it struck me all the same as a potent instance of the capacity of things to communicate to us across time and space, to embody what Susan Stewart calls 'a memory standing outside the self' and thus to promote emotions out of all proportion to their material paltriness. While I could only guess at its literal significance to my father, who had hardly ever spoken to me about his early life, the 1935 bus-ticket had for me an unmistakable aura, stimulating an indistinct yet perfectly vivid sensation of contact with an epoch before I was even born. There exists a variety of nostalgia directed at circumstances one could never truly have known, even at what never really happened.

In a poem entitled 'Inventory', the Argentine writer Jorge Luis Borges speaks of visiting an attic crammed with the bric-à-brac of several generations. His patient listing includes such forlorn items as

A Paraguayan hammock with tassels, all frayed away.
Equipment and papers.
An engraving of Paricio Saravia's general staff.
An old charcoal iron.
A clock stopped in time, with a broken pendulum.

A peeling gilt frame, with no canvas.
A cardboard chessboard, and some broken chessmen.
A stove with only two legs.

What might we hope to find in such a situation, he goes on to ask, beyond 'the flotsam of disorder' ? Who now has any idea who Paricio Saravia was? What possible portrait or landscape could once have dignified that decrepit frame? A whole context of richly layered experience has simply dropped away without recall. To peer back down the corridor of time is to glimpse the futile vestiges of human joy, aspiration and suffering. This disjunct catalogue of remnants may constitute a memorial of sorts, but equally it conduces to frustration and meaninglessness. Borges's poem is in truth more a commemoration of oblivion, an elegy to impermanence.

It would seem that the human species has always distinguished itself by a propensity to honour and preserve unusual objects. In *The Art of Prehistoric Man in Western Europe*, André Leroi-Gourhan speaks of the purposiveness with which the Paleolithic occupants of the Grotte de l'Hyène gathered together the eye-catching curios of their environment - things like shells, fossils, lumps of pyrite, or quartz crystals. Throughout the centuries, humans have persistently held onto objects of limited utilitarian value and devised sites of security wherein to keep them. The locked drawer in the teenager's desk and the attic, cellar or garage in the family house are but the more homely manifestations of a phenomenon which, across history, has inspired the mausolea of Egyptian kings, the great treasure-houses and archives of royal, ecclesiastical and commercial institutions, the Renaissance cabinets of curiosities, and, of course, the modern museum, with its vitrines and dioramas, not to mention its out-of-sight stock-rooms. And we should not forget all those other sites through which man shunts objects in the course of increasing or extinguishing their value, from the auction-room and the bank-vault to the flea-market and the rubbish-heap.

To be a collector is, even if unwittingly, to show that one cares about objects; only the superficial accumulator remains impassive and cool. Usually, genuine collectors have a shrewd idea of their preferences and ambitions, whereas to accumulate is really no more than a negative activity, a 'not-bothering-to-throw-away', albeit some hoarders, embarrassed by the spectacle of pointless junk, find justification in the old saw whereby 'you never know when a thing might come in useful'. Once inducted into a formal collection, an object is usually excused from further service (though occasionally a seamstress, say, may ceremonially try out the precious thimble handed down by her great-grandmother). It is axiomatic that the collected object embodies value only in so far as it registers a connection with an order beyond itself. Sometimes this order is the collection at large, for, if we are to believe Jean Baudrillard, collectors tend to cherish objects less for their intrinsic interest than for the fact that they are members of a defined set or series: hence the thrill felt by the stamp-collector upon completing a 'run' of a particular issue. (We may note that postal authorities nowadays offer reassurance to the panicky philatelist by marketing well advertised and impeccable sets.) Very often, though, the 'series' to which an object belongs is that stratum of past time from which it has emerged, as a surviving material witness. In so far as the import of a collected object is accelerated by the human impulse to clutch at the past, we can say that many collections are attempted memory systems. At first glance chaotic, Borges's inventory eventually yields its common denominators: each of those relics is ancient, each has played a part in the lives of people now dead, each participates in a tacit narrative, an ancestral history (albeit a faulty one).

There seems to come a point when the indistinct drive to collect is refined by a passion to systematise. Collectors begin by discarding early acquisitions which have in the meantime proved disappointing. They then proceed to more zealous acts of organisation, establishing classifications, writing labels and descriptions, and drawing up a numbered inventory or even a catalogue. Of course, private collectors are under no obligation to respect convention, and often invent odd ways of sorting, preserving and displaying their trophies. A friend of mine collects glass objects, from ashtrays to dangling crystals, and distributes them about the rooms of her house by reference not to their size, provenance or original use, but by their colour. Thus, in summer, her bathroom becomes a veritable sea of luminescent blues. The more ornate and extensive the collection, however, the more pressure there is to link it to some project or explicit principle of understanding. The numismatist who normally conceals his golden treasures from the eyes of the world may be forced not only to list them for insurance purposes but to think about safeguarding the collection's future by bequeathing it to a public museum. As for the *Wunderkammer*, or cabinet of curiosities, with all its heteroclite marvels, recent years have seen a re-appraisal of its supposed disorderliness and irrationality in favour of the view that it manifests a quest for coherence foreshadowing the mission of the modern museum curator - which is, roughly speaking, to elicit sense from the world in a co-ordinated fashion.

Nowadays, public collections are obliged by social and cultural pressure to eschew caprice and to apply lucid criteria to their holdings, initiating collecting strategies which facilitate scholarly narratives and consequential explanations. Curators typically seek to place objects of varied provenance within decisive constellations of meaning; or, to use a different image, to harmonise the weak murmurings of individual objects within a chorus audible enough to evoke a wider context which would otherwise escape the visitor's earshot.

To preserve memorabilia, or things which represent the past to us, is an undertaking premissed on the capacity of objects to act as signifiers of their original circumstances as well as on that of collectors to latch onto such significations (and indeed to celebrate and enhance them through display and attentive commentary). Edwina Taborsky speaks of the 'discursive object', while Krzysztof Pomian has coined the neologism *semiophore* to denote the object in its function of 'sign-carrier', that which solicits our semiotic response. For his part, the poet Gerard Manley Hopkins dreamed of penetrating what he termed the *inscape* of objects, their unique essence or secret design which, in turn, could inform an aesthetic counterpart in the shape of a poem. To the archaeologist, a rusty sword from antiquity no longer asks to be wielded; its new role is that of veteran of a distant campaign, its meaning dependent on its loquacity and the lucky chance of its survival. To the ephemeralist, the nineteenth-century play-bill with its printed image and blurb offers imaginative access to a once live performance at a particular theatre on a particular night. To the anthropologist, the carved prow of a Melanesian canoe or the featherwork crown of an Aztec monarch can be pregnant with the intensity of a remote society's aesthetic and spiritual expectations. To uninformed twentieth-century Europeans, such objects constitute so many blurred messages from an Elsewhere whose temporal, geographical and cultural parameters confound casual appreciation. The museological challenge is to try somehow to draw the enigmatic object into focus, to bridge the gap between utterance and puzzled listener.

As a true connoisseur of particularity, Hopkins expressed a commitment to the object 'in its delicate and surprising uniqueness'. Every unique or very rare object cries out to be given a personal name; in Western culture, the names we give to things (designations, nomenclatures, titles) tend to get written down. Catalogues - which translate objects into texts - seem an inevitable outcome of concerted collecting. There is a peculiar fascination, even a compulsion about the making of lists (indeed, the present essay labours under this very compulsion). Documents like Borges's attic inventory seem to want to coax singularities into an avowal of simultaneity and unison; yet they cannot dispel sparks of discord, which allow absurdity and alienation to encroach. Cohesion is a matter of time and patience. In his famous study of the lives of Alabama sharecroppers during the Depression, *Let Us Now Praise Famous Men*, James Agee spends page upon page enumerating the specifics of poor people's overalls and shoes, their broken-down beds and furniture, their humble kitchen implements, and succeeds in drawing beauty out of the very shabbiness of these material possessions. A set of accompanying photos by Walker Evans confirms Agee's intuition, demonstrating that a noble eloquence can inhere in the lowliest artefacts, provided they are entwined with human destinies.

Of course, not all objects aspire to be semiophores - if they did, the world would become unmanageable, overdosing us on meanings. Objects as it were 'in the raw' or 'in themselves', objects with no bearing on our lives, are surely mere clots of matter. Of the countless things in the world, it is obvious that the vast majority send out no signal; and it seems right that what is unremarked and redundant should remain mute or nameless. Few humans could contemplate an intelligent inventory even of the possessions in their personal room; although the writer Xavier de Maistre did compose *Voyage autour de ma chambre* as a spoof journey of exotic discovery, while the artist Daniel Spoerri solved the problem of the clutter on his table-top by glueing each item down and exhibiting the result as a kind of monument to contingency. Admittedly, once in a while, we are penalised for our neglect of things. It is perfectly sensible, we might suppose, to ignore the myriad bits of grit and litter along the motorway. But what happens when an insignificant nail penetrates the tyre of our car? It is likely to usurp our attention in a quite dramatic reversal of its prior fortunes. Conversely, the nursery rhyme reminds us that a whole kingdom can be set at risk for want of a single nail: thus, from time to time, the most peripheral things exert enormous influence as signifiers vital to the human endeavour.

A specialist in this paradox of reversed values, the poet Jean Follain has written persuasively about porcelain plates and crystal glasses arrayed on old dressers in provincial French houses, or the intimate contents of a traveller's pockets: a pocket-knife, a small notebook, a coil of string, a tiny screw. Follain loves to list such ephemera and to muse on their potential as semiophores of great poignancy: 'a song arises out of each and every object' is his maxim. A century earlier, Josef Freiherr von Eichendorff had given the same thought a Romantic twist, suggesting that

A song lies dormant in all things,
Which keep on dreaming, on and on;
And the world will start to sing
If you but voice the magic word.

The Romantic world-view envisions any given object as the threshold to the entire cosmos: the single modest thing represents a magical microcosm of the totality of things, and as such sheds its anonymity and assumes a revelatory distinctiveness. In one of Borges's teasing allegories about an everyday brush with ultimate meaning, a short story called 'The Zahir', the narrator relates how he came across the obscure yet ultimate Zahir - the key to the universe - in the form of an Argentine twenty-centavo coin bearing the date 1929 and with the letters NT and the digit 2 notched on it with a knife. (At earlier points in history, he adds, the Zahir had manifested itself as a tiger, an astrolabe, a compass wrapped in a strip of turban...) Ever since reading Borges's tale, I have often inspected my small change, and wondered.

The dream of a secret secondary dimension to the phenomenal world flows through the nineteenth-century imagination and has left a noticeable tinge on the arts of our own century, from Kandinsky, Franz Marc and Maeterlinck to Edward Weston, Octavio Paz and Andy Goldsworthy. The tenderness with which such creators treat the world of objects points to the hypothesis that practically any specimen we handle, once properly addressed and contextualised, is capable of confessing an involvement in universal patterns. At which point the button in the gutter, the circle of heron's feathers or the spider's web lit by the sun can become a symbol of cosmic harmony; and perhaps partake of *mana,* that invisible magic power which, as Marcel Mauss tells us, non-European cultures envisage passing into stones, arrowheads and fishing-nets in daily use, as well as inhering in more rare (and usually painstakingly crafted) artefacts, such as the totemic mask, the sacred headdress, or the ritual weapon. And even if we are immune to the spiritual dimension of such objects, we should, at the very least, recognise that the iciest extremes of abstract thought still owe something to the world of material circumstance. As William Carlos Williams once codified it, 'no ideas but in things'.

In the interwar period, Surrealism laid particular stress on the import of *objets trouvés* - objects discovered by chance in shop-windows, at the flea-market or even in the gutter or the trash-can - defining them as precipitates of unconscious desire. André Breton tried to analyse his attraction to unlikely objects which crystallised some irrational impulse. An unlabelled metal mask, an abstruse three-dimensional graph, a glove cast in bronze but painted to resemble velvet, a wooden spoon with a shoe carved at the end of its handle, a root shaped like a human figure, a colourful butterfly - these were among the artefacts and natural configurations which he deliberately interspersed amid his collections of tribal and European avant-garde art. Breton's Paris apartment became a private museum of oneiric cast, dedicated to analogy and alternative ways of seeing, and each item earned its place in so far as it was the locus of an intimate reflex of surprise and passion. As Paul Valéry once observed of the connoisseur, 'certain men experience, with an especial delectation, the voluptuous sense of the individuality of objects'. When surrealist artists like Salvador Dalí or Meret Oppenheim began deliberately to construct surrealist objects, or 'objects of symbolic function', it seems inevitable that they should have produced assemblages saturated with erotic association - home-made fetishes, as it were.

If fetishists are people who derive a stimulus from the material presence and sensory textures of the object they hold dear - whether the ecstasy they achieve be deemed essentially sexual or spiritual - then collectors are indeed fetishists, for they love to gaze at, stroke and even whisper to the things they have come to possess. Walter Benjamin once remarked that 'for a collector, ownership is the most intimate relationship that one can have to objects'. The patina on a much-handled ceremonial carving, the iridescence on a nautilus shell, the surprising weight of a meteorite, the sheen on a satin gown, the densely dappled surface of an Impressionist painting - there is never an end to the sensations which collectors can draw and draw again from their trophies, and which afford a marvellous finger-tip hold upon a contextual reality to which those objects bear witness. Albeit this hold may owe a good deal to fantasy: for not every possessor of a silk scarf once worn by Elvis Presley can vouch for its authenticity.

The specialist's concept of authenticity functions as an intellectual balustrade, yet it can do nothing to prevent us from plunging happily and unreservedly over the edge if we are lucky enough to encounter an object which opens onto an event or situation in a time and space beyond ordinary access. A certified moon-rock, a Paleolithic bone carving, a Mongolian shaman's drum, the shoulder-blade of a *Megaceros*, a finch from the Galapagos Islands, a letter penned by Captain Scott's frozen fingers, an astrolabe of doubtful provenance - any of these can seduce and inspire us, so that we succumb to the thrall of Otherness and Remoteness. To extrapolate from such eloquent semiophores is to inhabit a context we are simultaneously reinventing. We are like Prometheus breathing into inanimate clay, or, better still, the ventriloquist kidding his audience that an inert block of wood is capable of speech: yet who is to say that such illusion points away from truth?

It is probably true that the potency of those auratic objects which arouse our deepest responses is relatively short-lived. We squeeze our precious mementoes in the hope of inducing a flicker of long-lost feeling. Marcel Proust noted the strange capacity of spiritual and emotional powers to take refuge within stones and other unlikely receptacles; he also discovered that it can only be involuntary memory rather than the systematic procedures of conscious reminiscence which affords any sort of palpable contact with what has vanished. We linger over the lock of hair or the discoloured snapshot - but souvenirs grown cold are but the corpses of curtailed desires. All our amorous memorabilia, once so vibrant that we treated them as evidence of reciprocal love, lose their flavour and potency with the passage of time. As Rilke would say, 'thus do we live, and are always taking leave'.

The travel writer Bruce Chatwin tells the apocryphal tale of a workaholic typewriter salesman who travelled back and forth between England and Africa, living out of a suitcase with apparent indifference to the comforts and securities needed by his colleagues. He seems to epitomise Chatwin's conception of the modern nomad, one who thrives on a minimum of possessions. Yet the man did cherish a point of origin to which his migrations periodically returned him: whenever he called back at his head office in London, he would lock himself in a closet and open up a black metal box in which was kept a rigorously marshalled set of souvenirs -

a teddy-bear, a photo of his dead father, a trophy won for swimming, a presentation ashtray. Each time he came back from a long haul, he would review the collection, adding one fresh item and throwing out an old one. 'He is the only man I have ever met who solved the tricky equation between things and freedom', is Chatwin's half-admiring, half-appalled comment.

Within the field of museology, debates have gone on for some while about the nature of the shift in the object's semiotic status once it has undergone the ritual of accessioning. In this regard, the institutionalisation of cultural artefacts, from paintings to pottery shards, is hardly any different from that of specimens selected from the natural world. Yet the indexing and numbering of pieces, their placement within categories and displays, along with the devising of solicitous captions, and in due course the organising of supplementary lectures, videos, conferences and catalogues - all these acts of secondary monitoring and celebration are surely the outcome of some primal experience of recognition. It is a rare privilege to stumble upon an object which focalises all our drifting thoughts, an object which provides a magnetic locus of revelation and enthusiasm. Curators are scarcely a separate breed from the rest of humanity, and may even be more prone than the average person to experience a rapture, very like falling in love, when a discovered object asserts itself as the epicentre of an earthquake of the sensibility, making emotion inseparable from thought. Sometimes a package will arrive at the museum, and be opened, layer by layer, to expose a rare and eloquent piece which dispels humdrum normality and radiates an irresistible sense of connectedness and clarity. Before we have time to spell out the signs which it transmits, we can come alive to the object's material presence, respectful of its resilience, eager to be attuned to a message we would like to think is addressed uniquely to ourselves.

To extol the virtues of touching is to flout the sacred rope of museum protocol. Of course, rare objects are typically fragile, and to install them for long-term public scrutiny must involve protecting them from mishandling. At the British Museum, I have watched the crush of foreign visitors fondling the Rosetta Stone, as if it were a sacred relic in the cult of international tourism. (The fact that the attendants don't seem at all concerned about these promiscuous caresses prompts the guess that the curators are ahead of the game, and have removed the real Stone to the cellars. Similarly, the caves at Lascaux and Altamira were saved by replicas.) In museums, the discourse of things seems delimited by verbal discourse, each label insinuating that 'all you really need is words - so surely you can forego touching!' Yet if, as the philosopher Garth Gillan remarks, 'the body speaks the language of the world, and the world the language of the body', then true signification must emanate from a subtler web of relationships, such that thoughts, emotions and perceptions may at some point venture into the cooler realm of the verbal, yet still rely on the material one for nourishment.

It is never the level of the mercury on the thermometer at our door which tells us whether we feel hot or cold as we step outside. Similarly, it is rarely the objective logic of factual explanation which makes an exhibit compelling. The semiotics of the museum-piece is too often seen as a matter of conceptual identification and detached appraisal. Intellectual cognition is fine, and theorising is certainly a necessary prelude to wider investigation; yet they would never flourish were they not fertilised by direct experience. We simply can't have interesting ideas about the world unless we breathe in and out as we think. As the writer Joë Bousquet puts it, 'the beauty of things is forged in the attentiveness we bring to them'. And, one might add, their intellectual meaning too, since it is attentiveness, fuelled by feeling, which in turn is fuelled by sensation, which first guides us along certain tracks of analysis and encourages us to persevere with our speculations, calculations and experiments.

It is important to envisage our engagement with material things in terms of dialogue. 'The meaning of an object', writes Edwina Taborsky, 'appears only within a discursive interaction of the observer with the object'. We may strain to catch the message we feel the object to be voicing, but nothing will come of our listening unless we answer back, or more precisely, solicit the fullest vocalisation of that message. To scrutinise a specimen dispassionately may well be scientifically justified, but to censor all subjectivism is to overlook the role our feelings *necessarily and unabashedly* play in our understanding of the world. Novalis, who was a poet and literary theorist, but equally a student of the natural sciences and a career geologist, jotted down this maxim in one of his notebooks: 'It is not knowledge alone that makes us happy, it is the quality of knowledge, the subjective constitution (*Beschaffenheit*) of knowledge'.

The world means more to us once we appreciate the eloquence of seemingly mute objects. While they still drew breath, so to speak, the 1935 bus-ticket and the Paraguayan hammock with its frayed tassels had much to impart. Even now, as tokens of long-lost meanings, they continue to haunt us with their indistinct whispers. Our struggle to touch the past is like a parley with ghosts, a conversation in fits and starts; our enlightenment feeds upon dwindling fragments. If the symbolic Zahir ever does turn up, it is likely to be in the least assuming form. Everything depends on the tenacity of our concentration on the messages we hear (or think we hear). Sadly, what we learn to decipher best is the syllables of our own mortality. Indeed, the lesson may be that, if classification is cultural, clutter is only too natural. We have to face the fact that all things, including ourselves, are doomed to be classed one day under the single ultimate heading: EPHEMERA.

Bibliography

AGEE, J. 1988. *Let Us Now Praise Famous Men.* London: Picador.

ANGLIVIEL DE LA BEAUMELLE, A., MONOD-FONTAINE, I. and SCHWEISGUTH, C. (eds), 1991. *André Breton. La Beauté convulsive.* Paris: Éditions du Centre Pompidou.

BAUDRILLARD, J. 1994. The System of Collecting. In Cardinal, R. and Elsner, J. (eds), *The Cultures of Collecting.* London: Reaktion Books.

BENJAMIN, W. 1973. Unpacking my Library. In *Illuminations.* London: Fontana.

BORGES, J. 1972. The Zahir. In *A Personal Anthology.* London: Picador.

BORGES, J. 1979. Inventory. In *The Book of Sand.* Harmondsworth: Penguin.

CHATWIN, B. 1997. The Morality of Things. In *Anatomy of Restlessness. Uncollected Writings.* London: Picador.

EICHENDORFF, J. [N.D.] *Sprüche.* In *Gedichte. Ahnung und Gegenwart.* Zürich: Manesse.

FOLLAIN, J. 1957. Objets. In *Tout Instant.* Paris: Gallimard.

GILLAN, G. 1982. *From Sign to Symbol.* Brighton: Harvester Press.

HARBISON, R. 1977. Contracted World: Museums and Catalogues. In *Eccentric Spaces.* New York: Alfred A. Knopf.

HOOPER-GREENHILL, E. 1992. *Museums and the Shaping of Knowledge.* London: Routledge.

HOPKINS, G. 1953. Journal. In *Poems and Prose of Gerard Manley Hopkins.* London: Penguin Books.

LEROI-GOURHAN, A. 1968. *The Art of Prehistoric Man in Western Europe.* London: Thames & Hudson.

MAISTRE, X. DE 1876. Voyage Autour de ma Chambre. In *Oeuvres Choisies.* Paris: Hachette.

MAUSS, M. 1972. *A General Theory of Magic.* London: Routledge and Kegan Paul.

PEARCE, S. 1992. *Museums, Objects and Collections: A Cultural Study.* Leicester and London: Leicester University Press.

POMIAN, K. 1990. *Collectors and Curiosities. Paris and Venice, 1500-1800.* London: Polity Press.

RILKE, R. 1931. *Duineser Elegien.* Leipzig: Insel-Verlag.

STEWART, S. 1984. *On Longing. Narratives of the Miniature, the Gigantic, the Souvenir, the Collection.* Baltimore: Johns Hopkins University Press.

TABORSKY, E. 1990. The Discursive Object. In Pearce, S. (ed), *Objects of Knowledge.* London: Athlone Press.

VALÉRY, P. 1957. *Introduction à la Méthode de Léonard de Vinci.* Paris: Gallimard.

Leon Underwood: An Artist Collector

Celina Jeffrey

Since the turn of the century, the collection of so-called 'primitive' objects has been principally motivated by ethnographic or aesthetic concerns which have re-classified them as either artefact or art. This essay examines the aesthetic re-evaluation of ethnography as 'primitive art'[1] using the example of the English artist and collector, Leon Underwood (1890-1975). Underwood was a prolific artist who worked largely within the 'Primitivist'[2] discourse, in which the aesthetic, philosophical and ideological engagement with so-called 'primitive' art led to an incessant desire to collect. The narrative of an artist-collector like Underwood serves to illustrate some of the key processes, which informed the relationship between aesthetic Modernism, Primitivism and visual anthropology. Here, particular relevance can be attributed to the role of 'primitive' art within the re-conceptualisation of Western notions of 'art' and the history of art during this period. I would like to argue that the narrative of Underwood as an artist-collector interacted and transacted with these paradigms in order to reconstitute the value and purpose of art within his own society. In this respect, we may perceive Underwood's collecting practices and their relation to his own artistic production as outward signs of an ideational shift, towards a reconfiguration of art as 'universal'.

The examination of Underwood as an artist-collector is best viewed as a complex and fluid set of responses to contemporary issues rather than as a rigid examination of particular ethnographic sources used as visual stimuli. In search of a universal notion of authentic art, Underwood travelled extensively to experience the cultures of Poland, Iceland, Spain, Mexico, West Africa and Turkey, which he believed were untainted by the social and moral decay of the modern western world. His collection of 'cultures' - of people, places and objects were transfigured within his artistic practice, philosophy and writings as examples of the dematerialised and spiritual, a symbol of a lost totality. These 'voyages' of discovery were enhanced by 'moments' of discovery - at the British Museum for example, or in antique shops, markets and auction houses, in which African, Asian, Oceanic and American arts could be consumed. For Underwood these objects served a dual function, becoming a source of aesthetic and spiritual inspiration to reinvigorate his own art and philosophy.

The aim of this paper is to engage with the underlying motivations, valuations and aesthetic biases that informed Underwood's collection as well as acknowledge some of their inherent contradictions. For

Underwood's collecting practices were informed by what may be deemed an aesthetic universalism in which technique, representation and notions of spirituality were used to ascribe meaning and value to his collection. Yet, his explanation of art remained within the European rendering of the world, rejecting the specificities of the original historical and cultural context. I will focus on three significant aspects of his career in order to illustrate this. Firstly, the narrative of Underwood as an artist-collector. Secondly, his theoretical concept of the universal expressed through his writings and comparative art exhibitions, and finally through an analysis of his collection of West African art.

An Artist-Collector

Underwood's career as an artist developed concurrently with his passion for collecting. His father, Theodore George Black Underwood, who was a numismatist and the owner of an antique shop (in Paddington), that also sold fine art prints nurtured his son's artistic tendencies and interest in collecting. However, as a student, Leon Underwood received little formal education and his training, at the Royal College of Art in 1910, consisted largely of copying antique casts. As an aspiring artist but wishing to 'escape' the dogma of his training and the current trend for Post-Impressionism, Underwood travelled to Russian Poland in 1913 to paint landscapes and portraits, and to study religious painting. Like so many artists of this era, however, his service in the Great War was to have an arresting and profound effect upon his career. He served in France and was later transferred to the Camouflage Section.

The experience of the terror of War was diagnosed in his art and writings as an expression of the malaise of modernity from which his supposition on the primacy of art in life derived. This avowal of art was intricately bound to ideals of emancipation and the re-assertion of the role of the artist in society, 'to us in the trenches, came our leaders' speeches, on the fight for freedom as the fruit of victory - freedom of expression in religion, music, poetry and painting' (Underwood N.D.).[3] The work that Underwood produced in response to the War demonstrates an assertion of his humanistic belief in the spiritual qualities of art. The sculpture *Dove* was conceived as a simple and effective means to communicate a notion of peace and reveals his ideal of the 'poetic truth' of the artist (1934: 4). Yet, its simplified, angular shape, carved directly into Caen stone also related to the Vorticist aesthetic and particularly to the work of Henri Gaudier-Brzeska (1891-1915), who made a significant contribution to the development of a British form of 'Primitivism' in the pre-war years. In the immediate post War period, Gaudier-Brzeska figured as a prominent influence upon Underwood, who began to place increasing importance on sculpture, the techniques of direct carving and the geometricisation of form as a direct expression of pure and vital creativity: qualities he identified in 'primitive' art.

Underwood began collecting in 1919 with a selection of Austrian and Slovene paintings on glass but soon developed an interest in and accumulation of sculptural forms closely identified with 'primitive' art. In 1921 he opened an unconventional life drawing school the *Brook Green School of Art* (1921-1954) at his home in Girdlers Road, west London. Underwood's holistic teaching methods, which included life drawing, wood engraving, art theory, philosophy and politics proved to be a striking source of inspiration to early pupils which included Eileen Agar, Jessie Aliston Smith, Gertrude Hermes, Rodney Thomas, Blair Hughes-Stanton and Henry Moore.

The majority of these artists also worked within a 'Primitivist' aesthetic and were undoubtedly stimulated by Underwood's collecting practices, while some, most notably Eileen Agar, Gertrude Hermes, Henry Moore and Blair Hughes-Stanton, became collectors of 'primitive' art. The proliferation of 'primitive' art in the immediate post-War period fuelled such collections and by 1925 Underwood was a recognised collector of African art (Ellwood 1925: 188). He acquired his collection mainly from markets and antique shops, but was also familiar with the dealers of 'primitive' art in London, most notably with the collector and dealer Sydney Burney. There were a number of private galleries that Underwood frequented, including the Sydney Burney Gallery, the Chelsea Book Club and the Goupil Gallery that exhibited African art in this period and would have encouraged his appreciation.[4]

It was in the then imperialist capitals of Europe that the concomitant avant-garde and 'primitive' art-culture system developed most forcefully. The formation of aesthetic 'Primitivism', led by Gauguin, Fauvism, Die Brucke, Picasso and Braque, was paralleled by the increasing prominence of ethnographic museums, leading auction houses and private dealers, which acquired and exhibited art from the colonies. The systems of value and exchange of these art forms were first established within Parisian artistic circles at the turn of the century. It is most likely that the Parisian exchange system influenced the development of the British market in 'primitive' art. Jacob Epstein (1880-1959), for example, who has long been identified as one of the greatest private collectors and the most renowned artist-collector in the British context, chose and acquired many of his finest pieces (on the basis of aesthetic merit) from Paul Guillaume and the Parisian circle (Bassani & McLeod 1987: 11). In the British context however, the distribution and consumption of 'primitive' art was limited and confined to a small number of dealers, collectors and curators. Its circulation in artistic circles also came late to Britain, occurring in the inter-war years and led by a few protagonists including Jacob Epstein, Leon Underwood, Henry Moore, Roger Fry, Eileen Agar, Lee Miller and Roland Penrose.

The ethnographic collections at the British Museum also acted as a rich source of discovery for artists like Underwood who responded with enthusiasm to the recent influx of 'primitive' art. Yet, unlike the Museé d'Ethnographie du Trocadero which was a separate ethnographic museum, providing the avant-garde with a distinctive source of the 'primitive', ethnography was situated in the British Museum next to British and Medieval antiquities. The eclectic display of world culture at the Museum provided a valuable source of stimuli for contemporary artists:

> *The British Museum itself, was a center and meeting place for artists and writers who had spent a few hours in the great domed reading room, or among the fragments of Grecian, Egyptian, Assyrian, Chinese, Oceanic, African, and other ancient and modern cultures of east and west* (Wees, quoted in Mack 1998: 76).

In many ways, Underwood's increasingly diverse interest in 'primitive' art, as expressed in both his collection and in his writings were reflective of the antiquarian's universal sensibility, more closely associated with the paradigmatic organisation of the British Museum.

Underwood's development as an artist was intricately bound to his passion for collecting, serving a number of conceptual purposes. Although Underwood's work in the inter-war period was diverse, practising within a variety of media, he was principally a sculptor working in wood, stone and bronze, and a wood engraver, creating simplified, expressive forms and allegorical themes that often pertain to a generalised 'Primitivist' aesthetic. Underwood's relationship with 'Primitivism' was complex however as his work rarely imitated the exact art forms that he collected. This was indicated in the art and literary journal *The Island* founded by Underwood and the poet Joseph Bard in 1931, in which art works depict an array of highly romanticised subject matter that embody notions of the purity of 'primitive' man and the modern artist as spiritual guide. Central to this philosophy, was the ideology of aesthetic universalism in which 'primitive' art was incorporated into the canon of Western art, thus he wrote that at no time 'previous to this century, would we have admitted into the same tradition the sculptors of Hoa-haka-nana-ioa and Chartres Cathedral together with Gaudier-Brzeska' (Underwood Sept. 1931: 42). Underwood's theoretical inquiry into a comparative history of sculpture stemmed from this theory and occupied him for much of his life. He planned a book, the *Cycle of Styles* in which sculpture from pre-history to the present was considered in terms of the changing relationship between art, religion and technology.[5] Conceived as a response to the problem of the impoverishment of art within his own society, Underwood sought to trace the development of sculpture in terms of cycles, in which the relationship between spirituality and creativity were on equal parity with technology and knowledge.

This enquiry into sculpture through time and place was to occupy him throughout his life, becoming a crucial factor in his desire to collect. He travelled extensively to research and collect visiting Iceland in 1923, the Palaeolithic caves of Altamira in 1925, the Mayan cities of Mexico and Yucatan in 1928, and finally, west Africa in 1945. Here he studied, wrote, sketched, photographed and collected instances of art that had been the product of pre-modern cultures, in which art, religion and science worked holistically. Throughout his life he collected over 600 objects, including an extensive collection of west African art and a small selection of Oceanic, Tibetan, Indian and central American art.[6] The collection in turn informed his writings, which incorporated philosophical tracts, poetry, a satirical novel, a trilogy of books on African art, numerous articles of an anthropological persuasion and *The Cycles of Style.*

Art and Life

In his philosophical treatise, Art for Heaven's Sake, of 1934, Underwood described the predicament that was facing the role of the artist within his culture:

> *No significant artist of today can work without a definite idea about the reconstruction of the world he and his fellows live in, for he realises that his function, in the future, is to bring about the replacement of War by the culture of Art as the first concern of the nations* (1934: i).

In this treatise, Underwood diagnosed a fragmented world in which the processes of modernisation, epitomised by the War, had resulted in the disunion of art, spirituality and life. The historical crisis presented by the Great War was considered by many artists of the period to be the catastrophic outcome of modern man's affirmation of rationality over the instinctual self. This ideology of cultural crises had led artists to a fascination with 'primitive' life[7] and a widespread response within the visual arts was a rejection of the modern scientific standpoint in favour of an anti-rational, radical subjectivity as a means to 're-create' the world. Such a summons to refine and purify the nature of art in order to make it meaningful within the general culture was of central concern to Underwood. It was within this paradigm that his collection became a relevant and meaningful way to mediate the disjunction between 'art and life'.

Central to Underwood's philosophy as an artist and collector was a belief that art had lost its value within modern culture, 'art and life have drifted apart...I infer that life (the masses) has no serviceable use for art as it once had' (Underwood 1934: Addenda). Underwood's somewhat utopic belief that art had 'once' formed a central aspect of life was a compelling force becoming the definitive factor in his philosophical engagement with a notion of the 'pre-modern' artist and it is here that the value of collecting so-called 'primitive' art is clarified. For 'primitive' art was perceived to have functioned within a dialogue of art and life, providing a means to identify a sense of imagination and instinct which he felt had been lost by the dominance of reason, science and technology in western culture. It was the artistic expression of feeling and thought, governed by 'imagination and intuition' that would provide a moral and spiritual guide to deal directly with the modern problem of the fragmentation of identity, in order to begin to re-address the problem of the divergence of art and life (Underwood 1934: 3).

Underwood's subjective engagement with the idea of the 'primitive' was informed by the ideology of 'Primitivism', which had emerged as a powerful myth of the modernist trajectory and materialised as a complex matrix within the avant-garde capitals of Europe. It was a general and specific movement, characterised by an aesthetic engagement with 'simpler' art forms, generically identified either within the arts of Africa, Oceania and the Americas, or found in the folk and popular cultures of Europe. Yet, it also evolved out of the Nineteenth century discourse of Romanticism and was characterised by a pervasive anti-rational ideology that functioned as a form of social critique and a means to attack dominant thought. The ideology of 'Primitivism', then was a 'complex network of sociological, ideological, aesthetic, scientific, anthropological political and legal interests' that developed multiple and complex meanings in different contexts (Perry 1993: 4). For Underwood, 'primitive' art and culture become a source of the sacred and authentic, representing ideas of continuity and totality that were held in opposition to modernity, and a means to explore the origins of art and alternative sources of creativity.

'Primitivism' allowed Underwood to create a perceived identification with the 'primitive' artist, which was emulated within his art as an expression of vitality over the classical values of naturalism and beauty. Underwood shared his ideals and practice with many artists of the period, but particularly with Gaudier-Brzeska, who prior to his death in the First World War, had began to reject the Greek and naturalistic tradition of art in favour of identification with the so-called 'primitive' artist. 'The modern sculptor' wrote Gaudier-Brzeska, 'works with instinct as his inspiring force....That this sculpture has no relation to the Classic Greek, but that it is continuing the tradition of the barbaric peoples of the earth (for whom we have sympathy and admiration) I hope to have made clear' (16, 1914: 118). The two artists had a similar conceptual understanding of the spiritual propensity of art and a regard for the instinctual and emotional capacity of the artist that led to re-evaluation of the Western canon of sculpture. Yet, through their use of stone and wood and the method of direct carving as a means to express the emotion of the artist, they also rejected notions of modern materialism and the commercialisation of art. The sentiment of truth to materials and its inherent value of workmanship as a means to achieve direct artistic expression, rejected classical ideals of beauty with its dependence on proportions and led to an identification with the vitality of 'primitive' art.

During the 1920's Underwood developed as an artist and collector in reference to such claims to universality and he may even have considered his work as a continuation of Gaudier-Brzeska's. Underwood's frame of reference as a collector, which derived from a growing theoretical interest in the investigation of sculpture throughout the ages seems to have been a conscious response to 'Vortex Gaudier-Brzeska' published in the issue of BLAST of June 1914. In this article, Gaudier-Brzeska describes the development of sculpture from Palaeolithic times to the present day 'Moderns'. He asserts that modern artists are heirs to the traditions of prehistoric, archaic and especially the 'masterpieces' of Oceania and Africa, produced in the 'Vortex of Fecundity' (Gaudier-Brzeska1914: 157). Like Gaudier-Brzeska, Underwood's work reveals a concern for volume, mass and simplicity of expression, yet this did not involve a direct imitation of 'primitive' art, as had been popularised by the artists of the Bloomsbury group and the influential critics Roger Fry and Clive Bell, declaring that 'they set about fostering the pastiche of tribal form on to our ailing Western tradition, to serve our own alien experience. This was not the renewal of style, it was just a spurious novelty' (Underwood N.D.). For Underwood then the artistic process within collecting was not confined to formal affinity, but was informed by a complex understanding of how his collection encapsulated forms of art that were originally governed by a spiritual value.

Underwood's rejection of the Fry and Bell model was further elaborated in the journal, *The Island* (1931), which explored the relevancy of 'primitive' art within contemporary culture, and exemplified the importance of such collections within their concept of the relationship between the poet-artist and the environment.[8] The *Islanders* wrote Bard; 'were united from the outset in a strong desire to stand together and to offer a joint resistance to commercial art....[and] believe in the power and significance of imagination, and in the realisation of the artistic self through an imaginative and spiritual existence' (Eustace 1996: 16). The journal was a symposium for the artists and writers who met at Girdlers Road. to express their engagement with a belief in the power of the imagination and in the notion of the artist as shaman. [9] Each contributor submitted written manifestos on their artistic credos, accompanied by poetry, art criticism, essays and images. There were no illustrations of ethnographic art however, but the majority of images produced by the artists used simplified forms to express mythic or allegorical subject matter that pertained to a general 'Primitivist' aesthetic as illustrated in figure 1. In Underwood's written contributions, the relationship between 'primitive' art and modern sculpture was not identified in stylistic terms of which he was deeply critical, but in the 'essential purpose of the artist', a role that was essentially metaphysical in which art could unify the dichotomies of the modern world. In the fourth issue on 'Art and Religion', Mahatma Gandhi contributed a symposium of his belief in the importance of art to man's spirituality; 'religion is the proper and eternal ally of art.... I believe firmly that both religion and art have to serve the identical aims of moral and spiritual elevation' (Gandhi 1931: 99).

In *The Island,* notions of pre-modern, spiritual art and culture became a counter-point to lost values within their own system of belief. Underwood's motivation to collect 'primitive' art seems to have been informed by this same desire to engage with an ideal spiritual consciousness from which his own world could be recreated, claiming that 'I collected tribal art, wishing to pursue the study of the imagery of belief in the spirit-world' (Underwood, N.D.). Underwood's somewhat utopian system of belief sought solace in distant and imaginary cultures embodying a simpler lifestyle, that he engaged with through collecting and travelling. In this perceived realm of 'primitive' essences 'Man' existed as a brotherhood without the pain, suffering, sickness and death that had shattered the European psyche during the War. In this respect, Underwood's collection may have served as a means of asserting a 'renewal of existence' (Benjamin 1999: 63) to re-articulate his role as an artist in a society that had began to reject the value of art.

Figure 1: Left: Leon Underwod, Cover for The Island, 1931. (Photograph: Celina Jeffery)

'My Ancient-Brother Artists'

From the fragments of Underwood's collection that are identifiable during the period of the 1920's and early 1930's, it is possible to recognise an artistic process, informed by a complex matrix of factors, amidst his collecting. In an attempt to regain validity, render art poetic and thus salvage his ideal of the integration of art and life, Underwood collated examples of 'primitive' art. From the immediate post-war period until his death, Underwood pursued the world for remnants of 'authentic' past and present traditions of art-making that could stimulate and legitimise his own aims as an artist. Collecting seems to have served a dual function for Underwood, combating his own sense of artistic alienation within society by invoking a sense of the profound and authentic within his own art. Yet, his concept of indigenous art practice was a highly subjective one that was largely romanticised. In this instance we might recall how, as Hobsbawm has argued, that the turn of the century was a period in which western Europeans and North Americans were engaged in 'inventing traditions' to legitimise their own historicity (1983: 1). The 'invention of traditions' was particularly applicable to 'Primitivism', in which the collection of 'primitive' art sought to establish points of linkage and mutual understanding regardless of cultural or historical context. This principle may also be said to have informed Underwood's collecting practices, in which 'primitive' art was consumed for its presumed primal aesthetic and spiritual qualities for the purpose of re-inventing 'modern' art. Collecting as a form of 'inventing traditions' then was a paradoxical product of 'civilisation' itself, in which continuity was, 'largely factitious' (Hobsbawm 1983: 2).

Underwood's search for cultural authenticity continued at the caves of Altamira in 1925, where he 'discovered' the extraordinary realism of its drawings and stone reliefs and declared 'the presence of my ancient brother-artists' (Underwood N.D.). The appeal of these caves for the imagination of archaeologists, anthropologists, art historians and artists in the early decades of the century was profound. Of crucial significance to Underwood was that they seemed to challenge the hierarchies of Western art, that had further been confounded by principles of evolutionary anthropology; 'Sautuola's discovery came as an innocent contradiction of the Darwinian assumption of crude and brutish antecedents' (Underwood N.D.). Underwood regarded this example of Palaeolithic art with admiration declaring a preceding age of artistic reverie and a source of ancient legitimisation for modern 'Primitivism'. As a result, he took numerous drawings and notes from the caves at Altamira and later produced casts of the pre-Palaeolithic 'Dusseldorf Venus'. The experience had evoked an inward sympathy and perceived understanding for 'primitive' art, which was re-assimilated as an aspect of his own sensibility as an artist and collector.

Underwood travelled extensively to pursue his interest in exploring the 'primitive' arts of the world. In 1928 he undertook a commission by Brentano Press to illustrate a book called *The Red Tiger* (1929) by Phillips Russell and toured Central America. Their route followed part of the pioneering expedition of 1839 led by the explorer John Lloyd Stevens and the artist, Frederick Catherwood, who illustrated the book, *Incidents of Travel in Central America, Chiapas, and Yucatan* (1843). They followed part of the original route through Guatamala, the Mexican states of Chiapas and Tabasco, and the peninsula of Yucatan. Their itinerary was influenced by their interest in the area as the birthplace of ancient civilisations rather than the home of contemporary indigenous cultures. They did not engage with the living cultures or the contemporary cultural and political revolution in Mexico, but with the remnants of Maya and Toltec civilisations – the 'idea' of an authentic Mexico in its pre-contact state.

The Ninth century Toltec-Maya site of Chichen Itza proved to be particularly fascinating to Underwood. He was undoubtedly attracted by the monumentality of the structure, with its combination of sculpture and extensive carvings, as evidenced in his detailed illustrations. He was also intrigued by the figures of the *chacmool* to be found at Chichen Itza, Tula and the were-jaguar or 'red tiger' in the Merida Museum. The obvious sculptural qualities of the *chacmool* and were-jaguar, their sheer 'stoniness', sense of gravity and simplified, direct forms were instantly identifiable with his belief in truth to materials. Moreover, the *chacmool's* flat, cubic surfaces and lack of three dimensionality seems to have reaffirmed his understanding of the dialectic between ancient and modern sculpture.

Unable to collect carvings from the sites, Underwood accumulated a number of 'souvenirs' during his tour, to represent his experiences of these cultures. He kept detailed notebooks; made extensive drawings of sites, individual sculptures and carvings and collected postcards. Underwood made a cast of the were-jaguar, at the Merida Museum and did extensive drawings of the *chacmool* that became a source of stimulation for many of his future works. The function of such pieces within his 'collection' was undeniably a reminder of his tour, yet they may also have served another function, in which 'such objects allow one to be a tourist in one's own life, or allow the tourist to appreciate, consume, and thereby 'tame' the cultural other' (Stewart 1984: 146). They informed an integral aspect of the art and art theory dominating his work for at least the next ten years.

Fundamental to this appreciation was a belief in the value of art as a central component of the spiritual life of the community. Indeed, the influence of the role of pre-Columbian art in the service of a community directly inspired the utopic *Cathedral* of 1930-2. *The Cathedral,* a wooden carving was designed as a project for an actual temple of the arts, two hundred feet in height, on the scale of a Mayan temple. In *The Island* Underwood described it as a, 'a sculptural realisation of an architectural project for spiritual belief in the future' (Jenkins 1979: 3). The angular head and central arch were modelled on the *chacmool,* while the breasts and face relate more to the Yoruba figurative wood carvings in Underwood's collection and the overall shape was evocative of a heddle pulley.

Figure 2: Right: African Madonna, Leon Underwood, 1934-35 (Photograph: Conway Library, Courtauld Institute of Art)

Although Underwood's collection was eclectic in nature, it included examples of Eastern European, African, American, Oceanic and Asian material, a significant proportion of the pieces derived from areas of British colonial rule in west Africa. That African art assumed a central position within Underwood's collection was undoubtedly informed by its status as the embodiment of the 'primitive' and 'the totem of the European avant-garde' (North 1995: 278). It was African art then that Underwood chose to collect as the central component of his enquiry into 'primitive' sculpture. Significantly, Underwood also revealed aesthetic biases towards wood, bronze and ivory statuary, masks and headdresses, all of which could be understood on a formal level in terms of 'art' objects. The emphasis on carvings, in particular, with an 'abstract' aesthetic was commonly identified amongst Modernist groups as being representational of 'African art', and its language was appropriated to challenge classical ideals of beauty and naturalism.

The concentration of figurative woodcarvings undoubtedly informed Underwood's own art during the 1920's and 1930's, when he produced sculptures in 'Africanised' forms using 'primitive' woods. Underwood's sculpture, *African Madonna* (1935), made from Lignum Vitae, was a seminal example demonstrating these concerns (fig. 2). George Harwood commissioned the sculpture for St. Peter's English Church native school at Rosettenville, Johannesburg. Underwood chose to depict the Madonna as a Bantu mother and described it as a sculptural interpretation of the 'ideal of universal motherhood, which has so influenced our Western civilisation and culture' (Rand Daily Mail 21.05.36: 28). The figure of a Bantu woman as the Madonna challenged western ideals of beauty with religious and political implications, causing a great controversy when it was placed in the church and was removed from display. However, by using his African collection as a source of aesthetic and spiritual inspiration within his own work, Underwood had deemed it to be an equal, if not, superlative form of 'art'.

Universalism

Underwood's experiences of collecting, travelling and theorising had been based upon a conviction that the meaning of art was universal - whereby perception, meaning and emotion are universally shared. Yet, a collection supersedes its cultural and historical context and meaning with a system of classification that denies temporality. Underwood's collection was similarly used as a means to transcend historical and cultural boundaries and explore the essential aspects of sculpture. The new sense of the world developed by such 'Primitivist' sensibilities no longer required a system of polarisation for its realisation, but sought to merge space, time and context in its consideration of 'primitive' creativity in art. Within Underwood's collection the individual properties of art from West Africa, Papua New Guinea, Tibet, India and Mexico were subsumed within a holistic conception of 'primitive' art. Yet, as James Clifford has argued, the practice of collecting is not a universal phenomenon,

> *A history of anthropology and modern art needs to see in collecting both a form of Western subjectivity and a changing set of powerful institutional practices. The history of collecting is central to an understanding of how those social groups that invented anthropology and modern art have appropriated exotic things, facts and meanings* (Clifford 1996: 220).

The concept of universalism as a subjective, philosophical and ideological construct organised Underwood's Primitivist world-view and by extension, his collection. His practice of collecting rendered a radically different sense of time, one which was conceived in its psychological aspect or 'the mental growth of mankind; that growth in which the mind of the individual is a microcosmic reiteration of his whole development' (Underwood 1934: v). This attempt to cut across time and ancient thought was expressed most poignantly in an exhibition, *Sculpture Considered Apart from Time and Place,* which Underwood curated at the Sydney Burney Gallery in 1932.[10]

In many ways, the Exhibition was a recognition of Underwood's connoiseurship in the area of comparative aesthetics. It was one of the first exhibitions of comparative art to be held in a British gallery, followed by the International Surrealist exhibition in 1936 at the New Burlington Gallery and *40,000 Years of Modern Art - A Comparison of the 'Primitive' and the Modern,* 1948 at the Institute of Contemporary Art in which Underwood acted in an advisory capacity. Underwood was a personal friend and acquaintance of Sydney Burney and it is likely that they met through their shared interest in collecting African art. Like the Parisian dealers, Burney was an enthusiastic dealer and collector of contemporary European sculpture as well as 'primitive' 'Eskimo carving, African and Polynesian art and Chinese terracottas' and the exhibition undoubtedly functioned as a means to demonstrate his broad engagement with this art market (Neve 1974: 166). A precursor of the 1932 exhibition was the 1928 show, *Modern and African Sculpture* which exhibited the works of British artists such as Epstein, Dobson, Skeaping and Hepworth alongside African figurative carvings. This was expanded in *Sculpture Considered* to incorporate over 150 sculptures through the ages, from regions in Africa, China, France, Greece, India, Mexico, Persia and New Zealand as well as from a number of leading modernist sculptors including Jacob Epstein, Henry Moore, Gaudier-Brzeska, Augustus Rodin, Edgar Degas, Barbara Hepworth and Underwood.[11]

The Exhibition, *Sculpture Considered Apart from Time and Place,* demonstrated a multitude of Primitivistic sensibilities - locating 'art' in a system of universal aesthetics regardless of time or cultural context. This was indicated in the introduction to the catalogue, in which Underwood explained that the aim of the exhibition was to, 'reveal, by concrete illustration, elements in sculpture that remain unchanged by time or by the style of master, school or period - elements that are combined harmoniously by what we have called '*sculptural consciousness*' (Underwood 1932: 7). This was a reaffirmation of his belief that the spirit of art and the artist could transgress time and space and be received on an independent aesthetic and philosophical level. The exhibition also highlighted the significance of sculpture for Underwood as a medium to express continuity and tradition, 'in a survey of aesthetic culture from the cave times onward, sculpture is a key position of a race and its relative importance. Back and forth along a gradated scale of the various modes of approach, the history of the sculptor's search for self-expression swings slowly like a pendulum' (Underwood Sept. 1931: 41). The idea that sculpture could communicate qualities of expression or spirit regardless of time or origin, was the guiding principle of the choice of exhibits and their thematic organisation and display. Three factors informed this *consciousness*; the material, motives and the quality of the sculptor's personal vision. Consequently, the exhibition was arranged according to two further principles corresponding to the division of the sculptor's motives; the *repose* or static motive and the *dance* or dynamic motive. The *repose* room displayed examples of sculpture that were static in form, with materials which included stone, wood, plaster and some metal. Sculpture in the *repose* category included a stone Egyptian squatting figure with a stone sculpture, *Crouching Woman* by Barbara Hepworth. The idea was undoubtedly informed by Underwood's experience of monuments and sculpture in Mexico, in which his fascination with carving using simple tools emerged in his choice of exhibits such as the Aztec stone figure of a kneeling man and the stone figure of a woman by Moore. There was also a number of African wooden figurative carvings in this display. The *dance* motive room exhibited sculptures with dynamic forms such as a fourteenth century Madonna and Child, work by Gaudier Brzeska and Brancusi, in materials which included metal, wood and terracotta. A metallic figure of *The New Spirit* (1932) by Underwood with an Indian metallic Dancing Siva from the 12 Century BC were compared to illustrate movement and energy.

The Exhibition also reflected changing notions of 'art' that Modernism had given rise to in its engagement with 'Primitivism'. By displaying 'primitive' sculpture alongside 'western' sculpture within a gallery space, the exhibition elevated these artefacts to a position of 'art'. A photograph of the exhibition reveals an aestheticised display with each sculpture shown in the round to enhance the sculptural qualities of pieces, and notably without contextualising information or text, as would have been evident in museum displays (fig. 3). The exhibits photographed here include a Chinese Quan Yin figure, alongside a Sixteenth century Italian figure, 'The New Spirit' by Leon Underwood, 'Dancer' by Gaudier-Brzeska, a Twelfth century Indian Dancing Diva, a Dogon figure from west Africa, a Third century Chinese figure and 'Herring Gulls' by Maurice Lambert. This dialogue between sculpture through the ages had a dual effect: firstly, the modern Western sculptures gained in profundity and secondly the status of the 'primitive' sculptures was elevated within a timeless aesthetic standard of 'art'.

In *Sculpture Considered Apart from Time and Place,* Underwood demonstrated a utopic vision of art transcending cultural boundaries, uniting the art of humankind. It was from this trans-historical form of aesthetic and spiritual meaning that Underwood sought to recapture the kinds of representational and symbolic strength that he felt had been lost in the art of his own culture. The exhibition alluded to the fundamental value of his own collection and may have been a rendition of his ideal collection in which he could act out his aesthetic and philosophical enquiries.

Underwood's notion of universal aesthetics, in which anyone with an 'eye' could appreciate and engage with 'primitive' art, conflicted with the contemporary discourse of social anthropology. The resultant negation of the study of the art and material culture of 'primitive' peoples created a lacunae in which Underwood was able to develop an inter-disciplinary approach to the re-evaluation of 'primitive' art. His collecting practices, involvement in comparative art exhibitions and emulation of 'primitive' art were outward signs of an ideational shift. So called 'primitive' sculpture had assumed a position as *art,* which he suggested had 'a place in the gallery of world masterpieces: and by this we may enrich our store of precedent and meaning of tradition' (Underwood 1948: 185). This concept was asserted most forcefully during a collecting and lecturing tour of West Africa in 1945,[12] which gave rise to an influential trilogy of books on West African art and developed his career within the field of ethnographic museology.

Africa

As is evident from his collection, 'Africa' had occupied Underwood's imagination for many years. In many ways, 'Africa' represented Underwood's imaginary 'Other' - an appeasement of his own 'decadent' and alienated society and a means to re-construct the self. It was African art, particularly the art of west and central Africa, that Underwood chose to collect, represent, imagine, theorise and finally develop as an academic interest relevant to both the art historical and ethnographic disciplines of his era. It is within his collection of African art then, that we come closest to understanding his particular subjective, aesthetic and philosophical taxonomies and their relationship to the wider paradigmatic sphere.

In 1945, under the auspices of the British Council, Underwood undertook a tour of West Africa, with the purpose of developing a means of protecting local art making traditions.[13] Travelling through areas of British and French West Africa such as Ghana, Sierra Leone, Côte d'Ivoire and Nigeria, Underwood observed the art of the regions, lectured and collected. His lectures on *Art and Africa, The History of Printing and Technical Improvements* and *Tradition in Art* were given in schools, colleges, clubs and societies to encourage the appreciation of both the African and European cultural heritage. In his lectures, Underwood identified the 'present day decline' of West African art and spoke of the need to maintain standards and retain a traditional framework within which to produce their art (1945: 2). A subsequent report to the British Council spoke of the effects of Western influence on indigenous art, in which missionaries, travellers, anthropological collectors and the rise of the art market resulted in a fragmentation of local identity and an increasing awareness of commercialisation. He did not accept any accountability for his role within the art market and thus the development of 'art consciousness' amongst artists, but paradoxically considered his connoisseurship to be of value in instructing these peoples of the value of their traditions 'to the Empire and to the World' (1945: 7). Underwood's recommendations involved the distribution of reproductions of superior examples of art, followed by long term plans for restitution, legislation preventing the exodus of further significant works, the setting up of museums and education outreach to encourage traditional practice. However, this did not prevent him from collecting a substantial number of objects during his visit which were eventually sold on the art market.

During his tour, Underwood collected a considerable number of wood and ivory carvings, pottery and textiles, amassing some twenty-five cases. Underwood travelled extensively to collect these objects, going by foot to remote areas in the northern regions hoping to gain a more 'authentic' experience of art making outside of the Westernising influences on the coast. His collection included arts from a variety of regions such as Abidjan, Côte d'Ivoire, where he embarked upon his journey to the northern most region of Sierra Leone, west to Lagos and east to Benin. The collection did not represent a 'comprehensive' taxonomy, and would better be described as representing a subjective aesthetic bias towards figurative carvings, masks and headdresses. The majority of the collection, were from the Yoruba regions of Nigeria, which he described as having retained it's localised tradition and authenticity. As a result, Underwood collected an extensive range of Ibeji figures, a large number of masks and headdresses, including an elaborate Epa mask, and many carved figurative pieces.

A highly distinctive example of the kind of objects that he collected was a Yoruba Shango headdress, which Underwood found in a Shango temple at Ogbomosho in Northern Yorubaland (fig. 4). It was illustrated in his book *Figures In Wood of West Africa* (1947) in which he described it as *The Earth Feeding Mankind* (1951: xiv), a title that pertained to a supposed universal meaning of fertility. It is likely however, that such a piece would have been used in a Shango ceremony, as the double axe motif on the coiffure is a metaphor for thunderbolt to Shango, the *orisa* (god) of thunder and lightening (Picton 1995: 422). That Underwood felt capable of attributing meaning on the basis of his connoisseurship is demonstrative of the problematics of his engagement with universal aesthetics. For Underwood, such pieces were superlative examples of art and spirituality, which were believed to possess a 'fourth' dimension, or spirit that could transcend time and place. Underwood's understanding of the value of West African art within the expression of religious and social ceremonies may account for the concentration of masks and headdresses that he amasses from the Ibibio, Dan, Senufo and Yoruba.

During the tour Underwood also visited a number of schools and colleges where he collected paintings and drawings by students. The schools and colleges visited included; Bishop's Girls' School, Accra, Wesleyan Training College, Bunumbu, Sierra Leone, Principal Government Training College, Ibadan, Nigeria, NA School, Omu, Illorin, Nigeria, Principal Edo College, Benin and Middle School Jefferies, Bauchi, Nigeria.[14]

Figure 3: Right: Leon Underwood, view of Sculpture, Considered Apart from Time and Place, 1931, (Photograph: Conway Library, Courtauld Institute of Art).

During his visits, Underwood collected 107 drawings and paintings by pupils, which he used in an exhibition of African art in Lagos.[15]

Many of the examples show the influence of western art training – painting and life drawing being predominantly western art forms, while also engaging with local subjects such as market places or cultural beliefs rendered in strong colour and patterned compositions. Underwood held the exhibition in August 1945 at the British Council Reading Room in Lagos, to an audience of about one hundred people.[16] The exhibition included a number of watercolour drawings by pupils of various schools that Underwood had visited, alongside an array of the sculptures, weavings and pottery that he had collected primarily in Nigeria (Underwood 1946: 220). In an article, *Nigerian Art,* written for the Quarterly magazine, *Nigeria,* Underwood described the impact of African on European art but more significantly he spoke of the problems of the impact in reverse, suggesting bleakly that 'westernisation descends upon them' (1946: 216).

In particular, Underwood was critical of the western art education system that was being developed. As such Underwood met a number of artists during his visit, including Kponton in Lome, Zaganado, a Dahomian carver, Makide in Lagos and Bamgboye in Omu, Illorin, to assess the impact of 'westernisation' on their 'traditional' art making. Bamgboye, later to become a well-known Yoruba artist, who also taught at the first governmental experimental school, run by J. D. Clarke, was accused by Underwood of having acquired an 'art consciousness' (Underwood 1948: 15). For example, Underwood critiqued the artist for producing Ifa divination tables for the western market, suggesting, 'so soon as a traditional carver is made art-conscious-by European notions of art as something specialised-apart from ordinary life-his powers of expression decline' (Underwood 1948: 16).[17] Underwood had indicated both a rejection of art education as well as a fear that increasing commodification of African artefacts as 'art' would lead to the loss of its inherent value. But what was the intrinsic meaning of African art for Underwood and how may we account for it?

Underwood's criticism of art training and commercialisation suggests that he valued the perceived untutored creativity of the African artist, which crucially he linked to the ritualistic power of the African object. Unlike art in the modern west, which he believed had lost its 'imagination and intuition' in the course of its commercialisation, African art was deemed to have retained its singularity and ritual power or 'aura' as Walter Benjamin described art in its pre-commodified state (Underwood 1934: 3).18 Igor Kopytoff has described the process of commodification as 'anti-cultural' and conflicting with 'the essence of culture' which is concerned with the value of discrimination.19 In this sense, the African art object as non-exchangeable and ritualistic directly appealed to Underwood and to others like him, as Errington elaborates:

> *They are viewed as unique and irreplaceable, usually stable in space, and were intended to endure through duration with minimal change in location or meaning... Objects in capitalism, and therefore in nation-states, by contrast, are prototypically commodities, that is, exchangeable for something else, preferably money* (1989: 54).

Of significance in understanding this dynamic was how the notion of the African object as sacred appealed to a sense of authenticity that was felt to be lost within western art. The association between the 'unique value of the 'authentic' work of art with ritual, which Benjamin described, may be linked to Underwood's anxiety with the inauthentic sentiment of western art and thus the value he gave to west African art.20

The notion that the authenticity of African art was threatened by the impact of westernisation pervaded Underwood's ideology, and indeed that of many African art collectors within the first half of the century, giving rise to the highly paradoxical discourse of collecting as a process of salvage or protection. Thus Underwood described the 'present day decline' of African art and spoke of examples of Benin art as 'degenerate' due to western influence.[21] The desire to preserve traditional examples of African art from degeneracy seems to have informed Underwood's motivation to collect. The desire to 'salvage' that which is believed to be lost or under threat has been described by James Clifford as a definitive characteristic of collecting practice in the field.[22] Clifford describes how collecting as a means to relinquish that which is believed to be in danger of being lost is associated with an historical consciousness; 'authenticity in culture or art exists just prior to the present, but not so distant or eroded as to make collection or salvage impossible' (1987: 122). Underwood similarly believed that the culture he was studying was on the cusp of change from tradition and authenticity to a process of modernisation that induced the synchretisation and commodification of culture.

Underwood's concept of the authenticity of African art and his desire to 'salvage' this through collecting may also be understood in terms of the concept of the 'death of culture' which penetrated both anthropological and art discourses of the period. As Steiner has argued:

> *The concept of the 'death of culture' was used by early anthropology as a means of legitimating its burgeoning status as a science of preservation, where artefacts stood as visible symbols salvaged from the ravages of a decaying modern world. The same concept however, was also necessary to twentieth century artists who could only 'discover' African art in a context freed from the encumbrance of a living African artistic counterpart with an alternative voice, and a different evaluative language* (1994: 105).

Collecting here becomes a powerful hegemonic discourse, in which objects are stripped of their original meaning and conditioned to comply with the agenda of the collector. The paradox of this ideology was that Underwood's act of collecting exchanged the 'sacred' value of these objects with a status as 'art' in its western sense, further contributing to the art market in 'primitive' art and the subsequent 'decline' of the traditional culture that he was seeking to preserve.

These objects were considered to be neither 'aesthetic' nor 'artistic' in their original context, having been chosen on the merit of their authenticity, that is their condition, usage, uniqueness and rarity, but became so in Underwood's collection. As an artist and theorist of art, Underwood's identification with the art of west Africa revealed an inevitable bias towards sculptural works, such as the Yoruba figure of a female water carrier carved by Bamboya. A significant proportion of Underwood's collection also consisted of carved figurines with a simplified, abstracted treatment of form and use of primary colours, such as the Bambara antelope headdress that had provided such artist-collectors with a strong notion of 'African' art. Underwood also collected a number of rare objects including several Ibibio 'sun' masks, which were later 'faked' to comply with the demands of the art market as a result of their scarcity. Underwood's collection of African art thus saw the transformation of the objects in their 'traditional' phase as ritualistic in a sacred context and its modernist phase as 'objets d'art', effacing the social history of its production. Furthermore, it was Underwood's apparent connoisseurship in west African art that had allowed him to conduct the tour and to identify the 'Art' of the region and thus to diffuse 'African culture in Africa', revealing another powerful instance of the paradox of his collecting practices (Underwood 1946: 215).

Underwood published three short books on the art of West Africa as a result of his tour and indeed his long-term engagement with collecting African art.[23] The trilogy, *Figures in Wood of West Africa* (1947), *Masks of West Africa* (1948) and *Bronzes of West Africa* (1949), incorporated essays which discussed the art of each region within the context of their influence on western art, while engaging with issues of representation and interpretation. They represent a subjective response of an artist, in which Underwood admires the artistry of the work - describing the 'complexity' of his Epa mask for example, but is unable to clarify or interpret symbolic codes within such pieces. As such, many of his valuations of African art are primarily aesthetic and poetic rather than concise or 'factual'. However, where possible there is an attempt to authenticate the material to individual artists, the Epa head-dress being attributed to the now, well known artist Bamboya, dating from the 1930's in the region of Omu, Ilurin. A number of pieces from his collection were illustrated in the trilogy and discussed in numerous articles which he published in MAN and in The Studio, further suggesting that Underwood desired to propagate his belief in the value of 'African art'. In November 1945 Underwood also appeared in a documentary, displaying his collection of African art and exploring the idea that African artists had much to teach the development of the foundations of modern artistic expression.

Figure 4: Left: Yoruba Shango Figure, (Photograph: Conway Library, Courtauld Institute of Art).

Underwood collected over 550 objects, predominantly during his trip to West Africa in 1945 and he continued collecting into the 1960's. Some of the collection resided in his studio in Girdlers Road. (fig. 4) however the vast majority was sold on the 'primitive' art market in the late 1950's and 1960's. He sold a number of pieces to museums and galleries, including the Shango figure and an Ibo mask which are now in the Metropolitan Museum of Art, New York and the Bambara Antelope headdress which is now at the Field Museum in Chicago. Thiry-five pieces were sold through the Carlbach Gallery in New York in 1952 and 49 pieces were sold through the Wengraf Gallery in 1961, where the majority of pieces were sold to international dealers. fifty of the craft pieces went to the Museum of Mankind between 1949 and 1969. The rest was dispersed privately.

Underwood had set out to challenge the debased opinion of African art, declaring his 'discovery' of these art forms to be a decisive factor in their re-assessment, 'lost as mere 'fetish figures' in a more material world; African work depended for its rediscovery as works of art upon bridging the gap between European and African ideas, involving a less stigmatised interpretation of the word 'primitive' (Underwood 1951: xiii). This he suggested could be achieved by creating an inter-disciplinary approach to the study of west African 'art' within the categories of wood carving, masks and bronzes, that merged ethnography with aesthetics. In many ways, Underwood represented a new specialist of the subject, part art historian, and part ethnographer that attributed the status of 'art' to African carving.

Underwood's particular merging of aesthetics with ethnography, developed through his collection and promulgated through exhibitions, academic essays and books, was a significant contribution to the development of inter-disciplinary studies of African art. Thus, one of the first inter-disciplinary conferences was in 1949, with a discussion organised and led by Edmund Leach, Leon Underwood and Roland Penrose. This integration of art history and ethnography was an important development in the 1950's for the anthropology of art, which began to qualify African artefacts as art. This involved the attribution of aesthetic qualities resulting in an appreciation of the individual creativity of the artist and a further awareness of contemporary art practice.

Underwood's influence in this area was most evident in the work of William Fagg who described the artist as his 'mentor' (Maclancey 1988: 168). Underwood's influence was particularly apparent in Fagg's engagement with issues of representation and interpretation of African art. They published an article together, *'An Examination of the So-Called Olokun Head of Ife, Nigeria'* (1949), in MAN, and Underwood was consulted and acknowledged on many occasions within Fagg's writings. Underwood also acted as an advisor to Fagg's exhibition, *The Tribal Image: Wooden Figure Sculptures of the World* in 1970 at the Museum of Mankind, for which he selected 80 exhibits on the basis of their 'sculptural interest and quality' (Fagg 1970: 1). As in Underwood's collection, the individual historical and cultural attributes of each object were subsumed within the universal notion of 'primitive' art.

His collection amassed over a fifty-year period, illustrates the changing motivations, valuations and aesthetic biases that informed the re-conception of 'primitive' art as 'Art' in the inter-War era. The narrative of Underwood as a collector should be considered an aspect of the 'primitivist' channel, which involved its own particular discourse and mode of representation. Ostensibly, Underwood's collection could be considered to have functioned autonomously within the artist's creative process. However, as I have argued, Underwood's collecting was encouraged by an atavistic desire to revitalise art through a regression to more direct modes of expression, that was informed by philosophical motivations, which interacted and transacted with wider cultural and historical developments. Underwood's collection emerged from a crises in his historical consciousness concerning the separation between art and life and the displacement of the artist in contemporary society. Underwood valued the authenticity and ritual power or 'aura' of 'primitive' art, which he believed, had been lost in western art. As such, Underwood's collection was encouraged by an atavistic

Figure 5: Left: Leon Underwood, view of studio, 1960's, (Photograph: Conway, Courtauld Institute of Art).

Figure 6: Right: Leon Underwood, view of library, (Photograph: Conway Library, Courtauld Institute of Art).

desire to revitalise modern art through an appropriation of the authenticity of 'primitive' art. This was governed by a concept of universality, as demonstrated in his exhibition *Sculpture Considered Apart From Time and Place* which aimed to demonstrate that meaning and value in art is capable of transcending cultural barriers. This informed his tour of British west Africa in 1945, during which he aimed to demonstrate the value of African 'art' to Africans in order to develop a means of protecting local art making traditions from westernising influences. Paradoxically, Underwood's desire to collect, which derived from a need to 'salvage' the remnants of this 'traditional' art, contributed to the increasing commodification of African 'art' that he sought to critique. Thus, once these objects were absorbed into his collection they were endowed with the value of art and were eventually placed within the schema of the western art market, resulting in the loss of the sacred aura of their intended value. The individual objects assume a dialogue with one another becoming a means to transcend their time and place of origin in favour of the artist's aesthetic and philosophical appropriation. A photograph of Underwood's library shows the ease with which Underwood's own artwork rests with the 'collected' objects, the display emphasising the artistic qualities of each piece (fig. 6). The example of Underwood as an artist and collector of African art, serves to illustrate the transition of African artefacts as ritual objects to Modernist 'objets d'art'. It also demonstrates the highly paradoxical discourse of the cross cultural exchange that took place in this transition, that reveals more about the ontology of the collector than the collected.

Notes

1. The term 'primitive' is used to maintain the contemporary language, it is not considered an appropriate term.
2. 'Primitivism' is a highly debatable term that has been used to describe the appropriation of ideological, aesthetic and philosophical traits attributed to so-called 'primitive' societies, generically identified with the classic evolutionary classification of the Pacific, Africa and the Americas. It has a historical lineage tracing back to antiquity but gained dominance in the late nineteenth century, during the height of colonialism and its associated epistemological debates concerning the nature of human society. Visual 'Primitivism' was central to the development of the avant-garde and Modernism in the inter-war years.
3. Much of the primary material quoted here is sourced from one of the Underwood archives which is currently being held by the Conway Library, Courtauld Institute.
4. The Sydney Burney Gallery exhibited 'primitive' art throughout the 1920's and early 1930's, while the Chelsea Book Club and the Goupil Gallery exhibited African art in the early 1920's.
5. An article on *The Cycle of Styles in Art, Religion, Science and Technology* in pre-history was published in the Annual Report of The Society of Sculptors 1960-61. The final version of the book was never completed.
6. It is difficult to clarify the exact number of objects in the collection as many were dispersed privately before and after his death. However, a selection of material now resides in the Field Museum in Chicago, The Metropolitan Museum of Art, New York and The British Museum. The vast majority, however, was sold on the private market in London and New York in the 1950's and 1960's.
7. See Barkan and Bush, *Prehistories of the Future: The Primitivist Project and the Culture of Modernity.* Stanford University Press. 1995. Pg 14.

8. The Island was sponsored by Underwood, edited by the poet Joseph Bard and financed by Eileen Agar. It ran for four volumes from 15 June 1931 and was most likely to have been based on the journal *Theatre Arts Monthly.*
9. Contributors included Underwood, the thespian Velona Pilcher, the painter-poet and mystic, Ralph Chubb, the painter and sculptor Eileen Agar, the former Imagist poet John Gould-Fletcher and the artist Henry Moore.
10. The Sydney Burney Gallery was a private gallery in St James's Place, London. The exhibition ran from November to December.
11. Lenders included Roger Fry, Augustus John, Eric Kennington, Samuel Courtauld and Henry Oppenhiem (Neve 1974: 166).
12. Neve states that Underwood was in Africa in 1944 (1974: 218). However, both the report and several documents referring to Underwood's trip in British Council papers state that it took place in 1945.
13. Underwood, *Provisional Report on Art in British West Africa'* for the British Council, 1945.
14. Underwood, Ibid. 1945.
15. These now reside at the Pitt Rivers Museum.
16. See *Provisional Report on Art in British West Africa,* Part 2: 5.
17. However, Underwood collected several of Bamgboye's work, including an elaborate Epa mask produced before the period of his supposed commericalisation.
18. Walter Benjamin *The Work of Art in the Age of Mechanical Reproduction.* Illuminations, Pimlico, 1999: 215.
19. Igor Kopytoff: *The Cultural Biography of Things: Commoditization as Process.* In Appadurai *The Social Life of Things,* Cambridge University Press, 1986: 73.
20. Walter Benjamin *The Work of Art in the Age of Mechanical Reproduction.* Illuminations, Pimlico, 1999: 217.
21. See *Provisional Report on Art in British West Africa,* Leon Underwood. November 1945. Part 1, Section 2: 2
22. See James Clifford, 1987: 121.
23.Underwood planned to publish another book on the art of West Africa, including material on these areas as well as a section on the Ife, Olokun heads.

Acknowledgments

I would like to thank Garth, Jocelyn, Tiggy and Joshua Underwood, Ron Wiffen and the Conway Library, Courtauld Institute of Art for allowing me access to the Underwood archives. Also, Professor Dawn Ades of the University of Essex, Anthony Shelton and Angela Fagg for their advice and support.

Bibliography

BARD, J. and UNDERWOOD L. 1931. *The Island.* Volumes I to IV

BASSANI, E. MCLOED, M. 1987. The Passionate Collector. In *Jacob Epstein: Sculpture and Drawings.* Leeds and London: Leeds City Art Galleries. Whitechapel Art Gallery.

BARKAN, E and BUSH, R. 1995 *Prehistories of the Future: The Primitivist Project and the Culture of Modernity.* Standford: Stanford University Press.

BENJAMIN, W. 1999 *Unpacking My Library.* In *Illuminations.* London: Pimlico.

GAUDIER-BRZESKA, H. 1914. Letter to the Editor The Egoist, March 16.

GAUDIER-BRZESKA, H. 1914. Vortex Gaudier-Brzeska. *Blast* **1**.

CLIFFORD, J. 1987. Of Other Peoples: Beyond the Savage Paradigm. In Foster, H. (ed), *Discussions in Contemporary Culture.* Seattle: Bay Press.

CLIFFORD, J. 1996. *The Predicament of Culture: Twentieth -Century Ethnography, Literature, and Art.* Cambridge: Harvard University Press.

ELLWOOD, G. 1925. *Leon Underwood. Drawing and Design.* November.

ERRINGTON, S. 1989. Fragile Traditions and Contested Meanings. *Public Culture.* Vol. 1. Issue 2.

FAGG, W. and Underwood, L. 1949. An Examination of the So-Called Olokun Head of Ife, Nigeria. *MAN.* **49**. No 1.

FAGG, W. 1959. *African Art for God's Sake.* Liturgical Arts

FAGG, W. 1970. *The Tribal Image: Wooden Figure Sculpture of the World.* London: The British Museum Press.

GANDHI, M. 1931. Religion and Art. *The Island.* Vol.**1** no.4.

HOBSBAWM, E. and RANGER, T. 1983. *The Invention of Tradition.* Cambridge: Cambridge University Press.

MACCLANCEY, J. 1988. *A Natural Curiosity: The British Market In 'Primitive' Art.* RES (15).

MACK, J. 1998. *Kuba Art and the Birth of Ethnography.* In *The Scramble For Art In Africa.* Schildkrout, E., Keim C. A. (ed.'s). Cambridge: Cambridge University Press.

NEVE, C. 1974. *Leon Underwood.* London: Thames and Hudson.

NORTH, M. 1995. Modernism's African Mask: The Stein-Picasso Collaboration. In Barkan, E. and Bush, R. (eds), *Prehistories of the Future: The Primitivist Project and the Culture of Modernism.* Stanford: Stanford University Press.

PERRY, G. 1993. P*rimitivism and the Modern, Primitivism, Cubism, and Abstraction: The Early Twentieth Century.* New Haven: Yale University Press.

PICTON, J. 1995. *West Africa and the Guinea Coast.* In Phillips T. (ed), *Africa: The Art of the Continent.* London: Royal Academy of Arts.

READ, H. 1948. *40,000 Years Of Modern Art.* The Institute of Contemporary Arts.

STEINER, C. 1994. *African Art in Transit.* Cambridge: Cambridge University Press.

STEWART, S. 1993. *On Longing: Narratives of The Miniature, The Gigantic, The Souvenir, The Collection.* Durham and London: Duke University Press.

UNDERWOOD, L. N.D. *Underwood Papers.* Underwood Archive. Conway: Conway Library, Courtauld Institute.

UNDERWOOD, L. 1931. Sculptural Convictions. *The Island.* Vol. **1** no. 2.

UNDERWOOD, L. 1932. *Sculpture Considered a Part of Time and Place.* London: The Sydney Burney Gallery.

UNDERWOOD, L. 1934. *Art for Heavens Sake: Notes on the Philosophy of Art Today.* London: Faber and Faber.

UNDERWOOD, L. 1936. 'Letter to the editor' *Rand Daily Mail* 21 May.

UNDERWOOD, L. 1945. *British Council Report on Art in British West Africa.*

UNDERWOOD, L. 1946. *Nigerian Art* In *Nigeria, A Quarterly Magazine of General Interest.* No. 24.

UNDERWOOD, L. 1948. *Abstraction in African and European Art.* The Studio. December.

UNDERWOOD, L. 1949. *Bronzes of West Africa.* Alec Tiranti Ltd.

UNDERWOOD, L. 1951. *Figures in Wood of West Africa.* Alec Tiranti Ltd.

UNDERWOOD, L. 1952. *Masks of West Africa.* Alec Tiranti Ltd.

UNDERWOOD, L. 1961. *The Cycle of Style in Art, Religion, Science and Technology.* London: Royal Society of British Sculptors: Annual Report.

WILKINSON, A. 1984a. *Lipchitz, Epstein and Gaudier Brzeska.* In Rubin, W. (ed), *'Primitivism' in Twentieth Century Art: Affinity of the Tribal and the Modern.* Volume I. New York: The Museum of Modern Art.

WILKINSON, A. 1984b. *Henry Moore.* In Rubin, W. *'Primitivism' in Twentieth Century Art: Affinity of the Tribal and the Modern.* Volume I. New York: The Museum of Modern Art.

Archives

Leon Underwood Art Garth Underwood
Leon Underwood Art and Collection Jocelyn, Tiggy and Joshua Underwood.
Leon Underwood Writings Ron Wiffren, Conway Library, Courtauld Institute of Art
Leon Underwood Photograph Conway Library. Courtauld Institute of Art

The Dogs of Fo: Gender, Identity and Collecting

3

Sarah Cheang

Dominating the dining room of Preston Manor, Brighton, are one hundred and twenty-five Chinese figures known as the 'Dogs of Fo' (fig. 1). Visually arresting in their dark, mahogany cabinet, this gleaming collection is entirely made from *blanc de Chine*, a white, thin-walled, lustrous porcelain produced by the kilns of Dehua in Southern China. One hundred and twenty-four of the figures are lions, derived from buddhist iconographies and varying in height from 11cm to 51cm, whilst the remaining piece is an 11cm *qilin*, a Chinese mythical beast resembling a scaly unicorn. Manufactured in China and exported to Europe during the late-seventeenth and early-eighteenth centuries, these creatures were finally gathered together by Lady Ellen Thomas-Stanford (1848-1932), mainly between 1910 and 1914, forming what is probably the largest collection of its kind in existence. However, the single most defining element of Preston Manor's 'Dogs of Fo' is that, whilst not exactly identical in size and style, Ellen Thomas-Stanford's porcelain lions are all pretty much the same. Setting aside the one *qilin*, and two lions which are in a standing position, we have one object repeated one hundred and twenty-two times - a white, porcelain lion, sitting on a rectangular base.

Figure 1: Nine Lions from the one hundred and twenty-five piece 'Dogs of Fo' Preston Manor. ((Photograph: Sarah Cheang and Royal Pavilion, Art Gallery and Museums, Brighton and Hove Borough Council 1999)

In 1932 Preston Manor and its contents, including the 'Dogs of Fo', were left to the town by bequest. The house and grounds were opened as a museum in 1933, and since then there have been only four curators, each of whom has quite naturally sought a different emphasis, from eighteenth-century excellence to Edwardian reconstruction. Furniture and objects have been added or removed over time, and even entire interiors displaced in order to create new ones (Beevers 1999). Yet, the 'Dogs of Fo' have remained continually on show where their collector left them, looking out from their huge cabinet with no apparent regard for their frame of reference. This continuing presence, this pocket of stasis within a changing space, seems almost to hint at an excess rather than an absence of meanings - meanings so far beyond an immediate context that rather than grapple with the physical and conceptual problems of 'how does this collection fit within my vision for Preston Manor?' or 'where shall we keep these things?' curators have chosen to maintain the integrity of the collection and its collector, allowing the 'Dogs of Fo' to preside over the room come what may. At the same time, this collection has no renown within collecting circles of Chinese ceramics, and indeed seems generally to have been passed over. Save for one short article written within Brighton's museum service (Hershberg 1993), the collection has proved resistant to publication. Even P. J. Donnelly (1967), whose definitive guide to *blanc de Chine* begins by listing all public and private collections of this ware in Britain, seems to have been unaware of its existence.

That this collection has simultaneously transcended and circumvented the curated and connoisseurly spaces of the museum is significant. The incorporation of overtly Chinese displays into English, upper-class interiors begs many important questions concerning the history of mercantile and imperialistic relations between Britain and China. However, the apparent marginalisation of such a large collection, this elision of the super-abundant, also calls for a consideration of the collection's positionings within a gendered history of collecting and collections. Within certain contexts of 'good' and 'bad' collecting, 'useful' and 'useless' collecting, the drive for Ellen Thomas-Stanford, an upper-class Edwardian woman, to achieve a collection which was carefully displayed within a cabinet yet highly repetitive, is awkwardly positioned. Here, at Preston Manor, the identities of collector and museum are forced to interact. This essay asks whether it is in the creation and maintenance of complementary and gendered discourses of professional public collecting and amateur private accumulation that this collection's elision, its resistance to interpretation, has been grounded.

Investigating gendered collecting

Gender identity has been found to profoundly affect collecting, revealing itself in the type of objects collected, the ways in which these objects are arranged, displayed and related to, and the values placed upon those collected objects by society (Belk and Wallendorf 1997; Csikszentmihalyi and Rochberg-Halton 1981: 105-120). Collecting seems to provide a material display of social values, making the invisible visible through the arrangement of selected material culture in meaningful juxtaposition (Pomian 1990: 7-44). Thus Belk and Wallendorf (1997: 24) conclude that one of the social purposes of collecting is the reification, integration and maintenance of a 'gender dialectic'. It has further been advanced that there are two modes of collecting: the feminine mode which is relational and unemphatic, and the masculine mode which is intense, specific and serious (Pearce 1999: 210). Feminine collections express a material unity between the collection and the home, such as a display of plates on a sideboard or a collection of mouse replicas positioned about the house, which unlike masculine collections are not spatially or conceptually divided off from normal living, reflecting women's social positioning within the domestic sphere (Pearce 1999: 207-208; Wilkinson 1997: 97). The effects of aligning female collectors with domestic amateurism, and male collectors with public professionalism are twofold. Firstly, the museum institution provides collectors with an 'educational alibi' for what might otherwise be seen as extravagant or selfish spending, so that activities which mimic museum practices such as classifying, cataloguing and labelling a collection, connote a socially justifiable, 'good' collection (Belk 1995: 73-77; Wilkinson 1997: 85; Pomian 1990: 43). Thus feminine collecting, if disassociated from the museum and defined as the converse to educational collecting, becomes 'bad' collecting. Secondly, if the museum is considered to have become the professional institution which legitimises and authenticates collecting, a definition of collecting is made which mitigates against the very existence of feminine collectors. To say that a collection is a set of objects 'afforded special protection in enclosed places adapted specifically for that purpose and put on display,' (Pomian 1990: 9) precludes a feminine mode of collecting where objects may be integrated within general domestic displays.

But the identification of gendered modes of collecting does not mean that women can never collect in the masculine mode - can never be acknowledged protagonists in museum collections - or that men can never collect in the feminine mode. Helen Wilkinson (1997: 107) finds that the weighing up of 'good' and 'bad' collections within narrative fiction presents authors with an effective way of negotiating gender identities through stereotypes of collecting. This serves to underline the point that femininities and masculinities are ideologies of gender, socially constructed and embedded within a network of binary oppositions. Collecting, already gendered according to definition, becomes a fertile site for the contestation of these ideologies, both in the practice of collecting and in its literature.

Until fairly recently, history's lesson has been that only men can be great artists (Nochlin 1971). Similar assumptions, based on the privileging of wealth, social prestige and notions of genius, have also been extended to the field of collecting and need to be challenged. Studies of art collecting such as Pierre Cabanne's *The Great Collectors* (1963) and Lord Eccle's *On Collecting* (1968), have portrayed male collectors as combining an inner passion for art with the munificence to enable public access to their collections. However, female collectors, such as Catherine the Great and Peggy Guggenheim, whilst admitted to be capable of knowledgeable collecting, have not been accorded the same great and intense passion for possession of art as men, being either the selfless nurturers of the nation or possessions in themselves. Furthermore, it seems that as potential collectors, women communicate well and have a good 'eye' - the result of practising the art of looking on 'clothes, flowers, joints of meat, the laying of the table, herself in the mirror' (Eccles 1968: 70-76), whereas men, who are more likely to have been studying, will know more about the objects they look at.

Thus masculine collecting is informed and serious, and feminine shopping, whilst requiring certain skills of selection and communication, is uninformed, trivial and can never lead to greatness without stepping outside of gender roles. Eccles and Cabanne have not read the (female) consumer's urge to acquire as in anyway comparable with the (male) collector's passion, and it could be proposed that it is in these gendered distinctions of consumption practices that the notion of genius in collecting is created. The eighteenth-century European tradition of genius has been shown to have evolved by the end of the nineteenth century into a deeply gendered concept (Battersby 1989). Genius, the creative force which distinguished poetry from verse, science from technology, and art from craft was seen to be a male trait requiring notions of female non-genius as its foil. Therefore, it could be proposed that the quality necessary to raise collecting from mere shopping to high art is male genius, and that the female collector who does manage to achieve public prominence cannot be truly acknowledged as a 'great' collector, for this would be to threaten the very concept of male genius.

In a study of the late nineteenth-century artist Marie Bashkirtseff, Tamar Garb (1987-88) finds that self-representation for a female artist in patriarchal society presents many issues of masquerade, and few of whole, unfragmented identity. Bashkirtseff felt compelled to disguise her sex in order to negotiate prevalent discourses of masculinities and femininities, yet defences of the validity of her work also had to make use of feminine constructors such as 'prettiness' in order to legitimate her as a properly 'womanly' woman (Garb 1987-88: 82). In a similar vein, Pearce (1999: 210) proposes that feminine modes of collecting are adopted by mature, adult 'womanly' women in the role of domestic nurturer, whilst women who collect in the masculine mode are seeking other roles through their collections such as 'the child bride' or 'the vamp'. However, both alternative female roles suggested by Pearce seem to be partial attributes of the hyper-feminine, supporting the notion that an important factor in the generation of anxiety over female collecting is indeed the maintenance of gendered social boundaries. Feminine identities, produced, denied, contested and inscribed in the activities of collecting, seem in a constant state of emergence analogous to the identity of the colonial subject within colonialism for whom identification 'is always the return of an image of identity that bears the mark of splitting in the Other place from which it comes' (Bhabha 1994: 45).

If female identity is understood to be multi-faceted under patriarchy, then the identity formed through collecting must be equally multiple and/or partial. Susan Stewart (1993: 158-159), in her study of objects, collecting, narrative and desire, writes that the ultimate referent of the collection's selections and arrangements is the interior of the self. The collected objects, in fact, represent a surplus of the interior whose boundary with the exterior (the not-self) is being extended and marked by a material perimeter which both furthers and contains the self. Therefore, the collection is the self, but it is important to remember that this reified self, created by the will of the collector in response to both conscious and subconscious desires, represents the desired self; an ideal self. Thus, whatever longing has produced the collection, the collection can be seen as a way of providing a controlled cohesion of identity which is otherwise fractured and unstable. This self-possession through possessions is so strong that loss of the collection can be likened to loss of self (Wilkinson 1997: 106; Pearce 1999: 175). Hence, the collection also offers an opportunity for immortality, as the materiality of the collection, if preserved intact, can ensure the continuing integrity of the collector's identity after his/her death and mortification. Indeed, it was Ellen Thomas-Stanford's specific request that the 'Dogs of Fo' should always be displayed as she had left them (Roberts 1933).

Thus we can see that collections provide a material encoding of the collector's desired identity, including a desired positioning within the ideologies of gender and class. Yet the activity of collecting has also been seen as a vice, and an expression of social shortcomings (Cabanne 1963: viii). Stewart (1984: 163) writes: 'The boundary between collecting and fetishism is mediated by classification and display in tension with accumulation and secrecy,' reflecting the 'respectability' of collecting which tends towards museum practices. But as female access to the masculinities of 'respectable' museum-type collecting is problematic (Schor 1994:

257-258), and 'good' feminine collecting has been differently defined as the collection which integrates with the home, 'bad' feminine collecting has similarly been excluded from fetishism, so that alternative definitions are sought.

The Freudian concept of fetishism has, by the very roots of its argument, excluded women due to its innate phallocentricism. Women, by genital definition, cannot be fetishists since their 'lack' of penis denies them entry to the primary castration scene. Pearce (1999: 203-205) observes that for female collectors, terms such as 'accumulation' and 'obsession' are used in place of 'fetishism', and she suggests that this is because women enjoy a special relationship with the material world which enables them to invest objects with meaning without being fetishistic. But the very notion that female fetishism exists issues a challenge to Freud's phallocentricism, and in fact the actual potential of Pearce's statement lies in a partial acknowledgement that gendered discourses of psychoanalysis and consumption are implicated in the devaluation and disavowal of female collecting. Recent studies have explored and combined other readings of the fetish derived from Marxist commodity fetishism, and the field of anthropology, to formulate an understanding of how female fetishism can be theorised (Gammon and Makinen 1994). Taking colonial contact and conquest as her focus, Anne McClintock's study concludes that the fetish emerges in spaces of cultural ambiguity where social expectation and personal experience refuse to harmonise:

> *The fetish thus stands at the cross-roads of psychoanalysis and social history, inhabiting the threshold of both personal and historical memory. The fetish marks a crisis in social meaning as the embodiment of an impossible irresolution. The contradiction is displaced onto and embodied in the fetish, which is thus destined to recur with compulsive repetition. Hence the apparent power of the fetish to enchant the fetishist. By displacing power onto the fetish, then manipulating the fetish, the individual gains symbolic control over what might otherwise be terrifying ambiguities. For this reason, the fetish can be called an impassioned object* (McClintock 1995, 184).

These conclusions have profound consequences for a study of female collecting, for what is an obsessively collected object, if it is not an 'impassioned object'? The positioning of the fetish on the threshold between psychoanalysis and social history is also important for the potentially contradictory or unstable meanings which collections may hold, for the meaning of a collected object is neither fixed nor certain. As Stewart (1993: 32) writes: 'It is not through any intrinsic quality of the sign but rather through the interpretative acts of members of the sign community that the sign comes to have meaning [...].' Therefore the temporary sense of control achieved by the acquisition of fetishised objects may be in harmony or conflict with the 'interpretive universe' (Stewart 1993: 32) which gives meaning to ownership of those objects within a particular society, or even within the 'symbolic ecology' (Csikszenmihalyi 1996: 119) of a particular household.

To acknowledge that a female collector's activities may be fetishistic is to challenge that collector's access to feminine social roles. A further reading should therefore be made of Pearce's assumption that a special relationship exists between women and objects, capable of eliding both fetishism and masculine collecting modes. Wilkinson (1997: 100) concludes that it is A. S. Byatt's awareness of how 'women's lives in particular may be shaped and constrained by material,' which provides her writing with an unusual depth and resonance, allowing for material as well as verbal communication between characters. The notion that objects perform a special part in women's lives can also be found in studies of eighteenth-century consumption, where women have been shown to actively lay claim to the social role of consumers (see Vickery 1993: 274-301). This annexation of domestic consumption as feminine can be interpreted as an empowerment of women, in command of a specifically female space where male intervention is effectively marginalised. However, consumption has also been understood in direct opposition to production, where in patriarchal capitalist societies, production has been valorised as 'men's work,' and consumption correspondingly trivialised as 'women's work'. Furthermore, in the exchange economy of Western capitalist societies, consumption is abstracted from production and therefore from concepts of labour (Stewart 1993: 164). Yet private collecting, fundamentally an action of systematic domestic purchasing, is presented as an activity where, piece by piece, the collection is earned through a labour of consumption. Paradoxically, collecting simultaneously seeks to deny that act of consumption through a vocabulary which stresses the 'lucky find' and the 'acquisition' above the 'skilful purchase' or the 'bargain', prompting Stewart (1993: 164-165) to suggest that collecting further erases labour to produce the most abstracted form of consumption there is. Therefore, the 'good' collector transforms feminine acts of consumption into masculine acts of labour. If we are to understand collections as gendered signs of social achievement, then assessments of 'good' and 'bad' collecting might also reflect the degree to which a collected object is allowed to retain its connection with commodity status, failing to sever its link with consumption.

The interconnection of concepts of collecting and ideologies of gender produces an elision of female collecting. Therefore, the acknowledgement of women as collectors not only has the power to unseat gender bias in definitions of collecting, but also to challenge the social construction of diametrically opposed gender identities and even, as Belk and Wallendorf (1997: 9-10) find, to threaten male control of capital and power through an undisguised unity of production and consumption. The female collector, like the female fetishist, has fractured the masculine and feminine identities rooted in dichotomy. Perhaps, then, the identity of early twentieth century female collector Ellen Thomas-Stanford, reified in a massed display of *blanc de Chine* lions, negotiates a complex pathway through these networks of fracturing binary constructions.

Ellen Thomas-Stanford: identity and collection

On the evidence of receipts, invoices and letters preserved at Preston Manor, Lady Ellen Thomas-Stanford formed the bulk of her collection over a five year period, acquiring at least seventy-four of her lions between 1910 and 1914. The last purchase for which there is a record occurred in 1923, however, as can be seen in a photograph taken by the collector, when the collection had reached one hundred and sixteen pieces it was already extremely substantial, filling the cabinet (fig. 2). Ellen's photographed arrangement of the 'Dogs of Fo' shows an interest in a display which emphasises differences in style, so that, for example, those with pierced bases are grouped together on one shelf and those with relief decoration are on another, whilst across the cabinet the sizes of lion and therefore shelf heights are more or less symmetrical across a vertical axis. Her interest was hence one of visual effect rather than of scholarly separation into earlier and later wares, subtle glaze differentiations, or other more detailed analyses besides basic form.

That which distinguishes collection from accumulation is said to be system or purpose, so that when a new object is added to the collection it is severed from its origins and takes on the meanings generated by its new context - the context of the collection (Stewart 1993: 151-153). Each element in the collection works to create the meaning of the whole, and the sum of the collection is equivalent in value to that missing piece which the collector is continually in search of and which can be seen as a positive, motivational force behind the act of collecting (Baudrillard 1994: 13, 23). However, the 'Dogs of Fo' are said to have been collected until the cabinet was full (Roberts 1999), so that the collector imposed a physical rather than conceptual boundary on her activity. At the same time, a subtle integration of collection and room exists, for Ellen selected reproduction eighteenth-century dining room furniture with ball and claw feet, echoing the paw on ball postures of the lions, and there is also chinnoiserie lattice-work on the side tables, and an etching of African lions on the wall. Ellen claimed that the cabinet itself originated from George IV's sumptuous and 'oriental' Royal Pavilion at Brighton (Roberts 1957: 30), royal connections which have since been disproved but which frame the 'Dogs of Fo' within schemes of eighteenth-century chinnoiserie. Furthermore, a massed display of late-seventeenth and early-eighteenth century *blanc de Chine* lions, encrusted with ornamentation like piped-icing, could be read as a lavish and 'feminine' baroque design arrangement where a massed effect is far more important than individual pieces (Shulsky 1998: 27, 33). Therefore, the motivation to acquire, and the value of the last piece seem dependent upon judgements of domestic decoration and display, rather than issues of taxonomy. This is suggestive of Pearce's feminine mode of collecting, where collecting boundaries are integrated into the home. However, male late-Victorian and Edwardian collectors of Chinese porcelains also laid great emphasis on the collection's role within decorative and furnishing schemes. William Lever sought symmetry above taxonomy, and Frederick R. Leyland commissioned architect Thomas Jeckyll and artist James McNeill Whistler to create interiors which incorporated his collection (Impey 1992; Merrill 1998). It could therefore be proposed that the 'Dogs of Fo' represent the femininity of

Figure 2: The 'Dogs of Fo' by Ellen Thomas-Stanford c.1914. Archive, Preston Manor. (Photograph: Royal Pavilion, Art Gallery and Museums, Brighton and Hove Borough Council, 1999)

Edwardian Chinese porcelain collecting, as well as a feminisation of fetishistic collecting.

For the *blanc de Chine* collector there is a whole range of objects to collect, from wine cups and bowls to gods and goddesses (Donnelly 1967; Kwok 1993). Dehua clay possessed a greater elasticity than that of China's much larger ceramic-producing centre at Jingdezhen, allowing more detailed and deeply incised figure-work to be produced as well as fine relief decoration on cups and bowls, so that the best *blanc de Chine* figures have been seen as 'an object-lesson in the principle that beauty in a porcelain figure depends absolutely upon beauty in the material of which it is made' (Honey 1944: 134). But the majority of Preston Manor's 'Dogs of Fo' in fact demonstrate significant signs of poor construction and lack of finish, such as visible seams from the processes of press-moulding. Most have also sustained damage seemingly consistent with a lack of care by previous owners, so that one could speculate that these lions are representative of the lower end of an export market which, during its peak years of 1700-1705, saw four to five million pieces of Chinese porcelain imported into London (Kilburn 1998: 72-73).

Blanc de Chine figures, like other Chinese ceramic imports of the Kangxi reign (1662-1722), were seen in Britain as novelty ornaments especially befitting ownership by women (Somers Cocks 1989: 204-207; Kerr 1989; Marschner 1998). By the early eighteenth century, as porcelain prices fell due to market saturation (Kilburn 1988: 73-74), the well-to-do woman and 'professional' consumer of domestic commodities was already established as the main consumer of Chinese ceramics. Thus, it can be said that the history of Kangxi export wares, although by no means the exclusive province of women, is marked by a gendered consumption. However, twentieth-century modernist taste cultures have been seen as defining themselves in opposition to feminine taste cultures, thus marginalising 'feminine' taste (see Duncan 1995: 113-114; Light 1991). Modernist aesthetics in the collecting of Chinese ceramics, exemplified by the activities of the Oriental Ceramics Society founded in 1921, demanded a rejection of Kangxi export wares with their consumerist implications. These interwar collectors embraced newly discovered older wares from the Tang (618-907 CE) and Song dynasties (960-1260 CE) which, removed from Chinese tombs (with or without permission), represented quasi-Primitive, precapitalist qualities which can be defined in opposition to the 'trivialities' and materialism of Western consumerism (Torgovnick 1990: 8-9). These older wares were also seen to be more 'vital', able to capture the authentic spirit of the Chinese potter in their uneven surfaces and therefore revitalise a western aesthetic sense grown stale through the social rupture of industrialisation (Clunas 1997: 6). Situated at the other extreme, such is the mass-produced nature of the 'Dogs of Fo' that many of them really do seem to have come from the same mould, negating notions of the potter's spirit (fig. 3). This undisguised display of factory produced commodities, turned out with European markets in mind, and hence positioned within an export rather than artistic economy, has the effect of uniting the Preston Manor collection with feminine taste cultures of consumption and domestic display, rather than masculine taste cultures of genius and museum professionalism. This effect is further enhanced when we consider what these lions called 'dogs' may have represented for their collector.

The 'Dogs of Fo' are characterised by a sitting posture, a ball under the left or right front paw, a large head with snub nose, a wide gaping mouth, a harness decorated with bells and tassels and a stylised mane trailing

Figure 3:Four Lions, possibly from the same mould. Height 33cm. Accession numbers (Left to right): 325381, 325355a, 325345b, 325282. Preston Manor. (Photograph: Sarah Cheang and Royal Pavilion, Art Gallery and Museums, Brighton and Hove Borough Council, 1999)

all the way down to an uplifted tail. Each lion is mounted on a rectangular *blanc de Chine* base, usually with a tube attached which is ostensibly for holding joss-sticks. This form of lion is said to have been derived from Buddhist iconographies, and was termed 'of Fo' because 'Fo' has sometimes been used as a name for Buddha (Collier 1921: 90-122). However, the lions of Chinese Buddhism are often seen to exhibit the tendencies and uses of loyal and obedient dogs by standing guard at Buddhist temples and by playing with balls. The fact that some Chinese dogs with shaggy coats are named lion-dogs does not mean that Chinese lions should be seen as dog-lions. However, western 'experts' such as V. W. F. Collier (1921), concerned with piercing the veil of Chinese willful obscurity, have read palindromically and 'decoded' Chinese lions as dogs. By inverting their belief that Chinese people, lacking real lions in their own country, intended certain dogs to stand for the lions associated with the Buddhist faith, Chinese Buddhist lions were seen by British collectors as Buddhist dogs, so that they were restyled from 'lyons' in inventories of the seventeenth and eighteenth centuries (see Kerr 1992: 149) to 'Dogs of Fo' by the late-nineteenth century. To twentieth-century writers, Chinese representations of lions looked so much like Chinese dogs that R. L. Hobson (1933), keeper of ceramics and ethnography at the British Museum, could best describe Chinese lions as 'Pekingese-dog-like creatures'. Winifred Tredwell, in *Chinese Art Motives Interpreted* (1915: 86), stated that the Chinese lion 'usually toys with a ball and looks so much like a stuffed puppy that it is often spoken of as a dog of Foh ---- or Buddha.' However, it was also common practice for dealers and auction houses to sell these dogs of Fo as 'kylins' - another name transference, this time from the unicorn-like *qilin* which had become a generic term for any Chinese mythical creature. Therefore Ellen Thomas-Stanford always referred to her *blanc de Chine* collection as 'kylins', and in a gesture which ties all crossed-conceptions and appropriations together, she also owned a Pekingese dog which she named Kylin.

Pekingese dogs were widely understood in Edwardian Britain to have been developed, bred and even revered by the imperial Chinese court for their lion-like appearance (Collier 1921: 143-154), and Ellen's possession of the dog Kylin from 1908 to 1923 coincides with her period of 'kylin' collecting. Clearly, then, the dog and the collection were linked in the mind of the collector, suggesting that the 'Dogs of Fo' may also have been a reification of the class and gender-specific values which adhered to Pekingese dogs at the time. Thorstein Veblen (1994: 85-87), in 1899, condemned expensive dog breeds as part of the 'pecuniary canons of taste', and Pekingese dogs were certainly championed by upper- and middle-class ladies' magazines as 'the aristocracy - the créme de la créme - of dog-dom' ('Lady Algernon' 1900: 238). Moreover, one of the first Pekingese dogs to be imported into Britain was brazenly christened Looty and came as a gift for Queen Victoria along with other possessions of the Chinese emperor Qianlong, which had been taken from Yuanming Yuan (known as the Summer Palace) by British and French forces in 1860 (Hevia 1994: 327). As the following extracts from Ladies' Field illustrate, in this female arena, the discourses of imperial looting with their righteous theft and conquest (Hevia 1994), and discourses of Orientalism with their duplicitous and superstitious Chinese (Mackerras 1989) combine to produce an ideology of feminine, upper-class imperialistic identity through mythologies of lap dog ownership:

> *... the Pekinese of pure blood have for centuries past been most carefully preserved from any possible contamination in the Royal Palace of China ... it was not until the secrets of the jealously-guarded Summer Palace were exposed on the occasion of its looting by our troops - the King's Dragoon Guards - in 1860 that the true sleeve dog became known to us ....* ('Lady Algernon' 1900: 238).

> *So attached are the Chinese to this one breed of dogs, that to them they are almost sacred. You might as well ask a Chinaman to give you his pig-tail as his dog - either would be an impossibility. They are kept with great care absolutely pure in all high families, from Royalty downward. I have been told that it is only by bribery that they can be obtained. The plain truth is that they have to be stolen, and it often takes months before a favourable opportunity offers* ('Pekinese Spaniels' 1901: 489).

In positioning the Pekingese dog as 'almost sacred' in China, for reasons of social stratification as well as for religious belief, a similarity emerges between British ownership of the talismanic, lion-like Peke and British ownership of the dog-like *blanc de Chine* lion of Chinese Buddhism. In addition, both Pekingese dogs and *blanc de Chine* lions pertained to feminine taste cultures, so that ownership of these items created a feminised space within imperialism (see Lewis 1996). In turn of the century writing about Pekingese dog breeding, one can also sense a metaphor for aristocratic concern regarding the regulation and restriction of their own, human gene pool and concommitant possession of power and land.

Preston Manor was home to numerous breeds of dogs whose graves can be seen in the walled garden, but Kylin was Ellen's favourite (Roberts 1935). The most photographed of all the dogs, Ellen even had a picture she had taken of Kylin, with Jock the Airedale, printed on her menu cards. Interestingly, the dogs are shown arranged on the stone mounting block outside the Manor, and the similarity to the 'Dogs of Fo' on their rectangular pedestals is striking (fig. 4). Only one menu card has been preserved, from a dinner given on 10th November 1912, and the existing receipts show that by that date, forty-two lions had been purchased, in addition to any others which may also have already been in the collection. Therefore, at formal dinners, a cabinet display of at the very least forty-two *blanc de Chine* lions was being complemented on the table by an image of dogs posing on a white pedestal, so that the diners were effectively being fed 'Dogs of Fo' along with their meal. With each repetition of the *blanc de Chine* lion, and with each reproduced image of Kylin the dog, Ellen reiterated her statement of belonging to an upper class whose pedigree was as exclusive as her Pekingese dog, the importance of which becomes clearer when we consider that, whilst Ellen was only the second generation of Stanfords to be born into a landed status, she regularly entertained royalty as well as nobility, and her second husband Charles was Mayor of Brighton from 1910-1913, and then a Member of Parliament until 1922 (Beevers 1999). Therefore Ellen's collection, although private, was displayed to socially prestigious audiences in a room which was rather more public than others.

Figure 4: Kylin and Jock from Ellen's Albums c.1909. (Photograph: Royal Pavilion, Art Gallery and Museums, Brighton and Hove Borough Council, 1999).

Besides being said to be a gifted garden-designer and an excellent horsewoman, Ellen Thomas-Stanford was perceived to be a good photographer ('Mr. and Mrs.' 1911-1912), and using her bathroom as a darkroom, made many images of the Manor between 1905 and 1929. Her pictures are characterised by an absence of people, as she almost always chose to focus on empty interiors and unpopulated gardens, so that the occasional pet and a single, face-on image of the 'Dogs of Fo' stand out as portraits within a documentary of possessions. However, most of her pictures, with their unoccupied chairs and deserted vistas, express a kind of casual formality, where an untidy pile of books suggests that the reader has just departed, and mantelpieces offer their symmetrical loads for examination. It is as if Ellen had sought to capture and record, not the occupants of the house, but their lifestyles, so that the human figures are missing but the contextualisation remains. These photographs form a virtual tour of the house and grounds, an effect which is heightened by the use of albums which provide a linear sequence of experiences and seem to have a great deal in common with illustrated tours of great houses found in upper-class and aspirational middle-class magazines such as *Country Life*. Identity in the photograph has been seen as a doubling of self analogous to Lacan's theory of the mirror stage (Smith 1998: 74-75). However, absent from her mirror/photography, Ellen recognises herself and identifies her family not in the mirror, but in the Manor. And, unlike the mirror, but in common with the collection, the photograph with its stagings and its selections constitutes a socially constructed self.

It was clearly important to Ellen that her work was seen, as, in addition to the menu card reproductions, she gave her photographs away to friends and family, allowed her images to be used to illustrate an article in a Society journal, *Brighton Season* ('Mr. and Mrs.' 1911-1912), and also made at least one entire album as a gift, its leather cover tooled with the words 'Preston Manor'. Thus her circle of communication was expanded outside the physical boundaries of the Manor, and the photographs and the albums, like the space in the Dining Room, became both public and private. However, the female photographer is also a cultural producer who, like the female collector, places dichotomous sexual stereotypes on the horns of a dilemma (Bourdieu 1990: 19-41; Hirsch 1997: 154; Smith 1998). In this context, Ellen's photograph of her collection seems a double transgression of gender role, as well as a double statement of identity. Yet, although not strictly a family scene, the image of the 'Dogs of Fo' - called 'my kylins' by their collector - is also an evocation of her favourite dog Kylin, who surely must count as a family member, set within an album which stresses the domestic. Moreover, just as Ellen never exhibited her collection outside of the home, and did not belong to any collecting societies, her photographs were circulated entirely within feminine and domestic spaces of production and/or consumption: the album; the family gift; the menu card; the Society magazine. Therefore, her photographic and collecting practices, though both potentially transgressive, appear to have been conducted in ways which did not contest the contemporary discourses of upper-class feminine and masculine identities.

Whilst Ellen's photography extended the potential audience of her collection, it is important to note that she was not producing different views of her *blanc de Chine* lions, but was printing over and over again from the same glass negative. These multiples of a collection which in itself consisted of multiples are a reminder of the repetitious nature of collecting and of the massed effect which Ellen was creating - each lion duplicated in its pair, each pair duplicated several times on its shelf, each shelf duplicated several times in its cabinet section, each cabinet section but one of four that make up the bookcase. *Blanc de Chine* lions were not fashionable to collect in the early twentieth century, and were not seen in the quantities which Ellen achieved. In addition, Edwardian Society ladies may have doted upon their Pekingese dogs, but they did not generally amass huge collections of Chinese ceramic lions to complement this interest. For example, Society hostess Mrs. Greville of Polesden Lacey adored her many little dogs, including two favourite Pekingese, but her extensive collections of Chinese ceramics were of fashionable kangxi blue and white, *famille rose* and *famille verte*, with no particular emphasis on the lion (Rowell 1999: 54; Dearn 1999). Therefore, whilst anxiety over social status may have been one element in Ellen's motivation to collect, clearly the 'Dogs of Fo' had other significances to their collector, and other uses as fetishes which perhaps exceeded their role as signs of upper-class femininity.

The interplay between subjectivity and the socially produced self in collecting has been seen as a form of narrative within a semiotic system, where the practice of fetishism ultimately depends on the desire for control through the decontextualising of objects, and their subsequent recontextualisation within a narration of the collection/self (Bal 1994: 100-105). Thus, the fetishistic collector lacks social cohesion, and Jean Baudrillard

(1994: 10-11), expanding a metaphor of the recontextualised collected object as a faithful pet dog, observes that love invested in a pet is a sign of failure to establish normal human relationships. In addition, the spread of petkeeping itself and the cherishing and nineteenth-century sentimentalising of dogs as faithful companions, has been seen as symptomatic of the emotional incompleteness of modern European society (Thomas 1983: 118-119; Kete 1994: 82-83).

Ellen's husband's frequent absences on fishing trips in Norway have often been cited as a possible motivation for her collecting (Campion 1999; Roberts 1999; Beevers 1999: 14). This, in conjunction with the empty spaces of her photography save only for dogs, and the fact she was estranged from her son, seems to point towards a lonely life and an emotional dependence on pets. In addition, the love which Ellen had for Kylin her Pekingese comes into even sharper focus when we realise that Kylin was acquired as a young puppy bred by Mrs Benett-Stanford (Ellen's daughter-in-law), and so could be considered a kind of surrogate grandchild over which she had complete control. Ellen's mother had also been a great dog lover, so that Ellen grew up with the treasured souvenirs of dogs long departed, including dog portraits painted by A. J. Elsley (who also painted Kylin), two paper knives made from the stuffed paws of her mother's favourites, and the grave stones in Preston Manor's pet's cemetery where, by 1933, there were sixteen dogs and one cat. It could therefore be proposed that each lion she bought represented her dog Kylin, who in turn gave and received love and comfort in the absence of her son, her first husband, her living husband, her father, her mother - the family who do *not* populate her photography. Each acquisition of a lion brought temporary relief and control - a moment which could be extended through the keeping of receipts, and by her practice of labelling the lions with their place of purchase, for it must be remembered that the 'Dogs of Fo' were the only objects at Preston Manor for which Ellen ever kept receipts or made labels. The tone of Count Wrangel's (1913) short letter to Ellen, enclosed with a gift of a lion, seems highly suggestive of the strong animism to which the lions were subject:

> *Last summer when in Sweden I met a little white dog that might have some interest for you. I acquired it for you and send it for your inspection. If the little animal meets with your approval, it would give me great pleasure if you might give it a place at Preston Manor.*

The activity of labelling can be seen as a taxonomic process according masculine collections a 'professional' status by reflecting the collector's/institution's knowledge of an object's materials, origins and history. However, Ellen's use of the labels to record places of purchase does not demonstrate any knowledge of their production, but serves instead to tie the lions to points of consumption, conferring an identity of high-status consumer rather than learned collector. In addition, however important these places of purchase were to Ellen, the effort which she actually put into her purchasing appears to have been fairly minimal, as she did not attend auctions or travel in search of her lions, preferring instead to use dealers and agents who sent the lions to her on approval. This lack of active pursuit precludes Ellen's collecting from the hunting analogies which are said to lend the prestige of upper-class sport to the activity of collecting, and also obviates Baudrillard's notions of the art auction as a competitive arena which seals aristocratic parity (Pearce 1999: 183-4;

Baudrillard 1981: 117). Neither was Ellen interested in documenting her collection. As each lion was added to the collection, the receipt (if it was to be kept) was not filed away in a separate body of knowledge such as a catalogue or some other collecting record, but was instead folded up and stuffed inside the lion's hollow base, becoming an unseen, internal part of the lion.

However, Ellen did write a card label for her collection, just visible in her 1913 photograph, which reads: 'Kylins for holding joss-sticks. Period of Yung-Lo A.D. 1403-1426.' Here Ellen ascribed the production of her lions to the reign of the early Ming Dynasty emperor Yongle (1403-1425), a good three centuries too early. It is not known where Ellen obtained the information for her card label as most of her receipts show that dealers felt safest with the catch-all categorisation of 'old Chinese', but her mistake is understandable. Guides to Chinese ceramics could be extremely vague in the dating of Dehua *blanc de Chine*, whilst representations of lions did appear in early Ming ceramic production when a plain white porcelain was also much prized (see Blacker 1908; Willoughby-Hodgson 1907). However, the same increasing access to China and Chinese sources which brought about twentieth-century British interest in earlier, pre-export wares, also enabled an expansion of study, and ultimately produced a knowledge hierarchy in which the further an author was positioned from 'popular' knowledge and 'amateur' collecting, the less likely s/he was to use the term 'old Ming,' 'kylin' or 'dog' (see for example Collier 1921: 104; Honey 1944: 99). These competing systems of naming may also account for the presence of the *qilin* in a collection, sent to Ellen because she was known to be a collector of 'kylins', by a dealer whose understanding of 'kylin' differed to that of Ellen's. Thus Ellen's use of terminology was positioned within popular mythologies of Chinese ceramics - within consumer rather than connoisseurly understandings - and her fetishistic collecting was enunciated from within a feminine, Edwardian space.

Museum-making

In May 1924, Charles Thomas-Stanford (1924) wrote to Brighton Corporation suggesting that after he and Ellen had passed away, Preston Manor could 'be used as a subsidiary museum specially devoted to Sussex and Brighton collections.' This was formalised in March 1925 by Deed of Gift, stating that the Manor and its grounds be used in perpetuity by the town, and that a museum devoted to local history could be formed around Charles's personal library of books on Sussex. However, when Ellen died in November 1932, she bequeathed to the Corporation:

> *such pictures clocks furniture fittings and other effects in Preston Manor as the Director of the Public Library Museum and Art Gallery may select to be retained at Preston Manor and not to be removed elsewhere in order that future visitors to Preston Manor may have a correct idea of the appearance of the house as it was at the time when it came into the possession of the Corporation* (Roberts 1957: 5).

Ellen turned her husband's initial ideas around so that his intended museum of local history never materialised. His library of books relating to Sussex, known as the Sussex Collection, is displayed in part upstairs at the Manor, but is mostly in storage, and Ellen's decision to override her husband's wishes has several implications in terms of the status and meaning of her collection.

Firstly, to bequeath to the town not only her collection of lions, but also the entire contents and furnishings of her home, implies that the two were not conceptually separable so that whilst the collection was physically bounded by the cabinet, it was still very much integrated into the domestic interior in accordance with feminine modes of collecting. As a lasting immortality for Ellen's reified self, the 'Dogs of Fo' could not stand alone, but needed to remain within the 'symbolic ecology' of Ellen's household. Secondly, that Ellen chose neither to leave the 'Dogs of Fo' to Brighton Museum as a separate collection, nor to continue with Charles's plans whilst adding in her own collection, is further proof that she did not seek museum validation for her collecting. In fact, by prioritising the home above Charles' scholarship and research, Ellen succeeded in a feminisation of the museum, creating a domestic space in which the Sussex collection is almost entirely marginalised.

An interesting coda to this assessment is found in some photographs, taken shortly after Ellen's death to record the Manor exactly as she had left it. An image of the Morning Room, Ellen's private sitting room or *boudoir*, reveals the presence of a single, *blanc de Chine* lion positioned at one end of the mantelpiece. Its presence here is also confirmed by the 1933 inventory which records that in the Dining Room there were only one hundred and twenty-three lions and one *qilin*, but that there was another lion in the Morning Room ('Rough catalogue' 1933). Whether this lion was removed from the cabinet and placed here, whether it was a late purchase which was never added to the cabinet, or whether it had always been present in Ellen's *boudoir*, the secret of a more private space, it can be assumed that its meanings to Ellen were particular. However, the lion was not to remain there long. In the margins of the inventory, the first curator's handwritten records that the lion in the boudoir was 'put in case in Dining Room PM892.' In the museum of the house, this apparently aberrant lion could not remain on the mantelpiece, but had to be placed physically with the collection, and accessioned along with the rest. Even as Ellen was feminising the museum, the museum began a process of masculinising her collecting.

Conclusion: revenge of the *qilin*

In January 1999, David Beevers (curator of Preston Manor) and I rearranged the 'Dogs of Fo' according to the photograph taken by Ellen. This seemed to be a way of putting the collection, and hence the museum, into a more 'authentic' state and would also aid our understanding of the principles behind Ellen's collecting. We put the *qilin* out of the way, in the bottom left hand corner of the cabinet, together with any pieces which were left over, having been added after the guiding photograph was taken. However, in July 1999 we realised that museum staff could no longer easily find the *qilin*. They liked to show it to museum visitors as the one 'true' kylin in the cabinet, and so we moved it back to a more central location. The *qilin*, which I had habitually been overlooking, both in the museum and in my analysis of the 'Dogs of Fo', had revealed itself to be in some respects the most important piece in the collection. I still believe that for Ellen the *qilin* would have occupied a marginal position. However, this sequence of events illustrates how, in the museum environment, taxonomy is valorised and collecting sentiment erased.

Pomian (1990: 2) writes that the collection is a physical expression of society's values which forms a part of taste cultures and is thus not separable from notions of decor. However, the museum, by removing the collection from the domestic environment and positioning it in public space, appears by its very nature to sever these connections. But this can only be achieved by the positing of oppositional, mutually exclusive notions of private and public, which are elaborated, enunciated and maintained through discourses of gender. Therefore, to propound masculine and feminine modes of collecting is to suppress any decorative or consumerist aims amongst male collectors, and deny any 'serious' or fetishistic intentions amongst female collectors. However, Ellen should not be seen as a sexually political collector. Her collecting, like her photography, did not depart from upper-class, feminine identities of her day, especially at a time when the masculinisation of Chinese ceramics collecting was still nascent. Neither can Ellen's collection be neatly fitted into a single notion of high or low cultural value, since the *blanc de Chine* lion was symbolic of both mass-production and of wealth. Hence Ellen's collecting slips between the popular and the prestigious, the 'good' and the 'bad' in collecting, and the unfixed collection, occupying a multiplicity of cultural positions, ultimately lends itself to elision within the museum space.

Bibliography

BAL, M. 1994. Telling objects: a narrative perspective on collecting. In Elsner, J. and Cardinal, R. (eds), *The Cultures of Collecting.* London: Reaktion Books. 97-115.

BATTERSBY, C. 1989. *Gender and Genius: Towards a Feminist Aesthetics.* London: The Women's Press.

BAUDRILLARD, J. 1994. The system of collecting. In *The Cultures of Collecting.* In Elsner, J. and Cardinal, R. (eds), *The Cultures of Collecting.* London: Reaktion Books 7-24.

BAUDRILLARD, J. 1981. *For a Critique of the Political Economy of the Sign.* St Louis, Mo: Telos Press.

BEEVERS, D. 1999. *Preston Manor.* Brighton: Royal Pavilion, Libraries and Museums.

BELK, R. 1995. *Collecting in a Consumer Society.* London: Routledge.

BELK, R. and Wallendorf. M. 1997. Of mice and men: gender identity in collecting. In Martinez, K. and Ames, K. (eds), *The Material Culture of Gender, the Gender of Material Culture.* n.p.: Henry Francis du Pont Winterthur Museum. 7-26.

BHABHA, H. 1994. Interrogating identity. In Goldberg D. (ed), *The Anatomy of Racism.* University of Minnesota Press, 1990. Rpt. in Homi K. Bhabha, The Location of Culture, London: Routledge. 40-65.

BLACKER, J. 1908. *Chats on Oriental China.* London: T. Fisher Unwin.

BOURDIEU, P. 1990. *Photography: a Middle-brow Art.* Cambridge: Polity Press.

CABANNE, P. 1963. *The Great Collectors.* New York: Farrar, Straus.

CAMPION, D. 1999. Letter from David Campion, great-nephew of Ellen Thomas-Stanford, to author. 16 June 1999.

CLUNAS, C. 1997. *The Barlow Collection of Chinese Ceramics, Bronzes and Jades: an Introduction.* University of Sussex.

COCKS, A. SOMERS. 1989. The Nonfunctional Use of Ceramics in the English Country House During the Eighteenth Century. In Gervase, Jackson, Stops, et al. (eds), *The Fashioning and Functioning of the British Country House.* Washington DC: National Gallery of Art: 195-215.

COLLIER, V. 1921. *Dogs of China and Japan in Nature and Art.* London: William Heinemann.

CSIKSZENTMIHALYI, M. 1996. Design and Order in Everyday Life. In Margolin, V. and Buchanan, R. (eds), *The Idea of Design.* Cambridge, Mass: MIT Press. 118-126.

CSIKSZENTMIHALYI, M. and ROCHBERG-HALTON, E. 1981. *The Meaning of Things: Domestic Symbols and the Self.* New York: Cambridge University Press.

DEARN, Pl. 1999. Letter from Paul Dearn, house manager at Polesden Lacey, to author. 2 June.

DONNELLY, P. 1967. *Blanc de Chine: the Porcelain of T-hua in Fukien.* New York: Frederick A. Praeger.

DUNCAN, C. 1995. *Civilizing Rituals: Inside Public Art Museums.* London: Routledge.

LORD ECCLES. 1968. *On Collecting.* n.p.: Longmans.

GAMMON, L. and MAKINEN, M. 1994. *Female Fetishism: a New Look.* London: Lawrence & Wishart.

GARB, T. 1987-1988. Unpicking the Seams of her Disguise: Self-Representation in the Case of Marie Bashkirtseff. *Block 13*: 79-86.

HERSHBERG, S. 1993. All Manner of Strange and Hideous Monsters: Ellen Thomas-Stanford's Edwardian Cabinet of Curiosities. *Royal Pavilion and Museums Review.* **1**: 10-11.

HEVIA, J. 1994. Loot's Fate: The Economy of Plunder and the Moral Life of Objects From the Summer Palace of the Emperor of China. *History and Anthropology* **6.** 4: 319-345.

HIRSCH, M. 1997. *Family Frames: Photography, Narrative and Postmemory.* Cambridge, Mass: Harvard University Press.

HOBSON, R. 1933. Letter from R. Hobson, British Museum, to Henry D. Roberts, Preston Manor. 15 Nov. Archive, Preston Manor.

HOFFMAN, K. 1996. *Concepts of Identity: Historical and Contemporary Images and Portraits of Self and Family.* New York: Westview Press.

HONEY, W. BOWYER. 1944. *The Ceramic Art of China and Other Countries of the Far East.* London: Faber and Faber/Hyperion Press.

IMPEY, O. 1992. Lever as a Collector of Chinese Porcelain. *Journal of the History of Collections* **4.** 2: 227-238.

KERR, R. 1992. The Blanc de Chine Porcelain. In Murdoch, T. (ed), *Boughton House: The English Versailles.* London: Faber and Faber/Christie's. 149-161.

KERR, R. 1989. The Chinese Porcelain at Spring Grove Dairy: Sir Joseph Bank's Manuscript. *Apollo* 129 Jan.: 30-34.

KETE, K. 1994. *The Beast in the Boudoir: Petkeeping in Nineteenth Century* Paris. Berkeley: University of California Press.

KILBURN, R. 1998. Chinese Porcelain in Late Seventeenth Century English Inventories. In Hinton, M. and Impey, O. (eds), *Kensington Palace and the Porcelain of Queen Mary II.* London: Christies. 69-78.

KWOK, K. 1993. Blanc de Chine: the Hickley Collection. *Arts of Asia* **23.** Nov/Dec: 80-91.

'Lady Algernon Gordon-Lennox's Pekinese spaniels.' 1900. *Ladies' Field* 20 Jan: 238-240.

LEWIS, R. 1996. *Gendering Orientalism: Race, Femininity and Representation.* London: Routledge.

LIGHT, A. 1991. *Forever England: Femininity and Conservatism Between the Wars.* London: Routledge.

MACKERRAS, C. 1989. *Western Images of China.* Hong Kong: Oxford University Press.

MARSCHER, J. 1998. Queen Mary II as a Collector. In Hinton, M. and Impey, O. (eds), *Kensington Palace and the Porcelain of Queen Mary II.* London: Christies. 49-58.

MCCLINTOCK, A. 1995. *Imperial Leather: Race, Gender and Sexuality in the Colonial Contest.* New York: Routledge.

MERRILL, L. 1998. *The Peacock Room: A Cultural Biography.* Washington DC: Freer Gallery of Art.

'Mr. and Mrs. Charles Thomas-Stanford "At Home."' 1911-1912. *Brighton Season.* Autumn-Winter.

MUENSTERBERGER, W. 1994. *Collecting: An Unruly Passion.* Princeton: Princeton University Press.

NOCHLIN, L. 1971. Why have there been no great women artists? *Art News* **69**. 9: 22-39, 67-71.

PEARCE, S. 1999. *On Collecting: An Investigation into Collecting in the European Tradition.* London: Routledge,

'Pekinese spaniels' *Ladies' Field*. 1901. 31 Aug: 489-491.

POMIAN, K. 1990. *Collectors and Curiosities: Paris and Venice, 1500-1800.* Cambridge: Polity Press.

ROBERTS, H. 1933. Letter from Henry D. Roberts, Preston Manor, to R. L. Hobson, British Museum. 30 Aug. Archive, Preston Manor.

ROBERTS, H. 1957. *Preston Manor (Thomas-Stanford Museum)* Brighton. (18th ed.), Brighton: n.p.

ROBERTS, M. 1935. The companionship of dogs: happy lives at Preston Manor. *Sussex Daily News* 26 Mar.

ROBERTS, M. 1999. Second curator of Preston Manor. Personal Interview. 20 June.

'Rough Catalogue of Preston Manor Pottery, porcelain &c. Mainly as Identified by Mr. Stewart Acton 13 July 1933.' Archive, Preston Manor.

ROWELL, C. 1999. *Polesden Lacey,* Surrey. n.p.: National Trust.

SCHOR, N. 1994. Collecting Paris. In Elsner, J. and Cardinal, R. (eds), *The Cultures of Collecting.* London: Reaktion Books. 252-274.

SHULSKY, L. 1998. Queen Mary's Collection of porcelain and its display at Kensington Palace. In Hinton, M. and Impey, O. (eds), *Kensington Palace and the Porcelain of Queen Mary II.* London: Christies. 27-48.

SMITH, L. 1998. *The Politics of Focus: Women, Children and Nineteenth-century Photography.* Manchester: Manchester University Press.

STEWART, S. 1993. *On Longing: Narratives of the miniature, the Gigantic, the Souvenir, the Collection.* 1984. Durham, NC: Duke University Press.

THOMAS, K. 1983. *Man and the Natural World: Changing Attitudes in England 1500-1800.* Harmondsworth: Penguin.

THOMAS-STANFORD, C. 1924. Letter from Charles Thomas-Stanford, Preston Manor, to Town Clerk, Brighton. 23 May. Archive. Preston Manor.

TORGOVNICK, M. 1990. *Gone Primitive: Savage Intellects, Modern Lives.* Chicago: University of Chicago Press.

TREDWELL, W. 1915. *Chinese Art Motives Interpreted.* New York: Knickerbocker Press.

VEBLEN, T. 1994. *The Theory of the Leisure Class.* 1899. New York: Dover Publications.

VICKERY, A. 1995. Women and the World of Goods: a Lancashire Consumer and her Possessions, 1851-81. In Brewer, J. and Porter, R. (eds), *Consumption and the World of Goods.* London: Routledge. 274-301.

WILKINSON, H. 1997. Mr Cropper and Mrs Brown: Good and Bad Collectors in the Work of A. S. Byatt and Other Recent Fiction. In Pearce, S. (ed), *Experiencing Material Culture in the Western World.* Leicester: Leicester University Press. 95-113.

WILLOUGHBY, H. 1907. Some Old Ming Porcelains. Part II. *Connoisseur* **XVIII**: 26-32.

WRANGEL. 1913. Letter from Count Wrangel to Ellen Thomas-Stanford. 27 Nov. Archive, Preston Manor.

Scholars and Connoisseurs, Knowledge and Taste.

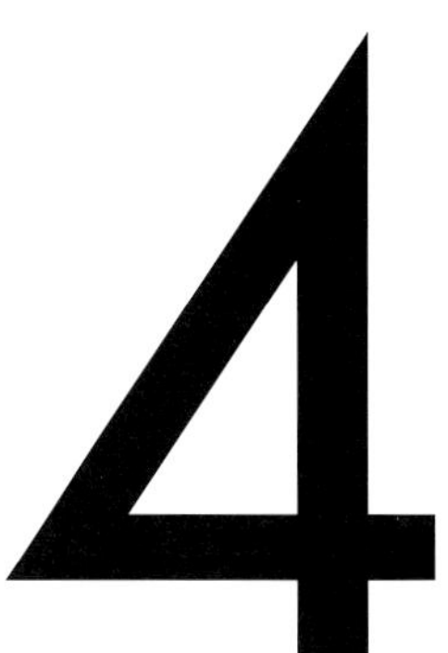

The Seligman Collection of Chinese Art[1]

Nicky Levell

At the age of eighty-two, less than two years before her death, the British anthropologist, Brenda Zara Seligman (1882-1965), signed a codicil to her will, which detailed the conditions relating to the bequest of her collection of Chinese art. This bequest constituted a unique arrangement, whereby the Arts Council of Great Britain, under the directorship of Gabriel White (1902-1988), was to hold the collection in trust for a fixed period of ten years; this was to be proceeded by the transfer of the collection to the trustees of the British Museum, who were endowed with the 'power to pass on to the Victoria and Albert Museum anything superfluous to their needs' (Gray 1965: 13).

At the commencement of the period of trusteeship, in accordance with the codicil's stipulations, the Arts Council organised a month-long temporary exhibition, 'The Seligman Collection of Oriental Art', which opened at their James' Square Gallery in London on 7 May 1966.[2] A representative selection of over two-thirds of the objects of the Seligman collection, some 351 exhibits, were shown.[3] In a contemporary review of the exhibition, Sir Harry Garner (1892-1977), the 'assiduous and discriminating collector' of Chinese art and the eminent aerodynamics engineer (Gray 1977: xxvii), lamented that it was unlikely that a collection of early wares (pre-Ming (Ming Dynasty, 1368-1644 CE)),[4] like that of the Seligmans', would ever be formed again. Without mentioning the inclement political relations or the concomitant restriction in the two-way traffic of cultural goods between China and the West, Garner blamed this future dearth on the younger generation of collectors, whose tastes were for later wares. He opined that 'the serious students and connoisseurs of Chinese art in the pre-war era have been largely replaced by the 'postage stamp' collector…to whom the condition of the piece and its freedom from the slightest defect is far more important than its intrinsic quality' (Garner 1966: 351).

When the Seligman collection moved into the public sphere, it was articulated as a representative, coherent body of plastic arts; delimited by cultural area and time-frame and, above all, by the collectors, Brenda and Charles Seligman. However a critical examination of primary and secondary sources reveals that the Seligman Collection of Chinese art had a far more complex 60-year biography than was betrayed by the 1966 exhibition. To a large extent, its life-history reflected the ever-changing patterns of knowledge and taste. To account for the mutability of 'taste', its potentiality to both control and respond to external phenomena, Bourdieu in his book *Distinction: A Social Critique of the Judgement of Taste* (1986), proffers an in-depth theoretical and empirical analysis of the competition or, what he terms, the 'symbolic struggles', between different groups and class factions, to attain distinction. However, Bourdieu stresses, *pace* Veblen, that individuals are not necessarily conscious of their participation in the competitive field. Nevertheless, these struggles for distinction constitute the fundamental dynamic of all social life; they determine tastes and, in turn, tastes are 'the generative formula of lifestyle[s]' (Bourdieu 1986: 173; Bourdieu 1993: 111). With this in mind, I will start by discussing the way in which the Seligmans, as members of the dominant class, with the requisite composition of economic and cultural capital, first entered and competed in the field of Chinese art. I will expose two distinct, mutually independent, phases in the growth and development of their Collection (from 1905-1965), in order to discuss the complex relationships between taste, knowledge, gender and collecting and the way in which the dynamics of these relations affect the circulation of Chinese art in both the private and public spheres. Before commencing, it is worth recalling Basil Gray's (1904-1989) perceptive synopsis:

Figure 1: Right: Charles Gabriel Seligman (1873-1940) (Photograph: The Royal Anthropological Institute of Great Britain and Ireland).

Figure 2: Far Right: Brenda Zara Seligman (1882-1965) (Photograph: The Arts Council of England)

> *the history of taste is a more elusive theme than that of knowledge; the landmarks may be the same, the great works written or discoveries made; but our quest involves the raising of such questions as why Chinese painting was the major interest in the early years of the century, but declined in the 1920s when Sung porcelain became the favoured art form; to be followed in the 30s by the ritual bronzes and archaic jades, and so on. Of course one cannot leave out of account availability; but taste does control, as well as respond to, what is to be seen in exhibitions or what reaches the market, even what sites are excavated* (1973: 19).

The originary moment

To locate the beginning of a collection, the 'originary moment', when the first object was acquired, necessitates the reconstruction of a biography of the collection. However, because the initial acquisition - be it a purchase, gift or *objet trouvé* – is 'arbitrary, contingent, accidental…[it is] only retrospectively, through a narrative manipulation of the sequence of events' that this originary moment is articulated as the beginning of the collection (Bal 1994: 101). The originary object in the Seligman Collection of Chinese art was a Ming beaker, a wedding present, given to them on their marriage in 1905 (L.C.G.C. 1941: 15).[5] It was this gift, that stimulated their interest in Chinese porcelain and 'from then onwards *he* began to look at things in museums and to buy a few oddments' (L.C.G.C. 1941: 15; author's emphasis]. Although obituaries consistently use the masculine singular pronoun when referring to the growth of the Collection; other sources indicate that collecting, as well as visiting museums, were just two of the activities they embraced as a couple. They visited the major ethnological and oriental collections in Europe and went on 'sorties in search of pieces for the collection' (Fortes 1965: 178-9). Herein lies the problematic: when collecting is a conjugal activity it is often difficult, if not impossible to determine which spouse, if any, is the dominant consumer, the taste-maker (Pearce 1995: 229). A critical analysis of two distinct phases in the biography of the Seligman collection of Chinese art, reveals how the cultural practice of collecting serves to reflect as well as construct gender identities.

From the outset, the Seligmans' propensity to appropriate Chinese art - either symbolically through visiting cultural institutions or materially through purchases - was practicable because of the amount of capital they had available to expend. Although it is not possible to gauge the exact amount of income the Seligmans had at their disposal, brief biographies indicate the nature of their class habitus, the high volume of cultural and educational capital they had available (Bourdieu 1990: 54), and the gendered dynamics of their conjugal and professional relationship, which fostered their collecting activities.

While both Charles and Brenda Seligman became noteworthy figures in the annals of modern British social anthropology, neither of them had any formal, academic training in this discipline. Charles, who became Emeritus Professor of Ethnology at the London School of Economics in 1934, started his career in medicine. The only son of Hermann Seligman, a London wine-merchant and his wife Olivia (née Mendez da Costa), he was educated at St. Paul's School, before gaining a scholarship to St. Thomas Hospital, where he held various positions – house-physician (1897), Salter Research Fellow (1899), and Director of the Clinical Laboratory (1901-1904) (Fortes 1941: 2; Myers 1949: 802). During his time at St. Thomas' his research focused on tropical pathology while harbouring a growing interest in physical anthropology. In 1898, he joined the ground-breaking Cambridge Anthropological Expedition to the Torres Strait. Only during the expedition, which revolutionised anthropological methodology, did Seligman receive his first anthropological training in ethnology, physical anthropology and experimental psychology under Alfred Cort Haddon (1855-1940) and William Halse Rivers (1864-1922). This was followed, six years later by a second period of fieldwork, under his (Seligman's) scientific leadership, in Papua New Guinea (the Cooke-Daniels expedition of 1904).[6] On returning to Britain, he was appointed on a three-year contract as pathologist to the Zoological Society of London as well as bacteriologist to the Royal commission, and he married Brenda Zara Salaman, the sister of his friend, Redcliffe Nathan Salaman (1874-1955), who was Director of the Pathological Institute at the London Hospital (Who Was Who 1941: 1215). The publication of his research undertaken during the Cooke-Daniels expedition, *The Melanesian of British New Guinea* (1910), 'definitely established his reputation as an anthropologist', and in 1910 he joined the London School of Economics, University of London, as Lecturer in Ethnology (Myers 1941: 630). In 1913 the lectureship was made into a part-time Chair for him, from which, due to ill health, he retired in 1934 (Fortes 1941: 4).

Brenda Seligman came from 'the section of middle-class Anglo-Jewry which, at the end of the century, contributed many notable personalities to English public and intellectual life' and her family was 'well to do with interests in the city' (Fortes 1965: 178). Her education reflected her class habitus: she was taught privately at home, before being sent to Roedean, after which she became a student on the pre-medical biology courses at Bedford College, London. However, she abandoned the latter in order to get married. The Seligman's marriage not only marked the inception of their collection of Chinese art, but also the beginning of collaborative, anthropological fieldwork in Sri Lanka (1907) and Sudan (1909-10, 1911-12 and 1921-22), with Charles specialising in physical anthropology, archaeology and history and Brenda in kinship and social organisation. Although Brenda 'looked on her own anthropological research as ancillary to her husband's'; Charles Seligman, as well as other anthropologists, acknowledged her contribution both to field-work and to the related publications (Fortes 1965: 178). In 1963, in recognition of her services to anthropology, she was the first person to be awarded the Royal Anthropological Institute's Patron Medal (Fortes 1965: 180).

From the outset, the Seligmans' intellectual and physical engagement with Chinese culture differed markedly from their professional engagement with other cultures. As anthropologists, during their extended periods of fieldwork, they had lived amongst, documented and analysed the Other and, at the same time, assembled representative collections of material culture for ethnographic museums in Britain (Fortes 1941: 5). However, their material appropriation of China, was diachronic, dislocated in time and space, and mediated, for the most part, by 'cultural brokers'.

In 1909, while *enroute* to the Sudan, they stopped off in Paris to visit a 'China shop', that had been recommended to them. In her journal entry, Brenda Seligman describes the way in which they were 'shown into a room full of early Chinese stuff, the floor was covered and the pieces were piled up on one another' (1909: 1). Coupled with her description of the two male vendors, her account gives the impression that this was a dubious, and somewhat illegal enterprise. This was confirmed by 'the fair man' who had been to Beijing where 'Early Ming and Sung graves are being dug up and fairly looted' (Seligman, B. 1909: 2). The ethical or moral implications of purchasing this material was not an issue for the Seligmans; they spent 'a glorious hour putting on one side pieces...[they] fancied'; and bought 'three warriors full of life and vigour [presumably Tang tomb figures]...some early Ming figures, a Sung [Song] dish and some bowls...and a celadon horse' (Seligman, B. 1909: 2-3), in total costing £150, a substantial sum in 1909 (the average wage was about £30 per annum).[7]

Even during their six-month trip to China (1929-30), they were removed, both linguistically and spatially, from the ethnographic field and repositioned as cultural tourists. Their journals and photographs bear witness to this dislocation. For example, for the first three weeks of their visit they stayed in the Grand Hotel de Pékin, Beijing, inside the walls of the inner city, in the Legation Quarter, along with Laurence Binyon (1869-

1943), Deputy Keeper of Oriental Prints and Drawings at the British Museum, and his wife, Cicely, Robert Lockhart Hobson (1872-1941), Keeper of Oriental Antiquities at the British Museum and the collector, Oscar Raphael (1874-1941). There they experienced what Binyon described as an 'Arnold Bennett millionaire style of life' (Hatcher 1995: 245). On their first evening, a banquet was held in their honour: their host was Ting Wen-chiang (1887-1936), former Director of the China Geological Survey; the guests included Li Ji (Li Chi) (1896-1979), head of archaeology at the Institute of History and Philology, 'Chang', Director of Archaeology; Wong Wen-Hao (b.1889), Director of the China Geological Survey; and 'Zen' the Director for the China Foundation for the promotion of Education and Culture, as well as 'Ma, Shen, Guan and Yü', employees from the Palace Museum, amongst others.[8] For the duration of the Seligmans' stay in Beijing, this elite corps of Chinese government officials, intellectuals, and museum professionals, organised a series of cultural activities for them. The Seligmans' material consumption of Chinese art was also mediated through a network of Chinese dealers. Whereas the ethnographic objects that they acquired in the context of ethnographic fieldwork, were documented, provenanced, and contextualised; the documentation relating to what they purchased in China is fragmentary. Their journal entries are often written using the plural pronouns, for example 'we bought five pieces' from Wu Lai Hsi (Seligman, B. 1930: 14), thereby precluding the possibility of discussing the complex relationships between gender, collecting, knowledge and taste.

The Karlbeck Syndicate

In the preface to *The Seligman Collection of Oriental Art* volume II, John Ayers noted that the Chinese ceramics included 'an outstanding *series* of tomb figure models' (1964: viii, author's emphasis). According to Baudrillard, a collection's seriality is always predicated on an 'internal systematic' whereby a 'formal' interest always replaces a 'real' interest in collected objects (1994: 22). From this perspective, when Seligman acquired the Tang tomb figures (Tang dynasty 618-906 CE), they no longer retained their original use value as funerary goods, rather, these commodities were diverted from their intended paths (Appadurai 1986: 26-7), and entered a new system of value, based on their scientific and aesthetic worth. For Seligman, Tang tomb figures were of 'anthropological value' because they shed light on the multi-cultural aspects of Tang society (1924: 113). This formal interest was articulated in his article, *An Amerind Type in China in T'ang Times* (1924). For Seligman, the subject of the article, a Tang whistle, which he had acquired sometime around 1909, 'so closely reproduce[d] the facial characteristics of the American Indian' as to provide material 'evidence' as to the existence of native American types in Chinese society (1924: 113). It was his enduring commitment to the 'traditional ethnological interest in the classification of races and ethnic groups' (Barkan 1988: 191; also see Kuklich 1984: 70), that not only marked him apart from the leading anthropologists of the 1930s (British School of Functional Anthropology), but was the intellectual rationale that informed his collection of plastic arts and photographs depicting Chinese racial

Figure 3: Tang figure 'Westerner Feeding a Bird', Seligman Collection (Photograph: The Arts Council of England).

Figure 4: 'An Amerind type in China in Tang Times' in Man August 1924. 'Fig. 1': Eumorfopoulos Collection. 'Figs. 2 & 3' Seligman Collection. (Photograph: The Royal Anthropological Institute of Great Britain and Ireland).

types during the 1930s. However, a systematic, 'scientific' motivation does not necessarily preclude an aesthetic sensibility; and for Seligman 'the T'ang was perhaps the age at which plastic art reached its apogee' (1937: 21). For him, the tomb figures were 'plastic portraits excellent in fidelity and often of great beauty' (1937: 21). A statement that helps cast doubt on the bi-polarised gendered interpretation which translates men's collecting solely in terms of a masculine, scientific, rational and serious activity, in contrast to women's collecting, which is articulated as feminine, non-rational, and based on relational and emotional responses to the material world. As Belk and Wallendorf argue 'within stereotypical gender role definitions, the activity of collecting is both masculine and feminine' and these categories of meaning...are more complex than a simple dichotomy' (1997: 10-12).

In terms of the stereotypical gendered approach, the serial collection, in contrast to the emasculated accumulation of objects, is defined by its incompleteness. It is the lack of a specific object or objects for the series that motivates the collector's 'quest and impassioned appeal to other people' for 'desiderata' (Baudrillard 1994: 23).[9] In the early 1930s, Charles Seligman's desire for Tang tomb figures, as well as glass and glazed beads, early jades and bronzes, for his collection, led him to enrol as a member of the Karlbeck Syndicate. This elite group, comprising of eleven private collectors and six cultural institutions, was formed to enable its members to acquire early Chinese art at source.[10]

In the early 1930s, the political situation in China forced Orvar Karlbeck (1880-1967), a Swedish civil engineer, to give up his work on the construction of the railway network across China, a career that he had pursued for almost twenty years. As a consequence of which, he embarked upon a 'new career of buying [Chinese] objects of art on behalf of a consortium of museums and private collectors', members of the cultivated classes, in Europe (Transactions of the Oriental Ceramic Society 1969: xv; also see Gyllensvärd 1981: 71-3). This was not, however, a totally new departure for Karlbeck. During his time as a civil engineer, he was collecting for 'Swedish museums and private connoisseurs' and sending reports of his research findings to Crown Prince Gustaf Adolf of Sweden (in 1950, King Gustaf VI Adolf) (Gyllensvärd 1980: 33). Although the construction of the railway networks in northern China has often been 'cited as a stimulus to changes in taste, by bringing to light tomb figures' and other mortuary wares, which were coveted by Seligman and his peers; such an ethnocentric explanation, fails to take account of the multi-factorial – the historical, political and socio-economic – dimensions of the actual (Clunas 1997: 7). Since the overthrow of the Qing dynasty and the establishment of the new Republic in 1911, there had been a series of civil wars and although 'by 1929 Chiang Kai-shek's Nationalist regime in Nanking [Nanjing] was recognised as the national government...it was under continual threat from the Soviets to the north, Chinese Communists, warlord coalitions, and Japanese expansionism' (Hatcher 1995: 245), as such it had neither the political or economic impetus to control the traffic in cultural property from China to the West.

In the course of four years, Karlbeck made two visits to China to source and purchase material on behalf of the Syndicate. The first trip was from October 1931 to November 1932, and the second trip, from May 1934 until December of the same year. These buying trips are well-documented in the reports that he regularly sent to Europe to be circulated to the members of the Syndicate. As historical documents, these reports provide information about the state of the art market in the various Chinese cities he visited, the faking industry, archaeological finds and sites, as well as details of the specific objects acquired and the prices paid by the members of the Syndicate. In total, Karlbeck purchased 1,236 objects on behalf of the members of the Syndicate (706 during the first trip and 530 on the second).

Out of the 122 objects that Karlbeck purchased on Seligman's behalf, exactly fifty percent were glazed or glass beads, particularly from the pre-tenth century (pre-Tang period). Seligman's formal interest in early Chinese glass was stimulated during his visit to China, 1929-30. As he recalled, whilst in China he recognised that 'glass might constitute an interesting feature of the incoming trade from the West', as such he documented all the specimens of western glass that he saw, and 'made enquiries as to the occurrence of glass beads and pendants and other small objects believed by the Chinese to be of considerable age' (Seligman, C. and Beck 1938: 1). At the same time, he acquired a 'small collection' of glazed and glass beads, which on *prima facie* grounds were pre-tenth century and the results from his initial investigation were deemed 'sufficiently encouraging to lead to further study' (Seligman, C. 1937: 15).

When Seligman 'struck out new fields of inquiry [he] did so with scrupulous attention to facts and theories', investigating 'every problem that confronted him by systematic methods akin to those employed by the physician or surgeon arriving at a diagnosis' (Myers 1941: 637); his approach to collecting and interpreting Chinese glassware was no exception. As Pearce explains 'systematic modes of collecting' 'draw a viewer into their frame, they presuppose a two-way relationship between the collection which has something public (not private to say), and the audience who may have something to learn, or something to disagree with' (1991: 149). Seligman was convinced that his collection of Chinese glassware had something public to say: it constituted 'evidence' of the early culture-contacts between the West and the Far East. He argued that the decorative patterns on early Chinese beads were derived from Western prototypes. Having subjected various early Chinese glass-bead fragments from his collection to gravimetric, spectrographic and microscopic analyses, at the Scientific Department of the Courtauld Institute, he was able to state that glass was being manufactured in China at least as early as the third century BCE. This being the case, he concluded glass-wares entered China on the same cultural wave that introduced iron. Despite the fact that Seligman could 'not read a word of Chinese' (Seligman, C. 1938b), he was able to contribute to sinological scholarship by using 'archaeological findings' to refute historical literary sources, which placed the inception of glass-making in China to the fifth century CE. Using both printed and oral media, Seligman was able to exhibit the collection and display his knowledge: a dual exposure which not only served to draw viewers into the frame, but simultaneously inscribed both collector and collection with a mark of distinction.[11]

Seligman's preoccupation with the diffusionist notion of culture-contact was manifest in the first paper he published on Chinese art, 'Bird Chariots and Socketed Celts in Europe and China', in which he suggested that these objects were derived from European prototypes of the Bronze Age (1920: 153-8; 1928: 247-254; 1938a: 86-7). In early twentieth century anthropology, there was a heated debate between evolutionary and diffusionist theorists. The former argued that the psychological unity of humanity accounted for the similarity of cultural features throughout the world; in contrast, the latter contended that cultural elements or traits had been invented in one particular geo-spatial area, and were transmitted elsewhere. The leading proponent of the diffusionist school, Grafton Elliott-Smith (1831-1937) propounded the heliocentric theory, namely that all civilisation had diffused from Egypt (Seymour-Smith 1986: 91-2). Although Seligman embraced certain elements of diffusionism, in order to explain the transmission of technology and ideas, such as metallurgy, glass-making, paper-making, printing, religion and myths, between the Occident and the Orient, he was not a staunch diffusionist like Elliott-Smith. For him, the process of cultural transmission was never mono-directional, and artefacts provided material 'evidence of the reciprocal influence of West and East' (1937: 23). He preferred the term 'culture mosaic' rather than 'culture-contact', to account for the way in which ideas are 'transmitted, distorted and reflected back again' (1936: 113-115). The objects that he asked Karlbeck to purchase were articulated as evidence of cultural transmission between the West and China. For example, the early glassware, bronze chariot fittings, and iron and bronze weapons, illustrated the spread of metal- and glass-making technologies, whereas the bronze mirrors and belt buckles, with their depictions of mythical beasts, such as the phoenix, were rearticulated as documents, which could explain the inter-cultural transmission and distortion of myths.

Figure 5: T'ang mirror 'Dancing Phoenix' Seligman Collection (Photograph: The Arts Council of England).

Although Charles Seligman's systematic, 'scientific' approach to collecting and interpreting Chinese art is gaugeable through his academic papers, it is too reductive and overdeterministic to interpret his collecting practices solely in the light of Baudrillard's phallocentric or Pearce's genderless serial/systematic modes of collecting.[12] Such a restrictive interpretation, by default, not only effaces Brenda Seligman's involvement in the formation of the collection, it also denies the far more complex dynamics that informed Charles Seligman's taste for Song domestic wares and his *dis*taste for Ming polychromes.[13] It also helps us understand his 'impassioned appeal' to Karlbeck to purchase along with 'the rarer racial types of T'ang figures…a good dancing T'ang lady' for which he specified 'she must be graceful, I want her on purely aesthetic grounds' (Seligman, C. 1932).

Private and public spheres

In December 1940, three months after Charles Seligman's death in an Oxfordshire nursing home, Brenda Seligman presented 'the whole of the collection of Chinese glass and some of the corresponding jades' to the British Museum (Hansford 1957: ix). Although Charle's death signalled the disposal of specific serial aspects of the collection, it did not engender its closure. Up until 1940, Brenda Seligman's involvement in the formation of the collection was inextricably bound up with her marital and professional partnership; a partnership in which she positioned herself in an ancillary, relational mode to her husband (Fortes 1965: 178; 180). However, notwithstanding her modesty and the biography writers' tendency to use masculine, third person and possessive, pronouns when describing the growth and development of the Seligmans' Chinese art collection, Brenda Seligman played a more proactive role than that she has been credited. Throughout her twenty-five years as a widow, she raised 'the aesthetic quality of the collection…by the addition of Chinese bronzes, jades and ceramics chosen for their fine quality as well as their representative character' (Gray 1964: xxvi), and in so doing confirmed that, as an individual, she had the competence, as well as the requisite composition of capital, to appropriate these luxury goods. Although she did not publish any articles relating to her collection, her engagement diaries and journal entries verify that 'without any pretensions to being a scholar, she was well enough versed in the technicalities of connoisseurship in the plastic and graphic arts of China and the Far East, and in the history of the civilisation in which they flourished, to feel at home among experts' (Fortes 1965: 177).

At the end of the war, Brenda sold the marital home, Ley Courtney in the village of Toot Baldon in Oxfordshire, which had been a congregational space for the cultivated elite: 'anthropologists…famous orientalists, collectors, psycho-analysts, physicians, artists, writers and men of affairs' (Fortes 1965: 177) and moved to a smaller residence, 22 Ilchester Place, in west London. Her move to London coincided with the inauguration of the Oriental Ceramic Society's (OCS) programme of bi-annual exhibitions.[14] Although Charles Seligman had been an active member of the OCS since the early 1930s, and was a member of the council when he died, Brenda Seligman's name does not appear in the Society's records until 1950; the year in which she was elected to serve as a member of its Council. Although she did not register for membership in 1933 when the Society became a limited company, this was not on account of her sex; as *The Burlington Magazine* stated in 1938, 'the society is open to dealers, museum officials and collectors of all sorts, including women'. Moreover out of the 131 individuals who registered in 1933, nine were women, and in 1935, the Seligmans' friend, Alice Mariquita Sedgwick, was elected, the first woman, to serve on the Council.[15] By 1947, the year of the OCS's 'Celadon Wares' exhibition, Brenda Seligman was a member of the Society and loaned thirteen specimens from her collection and it was later recorded that she 'was always at the fore in supporting these exhibitions and [attended]…almost every meeting and private view' (Gray 1964: xxvi).

In his introduction to the catalogue to accompany the 1947 'Celadon Wares' exhibition Arthur Lonsdale Hetherington (1881-1960), discussing the popularity of and demand for celadon, opined that 'the restful colour of the glaze, ranging from a bluish green through varying shades of greyish green to a sea-green and a deep olive-green, harmonises with furniture; and many of the utensils such as bowls, dishes, jardinières of varying sizes and shapes lend themselves well for the purpose they were constructed to serve' (1948: 5), and concluded that 'as receptacles for fruit on the dining table, for the display of flowers or for growing bulbs, and for adding *distinction* to a room containing old furniture, the celadons have no equal' (1948: 8, author's emphasis). This notion that the material or symbolic appropriation of early Chinese ceramics serves as an indicator of good taste was, of course, promulgated by members of the O. C. S. As Sir Alan Barlow (1881-1968), the Society's President from 1943-64 explained: 'the private collector...is helping in the accumulation and diffusion of knowledge and taste. Which, indeed, is one justification for the establishment of this Society' (1937: 95). It was this form of liberal idealism that prompted the Seligmans to present their collection to the Nation 'to advance the study and appreciation of Chinese Art'.[16]

By the late 1940s, however, the acquisition and reinscription of early Chinese wares into the domestic space was not a new concept. In 1909, Liberty and Co. had purchased archaeological 'loot' from the two dealers whom the Seligmans met in Paris. Their Regent Street branch had 'a pair of celadon horses' for sale (priced at £36) for the domestic interior (Seligman, B. 1909: 4).[17] In 1923, Hetherington published an article 'Celadon Porcelain its story and Decorative Value' in *Old Furniture Magazine*,[18] which included one colour and twelve black and white plates to illustrate different types of celadon ware and the way in which they could be incorporated into domestic interiors. One of the illustrated specimens, a Song vase (no. D181) with a floral scroll design in relief, which was credited to an unamed 'private collection' was owned by Charles Ernest Russell (1866-1960) (Ayers 1964: 88). Russell was the assistant editor of this periodical, a well-known connoisseur of Chinese ceramics and prominent member of the OCS. In July 1960, four months after his death, his collection of Song, Yüan and Ming celadons was sold at Sotheby's, and Brenda Seligman bought the Song vase (lot 142). By the time she acquired this object, it already had a distinguished 'cultural biography'.[19] Following its debut in Old Furniture, it was reproduced in Hobson, Rackham and *King's Chinese Ceramics in Private Collections* (1931) (which devoted an entire chapter to Russell's celadon collection); *Apollo* in 1947; the OCS's *Celadon Wares catalogue* (1947) and the *Sotheby Sale Catalogue* for12th July 1960. The reproduction of the Song vase and its cultural biography in the latter, augmented both the symbolic and economic value of the object, because as well as testifying to the aesthetic merit of the piece, the ascription of biographical 'attributes of depth, history and accumulated taste...offer[ed] a guarantee of authenticity linked with the prestige of the scholar' (Pearce 1995: 380). During the 1940s and '50s, Brenda Seligman purchased a number of celadon wares from Sotheby's, all with authenticated biographies,[20] enabling her to raise both the aesthetic quality, and symbolic and economic value of the collection, and position herself among the taste-makers: 'the group of well-informed and discriminating collectors of Chinese art who...made London a leading centre for all those interested in the arts of the East' (Gray 1964: xxvi).

Like other members of the cultivated classes, such as George Eumorfopoulos (1863-1939), Ferdinand Schiller (1866-1938), and Francis and Enid Brodie Lodge, Brenda Seligman had early Chinese ceramic wares on show, in her living space (Hardie 1997: 218-9; Kiddell 1969: xvi). By the early 1960s, the largest typological group of objects in the Seligman collection 'the unsurpassed range of Sung [Song] glazed wares', was displayed in her drawing room at Ilchester Place (Ayers 1964: viii). However, Brenda Seligman did not regard the Collection as *materia domestica*, as such she does not slot into the gendered categorisation which views women's collecting practices as 'a largely domestic history...in which collected material mixes...with other kinds of goods, and the whole forms a unity to which no dividing or specifying self-consciousness is attached' (Pearce 1995: 207). From one perspective, it could be argued that she regarded the collection as a bounded unity, a 'hermetic world' which was 'both full and singular, which ha[d] banished repetition and achieved authority' (Stewart 1993: 152). Her conception of the collection as a discrete entity was revealed when she decided upon the fate of the Ming roof tile, which had stood on the mantelpiece, both at the marital home in Oxfordshire, and later at her London residence. Robert Seligman, the Seligmans' only child, asked if he could have the tile as a 'momento' because he had 'considerable affection for this piece…[having] known it since childhood', however, after some consideration Brenda decided that on her death the tile was to remain in the Collection (Cohn 1965; Ayers 1965a). For Robert Seligman the tile constituted a souvenir, it was 'not an object arising out of a need or use value; it [was] an object arising out of the necessarily insatiable demands of nostalgia' (Stewart 1993: 135), whereas for Brenda Seligman the tile formed part of the collection, and the collection was ultimately greater than the sum of its parts.

One aspect of the collection, which she did not include in her bequest was her holdings of Chinese paintings. In her will however, she stipulated that these should be offered at cost price firstly to the British Museum, then to the Victoria & Albert, Bristol City Art Gallery and the Royal Scottish Museum, Edinburgh (V&A 1962). Although the Seligmans had bought 'some really good paintings' from a dealer in Beijing in 1929 (Seligman, B. 1930: 34), this area of their collecting was to remain undeveloped until the 1950s, when in her seventies, Brenda Seligman's 'interest turned increasingly to Chinese painting, which had always interested her and showed herself unafraid to venture in this field' (Gray 1964: xxvi). However, Brenda Seligman was not venturing into this field alone; in the 1950s and 1960s, Chinese paintings, which had long been valued and collected by Chinese and Japanese collectors and had been coveted in the West at the beginning of the twentieth century, were being appropriated, both visually and materially, in terms of exhibitions, publications and acquisitions, by the ''taste-makers' and their affiliated experts' (Appadurai 1986: 32). At the British Museum, Basil Gray (1904-1989), Keeper of Oriental Antiquities (1946-69) was 'greatly strengthening the [Museum's] collection of Chinese paintings', by purchasing from dealers like Jean-Pierre Dubosc (Ayers 1965b), and in 1953, Sir Percival David (1890-1964), the eminent connoisseur and collector of Chinese art, and a friend of the Seligmans, wrote to the Vice-Chancellor of London University, stressing the need for an acquisition fund for the Percival David Foundation (established in 1950), not only to 'fill in the gaps' in the ceramic collection (David 1940) but also to purchase the 'far more important aspect of Chinese art, that of Chinese paintings' (quoted in Whitfield 1995: 204). Likewise, at about the same time, another of Brenda's and Sir Percival's personal acquaintances, King Gustaf VI Adolf of Sweden, who was Patron of the O.C.S., who used to visit London on an annual basis to study and purchase Chinese art, started acquiring Chinese paintings (Gyllensvärd 1980: 41). Moreover, Brenda Seligman's interest in Chinese painting developed at a time when she was working closely with her 'devoted friend' Dr. Arthur Waley (1889-1966), editing Gordon Munro's manuscript on the Ainu. While Assistant-keeper in the Department of Prints and Drawings at the British Museum (1913-30), Waley had catalogued the paintings from Tun-huang in the Sir Aurel Stein collection and published *Introduction to the Study of Chinese Painting* (1923). It is significant that the latter was reprinted in 1958 (Barrett 1989: 97-8).

A notable event, in which Chinese paintings were given a high profile, was the 1954 'Exhibition of Chinese Art' in Venice. This exhibition, which was supported by 'nearly all the important British collectors' (Garner 1973: x), was organised by Jean-Pierre Dubosc, the 'well-known French collector-dealer' (Ayers 1965b). In 1955, the year after the exhibition, Brenda Seligman met Dubosc in London. In February of the following year, she travelled to Paris and stayed for a month as his guest and again, in 1957, she went to the Continent to spend a fortnight with him (Seligman, B. 1955; 1956 and 1957). On both occasions, virtually every day, Dubosc brought a selection of paintings for her to study, so that at the end of her stay she could make a discriminating purchase. In 1956, she purchased a scroll and two fans and the following year she bought a hanging scroll by 'Wang Yuan Chi' (Wang Yuanqi, 1642-1715 CE) and some fans (Seligman, B. 1956; 1957). Three weeks after her return, 'The Arts of the Ming Dynasty' exhibition, which had been jointly organised by the O.C.S. and the Arts Council of Great Britain opened at the latter's St. James' Square gallery. This purportedly comprehensive exhibition had a section on painting, in the Exhibition catalogue's forward, however, it was noted that this field of Chinese art was 'poorly represented in public and private collections' in Britain, the majority of exhibits in the pictorial art section had been loaned from museums in America, France, Germany and Sweden (Barlow and James 1957). This was a truism, out of the fifty-eight exhibits in this section, only nine were from private collectors in Britain, moreover, seven of these (one hanging scroll, two hand scrolls and four fans) were loaned by Brenda Seligman, who was a member of the exhibition's selection committee.[21] By acquiring several first rate paintings…a number of album leaves and fan paintings…which suited her taste for the scholarly and the 'artistic' (Gray 1965: 13), Brenda Seligman attained distinction as a well-informed, discriminating collector.

Conclusion

When 'The Seligman Collection of Oriental Art' exhibition opened in London in 1966, the selection of Chinese exhibits on display as well as the accompanying catalogue, projected an image of the collection as a coherent, representative body of Chinese plastic arts. In 1999, in the British Museum's Oriental Antiquities gallery, the only traces that remained of their collection were a few exhibits with accompanying labels; the latter gave a brief description of the object, its museum number and the source of acquisition, 'The Seligman Bequest'. Moreover, these exhibits were not grouped together, they were spatially divorced on different shelves and in different display cases. In 1940 and again in 1974, when the Seligmans' collections of Chinese art were absorbed into the British Museum's holdings, they were forced to relinquish their identities. Charles Seligman's collection of glassware, marked by its masculine, rational, scientific seriality is now in store; the main collection of early Chinese ceramics, sculptures, bronzes and jades, which spoke of their conjugal tastes and lifestyles, is divided between the British Museum and the Victoria and Albert Museum, and lastly, the collection of Chinese paintings, which reflected Brenda Seligman's aesthetic disposition, is divided between four different cultural institutions. Although the history of taste is an elusive theme, a reconstruction of the biography of the Seligmans' collection provides an insight into the changing patterns in cultural consumption, the circulation of objects between the private and the public spheres, the inscription of knowledge and value, and the dispositions of two 'serious students and connoisseurs of Chinese art' (Garner 1966: 351).

Notes

1. This paper is based on research undertaken in 1999 in the archives of the London School of Economics, University of London; the Far Eastern Department of the Victoria and Albert Museum; the Oriental Ceramic Society; and the British Museum. There are a number of people to whom I am indebted, for without their help, encouragement, and/or erudition this paper would not have materialised. In particular, I would like to thank Professor Craig Clunas (University of Sussex); Jean Martin, (Oriental Ceramic Society); Jessica Harrison-Hall (British Museum); Chris Wright (Royal Anthropological Society); Anthony Shelton, Ken Teague, Daria Neklesa, David Allen and Anne James (Horniman Museum); David Beevers (Preston Manor, Brighton); staff in the V&A's Far Eastern Department; archivists at the London School of Economics; Jackie Lomas, Arts Council of England; and last, but not least, Angela Levell for her continuing support.

2. The exhibition was accompanied by a catalogue: *The Seligman Collection of Oriental Art.* 1966. London: Arts Council.

3. The exhibits were: 79 Chinese bronzes, 30 bronzes from the Ordos (China-Mongolian border), Central Asia and Luristān (Iran), 31 Chinese jades, 5 Chinese sculptures, 1 Korean sculpture, 188 Chinese ceramics, 2 Chinese architectural ornaments, 11 Korean, 3 Indochinese (1 Vietnamese and 2 Thai) ceramics (Arts Council 1966).

4. In this paper, to avoid ethnocentrism, I have used the secular dating convention: 'CE' denotes 'Common Era', which is equivalent to Christian AD and 'BCE' denotes 'Before Common Era' which is equivalent to the Christian BC.

5. Elsewhere this has been referred to as a Ming vase (Ayers 1964: viii). Marriage also precipitated the Chinese collections of Sir Herbert and Lady Ingram (1908) and Mrs R.H.H. and Mrs Palmer (1924) (Gray 1973:.29).

6. In 1906, two years after the Cooke-Daniels Expedition, Seligman presented 46 objects which he had collected during his Papuan fieldwork (Horniman Museum numbers 6.136-6. 181) to the Horniman Museum.

7. David Beevers, personal communication, January 2000.

8. I have transcribed the names of individuals as they appeared in the Seligmans' journals.

9. Charles Seligman used the term '*desiderata*' in respect of the objects he wanted for his serial collection (Seligman, C. 1932).

10. The members of the Karlbeck Syndicate were: Museum van Aziatische Kunst, Amsterdam; Anders Hellström, Mölndal; Axel Lagrelius, Stockholm; Staatliche Museum, Berlin; British Museum, London; Professor C.G. Seligman, Oxford; David Weill, Paris; Dennis Cohen; George Eumorfopoulos, London; King Gustaf VI Adolf of Sweden; Louis Clarke, Cambridge; Malmö Museum, Malmö; Mrs. Robert Solomon, Chelsea; Oscar Raphael, London; The Royal Scottish Museum, Edinburgh; Capt. Spencer Churchill; The Museum of Far Eastern Antiquities, Sweden. Reports and correspondence relating to the Karlbeck Syndicate are held in the Far Eastern Department, Victoria and Albert Museum.

11. Seligman gave a series of papers (the first in 1932, with his collaborator Horace C. Beck, at the Congress of Pre-historic and Proto-historic Sciences held in London); he also published a number of articles on the spread of glasswares and glass-making techniques to China. (Seligman and Beck 1934, 'Barium in Ancient Glass'; Seligman, Beck, and Ritchie 1936, 'Early Chinese Glass from pre-Han to T'ang Times'; Seligman and Beck 1938, 'Far Eastern Glass: Some Western Origins').

12. For a critique of Baudrillard's sexist theory of collecting see Schor 1994: 256-258.

13. In recording his visit to the art museum in Beijing, Seligman not only compared the exhibits with pieces in his own

collection, he also mentioned the use of what he termed a 'beastly pink colour' in reference to an early manuscript, and commented that thankfully this colour was 'impracticable in porcelain 'til the 18th century' (Seligman, C 1930: 29).

14. For historiographies of the Oriental Ceramic Society see Hetherington 1948: 9-12; Impey 1998; Green 1998: 5-13.

15. The nine women who registered were: Mrs Bailey, Mrs L Clark, Lady David, Mrs Eumorfopoulos, Mrs Glyn, Lady Hoare, Mrs Middleton, Mrs Sedgwick, and Mrs Winkworth.

16. Clause 4, codicil to Brenda Seligman's will, dated 27 March 1963 (Far Eastern Department Archive, Victoria and Albert Museum).

17. Although Brenda Seligman referred to the ceramic horses on display at Liberty's as 'Celedon' (1904: 4); it is most probable that these equine figures were green/brown glazed Tang funery wares.

18. *Old Furniture Magazine* was in print from 1927-1930, after which it became *The Collector*; however this periodical did not survive long (Jenyns 1960: ix).

19. Appadurai argues that there is a distinction between the biography of objects and the social history of things; he argues that the former is applicable to specific things, whereas the latter refers to the wider historical trajectories of groups of objects (Appadurai 1986: 34).

20. Brenda Seligman bought from the following Sotheby sales: Joshua Collection (1945); P. Steiner Collection (1948); Bruce Collection (1953) and the Bennett Collection (1955) (see Ayers 1964: 84-100).

21.The other British collectors who loaned paintings were Sir Percival and Lady David and Sir Harry and Lady Garner.

Bibliography

APPADURAI, A. 1986. Introduction: Commodities and the Politics of Value. In Appadurai, A. (ed), *The Social Life of Things. Commodities in Cultural Perspective.* Cambridge, New York and Melbourne: Cambridge University Press.

ARTS COUNCIL. 1966. *The Seligman Collection of Oriental Art.* London: Arts Council of Great Britain.

AYERS, J. 1964. *The Seligman Collection of Oriental Art. Chinese and Korean Pottery and Porcelain,* Vol. II. London: Arts Council of Great Britain.

AYERS, J. 1965a. Letter to Dennis Cohen, 8 March 1965. Brenda Seligman Nominal File, Victoria and Albert Museum Archive.

AYERS, J. 1965b. Letter to C. Aldred, 17 Sept 1965, Brenda Seligman Nominal File, Victoria and Albert Museum Archive .

BAL, M. 1994. Telling Objects: A Narrative Perspective on Collecting. In Elsner, J. and Cardinal, R. (eds), *The Cultures of Collecting.* London: Reaktion Books.

BARKAN, E. 1988. Mobilizing Scientists Against Nazi Racism. In Stocking, G. (ed), *Bones, Bodies, Behaviour. Essays on Biological Anthropology.* London and Madison: The University of Wisconsin Press.

BARLOW, J.A.N. 1937. The Collector and the Expert. *Transactions of the Oriental Ceramic Society,* **14**, 1936-37.

BARLOW, A. and JAMES, P. 1957. Foreword. In *The Arts of the Ming Dynasty.* London: OCS/Arts Council of Great Britain.

BARRETT, T. 1989. *Singular Listlessness. A Short History of Chinese Books and British Scholars.* London: Wellsweep.

BAUDRILLARD, J. 1994. The System of Collecting. In Elsner, J. and Cardinal, R. (eds), *The Cultures of Collecting.* London: Reaktion Books Ltd.

BELK, R. and Wallendorf, M. 1997. Of Mice and Men: Gender Identity and Collecting. In Martinez, K. and Ames, K. (eds), *The Material Culture of Gender, the Gender of Material Culture.* Ann Arbor: University of Michigan Research Press

BOURDIEU, P. 1986. *Distinction. A Social Critique of the Judgement of Taste.* London and New York: Routledge and Kegan Paul.

BOURDIEU, P. 1990. *The Logic of Practice* (translated by Nice, R.). Cambridge: Polity Press.

BOURDIEU, P. 1993. *Sociology in Question* (translated by Nice, R.). London, California and New Delhi: Sage Publications.

CLUNAS, C. 1997. *The Barlow Collection of Chinese Ceramics, Bronzes and Jades: An Introduction.* Brighton: University of Sussex, History of Art Subject Group.

COHN, D. 1965. Letter to John Ayers, 3 March 1965, Brenda Seligman Nominal File, Victoria and Albert Museum Archive.

DAVID, Sir P. 1940. Letter to Brenda Seligman, 30 September 1940, The Seligman Papers, file 15/1/2, London School of Economics Archive, University of London.

FORTES, M. 1941. Charles Gabriel Seligman, 1873-1940. *Man,* **xli**, January-February, 1941.

FORTES, M. 1965. Brenda Zara Seligman, 1882-1965: A Memoir. *Man,* **216**, November-December, 1965.

GARNER, H. 1966. Chinese Works of Art from the Seligman Collection. *Apollo. The Magazine of Arts,* May 1966.

GARNER, H. 1973. His Majesty King Gustaff VI Adolf of Sweden. *Transactions of the Oriental Ceramic Society.*

GRAY, B. 1964. Mrs. B.Z. Seligman. *Transactions of the Oriental Ceramic Society,* 1963-4.

GRAY, B. 1965. Mrs. Brenda Seligman. *The Times,* Friday 8 January 1965.

GRAY, B. 1973. The Development of Taste in Chinese Art in the West 1872 to 1972. *Transactions of the Oriental Ceramic Society,* **39**, 1971-73.

GRAY, B. 1977. Sir Harry Garner. *Transactions of the Oriental Ceramic Society,* **41**, 1975-77.

GREEN, J. 1998. *'A New Orientation of Ideas'. Collecting and the Taste for Early Chinese Ceramics in England, 1921-1936,* unpublished MA dissertation, Birkbeck College, University of London.

GYLLENSVÄRD, B. 1981.Historical Introduction. *Arts of Asia* November-December 1981.

GYLLENSVÄRD, B. 1980. King Gustaf VI Adolf's Approach to Chinese Art. *Transactions of the Oriental Ceramic Society,* **44**, 1979-80.

HATCHER, J. 1995. *Laurence Binyon. Poet, Scholar of East and West.* Oxford: Clarendon Press.

HANSFORD, S. 1957. *The Seligman Collection of Oriental Art. Chinese, Central Asian and Luristān Bronzes and Chinese Jades and Scultures,* volume I.

HARDIE, P. 1997. Ferdinand Schiller – Jade Collector, 1915-3. In Scott, R. (ed), *Chinese Jades.* London: Percival David Foundation of Chinese Colloquies on Art and Archaeology in Asia, no.18.

HETHERINGTON, A. 1948. A History of the Oriental Ceramic Society. *Transactions of the Oriental Ceramic Society,* **23**, 1947-48.

HETHERINGTON, A.L. 1948. Introduction. in *Celadon Wares.* London: The Oriental Ceramic Society.

HOBSON, R.L. 1931. The Charles Russell Collection. In Hobson, R. Rackham, B. and King, W. (eds), *Chinese Ceramics in Private Collections.* London: Halton and Truscott Smith Ltd.

IMPEY, O. 1998. The Oriental Ceramic Society, London. *The Asian Art Newspaper,* June/July 1998.

JENYNS, S. 1960. Charles Ernest Russell. *Transactions of the Oriental Ceramic Society,* **32,** 1959-60.

JENYNS, S. 1969. Mrs Walter Sedgwick. *Transactions of the Oriental Ceramic Society,* **37**, 1967-69.

KIDDELL, J. 1969. Francis Brodie Lodge. *Transactions of the Oriental Ceramic Society,* **37**, 1967-69.

KUKLICK, H. 1984. Tribal Exemplars. Images of Political Authority in British Anthropology, 1885-1945. In Stocking, G. (ed), *Functionalism Historicized. Essays on British Social Anthropology.* London and Madison: The University of Wisconsin Press.

L.C.G.C. 1941. Professor C.G. Seligman. *Transactions of the Oriental Ceramic Society,* **18**, 1940-41.

MYERS, C. 1941. Charles Gabriel Seligman, 1873-1940. *Obituary Notices of Fellows of the Royal Society,* 10 December, 1941.

MYERS, C. 1949. Seligman, Charles Gabriel. In Wickham Legg, L.G. (ed), *The Dictionary of National Biography.* Oxford: Oxford University Press.

PEARCE, S. 1991. Collecting Reconsidered. In Kavanagh, G. (ed), *Museum Languages: Objects and Texts.* Leicester: Leicester University Press.

PEARCE, S. 1995. *On Collecting. An Investigation into Collecting in the European Tradition.* London and New York: Routledge.

SCHOR, N. 1994. Collecting Paris. In Elsner, J. and Cardinal, R. (eds), *The Cultures of Collecting.* London: Reaktion Books Ltd.

SELIGMAN, B. 1909. Journal, The Seligman Papers, file 1/4/3, London School of Economics Archive, University of London.

SELIGMAN, B. 1930. Journal of Japan, Korea and China, 1929-30, The Seligman Papers, file 5//1/6, London School of Economics Archive, University of London.

SELIGMAN, B. 1955. Engagement diary, The Seligman Papers, file 14/1/5, London School of Economics Archive, University of London.

SELIGMAN, B. 1956. Engagement diary, The Seligman Papers, file 14/1/5, London School of Economics Archive, University of London.

SELIGMAN, B. 1957. Engagement diary, The Seligman Papers, file 14/1/5, London School of Economics Archive, University of London.

SELIGMAN, C. 1920. Bird Chariots and Socketed Celts in Europe and China. *Journal of the Royal Anthropological Institute,* **50**.

SELIGMAN, C. 1924. An Amerind Type in China in T'ang Times. *Man,* **84**, August 1924.

SELIGMAN, C. 1928. Further Note on Bird-chariots in Europe and China. *Journal of the Royal Anthropological Institute,* **58**.

SELIGMAN, C. 1930. Journal of China, 1929-30, The Seligman Papers, file 6/1/1, London School of Economics Archive, University of London.

SELIGMAN, C. 1932. Letter to Orvar Karlbeck, 8 December 1932, The Karlbeck Syndicate papers, Far Eastern Department Archive, Victoria and Albert Museum.

SELIGMAN, C. and BECK, H. 1934. Barium in Ancient Glass. *Nature,* **133**.

SELIGMAN, C., BECK, H. and RITCHIE, P. 1936. Early Chinese Glass from pre-Han to T'ang Times *Nature,* **138**.

SELIGMAN, C. 1936. Patterns of Culture. *Man*, July 1936.

SELIGMAN, C. 1937. The Roman Orient and the Far East. *Antiquity. A Quarterly Review of Archaeology*, vol. **Xi**.

SELIGMAN, C. and BECK, H. 1938. Far Eastern Glass: Some Western Origins. *Bulletin of the Museum of Far Eastern Antiquities* (Stockholm), no.**10**.

SELIGMAN, C. 1938a. Chinese Socketed Celts. *Antiquity*, **12**, pp.86-7.

SELIGMAN, C. 1938b. Letter to C.W. Yih, 30 November 1938, The Seligman Papers, file 6/1/4, London School of Economics Archive, University of London.

SEYMOUR-SMITH, C. 1986. *MacMillan Dictionary of Anthropology.* London: MacMillan Press Ltd.

STEWART, S. 1993. *On Longing. Narratives of the Miniature, the Gigantic, the Souvenir, the Collection.* Durham and London: Duke University Press.

THE BURLINGTON MAGAZINE. 1938.Transactions of the OCS, 1936-37. July 1938, Cuttings File, Oriental Ceramic Society Archive.

V&A, 1962. Confidential memo, 12 October 1962, Brenda Seligman Nominal File, Victoria and Albert Museum Archive .

VON FAULKENHAUSEN, L. 1993. Historiographical Orientation of Chinese Archaeology. *Antiquity*, vol. **67**, no. 257, December 1993.

WHITFIELD, R. 1995. Landmarks in the Collection and Study of Chinese Art in Great Britain. In Wilson, M. and Cayley, J. (eds), *Europe Studies China: Papers from an International Conference on the History of European Sinology.* London.

WHO WAS WHO. 1941. *Seligman, Charles Gabriel, M.D. Who Was Who, 1929-1940,* vol. III. London: Adam Charles Black.

Naga Independence, Women and Radical Collectors: Themes in the Horniman Museum's Naga Collection

5

Andy West

Introduction

A large quantity of the portable material culture of the Naga peoples, who inhabit the borderlands of north-east India and north-west Myanmar (Burma), is to be found today in 43 public museum collections in the UK (West 1992). This material in the public domain comprises more than 7,000 pieces, and stands in addition to that which is in numerous private collections in Britain. When examined as a whole, this corpus of public collections informs the history and anthropology of Anglo-Naga relations. But each museum also has its own story to tell – even those museums which have minimal documentation for their Naga collection might at least recount the life and times of donors. The Naga collection at the Horniman Museum, which numbers in excess of 200 pieces, offers much more than a simple story: it engenders and encapsulates a variety of imperial and personal histories. This paper will discuss how the Horniman Museum material illustrates and illuminates the history both of the area and the Anglo-Naga relationship in general, and in particular how the collection emphasises two themes which have been often neglected in the past. First, the Horniman Museum's collection has a surely coincidental but probably unique emphasis on collections made by women. Second, the Horniman Museum's collection draws attention to a strand of radicalism within the British Civil Service, and among the British middle classes. Both of these themes merge to a third: the Naga quest for independence, or Naga resistance to external rule and dominance, which can also be explored in the Horniman Museum's collection.

Background

The Naga material culture now located in UK museums derives in the most part from a short period of time, the bulk of it having been collected in the fifty years before Indian independence in 1947. However, the total number of objects made and used by the Nagas which are in British public collections is still disproportionately high for a small population, and especially so given that the Nagas were living in a relatively inaccessible area on the fringes of empire. The quantity of material in museums provokes a series of questions, for example: 'why are these objects here?'; 'where exactly are they from?'; 'who made them?' and 'who used them?' Such questions lead ultimately to that of 'who are the Nagas?' (see West 1992 for some discussion of this). There is not space here for full discussion of these questions, but aspects of three fundamental issues in regard to museum collections are outlined below. The overarching context is British imperial and colonial activity, and within that the British construction of an idea of 'Nagas' (which had political and social consequences). Three fundamental issues underpinning this context are the geographical location of the Nagas, the apparent attraction of British officers to the Naga people, and the lure of the material culture itself.

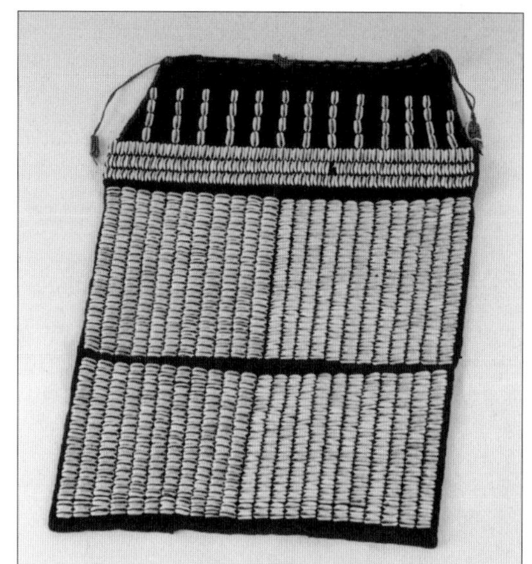

Figure 1: A man's apron, decorated with cowrie shells. A type worn by several Naga tribes including Lhota, Sema, Ao, Rengma or Angami. (Photograph: Horniman Museum).

The geographical location of the Nagas is important in any consideration of their identity and their relationship with the British. The highland area in which they live, being difficult to traverse, provided an almost impenetrable barrier between the plains of south Asia and the regions of east and south-east Asia. The Nagas' headtaking activities, along with the warlike reputation of other, adjacent hill peoples, enhanced the usefulness of the natural highland divide. The area presented such a distinct division, that the British laid down the boundary between India and Burma through these hills in the last part of the nineteenth century. The value of the hills was subsequently proved some sixty years later, when the attempted Japanese invasion of India foundered in the Naga Hills region in 1944. Perhaps rather fittingly, the final battle was partially fought across the District Commissioner's tennis court in the village of Kohima, the British administrative headquarters for the area.

The Nagas themselves consist of a number of 'tribes' or groups, such as the Angami, Sema, Ao, Phom, Sangtam, Konyak (see West 1994 for discussion of Naga identity and its relationship with the colonial past). The Nagas now live in the Indian states of Arunachal Pradesh, Assam, Nagaland, Manipur, and across the border in Burma.[1] The total population is, however, small[2] and the spread of the Naga population across several states and an international border is testament to ethnic and political tensions in the area they inhabit. The Naga peoples lived in comparatively isolated villages across the hills. Even those groups with which the

British became earliest acquainted had a contact period of less than one hundred years before India and Burma became independent. The export of such a large quantity of material culture from a small population over a short period of time indicates the enormous attraction it must have held for British collectors.

Figure 2: Wrap decorated with shells and goat hair. Angami. (Photograph: Horniman Museum).

Figure 3: Two hip baskets, for carrying bamboo spikes (*panjis*). Angami? (Photograph: Horniman Museum).

The British attraction to the objects made and used by the Nagas was connected with their feelings for the Naga people (see West 1994 for discussion of this relationship). The appeal of the Nagas to the British can be summed up in the sentiment of J.H. Hutton, one of the leading ethnographers of the Nagas. Hutton was a member of the Indian Civil Service who served for many years in the Naga Hills, and subsequently became William Wyse Professor of Anthropology at Cambridge University. For Hutton, the Nagas were 'a people in whose delightful company I passed what were probably the happiest years I had known since I left childhood for boarding school' (Hutton 1969: xii).

The appeal of the objects seems to have lain in their striking visuality, of form and colour. The material culture made and used by the Nagas was bright and distinctive, for example, the use of dyed hair, red and yellow basketry, shells and iridescent beetles wings. Especially popular among collectors were cloths (dyed, woven, often handspun cotton, decorated with dyed red hair, painted bands and shells), spears and *daos* (a type of axe) which were decorated with dyed red and black hair, conical red and yellow basketry hats with hair crests and other adornment, and a range of personal ornament from red and yellow basketry arm, leg, chest and ear ornaments, with additional decorations and ornaments using boars' tushes (tusks), shells, ivory, carnelians, metalwork – and dyed hair.

Naga material has become quite well-known and apparently easily identified by museum staff, specialists and non-specialists alike, because of its seeming distinctiveness (especially because of the frequent use of dyed red or black hair, and red and yellow basketry), coupled with the fact that so much exists in British museums. But along with such ready identification, there has grown a particular 'imagined geography', that is, the association of the Nagas with India alone has been reinforced. To research or simply 'look up' Nagas, books and sources on India are searched. Indeed, Nagas do not usually feature at all in general texts on Burma, whereas they may be the only one of many hill peoples of the north-eastern states to be included in works on India. This popular or semi-popular encompassment within India is important, and a significant feature of the historical construction of 'Nagas' and their connection with the British. The Nagas are linked to India, and India is linked to the UK through British colonialism and imperialism. It is to the empire that we first turn for an understanding of the Anglo-Naga connection.

India

The British empire in India had its formal origins in 1858 when, following the 'Great Rebellion' of 1857[3], the British Government replaced the East India Company and Victoria was proclaimed sovereign. This change of authority in theory did not affect the Nagas, since at that time the British had proclaimed they would have nothing to do with these hill peoples: the year 1858 falls in the middle of a period when the British withdrew from the hills.

The British first made particular contact with the Nagas about the 1820s, when searching for routes through the hills from the Indian plains to Burma and other states such as Manipur. The first European reference to the Nagas was probably made in 1822 which, based apparently on sources from the plains of Bengal, referred to them as 'extremely savage' (Hamilton 1822: 258).

In the 1830s and 1840s the British attempted to protect their investments on the edge of the Assam plains (principally tea gardens) from Naga raids, through undertaking military activities in the hills. At first, as they did so, there was an optimism about the hill environment and its commercial possibilities: 'a beautiful tract of country … thinly populated', with a 'climate congenial to European conditions', streams which 'abound in gold dust and masses of the solid metal', mountains which 'are pregnant with precious stones and silver' and good soil for silk, cotton, tea, coffee, sugar (M'Cosh 1836: 194). These startling assertions were found to be misplaced, and a change of policy soon occurred.

By 1851 it was evident that there was no direct economic advantage to be gained from the hills, and thus no funds to support policing or administering the area. Even the cost of military activity to protect plains settlements proved onerous, and provoked a change of policy: the British withdrew from the hills. Colonel Butler's recommendation on the matter stated that,

> *after mature consideration, it appears to me that our endeavours for some years to put down the internal feuds of the Nagah [sic] communities have proved a complete failure. I, therefore, beg leave to suggest that, for the future, we leave the Nagahs entirely to themselves, and wholly abstain from any interference with them* (1855: 202).

The British policy of non-intervention lasted some sixteen years, while Naga raids on plantations continued. In 1866 the British were back in the hills, in particular fighting the Angami Nagas. The Angami village of Khonoma, which had been attacked and captured by the British in 1850, had continued to remain powerful and dominate surrounding villages. Over the years succeeding the 1860s, the few British officers stationed in the hills slowly took Naga villages under their administration. They did so usually against the wishes of their superiors in the Indian Civil Service, who wanted to constrain expenditure, which meant curtailing any territorial expansion, especially of land without potential of economic return (albeit to protect adjacent areas), because the costs of administration and control had to be found elsewhere. Butler's focus on 'internal feuds' in his withdrawal recommendation (above) is apposite. These feuds were subsequently used as a rationale for taking Naga villages under British administration, in order to protect them from the attentions, raids and headtaking of their neighbours. Taking such villages into administration was often done by the officer in the field, on grounds of necessity, rather than first seeking authorisation. This process might almost be characterised (or perhaps caricatured) as a sort of 'protection racket', in which the British took over the roles of their Naga adversaries in dominating the weaker villages while providing protection against their stronger neighbours.

The 'protection' element was manifested in 'punitive' expeditions mounted against independent Naga villages which had attacked individuals and villages in the British-administered area. By the 1920s-30s civil officers had developed a practice of touring through unadministered country in addition to their regular travels through dependent areas for purposes of taxation and judicial hearings. Punitive expeditions were also mounted on the very rare occasions that a British officer was killed. It is important to note that there were no British 'other ranks' in the hills, only military and civil officers (see West 1994): a limited British presence in line with the policy of restricting access to the hills for all outsiders. The Horniman Museum has a Naga collection from Mrs Barker, recorded as having been brought back by her brother from the 1911 punitive expedition. This material is probably from the 1911-12 expedition against the Abors, a people to the north of the Brahmaputra River. The expedition was mounted in retribution for the killing of Noel Williamson, a British Political Officer, in March 1911. A considerable amount of Naga material was collected from this expedition.[4] Lhota Nagas travelled with the force to provide transport, and they also composed a song about Williamson's death (Hutton 1969: 369).

Military and civil collectors

The entry of the British into the Naga Hills region can be seen as the beginning of a military phase of operation in the area, with the military personnel accompanied by political officers. When the military presence became permanent, although limited, and after the western Naga villages were taken under protection, came a new phase. About halfway through the hundred years of British presence, around the turn of the nineteenth/twentieth centuries, an era dominated by civil administrators began. These men were part of the Indian Civil Service, and the Naga Hills was never their only posting. But many of the administrators who served in the Naga area had a particular interest in anthropology, and contributed to a culture manifest amongst those who worked there, of writing about the Nagas and making collections of their material culture

Figure 4: Carrying basket, decorated with tusks, goat hair and model heads. Angami (Photograph: Horniman Museum).

Figure 5: Cane helmet decorated with boar's tusks and goat hair. Chang or Konyak. (Photograph: Horniman Museum).

(see West 1992, 1994). Although they had generally regarded themselves as amateurs, several of the administrator-anthropologists went on to work in universities and museums in Britain. T.C. Hodson and J. H. Hutton took posts at the University of Cambridge, J.P. Mills at the University of London, W.G. Archer at the Victoria and Albert Museum (see West 1994).

The collectors of the vast corpus of Naga material now in museums included mainly military men, especially in the nineteenth century (and those who served in the area in the Second World War), in addition to administrators who dominate the collections formed in the 1920s and 1930s. The twin aspects of the military and administration characterised the British presence: a male presence, middle-class (with public school background), which emphasised masculine cultural features which they perceived in Naga society to be similar to their own cultural ideology and background (West 1994). This was the core group of people bringing Naga material back to Britain. But apart from what they saw as 'rescue' collecting in the face of social change, the Nagas also came to occupy a special place in the officers' lives. The Nagas were recognised as different to other Indian peoples, especially the Hindus and Muslims. The political and geographical marginality of the Naga Hill area, partly because of topographical impenetrability, was important strategically (West 1999). The Nagas were a hill people, located on the periphery of India and empire, with differences to plains peoples, but perceived similarities and links with the peoples and cultures of south east Asia, for example, with Borneo (Smith 1925).

The headhunting activities of the Nagas, while roundly condemned by the British, contributed to an exotic reputation manifested in Britain through some forms of popular literature, which probably encouraged collecting activities by those who only briefly visited the Hills. The British administrator-anthropologists were very much aware that a ban on headhunting meant social change, which would be visible in, for example, personal ornament associated with headtaking prowess. Similarly, they recognised that missionary activity was opposed to other forms of gaining social status and merit, and demonstrating personal prosperity, such as the public distribution of food at feasts of merit, and sexual prowess, all of which could be and were recorded in personal ornament and cloths. By the 1920s, the officers' awareness of social change reinforced the drive to collect what were seen as 'traditional' types of object, before they disappeared from manufacture and use. Parallel 'rescue' collecting in the face of social change, especially of rural artefacts, was in progress in Britain at the same time, following on from the collection of folk-lore and folk-music at the turn of the century and before.

At the Horniman Museum

The Horniman Museum collection of Naga material not only illustrates the main historical themes related to the military and administrative phases and activities in Anglo-Naga relations, but also highlights other important aspects. These additional emphases include: the problem of Indian and Naga independence, and the strategic importance of the region; British women as collectors of Naga material; and a strand of radicalism/liberalism among the British middle-classes who were involved in colonial and imperial issues. These three aspects – independence, British women collectors and middle-class radicalism - are interlinked. The Horniman collection also raises the issue of a conventional and Western 'imagined geography', noted above, which locates the Nagas predominantly within India.

These themes will be examined chronologically, following the pattern of growth of the Horniman Museum Naga collection. The bulk of the collection was acquired by the Museum after Indian independence in 1947: over 80 per cent was acquired by the Museum after 1950. The period of British contact with the Nagas through rule and administration was effectively the hundred years between the 1840s and 1940s. But although much of the material at the Horniman Museum arrived there after this period, nearly all was collected before 1947. As is frequently the case, the date of museum acquisition bears no resemblance to the date of field collection, and indeed, often serves to disguise the complexities, mechanisms, and processes through which material moves from creation in one place to display or museum store elsewhere.

The administrators

Only a few Naga pieces were given to the Horniman Museum before the First World War. Two early pieces which were originally designated as Naga, from the Museum's 'old stock', are probably not Naga at all. Such bold original attributions indicate how comparatively well known the Nagas were in the late nineteenth century, especially for such a small population. The first piece, a leather shield, has brass studs, which would certainly be atypical. The second piece is a heavy, ivory, 'archer's wristguard', which is inscribed, 'NAGA BOWMANS WRISTGUARD MANIPUR'. This is a big piece of ivory, cut to form a U-shape. It is unlike other Naga pieces, but comparable in size, form and material to a massive wristguard in the Pitt Rivers Museum, Oxford. The wristguard in Oxford was acquired by the Museum in 1929 and recorded as being 'already obsolete when collected': it is from the Kuki peoples of Assam.

The wristguard offers an example of an apparently minor question of identification, but one which begins to indicate the extensive confusion of names and peoples in the Naga Hills region, especially as experienced by the British since they entered the area in the first part of the nineteenth century. The term 'Naga' was never a clearly defined category for the invaders. The most convincing explanation of the term 'Naga' is that it derives from the 'Bengali word '*nangta*', meaning 'naked" (Butler 1875: 309, see also West 1992), and so is probably a term of derision for the hill peoples which was passed on by the plains peoples to the British. In the nineteenth century, the British at first pre-fixed the term 'Naga' to other identities they encountered on expeditions. This produced an apparent wealth of groupings (derived, it would seem, from the Nagas' primary self-identity by clan and village). For example, early explorers reported the Akook Nagas, Dyungiya Nagas, Loggjiang Nagas (these, and others, from Brodie 1845), the Jaipurias (Michell 1883), and the Bardnaria Nagas (Avery 1886). The clear designation of the bowman's wristguard in the Horniman Museum as 'Naga' might, therefore, indicate the notoriety of the Nagas being pre-eminent over other hill peoples such as the Kuki.

The first Horniman Museum Naga acquisition to be recorded by date, in 1909, came from W. Oldman, a London dealer, who claimed it to be a 'shellfish rake'. It was later redesignated simply as a rake on the basis of the description given by Hutton in his *The Angami Nagas* (1969: 78). This acquisition of a single and simple piece of agricultural equipment is in marked contrast to the personal ornament and cloths which represented the Nagas in many other early collections. The purchase may indicate the policy of the curator H.S. Harrison and his mentor Alfred Haddon of illustrating the range and development of tools and equipment. Harrison produced a booklet entitled *The Evolution of the Domestic Arts* (1925) for the Museum, in which he noted that, 'The implements used in the digging up of roots, or in the preparation of the ground and the planting of roots or seeds, range from a simple pointed stick to the complex machines of modern agriculture' (1925: 3).

The first substantial acquisition of Naga material redressed this agricultural focus, with a more conventional content of largely personal ornament and weapons. This collection, of over twenty pieces, came from the estate of Sir Henry Cotton in 1916: he died on the 22nd October 1915. It sets the usual tone of a collection formed by an administrator, as can be found in other museums. Cotton was born in India, in 1845, the son of a Madras civil servant. He passed examinations for the India Civil Service (ICS) in 1865, and went to Bengal in 1867. He held various posts in the north-east of India, ending his career in India as Chief Commissioner for Assam from 1896 to 1902. These latter six years, when he occupied such a senior post, are probably the most likely time when he acquired his of the Naga material. Otherwise, it is possible that he collected the material between 1878-80 when he was Magistrate and Collector of Chittagong, when he may have come into contact with other officers who travelled further north.

Cotton's collection includes material from the Angami and the 'Eastern Naga'. In the nineteenth century the Angami were the most powerful of the westernmost Nagas, dominating the groups to the south: Angami men were reported to travel as far as Calcutta, to acquire shells for personal ornament and for trade. From the Angami, Cotton's collection included their distinctive basketry leggings and armlets, made of red dyed and natural fibre strands, highlighted with interwoven yellow orchid stems. The leggings drew attention to the calf muscles, apparently much admired by Nagas as a sign of strength in hill walking, and such leggings were emphasised in Colonel Woodthorpe's nineteenth century illustration of an Angami warrior.

Cotton also possessed a wooden 'tail', which had no 'tribal' ascription, though fitted Hutton's description of the Angami version:

> *a tail of about a foot long is worn by veterans sticking straight out behind [worn at the waist]. This tail, ornamented with white seeds and long human hair as well as red goats' hair, contains a small receptacle at the root in which panjis [hardened bamboo spikes] are carried … the tail is regarded as the decoration of the warrior who has been the last to retreat before superior numbers* (1969: 31).

But such tails were known among other groups, for example, Woodthorpe (1881-82) described them in use among the Rengma but did not mention them among the Angami. This apparent discrepancy between two noted authorities, Woodthorpe and Hutton, illustrates some of the difficulties of ascribing undocumented material, the historical nature of 'ethnographic' collections, and the issue of change over time (West 1992). The difficulties serve as a reminder that Hutton's work, which has achieved high status, especially among many museum specialists and non-specialists, while still a useful reference, remains a snapshot of a period. It cannot be used to identify the whole corpus of Naga material over a hundred year period.

Cotton's 'Eastern Naga' pieces are two plain conical basketry hats, with red and yellow basketry side panels. Such hats are often referred to as 'helmets', as indeed they are in the Horniman Museum documentation: they were worn by warriors, but served no defensive purpose. These hats were not used by western Naga groups such as the Angami, who favoured the hair 'coronet' (a thick circle of black bears' hair), an example of which is also in the Cotton collection. The hats were traded from the easternmost Naga groups who were not directly in contact with the British (and possibly lived in Burma). In 1915, when Hutton had completed the manuscript of his book *The Angami Nagas*, knowledge of the easternmost groups was limited or non-existent. Hutton's division of the known (or imagined) Naga world included the Ao Nagas as the central Nagas, and the Konyak as the Eastern Nagas. The hats could have come from either group, but may have been traded from further east. (Cotton's collection includes a shield that is identified as Ao Naga). Perception of what was 'eastern' Naga territory, and which were the easternmost groups, shifted as the extent of British administration slowly expanded and the line advanced towards Burma.

Cotton's collection illustrates the main strategic points of British knowledge at the end of the nineteenth century: the powerful Angamis, and the Eastern Nagas who were a potential threat, living beyond the boundary. The eastern Naga threat was always there, even as the boundary moved eastwards, because the administered area never included all Nagas, nor even reached the Burmese border. Cotton's collection contained only male material culture, concerning war (spears, *daos*, a shield), and personal ornament associated with warrior prowess (chest ornament, tail, necklets). His collection perhaps summed up the conflictual nature of the Anglo-Naga relationship which characterised much of the nineteenth century.

Three other Indian Civil Service administrators gave Naga material to the Horniman Museum, but these men were of a later generation to Cotton. There is an important difference, because this next generation, who worked in the Naga Hills after the First World War, which built on the traditions established among the British officers in the nineteenth century to become the great collectors and describers of the Nagas (West 1994). Foremost was John Hutton, whose service in the Naga Hills began before the war, and who established strong links with Henry Balfour at the Pitt Rivers Museum in Oxford. Hutton wrote and collected a great deal, and was clearly a source of inspiration to his colleagues. But the Horniman Museum has only two pieces, celts, from Hutton himself. This is rather unusual, for Hutton amassed some 2,500-3,000 pieces for other museums, largely for the Pitt Rivers Museum in Oxford through his connection with Balfour.

There is a small collection, probably from the Naga Hills' administrator Adams, that was given to the Horniman Museum via a Girls School. This collection consists of basketry leggings, armlets, two earrings, and a waist band – probably from the Angami and Ao groups. There are suggestions that Adams did not quite fit in with the officers' culture that was empathic to the Nagas, and was not part of what seems almost to have been a clique of administrators (West 1992). This group of male administrators of the later generation were also anthropologists (at that time considering themselves to be amateurs, but some later took it up as a profession). They included J.H. Hutton, J.P. Mills,[5] H.G. Dennehy, C. Pawsey, and others (West 1994). They all collected from the Nagas and wrote about them. It seems that although relations between Adams and this clique were strained – and hence it is surprising to find pieces apparently collected by him – he did follow their practice and the traditions of officers in the Naga Hills, if this collection is indeed from him.

Anthropology and folklore

One object acquired by the Museum in the 1930s illustrates something of the nature of anthropology and its relationships to other disciplines at that time. The object is a highly polished metal disc or gong, used by some Naga peoples as currency, and also as personal decoration, worn by men over an 'apron' of cowries sewn onto cloth. It came to the Horniman Museum as part of the large collection of A.R. Wright: this disparate collection was connected with his interests in folklore. Wright had been a President of the Folklore Society, and one of his books, on *British Calendar Customs*, was published posthumously in 1936.

Especially in the early part of the twentieth century, there was considerable interchange between the disciplines of anthropology and folklore. The administrator-anthropologists of the Naga Hills published articles and reviews in *Folklore* (the Journal of the Folklore Society) in addition to writing for major anthropological journals such as *Man* and the *Journal of the Royal Anthropological Institute.* Although many papers they published in *Folklore* had what would be seen as an explicit folklore content (for example, on 'customs', superstitions, and folktales) others, such as Hodson's 1909 paper on headhunting, might be thought of as more recognisably anthropological or ethnographical.

The boundaries of the disciplines connected with key British activities in the Naga Hills, such as administration, exploration and military expedition, were blurred (see also West 1994). However, Hutton attempted to maintain some sort of distinction, as illustrated by his review of Arensberg's *The Irish Countryman: an anthropological study*, and his disapproval of Arensberg's 'definite attempt to extend to folklore the general principles of the functional school of anthropology' (Hutton 1937a: 320). This passage in his review almost suggests an implied difference perceived to exist between folklore and anthropology, between research at home and research outside Europe. But although Hutton's concerns were with Arensberg's sociological use of folklore, 'the part played in customary conduct by the 'scheme of thought' [folk beliefs]' (Hutton 1937a: 320), the tone does suggest his belief in a separate place for folklore. Nevertheless, the interchange between anthropology and folklore continued fruitfully, at least for the administrator-anthropologists: their books were reviewed in *Folklore*, such as Mills' *The Rengma Nagas* (Hutton 1937b).

The anthropology-folklore connection extended further. The Council of the Folklore Society in 1937 included Alfred Haddon and Henry Balfour as Vice-Presidents, and J.H. Hutton as a Member. As an officer of the Council, Wright must have known Hutton and also Haddon: we could speculate on Hutton as a source of the Naga piece. Wright was living in Honor Oak and therefore local to the Horniman Museum. The Museum with its library may have stimulated his interest in folklore and collecting habit, and locality reinforced by acquaintance with Haddon may have nominated the ultimate destination of his collection.

Art

In contrast to the nature of A.R. Wright's interests, the focus of collecting for W.G. Archer, one of the last British administrators to serve in the Naga Hills before Indian independence, was art. Archer became Keeper of the Indian Section at the Victoria and Albert Museum in London. During his time in the Naga Hills, Archer maintained an interest in Naga art, particularly carving, and apparently intended to write a monograph on the subject. He certainly collected material for this project, and many of the pieces he acquired came to the Horniman Museum in the 1960s. Apart from objects such as *dao* holders and personal ornament, Archer's material includes a number of large bamboo vessels with anthropomorphic relief carving.

Archer's collection reflects the nature of Anglo-Naga contact at the end of the British period of control. The British were now at the furthest eastern extent of their administered, protected and controlled area in the Indian Naga Hills: the British never ruled all the way to the Indo-Burmese border which they had fixed in the nineteenth century (see below). In terms of material culture, many of the pieces Archer acquired, such as the bamboo vessels, were not made nor used by the western Naga groups. These western groups were those with whom the British had longest been in contact, and from whom the bulk of collections had been made. They were also the groups on which the historical construction of the Nagas rested: the later contacts with eastern Nagas, and collections by the British were insufficient to alter the pre-eminence of the westernmost groups in the literature and imagery, nor to lessen their subsequent political dominance in India. Furtermore, it was, the easternmost groups that were located in Burma.

War and the end of empire

Archer's collection is unusual insomuch that it was made between 1946-48, whereas most Naga material in British museums collected in the 1940s dates from the Second World War. In the 1950s and 1960s, apart from Archer's material, the Horniman Museum also acquired other large Naga collections all linked to the 1940s, but connected with the War. These collections particularly illustrate a number of themes: the military importance of the Naga Hills; the end of empire; the retirement and sometimes death of 'old colonials', that is, of commercial, civil, political and military officials.

The material in these collections stands as a reminder that the region inhabited by the Nagas formed such a significant physical barrier between large continental regions, that it was taken to constitute a political border as well as being a natural boundary. The Nagas were not only living on the boundary but straddled the border, which gave them a political, national and geographical marginality, yet also a military prominence. Their strategic importance was first recognised in the British need to control the Nagas from the nineteenth century; and then again emphasised in the 1940s when the Nagas were crucial as potential allies against the invading Japanese. Indeed, the British learnt methods and techniques of guerilla warfare from the Nagas and other hill peoples, and relied considerably on their support. The final victory in difficult terrain owed much to the hill peoples. But in the battle that turned the Japanese advance, in Kohima, the trench dug across the District Commissioner's tennis court signified the coming end of British involvement in the area.

Many soldiers who fought in the Naga Hills during the war returned with Naga material culture as souvenirs or 'trophies', and much of this was eventually deposited in public or regimental museum collections in Britain. These ex-military men often brought home small collections of especially portable material, particularly textiles and typical weapons. For example, the group of cloths given to the Horniman Museum in 1983, which had been collected at Kohima in 1945; or the *daos*, spear and cloths given in 1950. A few soldiers appear to have made extensive collections: the Horniman Museum has one such, which was made in the 1940s and given to the Museum in stages from the 1960s on.

After Indian independence, the continued acquisition of substantial quantities of Naga material by public museums in Britain, was largely derived from collections which were made before 1947. This is not only because of the withdrawal of the British from empire, but especially in the case of north-east India because the Naga area has been effectively closed to outsiders since the late 1950s. In closing the area, the Indian authorities were continuing the British practice of keeping the hill peoples separate from the plains, and upholding the old requirement for special permits to enter the hills, but the underlying reason for closure was because of guerilla and other activities undertaken by some Nagas in pursuit of liberation, and the Indian army response (see West 1999). The end of empire meant the end of a reason for the British and most other outsiders to be in the hill area (from the view of many Nagas), but legitimised the entry of plains peoples (from the view of many Indians).

The collections of Naga material brought home by officials, visitors and others, usually stayed with them for some time. The transition of these collections from home to museum has often marked the final retirement or death of a military or civil official. When moving house, some sorted out their possessions, while the collections of others were presented, on their death, by relatives to local museums. Yet others clearly decided to dispose of their collections at some point after retirement. For example, F.J. Salberg of Forest Hill worked on the Assam-Bengal and other railways in India from 1905 to 1944, when he retired at the age of 60 years. He passed his collection to the Horniman – his local museum – in 1952, but lived until 1964. On the other hand, the 'trophies' of Colonel T.C. Rowland-Hill were presented to the Museum by his sister, after his death in 1963.

Burma

Also given to the Horniman Museum in the post Second World War period was a small amount of Naga material from Burma. Although only a small quantity, material with such a provenance is significant because it opens up the question of Naga identity and location. Most Naga collections in British public museums are from India: where material in undocumented but recognisable as Naga, past attributions have usually suggested India, largely on account of the historical and popular construction of Naga in Britain, as noted above. But, as the Horniman Museum's collection indicates, Nagas are also to be found in Burma.

In the late nineteenth century, when Britain possessed an empire in both India and Burma, the British mapped the boundary dividing the two states. The British drew it through the Naga Hills, at a time when they had little knowledge of, or contact with the hill peoples. As the British advanced their administration in India, from the Assam plains eastwards, they took under their 'protection' villages and 'tribes', using the local identity as a prefix to the word Naga. The various peoples of the hills maintained relationships with each other, but the British helped create a broader and distinct Naga identity.

However, the British never fully ruled or administered the area up to their defined border, neither on the Indian nor the Burmese side. This factor, coupled with the other British legacy of an international boundary which passes through and divides the territory of the hill peoples, brought subsequent lengthy (and still unreconciled) political problems for both the Indian and Burmese governments. The boundary line through the hills determined who became identified as Indian Nagas or Burmese Nagas. At Indian independence in 1947, Nagas were living in several administrative districts in India, Burma and elsewhere in areas which were only nominally protected. In effect the British passed over to the new central governments in India and Burma, territory which they had never really controlled, and a people over whom they had no real authority. This sequence of events has contributed to the ongoing strife in the region. Perhaps not surprisingly, some Nagas proclaimed their own independence in 1947 and later (see West 1999).

On the Burmese side of the border, British contact with the Nagas had accelerated in the 1920s with a series of well-publicised expeditions to eradicate 'human sacrifice'. It is possible that some of the Burmese Naga material originated from these expeditions.[6] But one small collection did not, and in addition to illustrating the Burmese theme, it indicates other strands running through the Horniman Museum material: collections made by women and an association with radical liberal ideas.

Figure 6: Headdress, with hornbill feathers, seeds, shells. Eastern Nagas. (Photograph: Horniman Museum).

Women collectors

Because the British presence in the Naga area was essentially male, collections of Naga material culture made by women are few. A small Burma Naga collection, of a hat, spear and *dao*, came from the historian and political scientist Dorothy Woodman after her death in 1970. One of her books is an important history of Burma under British rule (Woodman 1962). In the 1930s, Woodman was engaged in the political fight against fascism and imperialism, and was active in the struggle for independence in India, Burma, Indonesia and Vietnam. She was described as being 'too much of a firebrand' for the Women's International League. Woodman and her companion Kingsley Martin (sometime editor of the *New Statesman* in its heyday) were 'the only unofficial British guests at the 1948 ceremony of hoisting the new Burmese flag in Rangoon' (Anon. 1970).

A second woman donor of Naga material (but from India) was Beryl Power, who had been a suffragette, and subsequently a civil servant focusing on labour relations. Her obituarist noted that 'she passed into the highest grade of the Civil Service when that was rare for a woman and her career was distinguished' (Mason 1974). In 1929-31, Power was a member of a Royal Commission on Indian Labour, and this was probably when she acquired the Naga textile. The cloth has a painted central strip, which is conventionally headhunting insignia, marking status of taking a head, but the cloth was probably purchased in a shop or market. This type of cloth, with a painted strip, is indicative of two western Naga groups.

A third woman associated with the Horniman Museum was Ursula Graham Bower (subsequently Mrs Betts). Bower had a long and important connection with the Naga Hills and her life encompassed a number of themes. She first visited the area in the 1930s, and became fascinated by the Nagas, about whom she had already heard. After her initial visit, she returned to the Hills to stay among the Nagas for a few months at least. Still in the area during the Second World War, Bower became involved in organising Nagas as a guerilla force against the Japanese. She wrote a popular book on her experiences in the Hills (Bower 1952). Bower also learnt much about the life of south western Naga groups. She studied and wrote about problems emerging from the Naga cyclical migration patterns in the colonial period, and its implications for land ownership and competition with outsiders (for example, distribution of supposedly unused land to incoming groups, caused unrest since it was land which the Zemi Nagas claimed and used in part of their long migration cycle).

These three women collectors present a different aspect of the Anglo-Naga relationship to that of the male collectors and their predecessors. The men mostly lived and collected in various official capacities, and even those who entered as explorers remained part of the establishment. These women visited for different purposes, linked to their beliefs or interests. Their focus was very much concerned with themes related to independence, anti-imperialism, resistance to invasion and labour relations. Their collections serve as a reminder of an alternative perspective to Anglo-Naga relationships, especially within the context of Empire, to that which might be surmised through the conventional lens of the administrator and military collectors. Nevertheless, even that conventional image is incorrect, as evidenced by the activities of Sir Henry Cotton.

Radicalism

One dominant theme emerging throughout the collection is that of Indian, Burmese and Naga independence. This is particularly found linked to the collections made during the Second World War. Independence was a major tension in Anglo-Naga relations, a tension bequeathed by the British to succeeding Indian and Burmese governments. Independence for the Nagas was raised at least as early as the late 1920s, but the issue took on particular significance during the Second World War when the British needed the help of the Nagas and other hills peoples in the struggle against the Japanese invasion. Independence was allegedly promised to the Nagas at that time. Some of the administrators were supposedly sympathetic to this idea of Naga independence, separate from that of India.

A strand of (middle-class) radicalism in British society, illustrated here by two women collectors, Dorothy Woodman and Beryl Power, can also be associated with the theme of independence. Support for independence is evident in the activities of Woodman, but her concern seems to have been for the more general independence for India and for Burma, rather than for the smaller groups of people who comprised minorities in each state.

However, even some of the older administrators clearly supported such ideas of independence, casting some doubt on the popular portrayals of old imperialists. Sir Henry Cotton, owner of the first substantial Naga collection to come to the Horniman Museum, exemplified a commitment to a new India, despite or perhaps because of his family's long connection with South Asia. When he retired from India, Cotton became a Liberal Member of Parliament for a constituency in Nottingham. He 'attached himself to the Radical wing' of the party, and 'became leader of the section which pushed Indian questions to the front'. Even before he left India, 'his sympathies with Indian nationalism were well-known, and when he left Assam in 1902 he received a vast number of addresses of gratitude from his Indian admirers' (Anon. 1916).

Conclusion

The Horniman Museum's Naga collection has certain particular and interesting characteristics (like many other public collections, it has its own idiosyncrasies). The aim of this paper has been to indicate just some of the rich themes that emerge through looking at the collection as a whole, elucidating its chronology, and placing the collectors in context. Not all of the collectors represented in the Horniman Museum's selection of Naga material culture have been considered here. Similarly the focus has been on only certain aspects of Anglo-Naga history, particularly through the perspectives of military and administrative officials, and their concerns with anthropology. But the alternative perspectives on independence, and the roles of women collectors, which necessarily emerge from consideration of the collection, illustrate the range of themes which underly its construction.

Even these particular themes take on different forms through the history of Anglo-Naga relations, and the development of the Museum's collection. The period of time over which material was collected and acquired by the Museum indicates the importance of paying attention to history and chronology. It highlights the problem of using collections in displays presented in an 'ethnographic present' when individual objects may have been made and used in quite different times, contexts and relationships. For example, some 50 years and two world wars separate the collections of Cotton and Archer, with all the subtle and overt social, cultural and political changes that the period implies.

Similarly, museum collections separated by many decades at the point of acquisition, may have another, much closer chronological relationship. One of the Horniman Museum's more recent (1985) acquisitions of Naga material is a cloth woven by a Rongmei Naga woman, and worn for special occasions. It was acquired by the Museum through the weaver's grand-daughter. The cloth was probably made around the time of Sir Henry Cotton's death, when his collection of Naga objects, perhaps then only some fourteen years old, passed to the Museum. Such a juxtaposition only begins to indicate the need to see makers, users, collections, collectors and their context as an historical whole.

The acquisition of this Rongmei Naga cloth was made by contact with cartworkers through a touring exhibition of crafts entitled *The Living Arts of India.* The exhibition included a Rongmei Naga weaver who used a backstrap loom: but the inclusion of a Naga craft and worker reinforced associations of the Naga with India, rather than with Burma. The widespread linking of the Nagas to India[7] indicates the need to recognise that the simple attributions and ascriptions of material to particular peoples can be merely a crude cypher regarding their (often subaltern) relationship to Britain, and the imagined geography of association. There are various individuals who are involved in the production and use of material culture, in its exchange and in the process of collection and incorporation in museums: their different personal identities, gender, backgrounds, roles and purposes suggest the multiple strands which have made up the relationships between places, in this case, Britain, India and Burma, and the Nagas. Changes in the form of collections over time partially reflect the changing nature of those individual, colonial, imperial, social and even touristic relationships. The Horniman Museum's Naga material indicates some of the rich and complex contexts which helped stimulate the making of collections.

Notes

1. The name Burma rather than Myanmar will be used throughout this paper, because the focus is largely on the main period of British contact with the Nagas, roughly the hundred years of the mid-centuries 1850-1950.

2. The total Naga population is difficult to estimate because of the spread across internal and external boundaries, and especially on the Burmese side of the border, and because of the Naga insurrection in support of independence. There is also the question of which groups should be included as Naga, and people's own sense of self-identity. However, the total population, even now would seem to be in the region of a few hundred thousand.

3. The 'Great Rebellion' (Burke and Quraishi 1995) is otherwise, especially in the past, known as the Indian Mutiny (Spear 1965, and many others).

4. Further work on this expedition and the Naga material if collected, is in progress.

5. J.P. Mills also facilitated von Fürer-Haimendorf's anthropological work in the Naga Hills in the 1930s.

6. Work on these expeditions is in progress.

7. This association between the Nagas and India remains among many museum personnel, including museum ethnographers (personal communications).

Bibliography

ANON. 1916. Obituary of Sir Henry Cotton. *The Annual Register for 1915.* London: Longman, Green & Co.

ANON. 1970. Obituary of Dorothy Woodman. *The Times*, 2nd October.

AVERY, J. 1886. The Ao Naga Language of Southern Assam. *American Journal of Philology* **8**: 334-36.

BOWER, U. 1952. *Naga Path* London: John Murray.

BRODIE, CAPT. 1845. Narrative of a tour over that part of the Naga Hills lying between the Diko and Dyang river. In a letter from CAPT. P.A.BRODIE, Commissioner to MAJOR JENKINS, Commissioner to Assam, Communicated from the Foreign Department. *Journal of the Asiatic Society of Bengal* **167**: 828-44.

BURKE, S. and QURAISHI, S. Al-Din. 1995. *The British Raj in India: an historical review.* Dhaka: Oxford University Press.

BUTLER, Capt. J. 1875. Rough Notes of the Angami Nagas and their language. *Journal of the Asiatic Society of Bengal*, part **1**: 307-46.

FÜRER-HAIMENDOR,F C. Von, 1946. *The Naked Nagas.* Calcutta: Thacker, Spink and Co.

HAMILTON, F. 1822. An Account of Asam [sic] with some Notices concerning the neighbouring territories. In Burder, S. (ed), *Oriental Literature.* London: Longman, Hurst, Rees, Orme and Brown. 193-278.

HARRISON, H. 1925. (second edition) *The Evolution of the Domestic Arts.* London: London County Council.

HODSON, T. 1909. Head Hunting Among the Hill Tribes of Assam. *Folklore* **20**: 132-43 + pl 4-8.

HUTTON, J. 1921. *The Sema Nagas.* London: Macmillan.

HUTTON, J. 1937a. Review of The Irish Countryman: An Anthropological Study by C.M. Arensberg. *Folklore* 48: 320.

HUTTON, J. 1937b. Review of The Rengma Nagas by J.P. Mills. *Folklore* **48**: 326-27

HUTTON, J. 1969. *The Angami Nagas, With Some Notes on Neighbouring Tribes.* London: Oxford University Press.

M'COSH 1836. Account of the Mountain Tribes on the Extreme North-East of Bengal. *Journal of the Asiatic Society of Bengal* **5**: 193-208.

MASON, P. 1974. Obituary notes on Miss Beryl Power. *The Times,* 15th November.

MICHELL, St J.F. 1863. *Report (topographical, political and military) on the north-east frontier of India.* Calcutta: Sup't of Government Printing.

MILLS, J. 1937. *The Rengma Nagas.* London: Macmillan.

SMITH, W. 1925. *The Ao Naga Tribes of Assam.* London: Macmillan.

SPEAR, P. 1965 A History of India, volume two. Harmondsworth: Penguin

WEST, A. 1992. *Nagas in the Museum: An Anthropological Study of the Material Culture of the Hill Peoples of the Assam-Burma Border*. Unpublished PhD thesis, University of Hull.

WEST, A. 1994. Writing the Nagas: a British Officers' Ethnographic Tradition. *History and Anthropology* **8**: 55-88.

WEST, A. 1999. The Most Dangerous Legacy: The Development of Identity, Power and Marginality in the British Transfer to Indian and the Nagas. *Occasional paper* no **34**. Hull: Centre for South East Asian Studies, University of Hull.

WOODMAN, D. 1962. *The Making of Burma.* London: The Cresset Press.

WOODTHORPE, R. 1881-82. Notes of the Wild Tribes inhabiting the so-called Naga Hills on our N.E. Frontier of India. Parts one and two, *Journal of the Royal Anthropological Institute* **11**: 56-73 and 196-214.

WRIGHT, A. 1936. *British Calendar Customs: England volume 1: Moveable Feasts.* London: William Glaisher for the Folk-Lore Society.

In The Shadow of The Palace: Frederick J. Horniman and His Collections

Ken Teague

Introduction – the Horniman family

Frederick John Horniman, the founder of the Horniman Museum lived in the shadow of the palace. But not the royal palace, where the means to preference were estates, the army and the church; rather, the alternative palace - the 'Crystal' or Peoples' Palace which lauded craftsmanship and application, and celebrated the Empire for its commercial possibilities as much as its political circumstances, and paraded the exotica of human evolution in terms of replica dinosaurs and archaeology, tourism and foreign peoples. Around this alternative heaven lived Frederick John Horniman's parents and other eminent, middle class people: Paxton, the architect of Crystal Palace itself, diamond merchants and engineers; whilst below them, in Forest Hill, Frederick Horniman lived with his own young family, along with other aspiring tea merchants such as the Tetleys.

During the latter part of the 19th century, the heyday of Victorian Britain, Horniman amassed one of the largest collections of ethnographic material in the United Kingdom - one of the last of the 'cabinets of curiosities'; created a museum to house it, and then donated the museum and contents to the People of London for their 'recreation, instruction and enjoyment'. The collections formed the basis of two museums subsequently administered by the London County Council: the Horniman itself, and the Geffrye Museum in east London. All of this was created on the basis of wealth derived from the Horniman family's tea packaging business.

Horniman, a compulsive collector, was the son of a non-conformist (Quaker) entrepreneur, and had only a basic, rather than an academic education. He left school at fourteen years of age to enter the family business, and spent his working life as a businessman in the tea trade.

Personal documentation, such as diaries and letters, is lacking, so to try to understand Horniman and his collection we must contextualise him as a product of his society, first looking to his broad biography to discern the major influences on his life and personality: his family and commercial life; and then to the wider social and cultural influences of his time. A collector does not appear *de novo*, even though his collections, as in this case, may appear to do so. The wider influences on Horniman also include the development of anthropology and museums, tourism and travel, *Japonisme* and the Arts and Crafts movement. These influences, in lieu of narrower personality-structuring systems, such as academic conditioning and a subject discipline, or membership of the army or church, must be incorporated in the attempt to outline his beliefs, behaviour and motives.

As one of the wealthiest men in Britain, and without the constraints of boards of trustees or local or national government officials, Horniman collected according to his own wishes and personality quirks.

Surviving photographs show father and son, John and Frederick Horniman, as sober-faced men in dark suits; prosperous and worthy members of society. The plaque commemorating the donation of the Horniman Museum, gives an equally worthy and rational impression. These impressions are true, but they are not the whole story (how could they be?) of the passions and compulsions involved in the formation of the Museum, and the fortune on which it was based.

Indeed, the members of several generations of the Horniman family could truly say, 'I did it my way !'[1] Although family folklore stated the Hornimans to be descendants of early -13th century religious dissenters in Germany, who sought refuge in England, the family's recorded genealogy starts with Robert Horniman who was born about 1725. Frederick's father, John Horniman, a grandson of Robert, was born in Reading in 1802 or 1803. John Horniman married his step-sister Ann in 1825 and died in Croydon at a ripe old age in 1893; Ann died in 1900. Frederick was born in 1835, married first in 1859, a second time in 1897, and died in 1906. Horniman's parents were thus almost a lifelong presence, resident on the other side of Crystal Palace, above Horniman's own house in Forest Hill.

John Horniman was a Quaker, from a Quaker family of cabinetmakers (Greer 1995: 28), who married into a Quaker family. Records of his early life are slightly hazy but give evidence of a peripatetic lifestyle. Educated at Ackworth School in Yorkshire, John successively and variously stated his occupation and residence as: 'a grocer of Northampton', when he married in Reading in 1825; then as a member of 'Horniman and Co.' when he established a tea business in Newport on the Isle of Wight the following year (probably in partnership with his wife's brother); then as a 'grocer of Birmingham' when he registered the death of his second child in Bristol in 1831 (John's first two children were born in Northampton); then as a 'cheese factor' when Frederick John Horniman was born in 1835, in Bridgewater in Somerset; and finally as a 'tea dealer' when living in Reading in 1840. John was resident in Newport, Isle of Wight, from about 1845 until he moved to London in 1852.

The tea company of 'Horniman and Co'. was established in 1826 in a room over a stable in Newport. Here, John and his brother in law, Job, packaged tea by hand and sold it through pedlars. There is a suggestion that John may also have sold their tea as a pedlar for a time, and one wonders, given his changes of residence, if he was also a field preacher for Quakerism. There was a *contretemps* with the law when Job was caught peddling without a licence, poorer pedlars[2] who specialised in a single line of goods such as foodstuffs were more likely to try to evade their licence fees than pedlars selling a range of goods (Passmore 1991: 44-5). John paid the fine and emerged from the affair with character references as to his upright personality, and the nickname 'Honest' John Horniman, which he retained for the rest of his life. Quakers were usually trusted and respected as businessmen.

'Honest' John Horniman subsequently invented a crude packaging machine, and he and his brother-in-law sold tea in sealed packets of guaranteed weight and purity, in a context of sharp practice and smuggling. Despite initial resistance from the chemists and confectioners who retailed tea, and made profits from its adulteration, John laid the basis of the family fortunes, and started his rise in status from small businessman to commercial magnate.

Commerce and society

The 1830s, the decade when Horniman was born, were a time of great changes for the Quakers and the tea trade, as well as for Britain and the wider world in general. These changes helped to form Horniman's milieu, as man and collector, for the rest of his life. His working life as a tea merchant, and as a collector, may be seen as part of a more general liberal crusade against social problems in Britain and abroad. Although always relatively few in number, the Quakers were an influential force in this campaign to improve social conditions, abolish slavery, and establish a Christian world for everyone (Bainton 1964: 175-6).

The first half of the 19th century was characterised in Britain by a rising population, from 12 to 21 million from 1811 to 1851, which enlarged some cities by two or three time, often with slum-dwelling artisans whose working practices could not compete with machine-made goods. Working conditions were generally miserable, with low wages, long working hours and child labour. Alcoholism was rife and was increased by the introduction of distilled spirits. The working class were not franchised and had no representation in Parliament to change these conditions. Since the established churches were supine on these issues, action was taken by individual liberals and non-conformist, evangelical sects such as the Quakers (Bainton 1964: 25, 259). The Quakers were strong campaigners for temperance, the abstinence from alcohol and its substitution by tea as a more civilised and civilising beverage.

In the early 1830s the East India Company (EIC) held a monopoly on the import of nearly 14m. Kilos of China tea into Britain. Between 1833 and 1835, the evangelical and free trade lobby broke this monopoly and opened up the China trade. The evangelicals also pressed for, and achieved, unrestricted access for Protestant missionaries in India (Neill 1964: 276). Tea imports and consumption rose, some 32.25m Kilos were imported in 1836, and strong rivalry developed between London tea merchants and tea merchants in 'outpost' cities such as Bristol, Liverpool and Glasgow, whose wealth had been established on the slave trade and sugar.[3] Statistics about the tea trade at this time are unreliable. Tea was a profitable and a political business, and a major element in the two 'Opium Wars', in which the British in India tried to force opium onto the Chinese market in exchange for, amongst other things, another addictive drug - tea. Tea smuggling was rife in Britain, and all amounts, whether legal or illegal in entry, were boosted by 'smouching' or adulteration with hedge clippings, used tea leaves, dung and colourings etc. Such unsavoury additives were mixed with tea and sold to the public from open chests and boxes. Whilst both the Chinese and the East India Company sold some adulterated tea, in Britain, ' ... a whole industry was devoted' to this activity (Goodwin 1990, 43-4). In 1800 an Act of Parliament condemned such practice as ruinous to native woodlands, trade and government revenues (Emmerson 1992: 9; Tannahill 1975: 276).

When 'Honest' John Horniman (ironically as a social reformer) contributed to the Industrial Revolution and invented his refined packaging machine (about 1840 to 1844), which delivered Horniman's 'Pure Tea' in air-tight, tin-foil catty packets, of guaranteed weight and sealed under his name, his fame and fortune quickly became established. Horniman's tea, sold in a range of packets from 56.70 grms. to 1.3608kgs (two ounces to three pounds) in weight, was increasingly stocked by chemists, confectioners and later wholesale grocers. Horniman's packets were also thin, by contrast with the heavy wrappings often used, enabling him to sell tea at nett weight. Horniman & Company's packaging was revolutionary.

John Horniman and his family came to live in Croydon in 1855, and moved to Coombe Road in 1859. Here John Horniman bought 2.835 hectares (seven acres) of land and built an Italian style villa, 'Coombe Cliffe', surrounded by landscaped gardens, transforming a 'wilderness into a paradise' (Shaw 1993: 71), in which he entertained poor families from the East End of London on day outings.

'Honest' John Horniman was an active public figure with his own distinctive style of life. He is said to have ridden to business in the City of London in Quaker garb on a black horse; even after the opening of the Croydon to London railway. He was a member of the Peace Society, a Parliamentary reformer, slavery abolitionist and a philanthropist. After his retirement from the Horniman Company in 1868, John Horniman travelled, and may have collected, in Africa and the Near East (Duncan 1972: 2). He retained a financial interest in the Horniman Company until 1889, and is said to have made a further fortune by shrewd investment (M. Horniman pers comm). John Horniman continued to contribute to charities, giving about £100,000 a year (Shaw 1993: 71) and strongly supported the Temperance Movement, until he died in 1893. At this time his estate was estimated to be valued at today's equivalent of around £30 million pounds (Greer 1995: 137).

Frederick John Horniman - and his cultural milieux

Frederick Horniman was born in Bridgewater in Somerset in 1835, two years before Victoria ascended the British throne and inaugurated a period of commercial prosperity and imperialism which formed the framework for the rest of Horniman's life. After his education at a Quaker school, Friends College, in

Croydon, Horniman entered the thriving family business run by his father at the age of 14 years in 1849. About the time that Horniman entered the family business tea cultivation was being developed in India, to break the Chinese monopoly, and in 1850 Messrs. Horniman & Co. received their first consignment of tea from Assam. Alongside parental influence and example, Horniman came under the spectacular influences exerted by the 'Crystal Palace' which was re-erected some seven kilometres to the north of the family home at Coombe Cliffe.

The locality was already a fashionable part of London. The medicinal springs at Wells Park in Sydenham, attracted numerous visitors including royalty. The opening of the Croydon Canal which ran from New Cross via Honor Oak, Forest Hill and Sydenham to Croydon in 1809 prompted the establishment of tea gardens, a popular feature in contemporary society, in the taverns along the banks. The closure of the Croydon Canal and its replacement with a railway line between 1836 and 1846, giving access to central London further contributed to the fashionable nature of this part of south-east London for the rest of the nineteenth century. Housing development following the introduction of the railway, (Pisarro painted Lordship Lane station in about 1900), and a number of wealthy people, merchants and manufacturers moved in to Sydenham and Forest Hill. The seal of approval was placed on the area by the transfer of the 'Crystal Palace', the structure which housed the Great Exhibition in Hyde Park, to Sydenham.

Prince Albert's 'Great Exhibition' of 1851 had aimed to bring the best of manufactured goods together, both as a celebration of the British Empire and as an inspiration to British manufacturers, commercial interests and artisans. The Great Exhibition, 'from start to finish ...was a roaring success' (Hobhouse 1937; 139). Over six million tickets were sold for the Exhibition, and on one day attendance was over 100,000 (Best 1971: 252). 'It attracted an incalculable number of foreign visitors and cheap excursions from all over the British Isles enabled the whole of the more deserving poor to enrich their minds with its varied treasures.' Curiously, Hobhouse (op cit 149-50) then concludes that the Great Exhibition had 'no importance', other than being 'just a glorious show'. However, its mixture of exhibits from across the world, including strong representations of Oriental and European furnishings, decorative arts and crafts, is mirrored in the collections which Horniman subsequently amassed.

The 'Crystal Palace' was re-installed on the summit of Sydenham Hill, the highest spot in southern London, and was opened by Queen Victoria in 1854. Crystal Palace then developed as a centre for the arts, painting and sculpture, with concerts given by leading musicians. There were gardens with tropical trees, refreshment rooms and amusement grounds. Exhibitions included Assyrian art and architecture: 'The Court of Nineveh', organised by Layard and Fergusson, fine arts courts, Egypt, China, European historical periods and Natural History displays including geology and the first life-size re-constructions of dinosaurs. Some of the displays and exhibitions also exemplified the imperial theme well into the 20th century (Hobhouse 1937; Reeves 1986).

Crystal Palace was at the peak of its popularity between 1854 and 1900, with average visitor numbers of 2 million per year for its first thirty years. Around 1870 it was the most popular centre of entertainment in

England, with visits by royalty, both British and foreign (the Shah of Persia was a repeated visitor), Londoners and holidaymakers (tourists) from the North and Midlands of England brought in by special excursion trains organised by Thomas Cook and other travel agents.

The Palace was also a venue for temperance rallies which drew thousands of people, and was a cause close to the hearts of reformist tea merchants such as the Hornimans, as well as to Thomas Cook and Paxton (Brendon 1991: 44). Temperance was seen as essential to a worthy lifestyle and the benefit of society at large.

Following the success of the Great Exhibition, a whole series of international exhibitions were held in Britain, on the Continent and in the United States. In Britain, the Oriental and Turkish Exhibition was held in London in 1854, and the London International Exhibition in 1862. Tea merchants were especially interested in and concerned with these large-scale exhibitions. The 1862 London International Exhibition included Japanese art which made a great impression throughout Britain and encouraged Frederick Horniman and his son Emslie's life-long interest in the country. Japan had only recently (1854) been opened to relations with the United States and Europe, but the Hornimans blended Japanese teas with others, and it was apparent to them that tea played an important role in Japanese society, both on an everyday basis and in ritualised form in the Tea Ceremony. On his visit to Japan in 1895 (see below), Horniman was able to engage his interests by purchasing a substantial collection there. In 1884 the Indian Tea Association had a pavilion at the London Health Exhibition; in 1886 the Colonial & Indian Exhibition at South Kensington included displays with samples and drinks of teas from India and Ceylon (Sri Lanka). After it closed Horniman bought a number of objects from this exhibition for his museum (see below). Ceylon Tea stands featured at exhibitions in Liverpool (1887) and Glasgow (1888) - London did not have the monopoly.[4]

Museum collections and exhibitions, developing from those of preceding centuries, were a major feature in Victorian life. The East India Company, for example, encouraged its employees to contribute specimens to its collections, which were founded in 1801 with the aim of promoting Asian studies. Other trading companies did likewise. The East India Company's collection was opened to the public in London and provided a major part of the collections exhibited in the Indian Pavilion at the Great Exhibition of 1851. In 1857 the East India Company's collection was transferred to the British Government, and became known as the India Museum. Much of this collection was later incorporated into those of the Victoria & Albert and the Science Museums.

The development of museums in Victorian Britain was inspired by a number of social forces, including civic pride and rivalry, especially in provincial cities, as well as philanthropic interests such as those exemplified by the Hornimans. The establishment of museums, libraries, mechanics institutes and board schools, was meant to benefit the less well educated and under-privileged members of society by promoting social harmony, particularly in urban contexts where the rigours of life in industrialised cities were well recognised. At the South London Industrial Exhibition of 1865, Lord Palmerston spoke in support of social mobility for artisans through their exercise of skills, good conduct, and perseverance (Best 1971: 255-8).

Frederick John Horniman as a collector

In 1859, aged 24, Frederick John Horniman married Rebekah, the youngest daughter of John Emslie of Dalston, Middlesex. Rebekah was ten years older than Horniman. A daughter, Annie, was born in 1860, and a son, Emslie, in 1863. 1868 appears to have been one of the significant 'moments' in Frederick Horniman's life. John Horniman retired from the family business but remained living at Coombe Cliffe, whilst Frederick moved his family into their own home: Surrey House, 100 London Road, Forest Hill, London SE.

With his new-found freedom from the parental home, and having paid his social debt by reproducing his family, that is by fathering a daughter and a son; and with the wealth he was deriving from the family business, Horniman was now able to follow his own interests in collecting. His motivations, like anyone's were presumably mixed. They probably followed on from childhood interests (he said himself that he collected birds' eggs, butterflies, moths and insects as a boy), and from the example of his father's collecting. Collecting also provided freedom, in the mind at least, from an oppressive atmosphere in his own home. The portrait of Horniman at home in this period which was presented by his daughter, appears to show him as 'anxious to achieve the social distinction to which his wealth entitled him...(he) lived in the midst of a good deal of pomp and ceremony' (Pogson 1952: 2). Annie Horniman told of his progress in religious matters:

> *My father was a Quaker. He became a Congregationalist so as to marry my mother. I was christened in a Baptist chapel and, aged eleven, was taken to a Presbyterian church, but when I was eighteen we had a handsome carriage and pair and that (in a London suburb) took us automatically to church. Dear papa became less and less a Quaker as he became more wealthy, until he decided a man of his position ought to belong to the Church of England* (Pogson Ibid.).

There were many taboos in the Horniman household. Annie was almost grown up before she saw a pack of cards. Of all the prohibited subjects one took precedence - the theatre. However, with the connivance of a German governess, the two young Hornimans went to the theatre in Crystal Palace. This event sparked Annie's devotion to the theatre for the rest of her life.[5] The Hornimans had their passions.

Evidence for the start of serious collecting by Horniman is lacking. Horniman's curator in the 1890s, Richard Quick, stated it began in the 1860s. There is some indication that John Horniman travelled in the Middle East and North Africa, made collections there, and imbued Frederick Horniman with the passion for collecting (M. Horniman pers comm). Unfortunately there are no records of these activities, and Frederick Horniman's collection from these areas, although present in small numbers, nevertheless has important gaps, for example in woven textiles from this region, even though these were becoming increasingly popular on the London market. The weakness of an Islamic element in Horniman's collection, and his relative indifference to collecting from the Islamic world, also gives rise to questions in view of the strong Islamic influence in the Arts and Crafts movement, which Horniman also supported. It may be that this absence of interest (to argue from silence) reflects the very few evangelical results which were obtained in the first half of the 19th century in the Near and Middle East (Neill 1964: 302-4), in contrast to the progress that was thought to have been made in India and China.

Apart from the stimulus of the Crystal Palace, other museums in London, such as those of Twining (another tea merchant) and Pitt Rivers (Lane Fox, who opened his collection in Bethnal Green in 1874) also provided examples of collections of everyday, typical objects, that is, 'ethnography', echoing the more general cultural impulse towards social realism which was developing at this time.

At first Horniman collected through other merchants, travelling collectors, missionaries, naval officers and soldiers; from London dealers such as: Oldman, Webster, Viewig, Lawrence, Inman, Fenton and Burton; and in the provinces and on the Continent. He also bought from the auction houses in London: Sothebys, Phillips, Bonhams and Fosters; and from major exhibitions, for example, in 1886, after the Colonial and Indian Exhibition closed, Horniman purchased Indian specimens, as well as Zulu beadwork and weapons. A few years later his friend, Sir Somers Vine, the organising secretary of the Imperial Institute of the United Kingdom, the Colonies and India, helped Horniman to acquire a large, carved wooden Indian arch, and made collections for him in west and south Africa. Horniman also exchanged objects with other collectors. From 1883 until 1890, Horniman employed C.D. Watkins as his Curator, then, between 1890 until 1897 Watkins' duties were restricted to the Natural History collections after, Richard Quick, was appointed as Curator for the ethnographic holdings (from 1891 until 1904).

In 1888, Horniman moved his family out of Surrey House, which could no longer accommodate both the Hornimans and the collections, into nearby Surrey Mount. Surrey House was then opened as a museum: open to friends by invitation, and to the public on Bank Holidays. It is worth noting that the Crystal Palace, formerly the most important centre of cultural life in South London, was now in decline, due largely to maintenance costs (Hobhouse 1937: 160). Horniman's Museum may be seen as an attempt to make good this deficit.

In 1890 Surrey House Museum was renamed 'The Horniman Free Museum', and was opened to the general public free of charge on three days each week. The opening was widely reported in the press. The Museum had a printed guide and labelled objects in 19 rooms (according to St. Stephens Review, 3rd Oct 1891); or 22 or 23 rooms (according to The Pictorial World, 20th January 1891). Whichever was the case, the collection was ranked by the press as second only to the British Museum, and in 1892 the Horniman Free Museum received some 37,000 visitors. At this time Horniman also had a house in Brighton with collections which equalled those of Surrey Mount.

The middle years of the 1890s were another significant 'moment' in Horniman's life, both in terms of personal relationships and in his collecting. In 1893, Horniman's father died and Horniman returned to live at Coombe Cliffe to give comfort and support to his mother. Horniman's collections now received a new boost. Over the winter of 1894/5, Horniman, aged 59, made his first journey abroad, a three-month trip to India and Sri Lanka. In India, Horniman visited the Jaipur School of Art, which had been set up by the Maharajah of Jaipur. Here he extended his Indian collections to include bidriware and Hindu deities made from painted marble, and, in Calcutta, a life-size papier- maché figure of Kali trampling Siva. Horniman travelled on to Darjeeling where he bought Tibetan lamas' clothing, hats and boots, carpets, a metal figure of Chauraigee (Chenresig), and Nepalese *kukris* and *kora* swords from the 'Tibetan Curio Depot' (probably Paul Mowis's shop in the bazaar). His collection from Darjeeling led him to telegraph Quick to, 'build another room' to house it. He also visited the Alloobari tea estate near Darjeeling - his first sight of a tea plantation.[6] In Sri Lanka Horniman spent a day purchasing objects of daily life from villagers working on a coconut plantation. His total haul from Sri Lanka consisted of 'eight packing cases of curios', including a number of masks. Almost immediately after his return to Britain, Horniman's wife, Rebekah, died after a short illness. In the same year he was elected as the Liberal (Reformist) Member of Parliament for Falmouth and Penryn, a seat which he held until 1904.

CHRISTMAS HOLIDAYS.
SURREY HOUSE
MUSEUM
OPEN FREE
ON
BANK HOLIDAY
FRIDAY, DEC. 26th, and on
SATURDAY, Dec. 27th,
from 10 a.m. until 9 p.m. also
EVERY WEDNESDAY & SATURDAY, 2 to 6 p.m.
EAST AFRICAN LIVE MONKEY "NELLIE."
PAIR OF LIVE BEARS "ALICE & JUMBO."
The NEW ZOOLOGICAL SALOON "BIRDS, BEASTS, and FISHES" will be OPENED on BANK HOLIDAY.

Figure 1: Poster for Surrey House Museum (Photograph: Horniman Museum)

From September 1895 until February 1896, Horniman made a second trip. This was a world tour: across the USA, then to Japan, China, Burma, and southern India. As he returned home, Horniman visited Egypt where he was escorted around the temples of Luxor and Karnak by Howard Carter, who later became famous as one of the men who discovered Tutankhamun's tomb. Horniman's visit is recorded in a letter from the Field Director of the Egypt Exploration Fund, Professor Edward Neville, to H.A. Gruber, dated 22nd January 1896:

> *We had yesterday Mr. Horniman's (of Horniman's tea fame) visit; he had luncheon with us. Carter took him over the temple, and he was so much interested and struck by the beauty and the size of the work that he said at once that he would give us one day's profit, £100, and an annual subscription of £5. He immediately took out his cheque book, and wrote out the enclosed cheque. I am bound to say that it is to Carter that the Society is indebted for that gift. It is he who made Mr. Horniman acquainted with the Fund, and who took him over the temple yesterday.*

Figure 2: The Horniman Free Museum at Surrey House, Forest Hill, London (Photograph: Horniman Museum)

The Gizeh Museum Administrator in Cairo also advised Mr. Horniman about the purchase of mummies and other antiquities (Reeves & Taylor 1992: 54).

After the trip of 1895/6, which Horniman recorded for publication in the press, his collections were said to include: birds, butterflies and insects; Egyptian and classical antiquities, coins, manuscripts, armour, glass, porcelain, oriental ethnography and musical instruments. Horniman's Curator, Richard Quick, also helped to publicise the collection, for example by giving, 'an interesting lecture on Bells' to a large audience at the Borough Polytechnic Institute. He illustrated his talk with 'Lime-Light Lantern Views' (Forest Hill & Sydenham Examiner, October 1896 Issue).

Horniman was now a member of several learned societies including the Japan-Britain Society, whose members he invited to view his collections; the Anthropological Institute, the British Archaeological Association, the Royal Historical Society, the Royal Geographical Society, the Linnaean Society, the Zoological Society, the Entomological Society, and the Society of Antiquaries of Scotland, as well as numerous other societies and associations. Duncan (op cit) attributes Horniman's various learned affiliations to his wish to appear as a 'man of culture', which indeed he was, if only in a self-educated way. He also lent objects from his collections to the exhibitions in Crystal Palace and entertained Burmese performers visiting the Palace at his museum. In 1897 Horniman married again, to Minifred Louisa Bennet. As a result of her age, she was much younger than Horniman's daughter Annie, Horniman and Annie became estranged (Greer 1995: 185).

The tea business - rivalries and uncertainties

In business terms, the Horniman company expanded. John was succeeded by his sons, William Henry and Frederick John, who acquired their father's interest in the company in 1889 when they registered it as a private company: 'W.H. & F.J. Horniman & Co.' In 1891, despite the strength of other tea companies such as Brooke Bond and Liptons, the Horniman Company was still described as 'the biggest tea firm in the world' (St. Stephen's Review, Jan. 3rd, 1891).

Figure 3: F.J. Horniman (Photograph: Horniman Museum).

Even so the tea trade had its uncertainties and rivalries, and it may be argued that the approaches required in the business mirrored Horniman's eclecticism in collecting. In 1891, Horniman, now the senior partner, described the secret of his success as follows;

We supply direct and employ no middlemen at all. We buy and sell for cash and 5% profit on the (huge) turnover. Quality is always maintained, like the labels say, and the price was lowered by 4d per lb. when tea duty was lowered (other tea houses only reduced by 2d per lb). 'Always good alike' is a saying which refers to the consistent quality of Horniman's tea.

Orders are sent out the same day as requested. Only men and boys are employed, on piecework .... women have not the stamina of men (Horniman Archive).

Despite Horniman's reassurances there is some gloss in his words. The tea business can be a hazardous gamble. Supply and demand is generally very fluctuant. In part this depends on the nature of tea itself: 'No tea is the same year after year; like wine it responds to variables of climate and skill. A blend must have the right combination of colour, strength and briskness and must be economically priced' (Goodwin 1990: 169,171). Storage is also a problem since tea rapidly deteriorates in quality. Due to this uncertainty, severe slumps have occurred in the industry at times, for example in 1879 and 1896. To offset these uncertainties, the Horniman company spread its interests widely, and, as well as having special agents in Britain, had agents and warehouses all over the world. The company blended teas from China, India, Japan, Java and Ceylon (Sri Lanka); it had its own fleet of delivery vans and printed its own advertising posters, circulars and labels. By the turn of the century Horniman's Tea Warehouses and Offices occupied almost half of one side of Wormwood Street, with a warehouse in Shepherdess Walk, and an Export Department at Paul's Wharf on Upper Thames Street in the City of London. The Company received tea at several docks and wharves in the Pool of London. Unlike other companies such as Lipton's, it did not have its own tea estates abroad.

Advertising was an important aspect of the business, and, as was the custom at that time, made use of public figures. One advertisement showed the Prince of Wales enjoying a 'Right Royal cup of tea'; another had the Prime Minister, Mr. Gladstone, Florence Nightingale and the renowned preacher Dr. Spurgeon gathered around a tea urn. The company also published: 'Tea. Its Mystery and History', by S.P. Day, with a foreword by 'Lo Fong Loh, Secretary to the Chinese Educational Mission in Europe. At the turn of the century, the word 'Hornimans' was synonymous with 'tea', and Horniman, nicknamed 'Freddy Chinaman', was at the height of his wealth, and described in the press as a 'merchant prince'.

Figure 4: A packet of 'Horniman's Distinctive Tea' (Photograph: Horniman Museum)

Horniman's collection analysed

After the Horniman Museum passed under the administration of the London County Council in 1901, the collections were assessed by the new curators, A.C. Haddon and H.S. Harrison, as:

...a General Collection and a Natural History Collection. The General Collection is miscellaneous in character... containing archaeological, ethnological objects (with an emphasis on oriental, and European folk and decorative art and some musical instruments), on a world wide basis (Report to committee: Horniman Archive).

Duncan (1972) gives a comprehensive survey of the development of the ethnographic collection, based on the Museum's archives and her experience as a past curator at the Horniman Museum (during the 1970's). She echoes Haddon's verdict, and regards Horniman, prior to his two trips to the East, as, 'a compulsive magpie'...and an 'armchair collector'. She states (1972: 1) that the collections were usually made, 'from personal predilection rather than according to any scientific plan or museum prescription'.

These views are only partially true in my opinion, and I think it time to contextualise and to re-assess Horniman's collection more systematically.

After the Horniman Museum became a public museum in 1901, the two new curators, Dr. A.C. Haddon (Advisory Curator 1902 – 1915) and Dr. H.S. Harrison (Resident Curator 1904-1937) revised the collections on the basis of the Pitt Rivers system which was then followed in Oxford. This system was further adapted according to the Blackwood (1950s) system of classification of activities of daily life, which is now in operation both at the Pitt Rivers and the Horniman museums, amongst others. On this basis, and in conjunction with a recent 'Geo-Global Survey' of the Horniman Museum's collections, we are now in a position to re-assess the status of Horniman's original collection. This work has produced a more systematic, and statistical breakdown of the ethnographic collection, which supersedes former, impressionistic views.[7]

The original Horniman Collection was made over a period of some forty years, from the 1860s to 1900 (although Horniman continued to make additions to it until his death in 1906). The collection may be sub-divided according to the material he collected by proxy: through the filter of dealers and agents; material which was pre-selected and made available for him by other people; the collections which he made himself on his 1894/5 and 1895/6 excursions, and those which he directed his Curator, Quick, to make on his behalf during the 1890s.

Before the collection and the Museum were formally handed over to the London County Council in 1901, Richard Quick, between 1897 to 1899, listed the collection in two bound registers. The 'Geo-Global Survey' of Horniman's ethnographic collection (the Archaeological collections are not included), which was made at the museum in 1997, lists a total of 7,920 objects in the original collection which may be sub-divided by countries of origin and by size as follows:

Asia

Total number of objects 3,349 (42% of the entire collection), as follows:

- India (1281); China (677); Japan (676)[8]; Burma (277 ?); Sri Lanka (198); Indonesia (106); Middle East (89); Tibet (43).

Europe

Total number of objects 2766 (35% of the entire collection), as follows:

- Britain (1457, 18% of the total collection); Ancient Rome (405); Greece (273); Germany (202); Holland (114); Norway (62); Denmark (44); France (36); Italy (35); Spain, Ireland, Switzerland and Austria (all between 20 - 30); Iceland, Portugal, Poland, Bohemia, Hungary, Russia and Yugoslavia (all less than 20).

Africa

Total number of objects 1018 (13% of entire collection):
North (336); West (111); South (97); Central (31); East (10).

Oceania

Total number of objects 429 (5% of the entire collection):
Melanesia (270); Micronesia and Polynesia (159).

Americas

Total number of objects 334 (4% of the entire collections):
North (129); South (91); Central 82); Other (32).

The size of the Asian collections, given Horniman's interests, is not surprising. What is noteworthy, given the context of British imperialism and colonialism, is the strength of the collection from countries and regions which were not subject to British imperialism at this time: Japan, Indonesia, Tibet, Turkey, and to some extent China. This calls into question the view that ethnographic collections are largely formed from the colonial areas of imperial powers, and that the contents of such collections reflect the colonial experience.

What is also noteworthy is the strength of the British and European collections. Horniman did not restrict his definition of ethnography to 'other cultures' outside Europe, as, for example the British Museum and Liverpool Museum did until recently. For Horniman 'ethnography' included social and local history as part of a universal perspective.

I turn now to a breakdown of collections from some individual countries to see if this may reveal more information about Horniman and his collections. This breakdown is based on the Survey and on curatorial handlists, which may be subdivided by the (Blackwood) categories which we currently employ. The Blackwood system consists of 48 categories which cover most human activities, largely but not completely in functional terms, from Agriculture ... through Clothing ... Lighting ...Textiles ... to Writing and Printing. Ninety-six geographical divisions, mostly by country, cross cut these categories. This provides a classificatory grid which has certain overlaps and minor problems in some parts, but nevertheless gives a working system suitable for ordering the collection for several purposes including collecting, assessment of strengths and weaknesses, storage and object retrieval. This application provides 'profiles' of collections which enables comparisons to be made between collections in different museums, and of a single collection and its development over time. When applied to Horniman's collections from the Asian countries which he visited in 1894/5 and 1895/6: that is, India, Sri Lanka, Burma, China and Japan, this framework reveals the following patterns:

India

Aids, Physical - (2) walking sticks.

Armour - (30).

Art - (80) paintings, models of animals and people; decorative panels.

Buildings- (4) wooden doorways; tiles.

Clothing - (27) shoes, hats, belts.

Containers - (232) trays (in quantity), bowls, plates (Bidriware), vases, jugs, boxes.

Currency - (4) purses and moneyboxes.

Domestication (2) goads; (2) bells.

Firemaking - bag with flint and steel.

Food Preparation (33) - tea and coffee pots, cups, plates and ladles.

Furniture - (11) desk, couch, stool, brackets.

Lighting & Heating - (36) lamps, candlesticks.

Locks - (2).

Religion - (62) figures: Hindu, Buddhist, Jain, altar furniture, votive spoons etc., and especially a life-size display of Kali trampling Siva made from papier maché; a rare example of ephemera; an almost life-size iron figure of Vishnu; and a marble figure of the bull, Nandi, which weighs about half a ton.

Masquerade - (20) papier maché Hindu heads.

Metalworking - (6) coils of wire.

Narcotics - (70+) hookahs, lime boxes.

Natural objects - (7) pieces of elephants tusks.

Pastimes - (18) - hawking, chess, toys.

Personal Adornment - (220) jewellry.

Personal protection - (12) fans, umbrellas.

Photography - (22) photographs of Hindus.

Potter - (42) plates, cups, vases.

Textiles - a box of bobbins.

Toilet - (3) backscratchers; (1) fingerbowl.

Tools - a set of netting needles.

Transport, Land - (18) models of carts, animal trappings and harness.

Weapons - (188) swords, daggers, axes, bows and arrows, guns (some of this is Himalayan, e.g. Nepalese, in provenance).

Writing (23) pen tray, inkstands, paperweights, seals.

Musical instruments - (15) bells, gongs and drums.

That is, sample collections were made in 29 of the 48 categories which have been applied after systematisation of the Horniman Collection. This, I would argue, approaches a fairly global sampling of many (two thirds) human activities in India, which it would be difficult to replicate today, and suggests a more systematic approach on Horniman's part rather than simply 'magpie' collecting (although the sheer number of 'containers' does raise a question about obsessionality).

China

Either 677 objects (Survey), or 732 objects (handlist).
The categories collected here are: art (including models of people and buildings), clothing, containers, lighting, religion, manufacturing process, narcotics - pipes, pottery, textiles, transport - models, weapons, writing; musical instruments.

Fewer categories were collected than in India, which perhaps reflects Horniman's limited access in China. Most derive from missionary contacts rather than from his own direct collecting (10 objects). A particular strength is the Davidson Collection. The Quaker missionary Robert Davidson of the Friends Foreign Missionary Association went to West China in 1886. In 1895 he sold about 300 objects to Horniman. These were numbered, provenanced and their function recorded by Davidson, and were, 'descriptive of life and customs in inland China.' The collection was supplemented by the publication of Davidson's book, *Life in Western China* in 1905.

Japan

Either 676 objects (Survey) or 470 (handlist).
The categories by percentage of the total of 470 are as follows: Armour (3%). Art (35%), including a very large pair of cloisonne vases, and a carved, gilded screen depicting the life of the religious leader, Shinran Shonin, made by a named craftsman. Clothing (3%), Containers (33%), Food Preparation (5%), Religion (10%), Masquerade (5%), Narcotics (5%).

Burma

277 objects (Survey) in the following categories:
Containers, Domestic implements, Manufacturing processes, Personal Adornment, Religion - almost entirely Buddhist religious art and apparatus; Textiles, Weapons, Writing; Musical instruments.

Sri Lanka (Ceylon)

About 190 objects (survey) in the following categories:
Agriculture, (Physical) Aids, Art, Containers, Food Preparation, Furniture, Locks, Religious figures, Masquerade, Narcotics, Personal Adornment, Land Transport, Water Transport, Weapons; Musical Instruments.

Leaving aside questions of accessibility, and the financial resources which enabled Horniman to purchase and transport large, heavy and numerous objects back to London (for example the '8 packing cases' from Sri Lanka and the figures of Kali and Siva, and Nandi), the categories of material collected by Horniman on his trips of 1894 and 1895/6 should indicate what he saw as representative or typical of the countries he visited, as well as reflecting his wider interests. Horniman's interest in Oriental art is obvious, particularly religious art which ran counter to his iconoclastic, non-conformist background. This material also indicates that he was interested in 'high' cultures, as an 'orientalist'. The number of weapons he collected reflects a more widespread Victorian, imperialistic interest. However, there is also a significant number of objects of daily life and cultural identity: clothing, food preparation, pots and pans etc. Horniman's collection cannot be simply dismissed as 'a collection of curiosities'.

The Middle East

There is some suggestion (Duncan 1972: 2) that John Horniman travelled and collected in the 'Middle East and North Africa', and so provided one of the inspirations for his son to become a serious collector himself. This notion does not match with Quick's 1897 - 1901 register of the collections.

John Horniman does not appear as a source in these lists, with three possible exceptions: a vase, a bowl and a pair of boots, from the Caucasus. These are attributed to 'Horniman', which could refer either to John or to Frederick, and could equally refer to objects purchased from a London dealer as much as to objects collected whilst travelling.

A more substantial collection from 'North Africa' consists of about 50 objects including weapons (which sits uneasily with Quaker pacifism if they were collected by John Horniman), horse trappings and musical instruments. Again, these objects could have been collected by Frederick himself. Apart from his collection of Ancient Egyptian material, Horniman also collected some 15 to 50 objects from 'modern Egypt' (the record is unclear) including weapons, dolls, toys, spinning equipment, and pipes etc. during his visit in 1896.

The 'Middle East' is fairly sparsely represented in Horniman's collection. The two most substantial collections are:

Turkey

About 40 - 50 objects (handlist) bought from London dealers which are primarily slippers and pipes, containers and weapons.

Persia (Iran)

About 30 objects (handlist), again bought from dealers, forming a miscellany of pipes, spoons, toys, tiles, talismans etc.

Elsewhere the 'Middle East' is represented by small miscellanies of objects: Arabia (3); Palestine/Jordan (5); Syria (1), all bought from dealers. The small scale and nature of these collections calls into question the notion of British 'imperialism' or 'orientalist' approaches (*pace* Said), as personified by Horniman at least, in this part of the world.

Europe

The European collection appears to have been substantially formed by Quick, presumably under Frederick Horniman's direction, with a minor input from Horniman's son, Emslie. This especially applies in the case of the British collection, where Quick appears to have collected over 300 (handlist) objects, and Emslie about 50 (handlist); both collected furniture, ceramics and 'bygones'. The rest of the substantial European collections came from a variety of donors and vendors.

The 'Horniman Free Museum'

The Guide to the 'Horniman Free Museum' in Surrey House (10th edition, dated about 1896, compiled by Quick), lists 22 display areas including rooms and corridors as follows:

Entrance - Chinese chairs.
Reception - Japanese.
Rooms 3-8 - European and British material: horse armour, Spanish torture chair, Elizabethan bedroom and fans; Old English Chamber and pottery; Orchestral Organ and Musical Room; Old English Parlour, and Old English Pantry.
Room 9 - Oriental Armoury.
Room 10 - Oriental figure and dress.
Rooms 11-11a - Antiquities including models, locomotion and an Irish Wishing Chair.
Room 12 - Ancient Urns.
Room 13 - mummies from Ancient Egypt.
Rooms 14-16 - Indian rooms with brass idols etc. and a carved wooden archway.
Room 17 - China; Room 17a -Bibles, coins and a Hell Scene from Japan.
Room 18 - Natural History.
Room 19 - Ethnography, with drawers containing insects.
Room 20 - Porcelain and Glass.
Rooms 21 -22 - Zoological rooms.

The overall impression is of a collection of Ancient Egyptian, Oriental, and European material, with some representation of material from Africa, America and Oceania.

Duncan (op cit) opines that: *'The only logical arrangement was geographical but within this ... there was neither system nor sequence.'* My own assessment is less harsh, since I see the organisation of the displays as indicating some systematisation, with objects grouped by geographical area and category of objects, even if they do not follow a strict storyline and sequence. In this format they resembled the types of display which are still present in many provincial museums and stately homes in Britain today.

Visitor numbers to Horniman's museum show a steady rise over the years. From January to August 1886, when it was still called 'Surrey House Museum', there were 1,200 persons; in Whitsun 1888 - 5,207. After it was re-named the Horniman Free Museum and was opened to the general public on Wednesdays and Saturdays figures rose to 36,394 (1892), to 41,801 (1893), to 65,329 (1894). Apart from individual members of the public, Horniman also admitted groups from schools, orphanages, societies and clubs, including nurses,

Freemasons, orphans, servants, local policemen and their wives and so on. Members of a women's group from Lewisham were treated to an unwrapping and discussion of one of the mummies, and each member was rewarded with a piece of the wrappings as a memento; whilst visiting members of the Japan Society were rewarded with mounted butterflies from the collection. Both Horniman and Quick were members of this Society.

In 1896, aware that his collections were outgrowing Surrey House, Horniman commissioned Charles Harrison Townsend to build a new museum on the Surrey House site. At the same time, Horniman persisted in his collecting. In 1897, only two months after the sack of Benin City, Horniman was able to display Benin bronzes and Ivory bracelets and other material from the besieged city. Visitors in that year numbered about 100,000.

In 1898 Surrey House was closed and demolished, and the foundation stone of the present museum was laid by the second Mrs. Horniman.[9] On the 8th February 1901 the new museum was completed, at a cost of about £40,000, and was officially opened by the Duke of Fife, Lord Lieutenant of London, on 10th June. At the opening of the museum, which was, 'intended chiefly for the benefit of the working class', Mr. F. J. Horniman was presented with an Illuminated Address by the South London Working Men's organisations. Then in July 1901, the Museum and Gardens (6.075 hectares or 15 acres of land), and six houses, were formally made over, as a gift, to the London County Council, 'for the recreation, instruction and enjoyment of the people of London'. This was the first museum to be received by the London County Council.

Collecting in Victorian Britain

Rather than judging Horniman's collections by contemporary standards and views about museums, particular historical circumstances need to be taken into consideration.

The impulse to form a 'cabinet of curiosities', a hoard or collection of rarities expresses, 'a mixture of attitudes: an interest in learning and an encyclopaedic approach to enquiry, inspirational values, privacy, secrecy, rarity, boastful costliness...and features connected with storage', according to Ripley (1970: 27); whilst Pearce (1992: 43; 55) argues that collecting is a way of living within, and transforming chaos into sense, and that a collection can both bring a collector prestige, whilst alienating him from his family and friends. Horniman appears to fit many of these assessments of private collectors apart from 'secrecy', which is contra-indicated by the displays and publicity he gave to his collection. His 'alienation' or not is very difficult to assess, and appears to me, if it was so, to be more of a general characteristic of some British men, both in the Victorian period and in contemporary society. Although one should note, conversely, that his strong predilection for religious art from India, Burma, China and Japan runs counter to the supreme iconoclasm of his Quaker background.

Cabinets were formed in China, Japan, and the Islamic world, and so were not particular to the Christian west. They were often developed as a result of foreign trade, and the personal wealth derived from it; as, for example, in the numerous 'closets' (cabinets) created in Amsterdam (Ripley op. cit. 29). In Victorian England, many households had a 'museum room' containing antiquarian, geological and zoological objects. In this respect Horniman was firmly embedded in his cultural context, his difference was in the scale of his collecting.

The strong connection between non-conformism and anthropology has already been touched upon. There was a similar association between tea merchants, temperance, tourism, exhibitions and ethnographic museums, that is, Horniman was not alone in founding a museum based on such socio-cultural elements. Thomas Twining, of a much older tea family than the Hornimans, formed a collection of domestic and sanitary economy, which was exhibited at the Exhibition of Domestic Economy in Paris in 1855, then, in part, handed over to the South Kensington Museum in 1857. Twining later established his own Economic Museum in the grounds of his house in Twickenham in 1860. The Economic Museum contained instructive displays of building designs and materials, furniture and utensils, food, fuel, sanitary materials, textiles and costume, which Twining intended for technical education; the content, like Horniman's museum was a combination of English social history and ethnography, for example the Andaman Islands were featured. Unfortunately most of the collection and his building were destroyed by fire in 1871 (R. Twining & Co. 1982: 25).

W.H. Lever (Lord Lever) also assembled a large private collection in the late 19th and early 20th century, which combined fine art, European material, fossils and ethnography (largely from the Pacific and Southern Africa, but with some 'Oriental' material). This was displayed in the 'Free Library and Museum' in Port Sunlight from 1903 (West 1992).

The sources of the Horniman Collection, whether from dealers, missionaries, exhibitions etc., or from Frederick Horniman himself and his curator, Richard Quick, all reflect and represent social and cultural processes underway at the time. As such the Horniman Collection, rather than simply being composed of, 'rare and original curiosities', provides a number of 'documents', about disposable wealth in Britain, its uses and display, and of local and social history, as well as missionary and imperial activity abroad.

The encounters in the history of this collection are not only between Frederick Horniman and his objects, but consist of many other encounters: between Horniman and his significant others, primarily his family, and other collectors, and by the scientific establishment, which according to Duncan did not take him seriously.

Museums, especially provincial museums, were subject to considerable criticism in the late 19th century. This is expressed most clearly in an address given by the Curator of the Manchester Museum, Professor W. Boyd Dawkins in 1876. He adversely compared museums in Britain with those 'well-organised museums' he had recently visited on the Continent. In Britain, 'a museum is a sort of advertising bazaar, or a receptacle for miscellaneous curiosities ... an accumulation of objects, valuable in themselves but valueless for all practical purposes.' Dawkins' critique was directed primarily at the private and society institutions which then comprised the majority of the country's museums (Lewis 1989: 1). It could not have been a more accurate description of the contents of Horniman's Museum when it was opened ten or twelve years later. Nevertheless, such views do not take account of the educational uses to which Horniman put his museum. The provincial museums subsequently formed the Museum Association in 1889. Horniman's curator, Quick, was a member and attended its meetings (Lewis op. cit.: 12), but does not appear to have been on any of the committees.

Showmanship was also part of Horniman's approach to his museum (as advertising was to his business). This element is perhaps best indicated by his natural history collections and their uses. Duncan (op. cit.) notes the presence of more extreme curiosities in Horniman's collection, that is, 'comically arranged specimens of Animal Life - Frogs at Play, Kitten Pies, The Crab Party' and so on.

Anthropomorphism has a long tradition in popular British taste, and is illustrated both in the media and formerly in museums. Politicians have been lampooned in the press for centuries, with their face superimposed on an animal's body to make comment on their policies and behaviour. This humour was often used in the Victorian period, when it was also found in some Pre-Raphaelite paintings, and persists in contemporary society, for example in depicting John Major as a poodle during his dealings with the European Economic Community.

In museums, the practice of presenting animals in human guise has an equally long history. In 1778 Sir Ashton Lever's Natural History Museum in Leicester House, London was a fashionable resort which contained a roomful of monkeys who presented visitors with an Italian song, another read a book and another posed in the attitude of Venus de Medicis (Milo), 'the most horrid of all and scarce to be looked on', was one comment (Ripley op cit 33). In 1851 at the Great Exhibition a group of stuffed frogs were arranged as a barber, his customer and a passer-by carrying an umbrella. They were described by Queen Victoria as 'really marvellous' (Gibbs-Smith 1950, fig. 108; Hobhouse 1937, 125).

In Forest Hill, Horniman also displayed his own animals, both stuffed, and live (he kept two live bears). Horniman was 'free range' in his approaches, not restricted to one pious line of education. His museum was for the 'recreation' as well as the 'instruction' of the People of London. 'The stamp of Horniman's personality was everywhere. He catered ... 'for the intense curiosity about all that was strange and exotic in the little known ... Empire ...(and) fed as well the (popular) fascination with the grotesque' (Duncan op. cit.).

In my view Horniman straddled or epitomised the two strands of showmanship and a more didactic, 'scientific' approach, both entertainment and instruction, which have been present in museums since their foundation. Horniman was a passionate, not a rational collector, although it would be a mistake to suppose the latter approach was completely absent. Janus-like, Horniman looked forward to social reform and increasing educational opportunities for the public at large, but he also looked back with nostalgia for disappearing craftsmanship in his support for the Art & Crafts ideas and approaches, as his museum bears witness. It is tempting to apply contemporary museological judgements to Horniman, but I think it would be a mistake to impute the same constraints which bear upon curators today to an extremely wealthy man and his very different circumstances of more than a century ago.[10]

Frederick John Horniman died on March 5th 1906. His grave, marked with a plain stone alongside Rebekah's, is in a cemetery on the other side of the hill from his museum, still in the shadow of the 'Palace'.[11]

Notes

1. The individualism of several members of the Horniman family was expressed in a number of ways, for example in John Horniman's daily statement of his beliefs made in his dress and behaviour by riding to work from Croydon to London in the distinctive Quaker fashion of black clothes and broad-brimmed hat, which made no concession either to contemporary fashion or the modern transport system.

   Horniman himself was a small, energetic, and enthusiastic, man with concerns about 'purity' and freshness in his publicly expressed views; not surprising in view of the packaging on which the family business was based. Did these attitudes influence his collecting, for example from Japan, which had only recently been opened to the west and so was more 'pure' or un-modernised and uncontaminated than other countries, and apparently retained high standards in craftsmanship? (Impey 1977: 185ff). Horniman's interest in the Arts & Crafts movement was a similar impulse to return to former purity in craftsmanship, which ran parallel to his interest in Japonisme and Art Nouveau - the style in which his museum was to be built. Levell (pers. comm.) defines this paradox of embracing innovation whilst striving to recapture the past, as the, 'creative impulse of the romantic ethos' which was one of the distinctive features of the Victorian age.

   I see evidence of Horniman's showmanship in giving away souvenirs from his collection: strips of mummy cloth and moths; and performing as 'Freddy Chinaman' to the press; whilst his habit of eating rice pudding every day to maintain his health illustrates almost a Taoist concept of human nature and the means to longevity, and may be regarded as eccentricity rather than showmanship.

   Horniman's children each made their mark in different arenas. Both Annie and Emslie were educated at the Slade School of Art in London, then went their separate ways. Annie Horniman became an entrepreneurial patron of the theatre. She introduced George Bernard Shaw's plays to London, and promoted the work of Yeats, Synge and other Irish playwrights, for whom she founded the Abbey Theatre in Dublin. Annie also introduced the Repertory Theatre movement into Britain through her own, 'Horniman Company', which performed at the Gaiety Theatre in Manchester, which she also founded. She has been the subject of several biographies.

   Annie had 'an unusual mode of evening dress (purchased from Liberty's), variously attributed to eccentricity and showmanship, and was accused of exhibitionism (Pogson 1952: 14). Annie's support of Liberty's indicates an interest in common with her father in favouring the Arts & Crafts movement, whilst her eccentricities in dress, like her grandfather, expressed her non-conformist attitudes to society at large.

   Frederick Horniman was much more conformist in dress, although he did wear rather racy Prince of Wales' check suits at times. Horniman's non-conformity came out in the scale of his collecting and its display to the public, which presumably did help to shape his personality (Pearce 1992: 66).

   Emslie Horniman followed more closely in his father's footsteps. He was also a philanthropist who became Liberal MP for Chelsea, and was a member of the London County Council. Emslie travelled widely throughout the world, and retained his shared interest with his father in Japan. In 1910 he was closely involved in the Japan-Britain exhibition shown at the White City in London, particularly the educational aspects, and subsequently acquired a small Ainu collection on behalf of the Horniman Museum. He was also a collector, and a benefactor to the Horniman Museum, providing funds to build the Library and the Lecture Hall (now the Emslie Horniman Gallery which from 2001 will be devoted to the history of the

Museum's collections).

2. Passmore (Ibid) also notes that pedlars who carried religious book and pamphlets had an 'enormous benefit ... on the development of reading habits among the poor'.

3. I have not gone into the nature of British imperialism and the political context of Horniman's lifetime. Apart from the two 'Opium Wars' with China, there were also the revolutions in Europe (1848/9) which resulted in an expansion in the multicultural nature of British society, the Crimean War, the Indian Mutiny and the American Civil war amongst others.

   There is a nexus, during this period, of commerce and culture: tea, temperance, anthropology, tourism and exhibitions, which is beyond the scope of this paper. This period saw the publication of Darwin's *Origin of Species* (1859), which started enormous controversy within British society and challenged the authority of the established Church; to the delight of Non-Conformists. It was also the time of the American Civil War, in which Quakers tended to support the north and its anti-slavery platform. This led to a split in the Ethnological Society (the precursor to the Royal Anthropological Institute) between the 'ethnologists' and the 'anthropologicals'. The ethnologists who supported Darwin included Huxley, Lubbock, Evans, Lane Fox (later to found the Pitt Rivers Museum), Tylor (later to be the first Reader in Anthropology in Britain), and Galton, were all from a Non-Conformist, evangelical, humanitarian background, for example Tylor was from a Quaker family. The 'anthropologicals', who tended to have racist views in thinking that 'negroes' were a different species from whites, supported the South.

4. Is it too far fetched, given the overwhelming popularity of Indian tea against China tea at that time (in 1857, 97% of tea imported into Britain was from China, whilst by 1890 Indian tea imports formed about 70% of the British market, Emmerson 1992: 12) to see Horniman's soubriquet of 'Freddy Chinaman' as slightly out of step? And to trace a similar non-alignment, or non-conformity, of the Horniman Museum vis a vis the rest of the museum world in Britain? One wonders if the old rivalry between the anti-slavery tea merchants of London, and the pro-slavery merchant-councillors of the 'outpost' cities of Bristol, Liverpool and Glasgow, which all grew rich on the Atlantic slave trade, continued to reverberate at this time. Further, was this rivalry echoed in the establishment of the Museum Association later in the 19th century, and remains so at the level of local government in Britain today? I wonder also if the worthies of the newly-founded Museums Association could not cope with a privately owned and funded cabinet of curiosities, which also parodied Natural History (the strong bias in the Museums Association at this time (Lewis op cit 11), with its displays of Kitten Pies and The Crab Family? Was Horniman and his museum not sufficiently 'politically correct' for the late 19th century? Can an institution shake off its history, even if its collections are rationalised? This is another topic which needs examining.

5. See note 1.

6. A note needs to be made about the mythologising of Frederick John Horniman which is taking place in books, lectures and presentations to schools. For example Horniman is described as a traveller for 'forty years' whilst amassing his collection (Greer 1995: 28, 32; Shaw 1993: 78; and Pogson 1952: 17). This is not true. Horniman made two extensive trips in the 1890s, but before this, for forty years of his working life, he was, as Duncan puts it, an 'armchair traveller'. Greer (idem) states that Horniman, 'always brought back his personal treasures (that is the collections he had made during his travels) in his tea ships…' Again this is not the case. The Hornimans did not own any tea ships, but simply received tea on the London docks. Secondly, Horniman was not a 'venerable old man with flowing white locks' of 68 or 69 when he saw his first tea gardens (Shaw idem). He was about 59 or 60 when he went to Darjeeling. His hair may have been white then, if he had

much, but it was certainly not flowing - his bust and photographs from this time show a bald man! Trivial points perhaps but they do tend to cast Horniman in more of a physically heroic mould than was perhaps the case.

Despite his move towards mainstream religion, as noted in Annie's comments above, Horniman apparently retained an interest in the occult. His library contains Blavatsky's volumes on Theosophy amongst other, similar books. There is a story that Mather MacGregor, a member of the occult sect: The Golden Dawn, worked as Horniman's Curator-cataloguer or Librarian for a time in 1890. Greer (op cit 73: 155) states that Annie Horniman, also a member of the Golden Dawn, brought MacGregor to the Horniman home, where he took an interest in Horniman's collection, and was appointed as a curator. However, the current Librarian of the Horniman Museum, David. Allen, reports that there is absolutely no evidence to support this story. One should also note that Annie had an intense interest in Astrology (Pogson 1952: 19). Popular and academic interest in the occult, was prevalent in Britain at this time; for example see Tylor's accounts of his investigations into spiritualism. David Allen, describes Horniman's library as 'a very fine working student's library with good holdings of classical reference books on natural history, architecture and travel, which was assembled either by Horniman or by someone working to his direction.' (pers. comm.). This is another viewpoint which contrasts with Haddon's assessment of Horniman's Library.

7. The Survey may not be completely accurate in that some un-numbered objects may have been included on the assumption that they were acquired by Horniman, rather than subsequently. For example the Japanese collection is listed as 670 objects in the Survey, but as only 470 objects in the curator's hand listing from the registers. Nevertheless the Survey provides a useful breakdown of the collection for working purposes, and is still in process of refinement.

8. See note 7.

9.The architect, Charles Harrison Townsend, was a prominent member of the Art and Crafts movement, who also built Bishopsgate Institute, the Whitechapel Art Gallery, and Blackheath parish church, near Guildford in Surrey. The Horniman tower is made of Bath stone, like Wells cathedral. Townsend used eyelid motifs everywhere, both on the Horniman Museum and the Whitechapel Gallery. Perhaps they are Bodhidharma's eyelids, the symbolic motif for tea plants. George Bridge, a craftsman, and a team of ladies laid the 117,000 pieces of the entrance mosaic, which was designed by Anning Bell. Townsend wrote of his preference for women to make mosaics in the 'Girls Own Paper'.

10. Author's note. In writing this paper I have found myself repeatedly regarding it as a journey into irrationality. That is, into an account of the man and his collection in terms of enthusiasms, passions and sensualities as the critical factors, not in terms of the mind and rationality. Horniman's time was a different age, when museums were not as they are now, when they are all apparently scientifically organised and operated. However, Horniman did provide the material on which such an organisation could be made by Haddon and Harrison, his successor curators, I agree with Duncan's evaluation in this respect. At the same time, scientific organisation etc. merely disguises the tolerance for cognitive dissonance which Horniman and any other modern museum curator must accept in their work. One might argue that all museums are journeys into irrationality, hence their potency.

11. See note 6.

Bibliography

ALLWOOD, J. 1977. *The Great Exhibitions.* London: Studio Vista.

BAINTON, R. 1964. *The Penguin History of Christianity.* v 2. Harmondsworth: Penguin.

BELL, Sir. C. 1928. *The People of Tibet.* Oxford and London: Oxford University Press.

BEST, G. 1971. *Mid-Victorian Britain 1851-1875.* London: Fontana.

BLOFELD, J. 1945. Tea Drinking in China, *Royal Central Asian Journal.* v **XXXII**, Pt II, May, 193-198.

BURTON, B. 1991. International Exhibitions and National Identity. *Anthropology Today,* v7, no.3, June, London: RAI.

COLE, J. 1972. *Geography of World Affairs.* Harmondsworth: Penguin.

DESMOND, R. 1982. *The India Museum 1801-1879.* London: HMSO.

DUNCAN, M. 1972. *A Historical Study of the Ethnographical Collections in the Horniman Museum.* London: Museums Association, unpublished thesis.

EMMERSON, R. 1992. *British Teapots & Tea Drinking.* London: HMSO.

FORREST, D. 1973. *Tea for the British.* London: Chatto and Windus.

GAIT, Sir E. 1926. *A History of Assam.* Calcutta: Thacker & Spinks.

GIBBS-SMITH, C. 1950. *The Great Exhibition of 1851.* London: HMSO.

GOFFMAN, E. 1959. *The Presentation of Self in Everyday Life.* New York: Doubleday.

GREER, M. 1995. *Women of the Golden Dawn: Rebels and Priestesses.* Rochester, Vermont: Parker Street.

GOODWIN, J. 1990 *The Gunpowder Gardens.* London: Chatto & Windus.

HARVIE, C. Martin, G. & Scharf, A. (eds) 1970. *Industrialisation and Culture 1830-1914.* London: Macmillan.

HEREN, L. et al, 1973. *China's Three Thousand Years.* London: Times Newspapers.

HESSE, E. 1982. *Tea: The Eyelids of Bodhidharma.* Dorchester: Prism Press.

HOBHOUSE, C. 1937. *1851 and the Crystal Palace.* London: John Murray.

IMPEY, O. 1977. *Chinoiserie.* New York: Charles Scribner's Sons.

JOHNSON, B. 1983. *Development in South Asia.* Harmondsworth: Penguin.

LEWIS, G. 1989. *For Instruction and Recreation.* London: Quiller Press.

MILLER, P. 1979. *Teapots and Coffee Pots.* London: Midas Books.

MITCHELL, R. & Leys, M.D.R., 1963. *History of London Life.* Harmondsworth: Penguin.

MUSEUM IN DOCKLANDS PROJECT, nd. *Gateway to the East.* London: Museum of London.

NEILL, S. 1964. *A History of Christian Missions.* Harmondsworth: Penguin.

PASSMORE, S. 1991. Chapman or pedlar. *Family Tree Magazine*, Dec. 44-5.

PEARCE, S. 1992. *Museums, Objects and Collections. A Cultural Study.* London: Leicester University Press.

POGSON, R. 1952. *Miss Horniman and the Gaiety Theatre Manchester.* London: Rockliff.

PULLEN, D. 1975. *Sydenham.* Burnley: F.H. Brown.

PULLEN, D. 1979. *Forest Hill.* Sydenham: Pullen.

REEVES, G. 1986. *Palace of the People.* Maidstone: Kent County Council.

RIPLEY, D. 1970. *The Sacred Grove. Museums and their Evolution.* London: Gollancz.

SAVAGE, G. 1959. *Pottery through the Ages.* Harmondsworth: Penguin.

SCOTT, J. 1964. *The Tea Story.* London: Heinimann.

SHAW, M. 1993. The Horniman Family: Its Achievements in Business, Museums and the Theatre. *Lewisham History Journal*, no. 1, 1993. 65; 85.

SIMKIN, C. 1968. *Traditional Trade of Asia.* London: Oxford University Press.

TANAKA, S. 1973. *The Tea Ceremony.* New York: Kodansha.

TANNAHILL, R. 1973. *Food in History.* London: Abacus.

TEAGUE, K. 1993. *Mr Horniman and the Tea Trade.* London: Horniman Museum.

TEAGUE, K. 1997. *Representations of Nepal.* In Abram S., Walden J., and Macleod D. (eds), *Tourist and Tourism.* Oxford: Berg.

TWINING, R. & Co. 1982. *Tea and Sympathy.* London: London Borough of Richmond on Thames.

UKERS, W. 1935. *All about Tea.* New York: Kingsport Press.

WEATHERSTONE, J. 1986. *The Pioneers 1825-1900. The Early British Tea and Coffee Planters and Their Way of Life.* London: Quiller Press.

WEST, A. 1992. The History of the Ethnography Collections of W.H. Lever. *Journal of the History of Collections,* 4 no. 2, 273-283.

WOLF, E. 1983. *Europe and the People without History.* Berkeley, Los Angeles and London: University of California Press.

Merchants, Musicians and Missionaries:

Contributors to the Musical Instrument Collection of the Horniman Museum 1898-1998

Margaret Birley

Central to contemporary museology is the imperative for studies of collectors (Pearce 1992: 6). It is argued that an examination of the meanings invested by collectors in their collections, their intellectual milieus, the historical and social contexts, and their methodologies of collecting is a pre-requisite for a critique of any corpus of knowledge that has been promulgated by a museum. In the case of the Horniman Museum there is a lack of extant data for the reconstruction of many of these parameters; here the primary sources are the published records of collectors' stated collecting objectives. This account of the history of the Horniman Museum's major collections of musical instruments during the past century will focus on the individuals and institutions who acquired them and their contrasting collecting objectives, which are reflected in the different types of instruments housed in the Museum today.

During the early history of the Museum, many instruments were acquired from institutions and collectors operating outside the world of music.

The merchant and Member of Parliament

The second half of the 19th century saw the creation of a number of galleries and educational institutions, such as the South London Art Gallery in Camberwell and Morley College, in the heart of the poorest parts of "'the great intellectual desert' of South London"; (Rossiter 1893: 2, in Smith 1993: 11), for the direct benefit of their inhabitants. Although the Horniman Museum was likewise established in the spirit of philanthropy it was set in a quasi-rural location, whose charm was enhanced by its proximity to the attractions of the Crystal Palace. In Forest Hill the groves of oaks remaining from the ancient Great North Wood were as much a feature of the area as the new mansions of wealthy city merchants. One of these was Frederick John Horniman

(1835-1906), the Museum's founder and the chairman of a successful Quaker family business, which specialised in packaging and selling tea. In 1895 he became the Liberal MP for Falmouth and Penryn. As a committed philanthropist, he gave much of his wealth to churches and schools.[1] The most generous of his gifts was his own collection and museum building, dedicated in 1901 'to the public for ever as a free museum for their recreation, instruction, and enjoyment'.[2]

Besides musical instruments, Horniman's gift included the natural history specimens which he had amassed since his boyhood. His passion for collecting[3] such material was shared by many other pupils at the Friends' School in Croydon, which he attended from 1840 to 1845.[4] Natural History was considered to be 'the matrix of all scientific study in Quaker schools', with 'religious principles at its centre - to attend to the creation, to discover its lore and its laws' (Campbell 1953: 48).

Horniman also donated to the public his library of books, ethnographic material, antiquities, and oriental works of art. The salerooms, and church missions had all been fruitful sources for this material. As a Fellow of the Zoological, Society of the Royal Geographical and other Societies, Horniman had useful contacts who helped him to further the growth of his Museum.

Figure 1: Mayuri (Hindi- 'peacock') long-necked fretted fiddle. North India, c.1890. Frederick J. Horniman Collection (3861). (Photograph: Horniman Museum).

Horniman's collections were first displayed in 1888 in his private house, in a series of room settings with varied themes, including 'The Elizabethan Bedroom', 'The Ethnographical Saloon', 'The Indian Gods Room', and the 'Musical Instrument Gallery'. In the entrance hall stood a fine orchestrion, a large barrel organ from the Black Forest factory of Imhof and Mukle, which had a repertoire of dances and overtures from popular operas such as Hérold's *Zampa*; its loud, spirited music echoed round the house during the visitors' tours.

By 1901 Horniman owned some 200 instruments. Among them were a handful of European bowed strings including a violoncello converted from a viol by Tielke dated 1687, archaeological material such as Roman bells, and English instruments dating from the early years of the nineteenth century. Many of the musical instruments in Horniman's collection originated from those African and Asian countries which had at that time been annexed, officially or unofficially, by Britain. Like most British museums with 19th century ethnographic collections, the history of the Horniman Museum is bound up with the country's history as a world trader and colonial power.

After he had retired from the tea trade, Horniman travelled extensively. India, America and Japan, were among his destinations and he made purchases from dealers in every port of call (fig. 1). The eclectic nature of Horniman's collection is indicated by his own summary of his personal collecting objectives: 'I collected whatever appealed to my own fancy, or seemed likely to interest and to teach a lesson to those whose circumstances, or inclination, prevented them from visiting distant lands'.

Given the constraints on his travel prior to retirement, Horniman's statement may in part be self-referential. His collecting aims may have been both didactic and autodidactic, since his formal education ended when he joined the family firm at the age of fourteen.

The organologist

Two hundred musical instruments originating from outside Europe, of which the majority date from before 1880, were transferred to the Horniman Museum by Britain's pre-eminent museum of the history of art and design, the Victoria and Albert Museum, in 1956. All are finely crafted and have strong visual appeal. Most of them were collected by that museum's first curatorial adviser for musical instruments, Carl Engel (1818-1882), an eminent scholar in the field of organology, who was trained as a musician and a composer (Schott 1993: 9). The Introduction to his catalogue of the Museum's musical instruments, written in 1874, reveals his breadth of vision. The large collection of instruments from Asia, Africa and America which he created is considered by him to be a latent catalyst for the improvement of European instruments or for the invention of new ones, as the *sheng*, the Chinese mouth-organ, dating from the second millennium B.C., had been for the development of free reed instruments in the West in the 19th century (Engel 1874: 4).

Figure 2: Kamanche, spike fiddle. Iran, c.1800 (ex. Victoria and Albert Museum, 940-73). (Photograph: Horniman Museum).

Engel considers that Asian instruments' 'elegant shape and tasteful ornamentation, and the beautiful designs with which they are embellished ... afford valuable patterns for study and for adoption in works of art' (Ibid: 4). The earliest-known *kamanche* (spike fiddle), made in Shiraz c.1800, with an intricate inlay of coloured woods and bone, may have been one of the examples which Engel had in mind (fig. 2). Another of Engel's objectives was to promote an understanding of the musics of so-called 'foreign nations', among Europeans. He saw the study of instruments as a means to this end (Ibid: 4).[5]

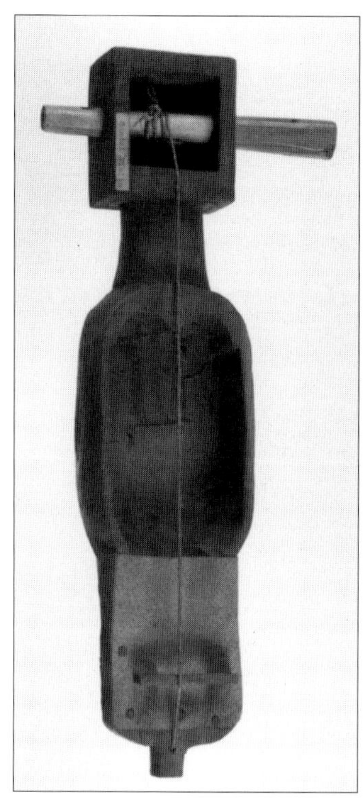

Figure 3: Banam, Santal, Fiddle N. India.Church Missionary Society Collection. (6.12.65/235) (Photograph: Horniman Museum).

The missionaries

The instrument collections in the Horniman Museum reflect the musical traditions of those peoples with whom collectors and their agents interacted. Both Engel's collection and Horniman's represent a wide range of instruments that featured in the context of religious ritual, and in the recreational lives of what were, by and large, the ruling classes. The collection of over 300 instruments that was amassed by the workers of the Church Missionary Society in Africa and in Asia, from the late 19th to the early 20th centuries, originated from peoples at the opposite end of the global economic spectrum. The documentation that was transferred from the Society to the Horniman Museum with the Indian instruments in 1965 indicates that they represented the musical traditions of the peoples that the missionaries termed 'out-castes', with whom they ostensibly had the most success in converting to Christianity.

Musical instruments, and other examples of material culture from the countries in which the missionaries operated, were supplied to the Lending Department of the Society in London for a series of loan exhibitions, beginning in 1882 and continuing until 1914. The exhibitions publicised the work of the Society and inspired new missionaries to come forward. The efforts of the CMS culminated in the massive 'Africa and the East' exhibition in London in 1909, staffed by 8,000 voluntary workers and attended by a quarter of a million visitors (Stock 1916: 504).

The Society's mission to the Santal people in Bihar in North-East India was established in 1860 by an ex-Cavalry officer, and it continued after India's independence. Among the Santal instruments collected by the missionaries for loan exhibitions were small drums, a Santal bowed lute *banam*, a transverse flute and duct flutes (fig. 3). One missionary describes his impression of Santal music:

> *Heard for the first time it tends to sound monotonous, owing to apparent lack of variation, but the simplicity of it ...can become very attractive* (Macleod n.d.: 15-16).

A similar description might well have been applicable to the image of the Santal people themselves which was projected by the relatively small, quiet-sounding instruments that were chosen from the Santal instrumentarium for the loan exhibitions by the Church Missionary Society. The missionaries also collected instruments such as ankle bells worn by dancers, cymbals and clappers, which are an integral rhythmic element of Indian music. Nineteenth century collectors such as Horniman, who had less culture contact than the missionaries, tended to overlook such instruments.

Systematic collecting

After Frederick Horniman's rather amorphous collection was passed to the London County Council in 1901, systematic collecting was inaugurated at the Horniman Museum with the appointment in 1902 of Alfred Cort Haddon, Lecturer in Physical Anthropology at Cambridge University, as the Horniman Museum's Advisory Curator. There was a radical shift in the collecting rationale, summarised in the annual report of 1906:

> *The object kept in view in the selection of specimens is that of making the Museum a teaching institution where the general public, scholars and school-children may be able to obtain information by the inspection of properly-labelled objects in a related series* (Harrison 1906).

Figure 4: Rebaba, Massawa, Eritrea. Jean Jenkins Collection.. (Photograph: Horniman Museum).

Many of the Museum's instruments were acquired in the field by anthropologists, as part of systematic collections of material culture. The interaction of the human race with the environment is a perennial theme of the published works documenting their collections.[6] Musical instruments were curated by the anthropology department's staff until 1960, after the ethnomusicologist, Jean Jenkins, was appointed in the mid-fifties as the Museum's Musicologist. She brought traditional music to a wide public through her broadcasts and her field-recordings which she made in Nigeria, Republic of Benin, Ghana, Côte d'Ivoire, Mali, Niger, Tanzania, Kenya, Uganda, Ethiopia, Syria, Jordan, Central Asia and Bulgaria (fig. 4). The exhibitions which she co-ordinated *'Eighteenth century musical instruments: France and Britain'* (1973) and *'Music and musical instruments in the World of Islam'* (1976) also served to raise the Museum's profile.

One of the most lucidly systematic collections of musical instruments illustrating an evolutionary series is represented by the gift of over 300 historic European wind instruments, which was presented to the Horniman Museum in 1947 by Adam Carse, Professor of Composition at the Royal Academy of Music in London. It consists of wind instruments used in European orchestral and military traditions from the 18th to the 20th centuries. In the introduction to his catalogue, Adam Carse states that the purpose of his collection is to demonstrate the gradual development of wind instruments, and to show the main lines of progress (Carse 1951: 13) (fig. 5). Carse's objectives have informed the interpretative schemes of the Museum's exhibitions of his collection since it was first displayed.

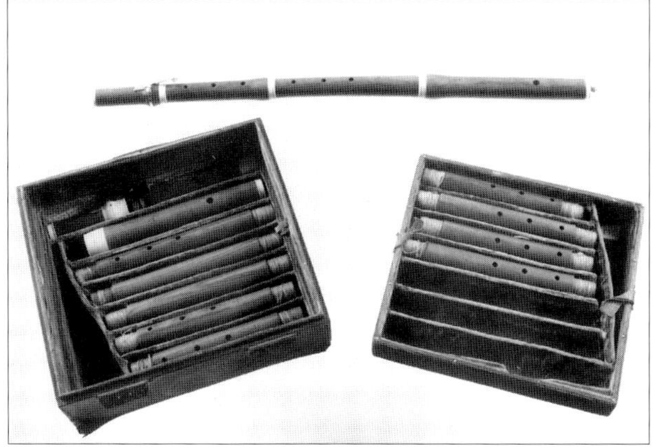

Figure 5: Pair of one-keyed flutes by Thomas Lot, Paris, c.1740. Carse Collection (14.5.47/263). (Photograph: Horniman Museum).

Another collection made specifically as an evolutionary series is the Wayne collection of concertinas and related free reed instruments, which was purchased in 1996, with the generous support of the National Heritage Lottery Fund and the MGC/Science Museum PRISM Fund. The core of the collection consists of 127 instruments created by Charles Wheatstone (1802-1875), a professor of Physics and the inventor of the concertina. Wheatstone's prototype concertinas which he was producing by the 1830s, and patent models, are featured in the collection. The work of other British and continental makers of the concertina is also represented, and the extensive archive which includes the Wheatstone factory daybooks and diary makes this collection a particularly informative one.

Musicians' collections

Among the major acquisitions made for the Museum by Frances Palmer, Keeper of Musical Instruments from 1978 to 1999 is a group of historic instruments used for performance by their owner, Arnold Dolmetsch (1858-1940), a pioneer in the field of early music. An appeal for the collection attracted support from bodies such as the National Art Collections Fund, the Victoria & Albert Purchase Grant Fund and the National Heritage Memorial Fund. The instruments were shown as a discrete collection in a temporary exhibition in the Horniman Museum in 1983, and subsequently, while a handful were incorporated into the permanent exhibition in the Museum, the bulk of them were displayed at Ranger's House, Blackheath from 1985-1995. The interest of the musical world in this musician and instrument maker led to the exhibitions about his life held in St John's Smith Square, London and in Le Mans, which Dr Palmer devised in 1991. Dolmetsch is famed as the re-inventor of the recorder in Britain, after his own, a Bressan dating from the middle of the eighteenth century, was lost in 1917. Needing a substitute for his concerts, he developed one in the early 1920s which became the prototype for the recorder now used in schools all over Britain. Dolmetsch was a skilled maker, and he played on a variety of the 17th and 18th century instruments in his collection, most of which he modified to suit his requirements.

Many musicians' instruments undergo some degree of restoration in the course of their working existence. The German baroque lute by Johann Christian Hoffmann of Leipzig, c.1730, that was given to the Museum in 1975, probably remained in original condition because it was not owned by a musician but was latterly the property of an artist, John Seymour Lucas, R.A. (1849-1923), who used it as a studio prop in his paintings of historical tableaux.

The collaboration of musicians and musical instrument makers in the acquisition of new instruments is an area of increasing importance for the Museum. Concert tours are a way of life for musicians from all over the globe; the current popularity of World Music and the economic dominance of western currencies are powerful forces drawing musicians from many traditions to London. Instruments acquired from Purulia and Seraikella Chaau dance ensembles from Bihar and Orissa, and from one of the leading classical music ensembles based in Tashkent have recently been purchased by the Museum from musicians on tour here. Video and audio recordings document both the professional musicians' performance technique and the contexts in which the instruments are played.

Musical instruments from the republics of the former Soviet Union are under-represented in the collections, and a series of fieldwork projects to collect material from these countries was initiated in 1994. It has brought the Museum substantial collections of both Belarusian and Uzbek traditional instruments, and recordings, purchased by the author from musical instrument makers and musicians in those countries.

Documentation: audio-visual recordings

The contemporary field collections from Belarus include such ephemeral objects as birch-bark flutes and clarinets made of bullrush stalks. These are as fragile as historic instruments, which, in order to achieve immutability, must remain for ever mute. The sounds of instruments, demonstrated by musicians within the culture at the time when they were collected, together with other kinds of information that can be mediated through audio-visual recordings greatly increases the value of field collections both as research material, and as objects for exhibition in the galleries. Audio-visual recordings can also enhance displays of older instruments. In the Music Room (1993-1999), the exhibition of the musical instrument collection that was curated by Frances Palmer, instruments from India and Iran, acquired by Engel, were displayed with the intention of introducing visitors to Hindustani and Persian classical music, (Engel's 'foreign nations') (Engel 1874: 4), and units for video illustrating professional musicians playing on their modern counterparts were integral to the showcases for these 19th century examples. Engel considered that 'the construction of the instruments reveals the nature of the musical intervals, scales and such like noteworthy facts' (Engel 1874: 4), but in his time the *kamanche* from Shiraz which he acquired for the South Kensington Museum would have had an almost exclusively iconic function, and it would have yielded little information about classical Persian music to the novice. Such connections, and many others, can now be made, when the sonic, kinetic and contextual aspects of performance on a musical instrument are mediated within its exhibition space. The technology of the late 20th century has immeasurably increased the value of Engel's gift to the future.

The collections today

The stated aim of the Museum today, as published in its current 'Corporate Plan' is 'to encourage a wider appreciation of the World, its peoples and their cultures, and its environments'.[7] This late 20th century development of Frederick Horniman's objective: to teach his visitors a lesson about 'distant lands', is achievable by virtue of the growth of the Museum's collections over the past hundred years.

Any object created or used for the production of sound may be considered to fall within the scope of the musical instrument collections. Many languages have no exclusive term for 'music', and the use of the adjective 'musical' is misleading within some cultural contexts. Western musical ensembles now encompass some instruments that were once used for signalling, like the french horn which evolved from an instrument associated with the hunt. The inclusion of sound-producing objects such as fog-horns and alarm bells enriches the breadth of the collections. The typological classification used for sound-producing instruments, which informed the organisation of both the past exhibitions of the collection, and its storage in the Museum's Study Collection Centre, is based on the Hornbostel and Sachs system (Hornbostel and Sachs 1914: 554-90), which is widely favoured by organologists dealing with collections from many different cultural areas.

The Museum now cares for some 60,000 ethnographical objects, 250,000 natural history specimens and over 8,000 musical instruments. The latter collection 'has some claims to being more comprehensive than any other in the UK' (Arnold Foster and La Rue 1993: 5,2,4). In 1997 the Museum was awarded Designated Status 'in respect of its musical instruments and ethnographic collections which are interpreted and communicated to a wide-ranging audience' (Museums and Galleries Commission 1997). The launch of the Horniman website in 1999 increased the Museum's public exponentially, bringing a new wave of websurfers to browse the virtual checklists of the Museum's collections of instruments via the internet. Among the challenges of the new millenium is the creation of the Museum's new musical instrument gallery, which is scheduled to open in 2002.

Notes

1. Horniman was born into a Quaker family, and like most Victorian Quakers he was 'in trade', which carried a social stigma in English class system. In her diploma thesis: *A Historical Study of the Ethnography Collections in the Horniman Museum, London* (1972: 6), M. Duncan argues that in creating his museum and converting to Anglicanism, Horniman was attempting to improve his social status.

2. Dedicatory plaque on the facade of the Horniman Museum, 1901.

3. 'Many boys had a passion for collecting. On walks this meant the amassing of specimens of all kinds. Back in School, this meant making a museum' 'F.J. Horniman was to recall all the boyish delights of specimen hunting' David W. Bolam, (1952: 92, 136) *Unbroken Community: The Story of the Friends' School, Saffron Walden.* Cambridge:: Heffer & Sons.

4. In 1879, Horniman was to have a butterfly found in West Africa, *papilio hornimanii,* named after him.

5. 'An acquaintance with the musical instruments of a nation conveys a more correct idea than could otherwise be obtained of the characteristic features of the nation's musical compositions' (Engel 1874: 4).

6. In 'The Mbuti Pygmies: an ethnographic survey', *Anthropological papers of the American Museum of Natural History.* 50/3 (1965: 166), Colin Turnbull stresses the predominance of the rain forest environment in the lives of Mbuti hunter-gatherers of Democratic Republic of Congo, from whom he collected a wide range of instruments. In 'Flourishing horns and enchanted tubers: music and potatoes in highland Bolivia' *British Journal of Ethnomusicology* 3, (1994: 35-48), the ethnomusicologist, Henry Stobart describes how strategies for survival are encoded in the seasonal usage of the pinkillos (duct flutes), which he acquired for the Horniman Museum in the Vitichi area of Bolivia in 1987.

7. Horniman Museum Corporate Plan for the Financial Years 1999-2001. p.2.

Bibliography

ARNOLD FOSTER, K. and La RUE, H. 1993. *Museums of Music.* London: HMSO.

CAMPBELL, S. 1953. *Quaker Education as Seen in their Schools in England.* London: The Epworth Press.

CARSE, A. 1951. *Catalogue of the Adam Carse Collection of Old Musical Instruments.* London: London County Council.

ENGEL, C. 1874. *A Descriptive Guide of the Musical Instruments in the South Kensington Museum.* London: Eyre and Spottiswoode.

HARRISON, H. 1906. *6th Annual Report of the Horniman Museum.* London: London County Council.

HORNBOSTEL, E. and SACHS, C. 1914. Systematik der Muskinstrumente. *Zeitshcrift für Ethnologie,* **xlvi**. English translation by A. Baines and K. Wachsmann. (1961: 3-29) *Galpin Society Journal,* xiv.

MACLEOD, A. (n/d). *The Santal Story.* London: The Overseas Missions Committee to the Presbyterian Church of England.

MUSEUMS AND GALLERIES COMMISSION 1997. *Museum Matters.* London: Museums and Galleries Commission, July 1997.

PEARCE, S. 1992. *Museums, Objects and Collections: A Cultural Study.* Leicester and London: Leicester University Press.

ROSSITER, W. 1893. A Summary of the History of the South London Art Gallery, Library and Lecture Hall, from its Foundation in 1868, a Quarter of a Century Ago. In Smith, N. 1993, A Brief Account of the Origins of the South London Art Gallery. In Waterfield G. (ed), *Art for the People: Culture in the Slums of Late Victorian Britain.* London: Dulwich Picture Library.

SCHOTT, H.1983. *Victoria and Albert Museum Catalogue of Musical Instruments.* Volume 1. Keyboard Instruments. London: Her Majesty's Stationery Office.

STOCK, E. 1916. *The History of the Church Missionary Society.* London: The Church Missionary Society of Africa and the East.

Quex for Adventure: The Powell-Cotton Family Enterprise from Field to Showcase[1]

8

Keith Nicklin

Percy Horace Gordon Powell-Cotton was born in Margate in 1866 and upon retiring from the army devoted his life to the systematic collection of zoological and ethnographic specimens. 'As a man, he was quiet, courteous and kindly' (C. Powell-Cotton & Lang 1988: 9), admiringly described by one who worked for him in the Cameroun rain forest as 'one of the coolest men and finest shots I ever knew' (Merfield 1957: 187). Between 1887 and 1939, the year before his death, he conducted no less than 28 collecting expeditions, first in Asia and later in Africa.

Figure 1: Portrait of Major P.H.G. Powell-Cotton, 1866-1940. Entrance Hall, Powell-Cotton Museum. (Photograph: Powell Cotton Museum).

He founded the Powell-Cotton Museum of African & Asian Zoology & Ethnography. This originated in 1896 as a single room, and by the 1970s the eighth gallery and part of Quex House, the Regency style family home, had been opened to the public. Since the founder's death in 1940, the Museum has been

Figure 2: The arrival of a mounted giraffe at Quex, October 1928. (Photograph: Powell-Cotton Museum).

administered as a trust (which was granted charitable status in 1962) under the directorship of the founder's son, Christopher Powell-Cotton, MC, CMG. The house and Museum are situated in Quex Park, a 250-acre oasis of mature parkland which breaks the monotony of the corn and cabbage prairies of the Isle of Thanet. As well as the Museum and gardens, Quex Park boasts the Waterloo Tower, with a peal of twelve bells, built by Squire Powell (John Powell Powell) in 1818, and a large collection of cannon made by the same ancestor.

The original pavilion, now Gallery 2, is in much the same form as when installed in 1896, complete with diorama depicting the Himalayas at dawn, and containing animals collected up to a height of 5,486.4 metres, (18,000 ft.). For many years this showcase surely represented the state of the dioramist's art, even in world terms. In the same Gallery are displayed ethnographic items collected in the course of the Major's visit to Ethiopia in 1899-1900, when he stayed in the palace of Emporer Menelik II, an experience described in his book, *A Sporting Trip through Abyssinia* (1902).

Major Powell-Cotton was 'a keen and sympathetic observer and systematic recorder of animals and their behaviour... a pioneer in the exhibition of the larger mammals against a representation of their natural habitat' (Powell-Cotton Museum 1990: 1). The taxidermic quality of the mounted specimens is of a superlative order, mostly carried out by the London firm, Rowland Ward. Completed in 1947, Gallery 1 is nothing less than a masterpiece of dioramic art, with four components as follows: African savannah and swamp, African desert and hills, African monkeys and apes and Indian forest by moonlight. Apart from the extraordinary spectacle of so many wild animals, large and small, offered to the public at close range in these showcases, there is much

Figure 3: Death Struggle' by Rowland Ward. (Photograph: Powell-Cotton Museum).

here to interest the specialist. For example, the inclusion of specimens from both East and West Africa illustrates variation in the pattern of giraffe markings; after acquisition the roan antelope on display was classified as a sub-species new to science at the time and named after Powell-Cotton.

Dating from 1908, Gallery 3 houses an equatorial Africa diorama dominated by a very fine bull elephant and including both white and black rhinoceros, and a further diorama of the African forest fringe which includes two duiker fighting a python, a scene taken from life. But the centrepiece is what some regard as among the best examples of the mounting skill in existence, namely a Central African lion locked in mortal combat with a Cape Buffalo. Both animals had a special connection with the Major, the buffalo formerly being recognised as a new sub-species, and so, named after him, and the lion being the one that mauled him in 1906. Incidentally, it was his thirteenth lion.

It is true that the older publicity material and exhibition texts reflect the derring-do aspects of Major Powell-Cotton's exploits, but this should not detract from his remarkable contribution to zoology. According to one report, 'From his material forty-one specific or sub-specific types have been described, a number of them having been named *cottoni* after the collector'[2] (Cooke & Barton 1957: 3). Whenever possible, he preserved not only the whole skeleton, skull and skin of each animal, but also representatives of both sexes and ages from foetal to senile. His field notes were made with military precision: specimens weighed and measured on the spot, and compass bearings taken.

Figure 4: Kuyu sculpture, ifya, used in Kébé Kébé performance; carried by a dancer wearing a long sacklike costume. Note representation of monitor lizard, cowrie shell on forehead, facial scarification, 'filed' teeth and carrying pole; monoxylous. Collected by Major Powell-Cotton in the then French Congo, 1927. (Photograph: Powell-Cotton Museum).

His methods of skinning, cleaning, preserving, packing and transport, using the best materials and methods of the time, were also impeccable, as was ongoing curatorial processing and care upon reception at Quex. In addition, many fine specimens were presented over the years to the British Museum (Natural History), and to the University of Oxford. Also, under the auspices of the Powell-Cotton Museum, many mammalian specimens, especially primates, collected in the field by F.G. Merfield in southern Cameroun, were forwarded to the British Museum and to the Royal College of Surgeons in London.

The Powell-Cotton zoological collection includes over six thousand mammalian specimens, almost one third of which are primates. Chimpanzee skulls number 187 (150 with post-cranial skeleton) and those of gorilla 204 (139 with post-cranial skeleton); colobus monkey specimens number 224. Almost half of the mammalian specimens comprise the Bovidae, including a number of excellent cline series showing, for example, bushbuck and duiker coat colour gradation. Bongo and gerenuk are among well represented rarities, numbering 30 and 34 specimens respectively. Cooke's survey of the mammalian collection in 1956 benefited from a newly issued *Catalogue of Mammals* listing all species represented with a summary of the material. The process of cleaning, numbering and packing skeletal material has been a long and arduous one, carried out to the highest standard and continuing to this day. The most recently completed group in this respect is that of Galago, not generally regarded by taxonomists as true primates at the time of acquisition.[3]

Despite the fact that the Powell-Cotton larger mammal series is 'the largest private collection shot by one man' a few did fall to Mrs. Powell-Cotton's gun (Pinfold: 1931). The then Captain Powell-Cotton met Hannah Brayton Slater whilst she assisted the completion of his second book, *In Unknown Africa* (1904). They married in Nairobi in 1905, and immediately set off to Uganda and the Congo. Hannah was virtually the first white woman known to have entered the Ituri Forest, and the contemporary press was full of reports of their honeymoon 'in the land of the pygmies'. In the course of the 'honeymoon trip', the bride made a significant collection of African insects, especially butterflies, which included some Ituri Forest specimens. The couple eventually returned home to a heroes' welcome at Birchington in 1907.

Although after his marriage some ethnographic collecting and documentation was in effect delegated either to his wife or children, Major Powell-Cotton habitually collected 'curios' among the peoples whose territories he traversed in the course of his zoological expeditions. For example, during 1926-27, in pursuit of gorilla, sitatunga and bongo in the French Congo, he collected 433 ethnographic specimens, including six 'fetish heads', *ifya*, used in the Kébé Kébé festival, from the Kuyu River area (Nicklin 1983: 55-9). With the precision of a military man and meticulous naturalist, the provenance is given as to village of collection (Ossango, 0 degrees 25' S, 15 degrees E, two hours fifteen minutes march from Linnegue), and name of carver and of owner. He also researched the use and meaning of the pieces, purchased the baskets in which they were stored and recorded the making and mending of this type of receptacle. Accompanying photographs tell us much about contemporary Kuyu village life, especially architecture and coiffure.

Of the four Powell-Cotton children, Diana, Antoinette and Christopher accompanied their father on some of his African expeditions. In the 1930s Christopher went with him to South West Africa and Antoinette to Zululand. Diana travelled with him to Red Sea Province, Sudan, in 1933, and to Italian Somiland in 1934, and stayed on eight months after his departure. Around this time Diana emerged not only as an accomplished markswoman, but also as a highly acompetent ethnographic collector and photographer.

The Powell-Cotton sisters conducted their own ethnographic trips to Angola in 1936 and 1937, making a large collection supplemented with black & white photographs. A selection of this material has been exhibited at the Museum since 1970. Upon their return to England they published a superb photo-essay entitled '*Feminine Coiffure in Angola*' (D. & A. Powell-Cotton 1937), a unique record of women's personal adornment among the Ambo peoples. Their father had started using a ciné camera in the field in the late 1920s, and this work was much extended by Diana and Antoinette. Documentary films (16mm, black & white, silent, with subtitles) produced by the Powell-Cotton Museum, including '*Kuanyama Marriage Ceremonies*' and '*Dombondola Pot-making*' were premiered at the Royal Anthropological Institute in London, and publicly screened for many years thereafter regularly at Quex. The originals of these films are lodged with the British Film Institute.[4]

After the death of the Major in 1940, a strong family connection with Africa continued for many years after World War II. After military service in East Africa and Burma, Christopher Powell-Cotton became Provincial Commissioner at Gulu, finally retiring from the Ugandan Civil Service as Minister for Security and External Affairs in 1962. Dr. Diana Powell-Cotton served as a physician in Uganda and Kenya, before retiring to Elementeita in the Rift Valley in 1967 to study and photograph birds; she died in Norfolk in 1986. After her work in Africa, between 1938 and 1974, with the help of other volunteers, Antoinette (popularly known as 'Miss Toni'), excavated significant Early Iron Age and Belgic pottery series from tidal sites at Minnis Bay near Birchington. These finds, and loan material from other sites in east Kent, are exhibited in the local archaeology section of Gallery 7. Miss Toni died in Margate in 1998.

From the early days of his travel and collecting, Major Powell-Cotton collaborated with the Ethnography Department of the British Museum and the Pitt Rivers Museum, Oxford, and presented specimens to both institutions. In particular, Dr. Braunholtz and Adrian Digby of the British Museum, and Henry Balfour and Beatrice Blackwood of the Pitt Rivers Museum became family friends, and would be invited to Quex to view new consignments from the field, and advise as to classification and the collection of further specimens. Diana established an especially close research and collection link with the Wellcome Historical Museum (Davies 1987). More recently, in 1982, formal association was established between the Museum and the University of Kent at Canterbury, leading to a post-graduate student attachment in the sphere of Angolan ethnography.

As the ethnographic collections became established at the Powell-Cotton Museum gifts of other material came in, often as significant collections in their own right. In this manner, for example, over three hundred important Ugandan items, collected by Archdeacon Walker from 1894 to 1910, were presented in 1970. Similarly, fifteen items collected by Captain M.W. Hilton-Simpson were given by his widow in 1938, including four superb masks from Zaïre which have been on display at the Powell-Cotton Museum for many years. As recently as 1995 the Crawford collection of over 300 South and Central African artefacts, acquired in the interwar period, was presented to the Powell-Cotton Museum.

Somehow, between expeditions, the Major found time to attend salerooms in order to augment his collections of cultural, though not zoological material. For example, the core of his extensive Asian weapon series comprises a collection made by Major-General Russell, purchased in 1940, and another made by Captain Mackay, R.N, bought in 1934. Much of the collection of domestic objects, weapons and cult items from the Pacific consists of a collection made by Admiral E.H.M. Davis in the late 19th century, purchased in 1938.

A few items of European porcelain collected by John Powell Powell, were supplemented by further pieces bought by the Major. In 1910 he also purchased the important Pope Collection of Chinese porcelain dating from the Kangxi to the Guangzu periods, 1662-1908. Much of this material was re-displayed in 1988, to coincide with the launch of a catalogue of the Chinese Imperial and Export porcelain collections at Quex, documented by Gordon Lang and Sonja Howlett, then Research Assistant in Fine Arts (Lang et. al. 1988).

Anyone entering the Powell-Cotton Museum cannot fail to be impressed by the 'old-fashioned' feel of the place. This is not simply because of the Entrance Hall display of the founder's portrait with accompanying selection of safari kit, but, rather, a distinctive, all-pervading atmosphere of 'stepping back in time.' The air is that of the Edwardian period, perhaps puzzling in view of the fact that apart from Galleries 2 and 3, the displays were mounted between 1955 and 1973, with some later modifications, and also that the presentation is not an ostensibly 'period' one. Herein lies the charm of the institution.

We shall return to this observation shortly, but first let us review some of the achievements of the Powell-Cotton Museum. The core of the Powell-Cotton Collection comprises over 6,000 mammalian and in excess of 19,000 ethnographic specimens, as we have seen mostly collected by the founder and his family and well-documented. Within this corpus are many rarities, and, unlike many collections in the UK, the material is by no means over-represented by former British colonies. Since having been open to the public in 1921 there has always been an exhibition guide booklet, updated from time to time. The specimens on display have been described using a variety of means: always accurate exhibition texts and labels, frequently contextual field photographs (usually taken by the collector), and in some cases the construction of large-scale representations of the local environment in the case of natural history, and costumed figures in the case of ethnography.

The founder published two books (Powell-Cotton 1902; 1904) on his earlier African exhibitions, and he and his daughter helped pioneer the use of ciné in the field as a valuable tool of documentation, the documentary films produced by the Museum for many years providing an adjunct to the displays. *The Catalogue of Mammals* (1964) and *The Powell-Cotton Collection of Chinese Ceramics* (1988) in effect provide the basis for a promising Powell-Cotton Museum publication series. Generations of scholars have benefited from the Museum's research facilities, not only in terms of readily accessible specimens and documentation, all on-site, but also with generous laying-out space, well-lit. In the early 1980s the Powell-Cotton Museum, with financial assistance from the Area Museum Service for Southeast England (AMSSEE), initiated the transcription of the founder's field notebooks for greater ease of scholarly access, a process only recently completed. During the latter half of the 1990s all of the ethnographic documentary films have been transferred onto video, in triplicate, for research and educational purposes, in-house and loan.

At its inception the Powell-Cotton Museum was obviously a product of its time, and had something of the character of a trophy hall, many specimens of mounted heads and skulls being prominent. But in reality it was always much more than this, on account of the Major's implicit interest in drawing the distribution map of the larger mammals of the African continent, at the Museum which he built for this purpose. At the time of his death there were very few 'gaps in the collection' in this respect. Given the fact that Powell-Cotton grew up during the Victorian era, the age, *par excellence*, of the peep- and freak-show, the Powell-Cotton Museum was rather unsensational, despite its proximity to booming seaside resorts such as Margate, Ramsgate and Whitstable, the source of most visitors (lower middle-class holiday-makers) to the Museum.

One of Major Powell-Cotton's obituaries (Anon. 1940) noted that 'the Powell-Cotton Museum has become a sort of family institute'. Although this observation is entirely appropriate, behind the success of the establishment was also the untiring dedication of two notable members of staff. G.F. Pinfold, the first curator, was appointed in 1921 (died 1945) and L.R. Barton, who began at Quex in 1930, was formally made curator in 1948; he relinquished fulltime curatorship only in 1980, continuing to work part-time there for several years before his death in 1988.

> *Messrs. Pinfold and Barton not only received and processed incoming specimens, but they also serviced his expeditions. In Lester Barton's words, 'I got to know Major Powell-Cotton very well. We worked together in... packing and checking tents, weapons and stores. After a trip we might receive 50 or 60 packing cases... things were hectic* (Wells 1978).

It would be unfair and inaccurate to call them family 'retainers'. Rather, Pinfold and Barton were putative members of the Powell-Cotton extended family, enjoying free accommodation within the Quex Estate and loyal to the hilt. Reputed to have died in harness whilst skinning a fox in the Museum workshop, Pinfold was a preparator of natural history specimens, formerly employed by Gerrards of London, and instructed Barton in these skills.

Pinfold established the twice-annual 'survey' of the collections, both reserve and displayed, the greater in the autumn, the lesser in spring. In the course of these surveys everywhere was inspected for possible damage by 'mould, moth and mite', and mundane tasks such as dusting the elephant, re-pigmenting dried vegetation, and rejuvenating gazelle muzzles with a concoction of 'French' polish with methylated spirit attended to. In her day, Mrs. Powell-Cotton undertook a supervisory role in this work, and later Miss Toni, especially in relation to the public part of Quex House. More challenging conservation matters and exhibition work were conducted largely during winter.

In this way, the entire collection was kept in tiptop condition and maximum time was left to receive the public during summer months. Lester Barton not only became knowledgeable in the preparation and preservation of mounted animal specimens, but also developed a talent for modelling human effigies, as seen in his display of Latuka and Dinka warriors, Gallery 3. Both utterly devoted to 'the Major', Lester also developed an especially close working relationship with Diana Powell-Cotton. In recognition of this, after a life-threatening illness, during the 1960s, Diana helped him convalesce at her home in Elementeita, Kenya.

During the greater part of its existence the Powell-Cotton Museum has been run by a full-time staff establishment of one or of two. Standards of preservation of the collection (in the absence of an in-house professional conservator) and its associated documentation (in the pre-computer sense) have been, throughout the 20th century, in general, first-rate.5 For much of this century, too, the Museum has catered for visiting interest groups and for schools of all types, and, bearing in mind its location in seaside Kent, multifarious language course students. This service has been mostly provided by the same curatorial duo, sometimes after-hours. 'Lifelong Learning' was practiced here long before it became a politicised slogan.

In recent years the Powell-Cotton Museum has been modernised. The underlying message from the galleries now is that of nature conservation (in truth nothing new, as the founder was associated with the concept of game management in its formative days) and a better appreciation of non-Western cultures (though one must read between the lines of Powell-Cottton family achievements!).

In an assessment of his father's character, the son of the founder, Christopher Powell-Cotton (1988: 9), describes him as 'a competent business manager' who successfully saw his estate through the agricultural depressions of the 1890s and 1930s. At his death the estate was prosperous, and the Museum which he founded properly endowed. In the same assessment we also learn that Major Powell-Cotton was, to those close to him, 'very fair, generous and sympathetic.' These are also qualities which might be applied equally to the person who wrote these words: that is, to Powell-Cotton, father and son.

It is almost inconceivable to see how a publicly funded body could have achieved all that the Powell-Cotton Museum has succeeded in doing during the century that has just passed. This is particularly true of the last fifteen years or so, when museum staff throughout this country have been tied to a ruthlessly imposed 'culture' of corporate management-speak and mode of operation. At the Powell-Cotton Museum it has been the practice, always, for its modicum of full- and part-time members of staff efficiently to do the necessary work in hand rather than talk about it in endless meetings and then spend much time composing and circulating formulaic reports. The Powell-Cotton Board of Trustees meets only twice per annum. Excellent 'value for money' has prevailed throughout the operation of most of its highly varied activities over a considerable period of time at the Powell-Cotton Museum, without the need to utter the phrase having arisen.

Although the Powell-Cotton Museum and Quex House has over the decades quietly changed with the times in order to retain its popularity (but never to become vulgar). Its unique historical atmosphere has been effectively nurtured over the years. Like the Pitt Rivers Museum ethnographic displays, those of the Powell-Cotton Museum are a cornucopean delight to its visitors and an adventure into the institution's stirring past.

As a whole, the principal exhibitions are, today, not so much a cutting edge statement about the two disciplines of zoology and ethnography, more a valuable reflection of a fascinating aspect of British social history, and, moreover, of the life and times of a philanthropic landed English family at the closing phase of the second millenium. Such comment should not detract from the immense scientific research potential of the core collection and its associated database.

Acknowledgments

This account draws freely upon previous writings about the Museum, including my own which are often far from original, and my period of appointment as Curator, 1980-82. It would not have been possible without pleasurable return visits to Quex from time to time and ongoing contact with staff there, notably the previous Curator, Derek Howlett, and his wife, Sonja, and the present Curator and Assistant Curator, John Harrison and Malcolm Harman. I should like to thank them, as well as Christopher Powell-Cotton; also my wife, Jill Salmons, who shared my life at Quex and helped in the writing and revision of this paper.

Notes

1. The title '*Quex for Adventure*' has been borrowed from the Powell-Cotton Museum press cuttings.

2. This figure has been considerably reduced by advances in biological taxonomy.

3. Much of this work has been accomplished by Malcolm Harman, who began work as a technician at the Powell-Cotton Museum at the age of 17 in 1972. He was trained in-service by Lester Barton and, upon his own initiative, become an accomplished taxidermist, with recent zoological field experience in Botswana, Zimbabwe and Transvaal. He has visited several of the founder's expedition haunts and is an authority on Powell-Cotton Museum history as well as local natural history.

4. The films were edited and subtitled by the Powell-Cotton sisters, with the help of Lester Barton, who, after the war, continued this work as well as servicing the Powell-Cotton documentary film programme.

6. For several decades the Museum has enjoyed a sound relationship with AMSEE and other professional bodies, and hence access to various specialist object-conservation facilities. Currently, the specimen-documentation riches of the Museum are poised for 'computerisation'.

Bibliography

ANONYMOUS 1940. Big game shot and naturalist; the late Major Powell-Cotton. *The Field.* July 20.

COOKE, H. and BARTON, L. 1957. The Powell-Cotton Museum of African Fauna and Ethnology, Kent, England. *South African Museums Association Bulletin.* Vol. 6, No. **11**: 1-8.

LANG, G. et al. 1988. *The Powell-Cotton Collection of Chinese Ceramics.* Birchington: Powell-Cotton Museum.

MERFIELD, F. (with Harry Miller). 1957. *Gorillas were my neighbours.* London: Companion Book Club.

NICKLIN, K. 198.1 Ethnography at the Powell-Cotton Museum. *Museum Ethngraphers' Group Newsletter.* No. **11**, 35-41.

NICKLIN, K. 1981a. *Powell-Cotton: Man & Museum.* Canterbury: Kent University Library.

NICKLIN, K. 1982. Fred Merfield and the Powell-Cotton Museum. *The Nigerian Field.* Vol. **45**, parts 1-3: 108-09.

NICKLIN, K. 1983. Kuyu sculpture at the Powell-Cotton Museum. *African Arts.* Vol. **17**, No. **1**: 55-9.

PINFOLD, G. 1931. Quex Park a romantic history. *Isle of Thanet Gazette.* March 18.

PINFOLD, G. 1929. Some notes on 'Fork Guards' *Man* no. **76**: 99-8.

POWELL-COTTON, A. 1940. Two handicrafts of Portuguese Angola. *Man.* Vol. **49**: 42.

POWELL-COTTON, D. & A. 1937. Feminine Coiffure in Angola. *Illustrated London News.* September 11.

POWELL-COTTON, P.H.G. 1902. *A Sporting Trip through Abyssinia.* London: Howland Ward.

POWELL-COTTON 1904. *In Unknown Africa.* London: Hurst & Blackett.

POWELL-COTTON C. & LANG G 1988. An historical note on the Powell-Cotton Museum. In Lang, G. et al. *The Powell-Cotton Collection of Chinese Ceramics.* Birchington: Powell-Cotton Museum.

POWELL-COTTON MUSEUM 1964. *Catalogue of Mammals.* Birchington: Powell-Cotton Museum.

POWELL-COTTON 1980. *Illustrated Guide to the Powell-Cotton Museum.* Birchington: Powell-Cotton Museum.

POWELL-COTTON 1983. *The Powell-Cotton Museum and Quex House.* London: English Life Publications.

POWELL-COTTON 1990. *Quex Museum House and Gardens.* Norwich: Powell-Cotton Museum & Jarrold Publishing.

WELLS, J. 1978. *A unique collection.* Thanet: Rostrum.

From the Fetish to the Specimen: The Ridyard African Collection at the Liverpool Museum 1895-1916

Louise Tythacott

On the 1st July 1895 Arnold Ridyard, a chief engineer with the Elder Dempster & Co.,[1] donated his first group of artefacts to Liverpool Museum. Twenty-one years and seventy-seven voyages later, he had transported almost six-and-a-half thousand objects from coastal regions of West and Central Africa to Liverpool (Clubb 1916: 1).[2] The collection comprised both natural history and ethnographic objects, of which the latter totalled around two-and a-half thousand -almost a quarter of the present-day African collection. Ridyard barely missed a voyage in twenty one years at sea, donating objects on a regular three to four monthly basis. He wasn't alone in his collecting efforts for he established a network of associates along coastal locales of Africa who donated via Elder Dempster to Liverpool Museum. An astounding total of 190 names are recorded in the Museum register as giving through this system of maritime transportation, including such prominent figures as the Governor of Sierra Leone, the Eastern Divisional Commissioner of Southern Nigeria as well as African kings, princes and chiefs (Tythacott 1998). So significant was the Ridyard collection, and so rapidly did it increase, that Annie Coombes has characterised it as...'one of the largest and fastest growing [African collections] in Britain from 1890 to 1913, second only to the national collection at the British Museum' (Coombes 1994: 129).

Numerous official documents attest to the rapid growth of the collections: from the 1909 Annual Report we learn that since 1896 - the year after Ridyard's first donation -11,371 ethnographic objects had been

Figure 1: Portrait of Arnold Ridyard, early 20th century, (Photograph: National Museums & Galleries on Merseyside, Liverpool Museum).

accessioned into the Museum (Annual Report 1910: 37), representing over a third of the present-day ethnographic holdings[3] in a period of only fourteen years. Though not all the acquisitions derive from Ridyard, the engineer remains the single most prolific donor of his time. In 1916 - the year of his retirement - the Museums Committee even named a section the 'Ridyard' Collection of African Ethnology and described it as...'probably the finest in the country' (Clubb 1916: 153).

This paper traces the formation of the Ridyard collecting phenomenon. It associates the particularity of this collection with the city that nurtured its growth and contends that only the world port of Liverpool could have fostered such a maritime associated collection. Ridyard was positioned at the interface of two changing museological worlds, and his collection was reconfigured over the twenty one year period by the new orderly Museum. At the beginning, he chose singularly powerful objects: there is an emphasis on so-called *ju jus* and masks, and particularly on the dramatic Central African *minkisi* - or power figures - embedded with nails, scissors and magical substances. Fifteen years after his first donation, Liverpool Museum established a more systematic framework for Ridyard's collecting activities. In 1910, a new Director - a natural historian - requested he focus on 'representative' examples of arts and industries that were thought to be dying out, in particular the 'primitive potter's art' (Annual Report 1911). The Museum intervened in the collecting methods of its most loyal and committed benefactor: an educational rationale was imposed on the engineer. The Ridyard collection thus came to be filtered through the gaze of a scientific natural historian and the lens of an increasingly pedagogical institution.

Global junctions: order, organisation, evolution

> *to no one spot in the civilized world are brought such a vast variety of substances -raw materials and worked fabrics - as to Liverpool...Liverpool...exhibits an amount of enterprise, such as, probably no other age, and no other place, has ever before shewn. The whole globe is scoured by these men and ships in search of whatever may conduce civilisation. The port itself is the largest in the world representing one-third of the commerce of England* (Collingwood 1862: 46).

During the mid-late 19th century, the ethnographic acquisitions at Liverpool Museum increased dramatically as a cornucopia of exotic curios were donated from maritime voyages around the world. The first ethnology accessions, recorded in 1852, comprised four 'amulets' taken from 'Malay pirates'. The 1858 Annual Report mentions purchase of a...'very extensive series of weapons of savage nations'...collected by a deceased Royal Navy Captain, said to have constituted...'one of the finest ethnographic series existing' (Annual Report 1859: 6). In 1861, Captain Mackay donated a large canoe from Malabar and a variety of Malay and Burmese objects were brought back by master mariners over the following years. From the mid-19th century, Museum registers frequently refer to curios donated by Liverpool traders and seafarers. Inevitably then, the maritime connections of the world's largest port influenced the profile of the city's ethnography collections.

As the century progressed, the influx of exotic objects was subjected to Victorian organisational principles, a trend towards order illustrated by a speech in 1862 to the *Liverpool Literary and Philosophical Society*:

> *One thing is certain...that no accessions of importance are derived to our museums and collections from the labours of sea-faring men. A piece of coral, a parrot, a shell or two, or something that has received attention from its oddity, is occasionally brought by the sailor...but anything of value or importance is not even to be looked at. No system of any kind marks the seaman's gatherings...It is this utter want of system - this absence of rudimentary information which renders the ordinary collections of seamen so entirely valueless* (Collingwood 1862: 48).

Collingwood's address culminated in a call for a more structured approach to collecting natural history specimens, for the instigation of...'a scheme for instruction on board ship' (Collingwood 1862: 53). A move away from chaos, disorder, the random nature of acquisition is introduced in the mid-19th century: taxonomy, systems of classification and order were increasingly evident. In their internal discourses and public displays, the Victorian Museum imposed new systems on otherwise disparate groupings of artefacts. The emphasis on individually rare curiosities was now supplanted by structured systems of collecting. Disciplines, such as ethnography, were formed in the mid-19th century to codify new forms of knowledge;[4] ethnographic artefacts were soon segregated and classified in museums for research and public display.

The order placed upon artefacts in the natural science museums of 19th century Europe was guided by Darwin's theory of evolution; ethnographic objects too were organised in terms of this developmental model. The products of human societies, along with those of the natural world, were arranged in a hierarchy with the simplest or most 'primitive' at the bottom and the highest order of development, the most 'civilised' at the top. Such a system, encoded in museum displays, visibly mapped out the justification for European racial hegemony and colonial rule. By the end of the century evolutionism dominated the arrangement of exotic artefacts in European museums and it would endure as the most entrenched organisational paradigm in 20th century ethnographic displays.[5]

At Liverpool Museum, the displays instigated by Dr. Henry Ogg Forbes corresponded with these contemporary racial ideologies. The most influential exponent of evolutionary theory of the time, Sir James

Frazer, was in close proximity for a short period, as Professor of Ethnology at the city's new University. Ridyard's African collection then was absorbed into the Museum displays in terms of the developmental model.

The early Liverpool Museum: 1860-1910

Established through the amalgamation of two key collections, Liverpool Museum from its beginnings combined natural history with ethnography. In 1851 the Right Hon. Edward-Smith, XIIIth Earl of Derby, bequeathed his zoological, botanical, geological and mineralogical collections to the town, as well as an aquarium. The Derby bequest was first exhibited in a small house in Duke Street and opened to the public in March 1853. The collections very soon required more space and in 1860 Sir William Brown funded the creation of an imposing neo-classical building in the centre of the city to accommodate them: by the end of the century, it was still amongst the largest museums in England outside the metropolis (Forbes 1898: 71). In 1867 the collections of the Liverpool goldsmith, Joseph A. Mayer, were presented and a large central court surrounded by three tiers of galleries was set apart for the bequest. Mayer's gifts included Egyptian, Assyrian, Greek and early Roman antiquities, Anglo-Saxon pottery, medieval ivories, Chinese and English ceramics, illuminated manuscripts, African ivories and a rare pre-Columbian manuscript; the Codex Fejérváry-Mayer. The two combined bequests merged to form the Free Public Museums of Liverpool. Ridyard's African donations, comprising objects from both the natural and cultural worlds reflected the dominant organisational structure of the Museum, mapping the institutions disciplinary synthesis of natural history and antiquities/ethnography.

The ethnographic collections of the Mayer Museum had already gained a high profile in the late 19th century prior to Ridyard's activities. In 1882 an Ethnographic Annexe at the rear of Liverpool's Walker Art Gallery was opened to the public, and the 1885 Annual Report noted...'the ethnographic Department...has become more fully developed than any other department in the Mayer Museum'(Annual Report 1886: 26). Despite this, the ethnography displays were dismantled in 1886 due to lack of space and the collections remained in storage for the best part of ten years. A new purpose-built Ethnography Gallery was opened in 1895.[6] The Annual Report of the preceeding year, in anticipation of its opening, announced optimistically... 'that when set out, it will, it is believed, rank next in importance to the National Collections' (Annual Report 1894: 24-5).

Indeed, by the end of the century Liverpool Museum had begun to see itself in competition with the national collections of the metropolis, with its 1898 Annual Report claiming more visitors than the British Museum. This sense of national importance was confirmed by the range of scholarly attention, both national and international, recorded in the official documents. The new Ethnography Gallery of 1895 in particular was admired by a number of distinguished scholars in its first year, including the highly influential Alfred Haddon, Reader in Anthropology at Cambridge University. Over the next four decades, Haddon became a frequent visitor to the collections.[7] In 1906, Dr. Meyer, Director of the Royal Museums in Dresden described the Ethnological Section as...'next to London, the most comprehensive, and in all respects one of the best in Great

Britain' (Annual Report 1906: 48). The ascendance of ethnology, and the significance of the African collection in the late 19th-early 20th century, was largely attributable to the collecting activities of Ridyard.

Conjunctures: Dr. Henry Ogg Forbes, Sir Alfred Jones, Sir James Frazer

Perhaps it is more than coincidence that in 1895 - the year the new Ethnography Gallery opened - the Museum received its first group of donations from Ridyard. Three influential personalities converged in Liverpool around this time, whose activities were formative in linking the city, the Museum and the burgeoning nexus of colonial interests in Africa: Dr. Henry Ogg Forbes, Director of Liverpool Museum; Sir Alfred Jones, Director of the Elder Dempster & Company; and Sir James Frazer, evolutionary theorist, author of the *Golden Bough*, who in 1907 took up the first Chair in Ethnology at the University of Liverpool. This triumvirate fused the city's powerful economic, intellectual and cultural concerns. Directly or indirectly, their activities nurtured Arnold Ridyard's activities. Indeed without the direct support of Forbes and Jones, the Ridyard collecting enterprise undoubtedly would not have occurred.

Dr. Henry Ogg Forbes joined the Museum in February 1894 - the year before Ridyard's first donation - and retired in 1910. Though best remembered for his ornithological work and an early specialism in diverse fields of natural history, he also took a deep interest in the emerging discipline of ethnology.[8] Forbes' scholarly reputation was well recognised: he produced *A hand-book to the Primates* (1896-7) and the *Natural History of Sokotra* and *Abd-al-Kuri* and founded and edited the *Bulletin of the Liverpool Museum* (1897-1901). According to Karpinski, he was the first British scholar to take an interest in the art of Benin, writing two articles on its cast bronzes in 1898 and 1900.[9] In 1905, he was offered the readership in Ethnology at the University of Liverpool, two years before Frazer was appointed as its first Professor.[10]

Under Forbes' influence Liverpool Museum was transformed. He spent most of his first year working on the redisplays: two large rooms in the basement of the building on the west side were arranged for the ethnographic collections (Annual Report 1894: 4). The Annual Reports from 1896 list accessions in terms of three main racial divisions based upon colour, and these were to become the dominant organising principle for the new displays - the 'Melanian' (black), 'Caucasian' (white) and 'Mongolian' (yellow). 'Melanian' specimens included those from Africa, New Guinea, the Solomon Islands, the New Hebrides, Polynesia, New Zealand, Micronesia and Matty Island; the 'Mongolian' race comprised South America, China, Japan, Burma and the Malay Archipelago; 'Caucasia' signified Europe, India and Egypt. The emphasis on racial typologies extended to the educational programme: in 1896 Forbes lectured on 'The Pedigree and Races of Mankind' and Peter Entwhistle, Curator of the Mayer Museum, gave talks on 'Pre-historic Man' (Annual Report 1896: 28). The same year, photographs depicting the different racial types from around the world were exhibited, and images of Kru-boys (sic.) from Liberia, apparently 'taken from life', were enlarged for display purposes (Coombes 1994: 139). According to the Annual Report three years later, such photographic enlargements illustrating the 'races of mankind' were actually...'inaugurated and first exhibited in England in this museum' (Annual Report 1899: 14). The emphasis on physiognomy reflected the dominant evolutionary framework of the Museum's displays.

The ethnography collections were increasing so dramatically from Ridyard's donations that by 1898 Forbes was reporting on the complete congestion of the exhibition rooms. In the 1899 Annual Report, he contended:

> *The West African Section has again necessitated the allotment of additional space for its better exhibition. It has been impossible to find room for the Australian and the New Zealand exhibitions, removed from the east side of the gallery to provide more vacant space for the West African collection, which continues to occupy the east side of the gallery as well as the central cases; additional space is consequently required for them* (Annual Report 1900: 34).

In 1900 he commented again on the increase in the West African collections and their encroachment upon other displays.[11] The new ethnography displays opened on 19 October 1906 arranged along Forbes' racial lines: the 'Mongolian' gallery was on the top floor, objects of 'Caucasian' origin in the Main Hall and surrounding balcony, 'Melanian' specimens in the basement and adjoining Ethnography Gallery (Coombes 1994: 141). Visitors encountered the Caucasian section upon arrival - those of the 'civilised races' - which, for Coombes, functioned as...'the standard against which to judge the relative stages of 'civilisation' of the other sections' (Coombes 1994: 141). The three racial divisions, as Coombes points out, corresponded to those identified by A.C Haddon in *The Study of Man*, which in turn had been developed from the four racial groups devised by Alfred H. Keane. Keane's racial conflation of physiological attributes with ethical qualities assigned the 'Ethiopic negro' the lowest division of humankind...'a sensuous, indolent, improvident, folk, fitful, passionate, and cruel, with no sense of dignity, therefore born slaves' (Keane quoted in Coombes 1994: 141). Now discredited as racist, 19th century Social Darwinist thought fused the physiological attributes of race with psychology. As Coombes writes the....'assumed interdependence of biological and moral characteristics consistently underpinned the ethnographic narratives in the Liverpool Museum and other collections nationwide' (Coombes 1994: 141). Such racial typologies would have been familiar to Ridyard: in particular, he was aware of the 'Melanian' displays in the basement exhibiting the Museum's African collection, most of which he had donated.

The Ridyard arrangement must have been ratified, if not established, by the Director of the Elder Dempster & Co. The time, space and energy this massive collecting project imposed on the life of a chief engineer could only have been sustained with the support of the Company. Yet it is difficult to trace the exact relationship between Dr. Forbes and Sir Alfred Jones as there is little written correspondence between the two, though the Museum's Annual Reports frequently attest to the links between Elder Dempster and the Museum. Several reports acknowledged Jones specifically for the growth of the African collection. Reference is made, for example, in 1898 to...'Messrs Elder, Dempster, & Co, for so kindly continuing their permission for these objects to come freight free' (Annual Report 1898: 34). Clubb's 1916 report, on Ridyard's retirement, concluded by acknowledging...'the public-spirited action of Messrs. Elder Dempster & Co, for throughout the whole period that Mr. Ridyard has been collecting for the Museum, the late Sir Alfred L.Jones, and subsequently other Directors of the firm have permitted the free transport of these objects from the west African coast and given various facilities to Mr. Ridyard in his work' (Clubb 1916: 5). An earlier report of 1902 had given:

> *special thanks to Sir Alfred Jones and through his personal influence with the members of the West African section of the Chamber of Commerce, for the great interest they have shown in it, and the most generous offer they have made to assist in rendering it as complete a representation as possible of the Ethnology of West Africa, the region with which Liverpool is so intimately in relation* (Annual Report 1903: 58).

Liverpool was deeply involved in West African trade in the late 19th century, its maritime reputation embedded in the popular imagination of the region. Sir Richard Burton, the great 19th century explorer, for example, recorded when visiting Benin City in 1867 that the War Captain of that town, 'to show his geography, inquired about the war in Liverpool' (Hunt 1972: 10).

From early in his career Jones had declared an intent to monopolise the entire maritime trade of the West African ports and by the 1890s he had absorbed all competitors: Elder Dempster became the foremost British shipping company operating in the area. Jones became a household name in the UK...'it was to Sir Alfred Jones that the great Colony of Nigeria owed its formation'...declared one newspaper in 1909 (Journal of Commerce 1909). Labelled variously the 'Napoleon' or 'uncrowned king' of West Africa, an obituary recalled:

> *it was mainly his agitation which rang the death knell of the Royal Niger Co. as an administrative corporation...it is an undoubted verity that every nook and corner in British West Africa bears testimony in some form or other to the untiring energy and indomitable resolution of the man who has been styled "the Napoleon of West Africa"... 'The wonderful success of the mosquito theory in the fight against the curse of West Africa, malaria, is mainly due to Sir Alfred's generous and determined espousal of the cause* (Journal of Commerce 1909).

Jones was renowned for his philanthropy and the energy he brought to charity and finance. He was the President of the Liverpool Chamber of Commerce, founder and Chairman of the Bank of British West Africa (1894), President of both the British Cotton Growing Association and Empire Cotton Growing Association (1902), Chairman of the Institute of Commercial Research in the Tropics (founded in 1900) and Chairman of the Liverpool Steamship Owner's Association.[12] His most famous charitable act was the origination and endowment in 1898 of the Liverpool School of Tropical Medicine to complement Joseph Chamberlain's in London. In recognition of services to West Africa and Jamaica, he received a knighthood in 1901.[13] It would have been typical of Sir Alfred Jones then to endorse a chief engineer's collecting activities for his local Museum.

Jones' death in 1909 - the year before Forbes' retirement - was reported as...'a great loss to the British

Empire and the world at large' (Journal of Commerce 1909). Flags were flown at half-mast in public institutions in Liverpool; national figures - Winston Churchill, Joseph Chamberlain, even King Edward, with whom Jones had shared conversations on West African affairs - were said to have been moved by the loss.

Two years earlier, Sir James Frazer - the greatest evolutionary thinker of the age - had moved from Cambridge to take up the first Professorship in Ethnology at the University of Liverpool. Though Frazer's tenure was shortlived - lasting less than a year - he was concerned to develop the potential of ethnography in one of the world's most active ports and establish links with the city's Museum. Frazer intended Liverpool to become a key centre for anthropology. In 1907 he wrote to Galton:

> *I have a scheme which I intend to advocate in my inaugural lecture, of establishing a fund for sending anthropological expeditions to collect information about savages before it is too late. Liverpool with its wealth and its connections with foreign lands is perhaps the best place in the country to launch such a scheme, but I would try to get the older Universities, the Royal Society, the Anthropological Institute and the British Museum to join in the work and help in the management of the fund* (Ackerman 1987: 209).

Initially identifying Spencer and Gillen for the first expedition to Western Australia, Frazer realised the former could not leave his post, and altered the proposal...'from the establishment of an expeditionary fund to the creation of an institute, on the analogy of the Smithsonian Institution, to study the primitive peoples of the Empire before their behaviour and beliefs were completely and forever changed by exposure to Europeans' (Ackerman 1987: 210).

Frazer echoes here a typical evolutionary perspective in which so-called primitive culture would crumble in the face of inevitable Western progress. His vision of a Smithsonian Institution in Liverpool was never realised and, in 1908, he left the urban and busy port city to return to the quiet of Cambridge. Yet his brief soujourn in Liverpool indicates the significance of the city during this formative period of British anthropology:

> *the fact that he would be professor in itself indicated the high value that the university placed on anthropology, which made a pleasant contrast to Cambridge, where its furthest penetration - Haddon's readership - had been established only after a long and wearisome struggle...the appointment plainly meant that the University of Liverpool was on the move, a place to be watched in the future'* (Ackerman 1987: 208).

The conjuncture of Frazer, Forbes and Jones denoted a decade of great economic and intellectual vitality in Liverpool. The port was the key conduit for the ingress of ethnographic objects and, as Frazer had pointed out, as a centre of a colonial web it might also nurture the incipient Victorian discipline of anthropology. Arnold Ridyard's African collection was enmeshed in this era of visionary aspiration.

The extent to which the lives of Forbes, Frazer and Jones intermingled remains a matter of conjecture.

Ridyard, the seafaring engineer whose existence was confined to one of perpetual maritime flux, would not necessarily have had direct dealings with Jones nor, of course, with Frazer. Yet the convergence of such influential personalities, the promotion of Africa, ethnology, trade and material culture undoubtedly facilitated Ridyard's ability to collect over such a prolonged period and on such a massive scale.

The enigma of Arnold Ridyard: an absent presence

> *The secret of Mr. Ridyard's success, in obtaining specimens, has been his complete understanding of the natives and his great consideration for their habits and customs. From conversations with Mr. Ridyard one learns that he quite endeared himself to many native officials of high standing, who were at all times anxious to show their obligations by obtaining specimens for him* (Clubb 1916: 5).

Apart from the thousands of natural history and ethnography artefacts which today bear witness to his presence in Liverpool, Arnold Ridyard left few traces of his personal motivations for collecting. Though a few letters and carefully recorded descriptions of some artefacts attest to a devotion to detailed provenancing, a two page hand-written letter to Sir Alfred Jones on 'Cotton growing in West Africa' is the only extant document in the Museum collection to explicitly indicate his written interests in the region.[14] No diaries or field notes are otherwise available to shed light on the motivations for a remarkable collecting passion.

Ridyard joined Elder Dempster in 1874 and served 41 years with the Company at sea. From 1874 to 1916, he worked as Second Engineer, chief engineer and finally Commodore Engineer on the *Niger*, the *Karina* and the *Tarquah*. A page of reminiscences from his grandson, T.E. Roberts, and a letter from a fellow seaman, Captain A.E. Webster, evoke a partial image of his personality and activities. Webster, who was traced by Charles Hunt in 1971,[15] had served with Ridyard as Chief Officer on both the *Karina* and *Tarquah* between 1907-14. In response to Hunt's enquiry, Webster wrote:

> *His one hobby was collecting fish and reptiles for the aquarium and museum from West Africa and he was well known to the Hausas on River Niger. He used to visit the second hand stores in Liverpool and buy all the old clothes, especially umbrellas, and trade with the natives for the live-stock they brought in canoes down the Niger River. We used to call at Burundi, a depot for the Old Niger Company, and the natives used to meet the ship, and Mr. Ridyard would go on the beach surrounded by natives and then the trading started. I remember the mud fish which burrowed in the earth and came out during the rainy season, and various fishes. He was a very eccentric man trusted by natives who at that time were cannibals* (Webster n.d.).

Webster provides a fascinating image of the trade in second hand Liverpool umbrellas on an African beach, though a less credible characterisation of 'natives'. T.E. Roberts alluded to his grandfather's cultural sensitivity in a letter to the Museum in 1981...'My Grandfather must have had an appealing character because of all the contacts he made and people, both black and white, who helped make his collection possible' (Roberts 1981: 2). Ridyard's devotion to transporting museum objects may, ironically, have contributed to his early retirement. According to Roberts, a monkey escaped on deck during one of the voyages and only his grandfather attempted to capture it. The animal bit Ridyard on the hand which developed into a growth, forcing his eventual retirement...'it was very clear that...my Grandfather was very improvident concerning his own affairs and spent all his spare money on his African collection. Clearly history and the Nation has gained by my Grandmother (who) was virtually a pauper when he died' (Roberts 1981: 2). Had Ridyard sold rather than donated some of the six-and-a-half thousand objects to Liverpool Museum he could have retired from service years before. The Benin Queen Mother Head for example, donated in 1899, is now considered one of the most valuable objects in the Liverpool Museum collection.

Ridyard also gave artefacts to the Chadwick Museum, Bolton[16] and amassed his own private African collection.[17] After a life devoted to seafaring and collecting, he retired from service in 1916, and died eight years later in 1924.

African routes and fetishes

For 21 years the Ridyard accessions dominated the pages of Liverpool Museum's registers. The lists of his objects, which appear almost every three to four months, are interspersed with sporadic accessions from other sources. Ridyard donations could comprise as few as six objects in one accession, or as many as 85,[18] the average numbering between 20-30 pieces. The quantity of goods brought back on every voyage was constrained by the available storage space on board ship and generally when larger objects were transported there would be fewer of them.

None of the six-and-a-half thousand objects transported by Ridyard were ever recorded in the 'Bills of Entry' in the maritime archives for the port of Liverpool. Some cargo lists refer to the arrival of boxes of 'curios', though none correspond to ships Ridyard worked on. One or two boxes were labelled for the British Museum during the period, others had no specific destination. It seems evident then that Ridyard's vast collection was not transported as cargo. Indeed, with the special arrangement between the shipping Company and the Museum, it is probable that the engineer stored artefacts in his own private cabin or in a special place allocated below deck.[19]

According to stockbooks, the chief engineer missed few voyages in all his 21 years at sea. The three to four month regularity of donations reflects the duration of the journey from Liverpool to Africa and back. The thousands of items provenanced to coastal sites in Africa, over the years, mapped the ports of call of Elder Dempster ships. Objects were acquired from the major European trading sites on the coastline at the time; they plot the routes of Ridyard's maritime journeys.

Ethnographic objects were derived from French, Belgian, German, Portuguese as well as British administered territories along the coastline, from Sierra Leone to the mouth of the River Congo. Unlike other

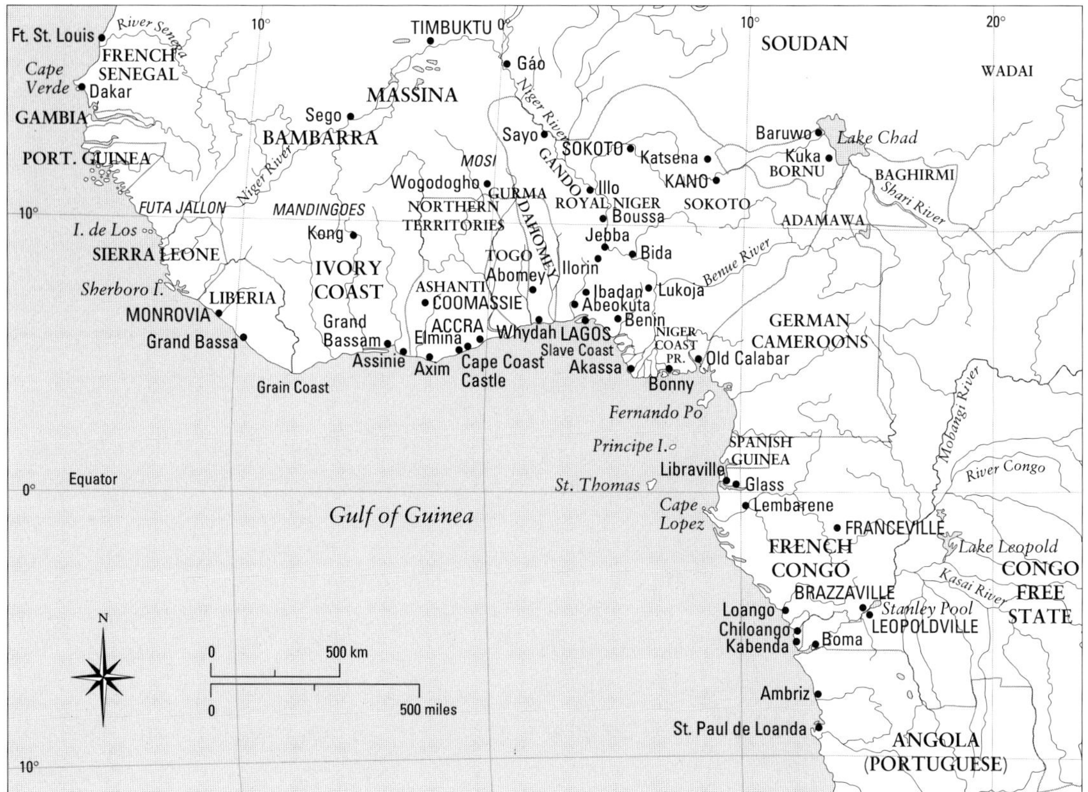

Map 1: Elder Dempster ships took a variety of routes along the coastline of Africa. The bulk of the artefacts from Ridyard were acquired from Freetown (Sierra Leone), Cape Coast Castle, Accra (Ghana), Lagos, Akassa, Bonny, Old Calabar (Nigeria), Loango (Gabon), Chiloango (Zaire) and on up the River Congo itself.

ethnographic collections formed during this period, the Ridyard collection was not embedded predominantly within the nexus of British colonial interests in Africa, reflecting instead wider maritime concerns. Predicated on coastal trade rather than British imperial domains, the collection transcended European colonial divisions. A high percentage of artefacts originated from the former French colony of Gabon, from the 'Belgian Congo', the 'German Cameroon' and 'Portuguese Angola'.

The single most important piece in the Ridyard collection is the early 16th century bronze cast of the Queen Mother Head from Benin, donated in 1899. Other important artefacts include a collection of seven Sande society helmet masks from the Sherbro and Mende peoples of Sierra Leone, Yoruba carvings and genre figures from Nigeria, polychrome Douala masks as well as groupings of Bafo and Bamileke carvings from Cameroon, white-faced masks from the Ogooué river area and Fang carvings from Gabon. It was during the first six years that Ridyard transported the most important *minkisi*, or power figures, made by the Kongo peoples of Central Africa. There is a range of *minkisi*, including a *kozo* (double-headed dog) and the powerful *Mungarka* (sic. *Mangaaka*) figure, as well as around 40 carved wooden figures from such coastal and riverine locales as Lualli, Mayumba, Cacongo, Landana, Banana and Boma, all in Central Africa.

It was these Central African 'fetishes'- or power figures - in particular that seemed to have caught Ridyard's attention, and for which he provides the most meticulous descriptions. The idea of the 'fetish' had long captured the European imagination as the embodiment of the irrational and the primordial. First put into

Figure 2: Head of a Queen Mother, Benin Kingdom, Nigeria, early 16th century, bronze, 35cm. Accn 27.11.99.08. (Photograph: National Museums & Galleries on Merseyside, Liverpool Museum).

circulation by 16th and 17th century Portuguese seafarers who referred to African charms and amulets as *feitiço*, the 'fetish' - a European invention - was soon applied derogatively to other aspects of 'primitive' cultures (Shelton 1995). Most prominently of all the carved *minkisi* or power figures, bristling with nails, came to symbolise the idea of the irrational fetish, objects which in reality formed part of divination systems amongst the Kongo peoples of Central Africa. These potent artefacts held a deep fascination for Ridyard and he reproduced dominant stereotypes in his register descriptions.

A year after his first collecting voyage in May 1896, he described two fetishes 'studded with nails' transported from Landana in present-day Angola - one a large 'wooden fetish called Coangi', the other labelled 'Cawso'.[20] He returned four months later with 12 objects including a 'fetish' carving from Gabon, a 'fetish cap' made of parrot feather, a 'fetish charm', a polychrome Douala mask and three figurative carvings from Mayumba country.[21] After his next trip, in January 1897, he donated a figurative carving and 'fetishes' from Gabon and Cameroon. Eight months and two voyages later, three important power figures were accessioned with the following descriptions carefully noted in the register:[22]

> *20.8.97.7 Wooden fetish in the form of a man with right hand raised in a striking attitude...The name is "Fulameconda". It is said to "attack its victims with dropsy and sleeping sickness".*

> *20.8.97.8 Wooden fetish figure in form of man with right hand raised in a striking attitude: on the stomach a projecting boss with mirror front, round the neck an iron link chain with a small composition ornament; on the figure are sundry wire nails. The head dress has had feathers stuck in it. The native name is 'Chicoca'. It is said to attack its victims with rheumatism & syphilitic sores & swellings.*

20.8.97.9 Similar to fetish no.8 - though smaller the head-dress is painted white. The native name is 'Mabialla Maupauha' and is said to 'attack the brain rendering its victims idiots'.

These register entries were augmented by notes supplied by A.M. Harbourne:

When anyone is attacked by one of these, he must first of course find a doctor...one of the family who own the fetish and then only by paying sufficient to satisfy them can he produce the remedy. Great care should be taken in handling these fetishes as cases are known of the above diseases attacking persons merely through placing their hands on them. I suppose owing to the medicine with which they are covered (Liverpool Museum register, accn 20.8.97.7).[23]

Figure 3: Head on top of a slit log drum. Sarongo people, Central Africa. 19th century, wood. 28cm. Accn 8.12.1897.13. (Photograph: National Museums & Galleries on Merseyside, Liverpool Museum).

Ridyard donated a further 41 objects including '*ju-jus*' and a fine Sorongo slit-gong[24] after returning from his next trip in December 1897. One of the most important Ridyard acquisitions, the *kozo* or double-headed dog, was acquired from Landana two trips later in August 1898. A highly important piece - one of only four known dogs in the country - the heads which look in opposite directions symbolise the animal's ability to mediate between the human and divine world. 'Dogs have 'four eyes', according to MacGaffey...'two for this world and two for the other' (1993: 43). The sculpture was labelled...'Fetish 'Ikoss' in the form of as double-headed animal afflicts offenders with a throat disease'.[25] Transported and donated on behalf of Mr. U. Shawcross, it arrived in Liverpool with a second power figure, (sic Mangaaka) destined for Peel Park, Manchester. In a letter to Ridyard from Chiloango, Landana, of June 1898, Shawcross wrote:

Herewith I send you the two fetishes as promised last voyage. I have been unable to get much information about them except that the smaller one is Ikoso a fetish, which when he chooses to be disagreeable, enables the offender to shuffle off this mortal coil, with the aid of a lingering throat sickness (animal fetish, Liverpool). The other one is not so gentlemanly, he goes under the title of 'Mungarka', and is one who possesses an unenviable power and notoriety in this district of Cacongo. He is worse than Berry; should his satanic majesty choose to deliver a verdict of guilty, the culprit blots himself out of the census return permanently, without even the necessity of calling in a doctor; a cheerful sort of chap ain't he? (Manchester). I had thought of attaching a label addressed to Mr. Ridyard, but fortunately remembering the law of

> *libel, I refrained from doing so. Mr. Dennett will very likely be on board with you in Loango as he wishes to take a photo of 'Mungarka' for reproduction in his new book. He is a great student of folk-lore amongst these natives and am sure he will only be too pleased to give you some reliable information about it. These fetishes are like the Spanish fleet, i.e. becoming very rare. I hope you will send 'Mungarka' to Peel Park museum as promised. Wishing you on this 50th voyage the best of health and luck* (Shawcross 1898: 1-2).

The Peel Park register recorded a note from Ridyard:

> *No doubt 'Mungarka' is fine, and you are a very lucky gentleman to get it. I asked for it 2 voyages back. Mr Shawcross gave me Mungarka, but I told him I would not take it on my account, but would present it in his name. This is a stroke of Policy, as he is in a good quarter for getting something for you... When bringing two of the fetishes from shore sometime back, there was a body of men working on the road where my man and I had to pass. On seeing the fetishes, one of them called out 'Cawso, Coangi' (kozo, Kwangi), and they immediately stopped work and took off their caps until we had passed. The Portuguese and French Governments are taking these Fetishes away by force as they stop the trade of the country* (MacGaffey 1993: 42).

Figure 4: Nkisi figure (originally labelled 'Mungarka'). Kongo peoples, Central Africa, 19th century, wood, nails, half scissors, mud compound, ceramic, pigment. 44cm. Accn 29.5.00.21. (Photograph: National Museums & Galleries on Merseyside, Liverpool Museum).

Figure 5: Nkisi figure (originally labelled 'mbungo dilu-ndilu'). Kongo peoples, Central Africa, 19th century, wood, feathers, nails, mud compound, textiles, glass, pigment. 50cm. Accn 9.3.1899.23. (Photograph: National Museums & Galleries on Merseyside, Liverpool Museum).

The Salford register indicates that a 'nkisi similar to Mungarka' was given to the Liverpool Museum. A 'large wooden bearded fetish labelled "Mungarka"' in the Liverpool collection was indeed transported by Ridyard, yet accessioned two years after this date in 1900, having been collected by Mr. O. Sonnenberg of Hatton & Cookson, Landana, Chiloango, not Shawcross.[26] The piece is probably the most important Central African carving in the collection.

Arnold Ridyard assiduously transported these 'fetishes' on almost every voyage during his early collecting years. In March 1899, six months after the double-headed dog was accessioned, a fine *nkisi* figure from Lualli, Chiloango, Landana in Portuguese Congo, with feathers, nails, glass, mud compounds and textiles attached, was donated, accompanied by a letter from Mr. Saunders of the previous January:[27]

> *Many thanks for your kindness. Letter safely to hand. Fetish. I herewith send you the small fetish I promised you. The name is 'mbungo dilu-ndilu',[28] which means something like man-eater. It is a private fetish in contra-distinction to the usual family-fetishes as there are in every town. The owner, of course, used it to make money out of its occult properties. It was obtained from the owner in a palaver made by the governmental representative at Lualli, a place about 20 miles distant from the coast. The town where it was found is situated on the Lualli-river, an affluent of the Chiloango. It is said to have killed several people amongst whom a woman educated by the missionaries which killing of people was also the reason to make the above mental palaver and to force the natives to hand over their fetish to the government. Further particulars are unknown to me* (Saunders 1898: 1).

Many of these accompanying letters reproduce stereotypes of *minkisi* as repositories of pernicious and alien forces. Three months later more 'fetishes' arrived - most notably 'Se Keh tem beh' - 'a female figure with small pipe, accompanied by a basket of various medicines from the Mayombi people, Lualli'.[29] In November Ridyard donated a 'Doctors outfit' on behalf of Mr. Sonnenberg - the collector who donated 'Mungarka' two voyages later - described in the register as 'Ingauga', 'fetish figure of a man with large headdress and protruding stomach inlaid with glass, the figure is bound round with strips of fur and has a cord for supporting it when worn round the neck; attached to the cord is a small tube with a feather in it, from Fute, Chiloango'.[30] Two more fetishes were included in this November accession - 'fetish figure of a woman - 'npemba'. It is said to talk and tell people what sickness they are troubled with, and to talk during midnight, 'Ncutu', Landana',[31] and a smaller fetish, 'Cossa Mabiella'[32] provenanced to Landana, described by Mr. J.M. Bastez in the accompanying letter:

> *Herewith the small fetish. In town...where they want to know who has robbed anything, they put these fetish between all the niggers, and the one which has robbed declared at once: Also if any women are very sick they care for these Fetishes and with two words which are the same as the Fetish name, the (women) will be better in a day* (Bastez 1899: 1).

H. Hirst, based at Nseri, Landana described a 'fetish' received in May 1900 as 'Mabella' - 'a private fetish; the owner of which is credited with extraordinary powers of endurance and fleetness of foot in escaping from enemies or wild animals. Such private fetishes no other person except the rightful owner may touch in fear of death or some frightful disease'.[33] On his next trip - September 1900 - Ridyard returned with two 'fetishes' and a...'Wooden fetish figure with a piece of mirror inlaid in the stomach, painted, Landana' . The last notable 'power figure' arrived at the Museum in June 1901 - a *nkisi* from Landana with the label...'Wooden fetish figure (*mangaea*) with piece of mirror inlaid in the stomach & studded with nails',[35] and 'a wooden fetish in the form of an animal with piece of mirror inserted in composition on its back, kept in the owners bedroom for protection'.[36]

Ridyard was obviously fascinated by the 'fetishes', donating pieces on almost every voyage between 1895 and 1901 and presenting Liverpool Museum with a spectacular Central African collection. The emphasis on these figures - and on large eye-catching sculpture in general however did not reflect the interests of a trained anthropologist with an intimate knowledge of everyday culture, but the capricious eye of the exotic voyager, the seafaring *flâneur.* Though describing the most impressive pieces and, as we have seen, diligently providing letters from interested collectors, the chief engineer was not concerned with the detail of ethnographic context. He transported artefacts of dubious authenticity: some masks were never used, others may even have been faked for sale to this well known British collector.

Annie Coombes likens the relationship of Ridyard to the Liverpool Museum with that of Emile Torday and the British Museum.[37] Yet the similarity between the two men is not as close as it may seem. Ridyard, unlike Torday, was not an African specialist. Acquiring no deep knowledge of peoples or languages, his collection was extensive rather than intensive, predicated on caprice rather than academic knowledge, on chance acquisitions rather than systematic and focussed research. It is the visual impact and the power of artefacts that seemed to have been the strongest guiding force.

Any analysis of Ridyard's collecting activities is ultimately hindered by the lack of personal details surrounding the life of this enigmatic engineer. The psychological and social motivations for spending 21 years acquiring thousands of objects for a local Museum seem never to have been recorded. One could speculate on desires for the accumulation of symbols of permanence with a life of constant flux, or a philanthropic need to donate to a public museum to educate others about African culture, or even an egocentric motivation to gain status through high profile presentations. But Ridyard remains silent. Nothing is presently able to explain his particular dedication, why he devoted almost his entire professional life to this extraordinary enterprise at sea.

The Ridyard donors

Elder Dempster & Co. had a vast network of agents working in the ports and riverine locales of West and Central Africa. The boats exported a variety of goods to Africa - candles, bars of soap, cotton sheets, umbrellas, sticks, nuts and bolts, combs, hats, bedsteads. Exotic monkey skins, ivory tusks, rubber, ebony and, most importantly of all, palm oil would have comprised the cargo for return journeys to the UK.[38]

From the late 1890s Ridyard developed his relationships with people who collected 'curios' for him while his ships traversed the coast. The network of African and colonial donors is perhaps the most interesting, and unique, aspect of this fascinating collecting enterprise. One hundred and ninety names appear in the registers as having donated *per* Ridyard to Liverpool Museum: there were ships officers, colonial administrators, missionaries, traders, army officers, legal professionals, African chiefs, princes and kings.[39] The first donor name appears in the register in 1897,[40] two years after he first began to collect; the last is in 1915, when Mrs Mayer-Griffith presented a Bamileke stool and chair in memory of her son, Major W.G. Mayer-Griffith, who had been killed in action in 'German Cameroon'. From the turn of the century on, in fact, the donors' dominate the pages of the Ridyard accession lists: as many as 22 names could be entered in a single accession. Some collected only one or two artefacts, others amassed collections of 50 or more, some repeatedly donated and transported via Elder Dempster over a period of years.

Through the huge variety of objects chosen and their accompanying descriptions, donors reveal particular preferences. Some, like Ridyard, were concerned with 'fetishes'. Rev. Ferguson, from Cape Palmas, for example, donated (an) 'elephant's tail, Fetish charms, Fetish Horn and 15 other charms' between 1905-1907. Mr. J.H. Frame, in 1900, collected '5 wooden fetishes from Bali, Cameroon'. Prince Adam Duke from Old Calabar, Nigeria presented...'wooden figures and a human skull said to be a '*juju*' of late King Duke, 4 leaves used in making '*juju*' and poison leaves' in 1909. Others had seemingly more mundane offerings: in 1900, J. Anderson from Landana collected wooden soup tureens, a knife, bamboo staffs and wooden stick.[41] Fellow seamen, Mr. E. Ashley, 2nd Engineer on the *Ekuro*, presented eight earthenware bowls[42] and W.J. Johnson, 2nd Engineer on the *Empire*, acquired three baskets from Nigeria for Ridyard to transport.[43]

Prominent and famous Ridyard donors included Sir Leslie Probyn, the Governor of Sierra Leone;[44] J.P.H. Brown, the African owner of the 'Gold Coast Leader' newspaper and leader of the African Rights Protection Society; C.D. Hotobah During,[45] creole lawyer and later on Vice-President of the National Council of the Colony of Sierra Leone and A. A. Whitehouse, the Eastern Divisional Commissioner of Southern Nigeria - it was Whitehouse who cultivated the closest links with both Ridyard and the Liverpool Museum. In February 1904, he collected 26 masks and figures of the western Ijo peoples in southern Nigeria during a 'punitive expedition' around Wilberforce Island in the Akassa branch of the Niger,[46] subsequently transported, via Ridyard, to the Museum. A year later in February 1905, 25 water-spirit headresses were presented to the Museum with the following description:[47]

> *From the Ikpaffia country, 3 miles up the Degema River, W. Africa. The whole of the headdresses are worn in the native dances and have had wide framework for the head, most of which are now wanting. Ikpaffia (Ekpeya) subtribe, Ibo tribe, neighbouring tribe Abua. Both having a play called 'Ogbukele' in which these headdresses appear These resemble more closely Abua than the Ikpaffia.*

These masks were originally intended for Ridyard, for in a letter to the chief engineer on 31st December 1904, Whitehouse wrote from his base in Degema...'I hope to have a few 'curios' shortly for the Liverpool Museum, from the IKPAFFIA Country some 30 miles or so up this River, and if you are returning in a few days I may have them in readiness for you'[48] (Whitehouse 1904). A letter to Henry Ogg Forbes in January

1905, however, indicated that the collection would be sent via another ship, the *Biafra*, instead.[49]

> *By this steamer I am forwarding 3 cases of curios for the Museum, which were obtained by the column detailed to subdue the late outbreak in the Ikpaffia Country in this Division. Nearly all of the articles, including the Alligators, are worn on the head during the country 'plays'. I intended to send these specimens with Mr. Ridyard, but they did not arrive in time!* (Whitehouse 1905).

With this ferment of seafaring activity between Liverpool and West Africa at the turn of the century, ethnographic objects could have been transported by any of the innumerable ships operating between these two maritime domains. Ridyard's vast donor network, spread from Sierra Leone to the mouth of the River Congo, and incorporating both African and European collectors, indicates a complex myriad of relations involved in collecting in Africa. According to Coombes, the extensive colonial relationships cultivated by the engineer...'are an exemplary demonstration of the diverse interests in the traffic in ethnographica in the late 19th and early 20th centuries...Evidently, the support and constant collecting activities of government officials or merchant employees, from at least 1897, was an essential ingredient in the success and expansion of Liverpool's Mayer collection' (Coombes 1994: 131).

From magic to science: the new pedagogic museum

Arnold Ridyard was situated at the intersection of two museological worlds - the pre-modern museum, where exotic curiosities were admired for their ability to provoke wonder and awe, and the modern pedagogical museum, in which objects are specimens integrated into ordered types and systems. In *The Birth of the Museum* (1995) Tony Bennett presents the modern museum as refashioning cultural artefacts in ways that facilitate specific didactic and ideological purposes. Bennett's incisive analysis, influenced by Foucault's ideas, maps the movement towards classification, order, control increasingly evident in 19th century museums.

By the early 20th century, Ridyard's eclectic collection was entangled in the shifting ideology of an Edwardian museum embracing the modern epoch. We have seen that the chief engineer had a prescient eye for startling, formally powerful artefacts, for those singular pieces that captured his sense of the primitive. There is an interest in the rare and exceptional, not typical and the everyday. Fifteen years after Ridyard began to collect, a shift occurs that is clearly marked within the internal discourses of the Museum. The 1910 Annual Report formally requested that he acquire specific types of 'specimens', in particular he was asked to:

> *pay special attention to the procuring of examples of the primitive potter's art as now carried on in Africa, an art gradually disappearing owing to the introduction of metalware* (Annual Report 1911).

The discourse of a 'disappearing world', a familiar trope in museums of the time, reinforced the educational necessity and urgency of systematic collecting. Accordingly, between 1910 and 1912 Ridyard collected around

100 earthenware pots and vessels from Oblogo near Accra in Ghana. As Clubb reported:

> *By request, Mr Ridyard made a special point of collecting representative examples of those arts and industries that are now fast dying out, owing to the rapid replacement of them with European goods. For example, the Blacksmith's Art in West Africa is illustrated in the Museums by the whole of the native workman's outfit, together with the actual charcoal and sand surrounding the native smith's hut, as well as photographs of the smiths at work. Another series - the Potter's Art - is complete from the raw clay to the finished wares, and the specimens illustrate well all the phases of the operations and the times taken for the various stages. The Art of Weaving is illustrated by a complete native loom, set up with its actual surroundings, as when in use by the fisherman - weavers of Jellah Coffee (sic. Dzelu Kofe)* (Clubb 1916: 4).

Clubb had long served as Curator of the natural history collections at Liverpool Museum and on Forbes' retirement in 1910, he was appointed Director. He brought with him a scientific perspective and an interest in emergent trends in public education. In his 1911 report, Clubb noted the frequent use of the Museum theatre by school teachers, and that the ethnography collections were of particular focus. Two years later, he was made joint secretary to a British Association special committee appointed to look at the educational side of museum work (West 1981: 11).

Liverpool Museum had been increasingly used by schools since the changes to the Education Code of the mid-1890s and the Education Act of 1902 which had allowed visits to the Museum to count as part of school attendance. Such changes stimulated debate within the Museums Association reflecting an increasing concern to attract a larger, more diverse public and to augment the role of museums within state educational programmes (Coombes 1994: 111). The promotion of a natural historian within the Liverpool Museum hierarchy was well fitted to an institution which was increasingly pedagogical.

Under Clubb, Ridyard's collecting behaviour conformed to the directives of the educationally-oriented museum. Ridyard's habits were clearly not systematic enough, there was no didactic principle guiding the accumulation of objects, though there was of course the evolutionary paradigm within which to ultimately display them. We have seen how hard Henry Ogg Forbes had worked to order the unruly influx of African material every three months into his racial classifications at the Museum. As the 20th century progressed Ridyard's unsystematic eye was replaced by systematic collecting policies. Echoing Collingwood's claim 50 years before that a disordered, haphazard collection was of little value, a more focussed approach by 1910 was clearly imposed. From this time on, Ridyard no longer transported spectacular individual pieces. Instead, utilitarian specimens of everyday African life increasingly appear: baskets, pots, paddles, calabashes, roots, gourds, fans and mats are listed frequently in the accessions register. The individualistic gathering of unpredictable, eclectic curios was remoulded by the 20th century Museum, resulting in an early collection predicated on intuition, caprice, aesthetic wonder to a later one based on order, types and structure. Arnold Ridyard had shifted from gathering magical *fetishes* on the coasts of Africa to collecting instructive scientific specimens.

Notes

1. Elder Dempster & Co. ran cargo liner services to West Africa

2. The collection totalled 6,450 objects consisting of 3,969 natural history specimens and 2,481 ethnographic artefacts. Of these 1,585 donations laid the foundation of the aquarium.

3. The ethnographic collections, until 1996, always included material from Oceania, the Americas, parts of South-east Asia as well as Africa.

4. In 1842 the Ethnographical Society was formed, the Anthropological Society of London was founded in 1863 and together they formed the Anthropological Institute in 1871. Ethnography did not obtain formal recognition as a scientific study, however, until the late 19th century in England.

5. This organisational principle is still present today in places such as the Public Museum in Warrington.

6. The new gallery was opened on 19th June.

7. Until his death in 1940, see West 1981: 7-8.

8. Before arriving in Liverpool, Forbes spent five years recording the flora and fauna on the Indonesian archipelago. His book, *A Naturalist Wanderings in the Eastern Archipelago* (1885) was the result of this research. His interest in the Pacific region developed during a three year stay in New Guinea, and deepened later on as Director of the Canterbury Museum in New Zealand. See Roy Ellen: 1978, 'The Contribution of H.O. Forebes to Indonesian Ethnography: A Biographical and Bibliographical Note' *Archipel* 16.

9. See 'A Benin Bronze Horseman at the Merseyside County Museum', *African Arts*, February 1984, vol. XVII, no. 2. In 1898, Forbes published an article, 'On a Collection of Cast-Metal Work of high artistic value from Benin, lately acquired for the Mayer Museum' and in 1900 published another piece, 'Cast-Metal work from Benin'.

10. Forbes' achievements were recognised through fellowship of the anthropological Institute: he contributed to its journal and became a member of its council.

11. Mainly Australia and New Guinea. In 1901, the Horseshoe galleries were completed and work began on redisplaying the natural history and local arcaeology collections in these area to alleviate some of the overcrowding. See West 1981: 9.

12. Jonese was also appointed to the Admiraly to inquire into the question of Naval Reserves and, most controversial of all, he was the Consul in Liverpool for King Leopold's Congo Free State. Jones had carried on King Leopold's notorious trade with a Belgian subsidiary of Elder Dempster.

13. He was conferred the degree of Honorary Fellow by Jesus College Oxford; created K.C.J.C of Spain in 1906 and presented with the Star of the Order of St. Stanislaus and the Cross of the same order.

14. The letter was written from Sierra Leone in 1903.

15. Former Keeper of Ethnography at Liverpool Museum.

16. Around 105 objects went to Bolton Museum in 1920 and 1921. Apparently, some items at his home were selected for donation to Bolton by P. Entwhistle, Curator at Liverpool Museum, when Ridyard moved there. In 1946 his daughter, Mary

Horrocks also donated material to the Museum.

17. When Roberts' father re-married, all the various African artefacts which his grandfather (Ridyard) had given to his mother were disposed of.

18. His collections ranged from 6 objects given on 28.6.901, to 85 donated on 19.4.1898, which may include a whole range of herbs and medicines carefully itemised and documented.

19. I am grateful to Mike Stammers at the Merseyside Maritime Museum for his generous advice on these matters and to Gordon Read for his help in the maritime archives.

20. 25.5.96.1-2.

21. 14.9.96.1-12.

22. Three months later 37 artefacts had come in.

23. The particulars were given by Harbourne to Ridyard. Harbourne, however, is not an acknowledged donor.

24. Labelled a Miloango fetish reputedly from Mussurongo tribe, Noqui district, Congo river, 8.12.97.13.

25. 9.8.98.43. It was accessioned as No. 43 in a group of 72.

26. 29.5.00.21.

27. 9.3.99.23.

28. Illustrated in *Astonishment and Power,* and described as *nkisinduda:* 1993: 98-99.

29. 26.6.9944, with a letter attached dated 4/5/99 which is difficult to transcribe.

30. 27.11.99.42.

31. 27.11.99.28.

32. 27.11.99.29 - at his piece was brought in in the same accession as the Queen Mother Head.

33. 29.5.00.20.

34. 24.9.00.6.

35. 24.6.01.3.

36. 24.6.01.3-4.

37. As paradigmatic of that between 'armchair' anthropologist and those in the field before 1920: 132.

38. The fruit of the wild palm trees grew in abundance in the forests along the coasts of Africa, its oil was used in the manufacture of soap and as a vital component of new industrial processes. Lord Leverhulme's empire was based on the manufacture of soap powder. Palm oil in the late 19th century replaced the earlier trade in slaves as the key commodity of trade from West Africa, certain of the Liverpool traders at the time being labelled 'palm oil ruffians'.

39. Africans that appear in the register include Prince Bassey Duke Epraim of Old Calabar, King Cudjoe Ababio IV of Accra,

King Amonoo V of Anamaboe, Gold Coast, Chief Squiss from Bonny, Chief Fred Greeen, Chief Frederick S. Ja Ja (who donated a wooden stool used by the late king of Ja Ja of Opobo), Chief Api Cookey Gam from Opobo Town.

40. 27.4.97- Mr. A. Forman.

41. 26.2.00.30-41.

42. In 1913.

43. In 1910 and 1911.

44. He donated 3 hats and 2 baskets in 1909.

45. He donated around 16 objects between 1906 and 1913, including wooden carvings, rattles, and gourds, Steatite figures and Mende masks.

46. 4.2.04.25-49.

47. 4.2.05.1-25.

48. The letter also mentions the journal Man which Ridyard had sent to the Divisional Commissioner. In 1904 Whitehouse published an article 'An African Fetish', in the Journal of African Society (Vol 4: 410-416) where a detailed description of so called '*ju ju'* rites and a *'ju ju'* house is provided. Whitehouse had previously destroyed this building with fire believing it to be Nigerian ritual, in the same journal.

49. 22.2.05 - handwritten transcript of letter.

Acknowledgments

I am grateful to Georges Bankes, Keeper of Ethnology at Manchester Museum for supplying information on the Manchester collections and to Mike Stammers, Keeper, Maritime Museum, National Museums & Galleries on Merseyside for his generous help and advice on seafaring. I am also indebted to Gordon Read, the archivist at the Maritime Museum for his help with research in the archives and to Dudley Reynolds and Roger Bailey for assistance with research. Zachary Kingdon and Lynne Stumpe read draft manuscripts and made valuable comments. Richard Kirkby has also made incisive editorial amendments.

Bibliography

ACKERMAN, R. 1987. *J.G. Frazer: His Life and Work.* Cambridge: Cambridge University Press.

BASTEZ, J. 1899. *Letter from J.M. Bastez to Arnold Ridyard* dated 1899, with reference to accession 27.11.1899.29. Liverpool Museum archives.

BENNETT, T. 1995. *The Birth of the Museum.* London and New York: Routledge.

CLUBB, J. 1915-16. Report of Curator of Museum on Collections made for the Liverpool Museums by Mr A Ridyard during a period of 21 years, 17th March 1916, Liverpool, City of Liverpool Proceedings of the Council 1915-16.

COLLINGWOOD, C. 1862. On the opportunities of advancing science enjoyed by the mercantile marine. *Address to the Liverpool Literary and Philosophical Society*, No.**16**.

COOMBES, A. 1994. *Reinventing Africa: Museums, Material Culture and Popular Imagination in Late Victorian and Edwardian England.* New Haven and London: Yale University Press.

ELLEN, R. 1978. The Contribution of H.O. Forbes to Indonesian Ethnography: A Biographical and Bibliographical Note. *Archipel* **16**, Paris: Redaction, 135-159.

FORBES, H. 1989. On a Collection of Cast-metal Work of high artistic value from Benin, lately acquired for the Mayer Museum. *Bulletin of the Liverpool Museums,* Vol **I**. Liverpool: Free Public Museum, 49-70.

FORBES, H. 1900. Cast-Metal work from Benin. *Bulletin of the Liverpool Museums*, Vol **II**. Liverpool: Free Public Museum, 13-14.

HUNT, C. 1972. A Link with Elder Dempster. *Sea - Journal of Elder Dempster*, January, Vol.8, No.3. Liverpool: Elder Dempster, 10-11.

JOURNAL OF COMMERCE, 1909. Death of Sir Alfred Jones, K.C.M.G., close of remarkable career. Dec 14.

JOURNAL OF COMMERCE, 1909. Obituary, Dec 10.

KARPINSKI, P. 1984. A Benin Bronze Horseman at the Merseyside County Museum. *African Arts*, February 1984, Vol **XVII**, No.2, Los Angeles: UCLA.

MACGAFFEY, W. 1993. *Astonishment and Power.* Washington D.C.: Smithsonian Institution.

ROBERTS, 1981. Memorandum on some remembrances of my Grandfather, Arnold Ridyard. 1853-1924. Dated 10th February 1981. Liverpool, Museum archives.

SAUNDERS, O. 1898. Letter from Mr Saunders to Arnold Ridyard to accompany accession 9.3.99.23. Liverpool, Museum archives.

SHAWCROSS, U. 1898. Letter from Mr Shawcross to Arnold Ridyard to accompany accession 20.8.97.7-8. Dated June 9th 1898. Liverpool, Museum archives.

SHELTON, A. 1995. *Fetishism: Visualising power and desire.* London and Brighton: Lund Humphries, The South Bank Centre The Royal Pavilion Art Gallery & Museums.

TYTHACOTT, L. 1998. The African Collection at Liverpool Museum. *African Arts*, Summer, Vol **XXXI**, No.3. Los Angeles: UCLA, 18-35.

WEBSTER, nd. Transcript of letter concerning Arnold Ridyard. Liverpool: Museum archives.

WEST, A. 1981. A History of the Ethnology Department, unpublished manuscript. Liverpool, Museum archives.

WHITEHOUSE, A. 1904. An African fetish. *Journal of African Society*, Vol **4**, 410-418.

WHITEHOUSE, A. 1904. Letter from A. A. Whitehouse to Arnold Ridyard dated 31 December 1904. Liverpool: Museum archives.

WHITEHOUSE, A. 1905. Letter from A. A. Whitehouse to Dr. H.O. Forbes dated 21 January 1905. Liverpool: Museum archives.

Annual Reports of the Free Public Museum of the City of Liverpool cited:

1859, 6th Annual Report for the year ending 31st December 1858.
1886, 32nd Annual Report for the year ending 31st December 1885.
1894, 41st Annual Report for the year ending 31st December 1893.
1895, 42nd Annual Report for the year ending 31st December 1894.
1896, 43rd Annual Report for the year ending 31st December 1895.
1899, 46th Annual Report for the year ending 31st December 1898.
1900, 47th Annual Report for the year ending 31st December 1899.
1903, 50th Annual Report for the year ending 31st December 1902.
1906, 53rd Annual Report for the year ending 31st December 1905.
1910, 57th Annual Report for the year ending 31st December 1909.
1911, 58th Annual Report for the year ending 31st December 1910.

Discontinuous Histories: 10

The Royal Albert Memorial Museum, Exeter, and its African Collection, 1868-1996

Nicky Levell

In Exeter, in 1862, an assembly of 'city and county gentlemen' formed a committee in order to establish a public museum, which, in their words, was to be:

> *a building which as regards architectural features and internal arrangements, shall be an ornament to the chief city of the county, and a fitting testimony to the progress and intelligence of the age* (Donisthorpe 1868: 11).

The dominant presence of the Royal Albert Memorial Museum (RAMM)[1] on Exeter's urban landscape undeniably stands as a testimonial to the Victorian period. Its biography however, reveals that it is not so much a monument embodying the 'progress and intelligence' of the age of Empire, but rather a product of the complex matrix of discursive practices that generated and fostered its form and content. From a Foucauldian perspective, it is not the historical 'progress' of a particular period that explicates the birth of public institutions but the discontinuities, which are often rendered invisible in a 'normal' historiography. Redressing this normative imbalance, this paper seeks to expose the ruptures and rearticulations that have occurred during the RAMM's 128 year life-span, thus constructing an effective history (Foucault 1974: 4).[2]

The RAMM is situated in Queen Street, in the centre of Exeter; over the years, its external appearance has

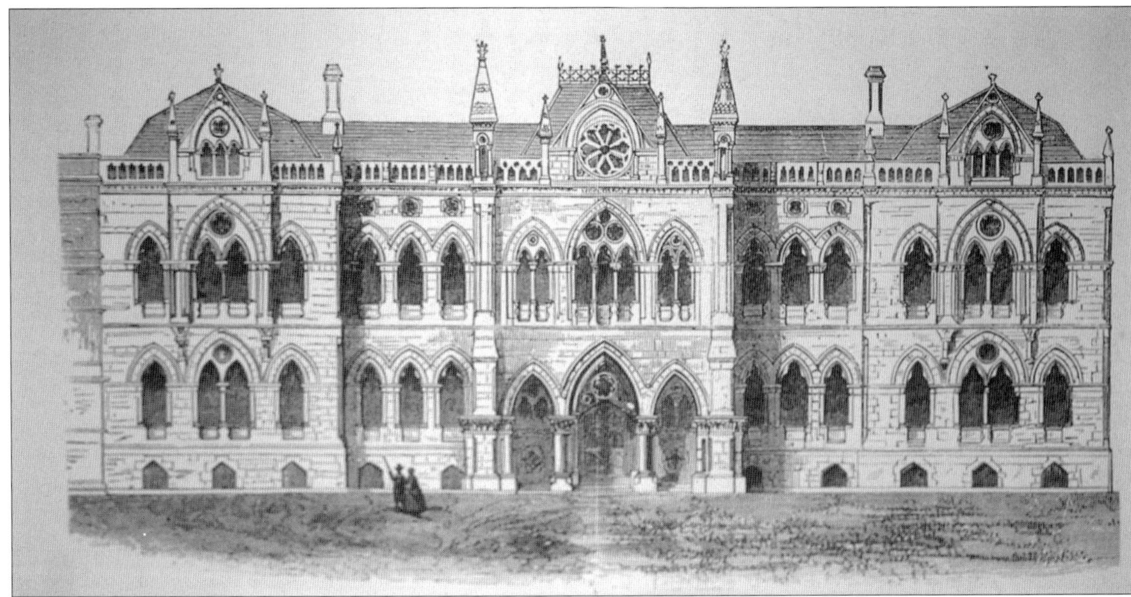

Figure 1: Front elevation 1888, Albert Memorial Museum, Exeter. (Photograph: Greenwood, 1888).

not changed greatly and, according to a recent brochure, 'the splendid Victorian Gothic building [still] exudes the self-confidence of the local philanthropists who raised the money for its Construction' (RAMM 1995a: 2). Yet, its 'internal arrangements' tell another story: a history of change in respect of the collection, confinement, classification, and arrangement of material culture, for the production of knowledge. By reconstructing a partial biography of the institution and its ethnographic collection, it becomes apparent that material things have no essential identity. Their values and meanings are contingent on the spatio-temporal, discursive relationships in which they are embedded. As such, at different times in their life-histories, they have been reclassified and rearranged, in order to generate new truths.

The RAMM has fifteen public galleries arranged over two floors. The six ground floor galleries display: Archaeology, Local History, Geology at Work, a Victorian Butterfly collection, World Natural History, and Devon Wildlife, and the nine first floor galleries are devoted to: temporary exhibitions, Clocks and Watches, Ceramics, Glass and Silver, Fine Art, Ethnography, Classical Antiquities, and Natural History (RAMM 1995b: 8).

The Museum houses the largest collection of ethnographic objects (totalling about 16,000 items) in Devon (Pole 1994: 2); the majority of these were acquired between 1868 and 1959. In September 1996, the ethnography galleries and the balcony area closed to the public and a major, lottery-funded, 1.7 million pound capital project to refurbish the space and redisplay the collections was initiated. This project culminated in the opening of the new World Cultures galleries in June 1999.[3] Prior to this rearticulation, there were two distinct ethnographic galleries: 'The Americas' combined material culture and natural history from the American continent and 'Ethnography' displayed material culture from Europe, the Pacific, Asia, and Africa. For the purpose of this paper, I will only review the changes in display that have occurred in the main ethnographic gallery which, in fact, housed the Americas collection until circa 1974.

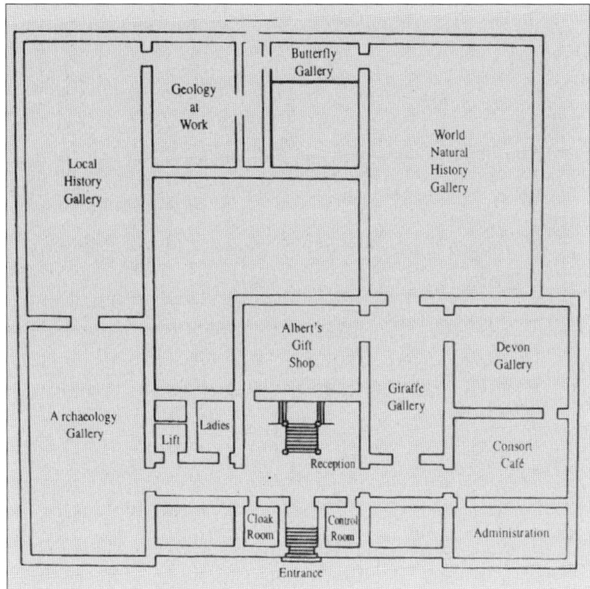

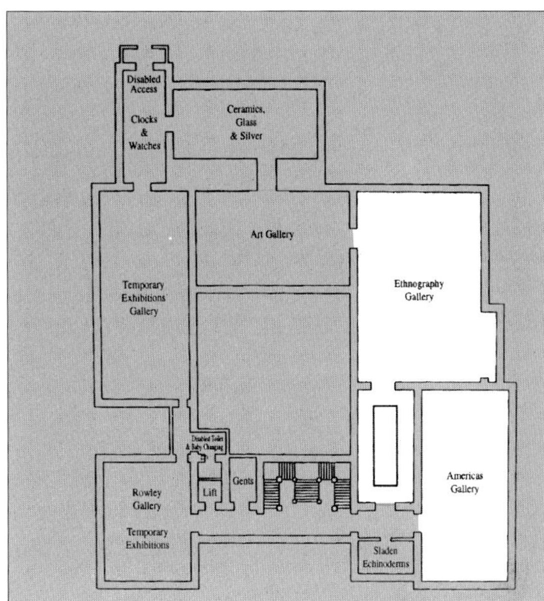

Figure 2: Far left: Ground floor plan, RAMM, 1996. (Photograph: Exeter City Museums and Art Gallery).

Figure 3: Left: First floor plan, RAMM, 1996. (Photograph: Exeter City Museums and Art Gallery).

The age of confinement

In his book, *The Order of Things*, Foucault describes the way discursive practices are located within specific 'systems of knowledge' (O'Farrell 1989: 54) or what he terms *epistèmes*. He suggests that, in western culture, there have been three major periodisations: the Renaissance, the classical, and the modern *epistèmes*, and 'each of these had quite specific characteristics, and the shift from one to the next represented a massive cultural and epistemological upheaval, a rupture that meant a complete rewriting of knowledge' (Hooper-Greenhill. 1992: 12). Unfortunately, Foucault's definition of an *epistème* has changed throughout his writing, in particular, he has rejected the idea that it constitutes a totalising and unified system underlying the knowledge of a particular place and time, rather he proposes that 'the *epistème* is not a general stage of reason. It is a complex relationship of successive shifts' (quoted in O'Farrell 1989: 59). For the purpose of this paper, I will use this as a working definition, in order to critically examine the way in which the RAMM, an institution born of the modern epistème, has rearticulated its space, subject positions, and objects, in so doing, effectively reflecting the successive shifts in reason and knowledge.

The Birth of a specialised space

> *An abrupt discontinuity can be identified as the invention of democratic culture* (Hooper-Greenhill 1992: 168).

The establishment of the RAMM was certainly a derivative of the newly emergent democratic, liberal ideology of Victorian Britain. When the 1862 committee first met, it proposed that an institution housing a Museum, Art Gallery, Free Library and School of Art (with provision for Science classes) would be a fitting memorial to the late Albert, Prince Consort. To this day, on entering the Museum, the first object the visitor confronts is a statue of Prince Albert, set into an alcove, which is often adorned with fresh flowers. Such an encounter poignantly conjures up the image of being in a cloistered, Victorian-gothic mausoleum. This royal icon had been the driving force behind the 1851 'Great Exhibition of Works of Art of All Nations', which, it was recorded, 'brought prominently forward the subject of Art Education ... in Exeter, as elsewhere' (Donisthorpe 1868: 7). The steering Committee was not, however, a neutral body of 'philanthropists'; some of its leading members had close connections with the state. In fact the Museum was first proposed by Sir Stafford Northcote of Pynes, Exeter, a Member of Parliament for Devon, who had been secretary to the Great Exhibition, and the site for the museum was donated by Mr Gard, then Member of Parliament for Exeter. Hence, from its inception, the Museum's steering committee was not an apolitical body of philanthropists, but a corps of influential men, closely connected to the state.

Apart from a grant of £500 from the Science and Art Department of South Kensington, the rest of the money (£14,241) was raised by public subscription. When the Museum opened to the public in 1869, sufficient funds had not been raised to complete the building; therefore the ethnographic objects were placed in 'a temporary museum or depot' (Donsithorpe 1868: 24). At this stage, the institution was still administered by the committee, however, the following year, it was taken over by the City Council, under the terms of the Free Libraries Act. From that date forth, it became a municipal museum, governed by a party of councillors and other members, and the admission fee (which had been a penny) was ceased (RAMM 1964: 1).

In effect, the RAMM was an exemplary product of, what Foucault terms, the 'disciplinary society'. In *Discipline and Punish* (1977), Foucault studies the development of new, systems of knowledge and forms of architecture, which created the conditions for social regulation, for the emergence of a self-regulating citizenry. These new disciplinary technologies, which emerged at the end of the classical *epistème*, were methods that divided and controlled time, space and movement. By relying on the distribution of individuals, in space and visibility, they became widespread procedures for surveillance, domination and control (Foucault 1977: 143). Foucault used the military hospital at the port of Rochefort to illustrate his hypothesis - an apt analogy can be drawn between the latter institution and the RAMM. At the military hospital, the first phase of the development prioritised things rather than people. Monetary policies were established, wards were created, medicines were purchased, their uses were registered, after which they were locked away. In comparison, at the RAMM, artefacts were acquired, they were classified and noted in a register,[5] then, they were arranged on screens (out of the public's reach). In both institutions, the organisation of space and the collection and storage of information provided the means for surveillance and knowledge-control.

Ironically, the people of Exeter had financed the RAMM, an institution which was a dual purpose governmental apparatus for regulating their conduct and disseminating ideologically-informed knowledge. It has been argued that the 'public museum emerged as one of the campaigns of the state to direct the population into activities which would, without people being aware of it, transform the population into a useful resource for the state' (Hooper-Greenhill 1992: 168). From the beginning, the RAMM was a political space; it embodied, amalgamated and consolidated numerous state-driven campaigns, such as, education for the masses and colonialism.

The specialised subject position

> *This new 'disciplinary museum' was on a far greater scale than in the past, and required specialised subject positions to maintain its momentum as an instrument of the state* (Hooper-Greenhill. 1992: 188).

In 1865, the committee had realised 'that the task of caring for an important regional museum was too much for volunteer assistants' (Boylan 1969: 3), consequently Mr W. D'Urban 'was appointed curator, to arrange, catalogue, and look after the already extensive collections' (Donisthorpe 1868: 25). This personnel rearticulation was a significant break off point; it provided the administrative infrastructure for the production of knowledge. A dichotomy ensued: the knowing subjects were divided into producers of knowledge (curators) and consumers of knowledge (visitors). In the public museum, the producing subject, wielding pedagogic authority, is often invisible to the public's gaze (Levell 1996: 10). At the RAMM it has been documented that:

> *much of the time of the curator and his staff is spent behind the scenes in preserving and annotating the collections that accumulate over the years. The results of this work are seen when the more public task is undertaken of arranging the material in the galleries* (RAMM 1964: 3).

Consequently, the consuming subject only had access to the 'edited' knowledge (the catalogues, displays and accompanying text) in the public spaces. The birth of the Museum, a purpose-built, seriated public space, facilitated surveillance and control: visitors were proffered knowledge for passive consumption. This point was made explicit: '[The RAMM's] special function is to show actual things, and to indicate the conclusions to be drawn from them in the light of competent opinion' (RAMM 1964: 3).

Educating the public

From its inception, the RAMM was conceived to be one of 'the agencies of national education' which was intended to 'exercise a beneficial influence all over the West of England' (Donisthorpe 1868: 17). In order to be valued as a serious educational asset, it was essential for the collections to be classified and displayed in a cohesive, informative manner. Exeter was only too well aware that other provincial museums of this period were 'usually little else than collections of curiosities' (Donisthorpe 1868: 18). To counter this prevailing trend, the RAMM was articulated as a pedagogic institution, centred on the provision of 'rational amusement', and, its core function was defined as:

> *[the] preservation of treasures which exercise an educational influence through the agency of a public exhibition, not furnishing entertainment alone, but imparting instruction* (RAMM 1887: 5-6).

In Exeter, as elsewhere, local people working as government officials, traders and missionaries brought back material culture from the colonies, which was subsequently institutionalised in these newly born public spaces. Such material tended to be classified and displayed in such a way as to validate colonialism, whilst simultaneously and indirectly providing a cohesive, cultural identity for the West. Thus, the RAMM's ethnographic collection not only provided a window onto the colonies, it also represented the local people's achievements in foreign lands and, from a wider perspective, also confirmed the empire's mission and worth.

Henry Townsend: missionary and collector

Colonialism engendered the emergence of a number of specialised subject positions; two such examples are the missionary and the trader. To some extent, in certain contexts, these new subject positions, which reflected the historic shift of power and knowledge, served to transform collecting practices. In the second half of the nineteenth century, two Exeter men, Rev. Henry Townsend (a missionary) and Richard Dennett (a trader) presented their ethnographic collections to the RAMM.

When the RAMM was founded in 1868, Rev. Henry Townsend donated his collection of Yoruba artefacts to the Museum. Even today, this collection is regarded as a major part of the Museum's Yoruba holdings. However, from one perspective, Townsend's donation is not a collection *per se*, but rather what Stewart terms a 'collection of souvenirs' (1984: 135), and in order to make sense of this idiosyncratic assemblage it is necessary to reconstruct a historically specific narrative, (to discover how these possessions were amassed), however 'it is not the narrative of the object; it is the narrative of the possessor' (Stewart 1984: 136), Townsend.

Henry Townsend was born in Exeter in 1815. At the tender age of twenty-one, he started his life as a missionary in Sierra Leone, with apparently 'no motives of any other kind ... than the salvation of immortal souls' (Townsend 1887: 2). In this colonial outpost, he devoted his time to converting liberated slaves who had been 'rescued by British cruisers and placed under missionary instruction' (Western Times 1886). These Africans wanted to return to Yorubaland, in their mother land Nigeria, and in 1843, Townsend accompanied a group of them to Abeokuta, a town inland from Lagos. According to his nineteenth century biographer, he was not only the first Anglican missionary in Abeokuta, he was 'the first white man they had ever received or seen' (Townsend 1887: 36). On his arrival he was warmly welcomed by the townspeople because he was bringing home their kinsfolk. Apparently, this amicable reception prompted him to stay and establish a mission, and it was during his time in Abeokuta that Townsend assembled his collection.

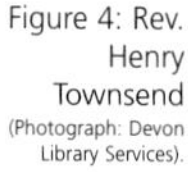

Figure 4: Rev. Henry Townsend (Photograph: Devon Library Services).

Abeokuta, in the Egba kingdom, was not a stable country;. many of the inhabitants were liberated slaves who lived under the constant threat of invasion from their neighbours, the Dahomians,[6] who had a slave-raiding army, and resided in the

Kingdom of Dahomey, to the west of Abeokuta. Townsend became actively involved in the politics of the Yoruba states, in particular, he undertook to strengthen the state of Abeokuta, by increasing the power of the *Alake* (Chief king or *oba*). Having an influence over the powerful chiefs and being 'thoroughly versed in the politics of the Egbas' (Townsend 1887: 143), he was successful in promoting a Christian convert, Ogubonna, as *Alake*. Whilst in Abeokuta, Townsend became a 'great favourite' of Chief Ogubonna (Pearce 1970b: 1), assisting him in the battles against the Dahomians. Although he did not actively participate in the fighting, he provided the Egbas with ammunition, which had been entrusted to him by the Consul (Townsend 1887: 75). In part, it is this narrative than can be generated from Townsend's souvenirs.

Townsend's souvenirs are metonymic objects inasmuch as they are partial substitutions for his first-hand experience in Abeokuta. As Stewart argues, the souvenir has a twofold incompleteness: 'first, the object is metonymic to the scene of its original appropriation in the sense that it is a sample' (1984: 136). In this respect, the slave chain in the Townsend collection, signifies the occasion in about 1850, when Townsend 'freed two captives and removed the slave chain from their necks'.[7] This object, therefore, not only signified the specific episode, the scene of the appropriation, it also reduced the larger, complex experience of the slave trade into a more comprehensible, miniature form (Stewart 1984: 141). Second, the slave chain constitutes an incomplete sign, which requires a 'supplementary narrative discourse'; thus the collector becomes the 'narrative agent' (Bal. 1994: 112) and the collection functions as a partial autobiography.

A number of parallels can be drawn between the collecting practices of Sir Hans Sloane and Rev. Henry Townsend. An effective history of the British Museum would identify: 'an articulation between the marriage of Sloane to a Jamaican heiress, his participation in the slave trade, and his financial abilities to collect' (Hooper-Greenhill 1992: 20).

Similarly, Townsend's ability to collect was facilitated by his friendship with Chief Ogubonna and his efforts to abolish the slave-trade. It seems feasible, however, to suggest that Townsend, working as a church missionary, did not have the 'financial abilities' to collect, as such one must assume that a lot of his souvenirs were gifts. Interpreting Townsend's souvenirs as 'gifts', reinforces the contention that souvenirs are objects which 'speak not so much to the time of production as to the time of consumption' (Stewart 1984: 144). The souvenir-cum-gift is no longer exchanged on the basis of its 'use value', it is physically removed, and its value is rearticulated at the level of social relations. For example, Chief Ogubonna gave Townsend an Eshu figure.[8] This figure used to stand at Ogubonna's door as a protective symbol, however, when this metonymic object moved into Townsend's possession, it proffered itself as a sample of the friendship between the missionary and the chief. Moreover, it also served to narrate Townsend's success story: he had realised 'his duty to promulgate a knowledge of the truth among the heathen' (Townsend 1887: 148).

In Abeokuta, as elsewhere in the Empire, missionary practices were embedded in the political, economic and ideological discourses of Victorian Britain. In 1848, Townsend returned home to appear before special committees at both Houses of Parliament, which had been established to decide the fate of the British preventative squadron. In giving evidence about his personal contact with the slave trade, Townsend publicly declared his support for the retention of the British squadron, which was, in his opinion, effective in 'checking' the illicit traffic in people (Townsend 1887: 150).

In a number of ways, Townsend's activities were bound up with imperial policies and, as such, he naturally assumed the role of a colonial agent, involved in the national drive to 'civilise' the African. In addition to his ecclesiastical duties, he spent time encouraging 'lawful commerce', agriculture, reading and writing (he even instigated the first publication of a bilingual newspaper in Abeokuta). These activities were recognised and commended by the monarchy: Queen Victoria sent a letter and bibles to the Egba people and Prince Albert sent a steel corn-mill and 'all these were delivered by the Rev. Henry Townsend, the promoter of Friendship between the English and the Egba peoples' (RAMM np: 53).

Although it seems that Townsend was well-liked and successful in converting many Egbas to Christianity, one wonders whether they were truly convinced by his Christian doctrine. Christianity might have just been regarded as a means to an end, that is to say, conversion to Christianity not only procured British protection against the slave-traders but it also 'became the means of improving the land' (RAMM, np: 49). With this in mind, it is worth commenting on two polychrome woodcarvings from Abeokuta, both of which depict a European missionary on horseback (Chappel 1981: 42). One of these carvings is part of Brighton Museum's holdings, while the other is housed in Hamburg's Museum für Völkenkunde. William Fagg has suggested that the Brighton carving was made before 1875 (Zwernemann 1985: 134), which corresponds to Townsend's time in Abeokuta. Moreover, what is interesting about the Brighton figure, is the carving of a blue figure behind the European missionary. Dr. William Rea has speculated that this blue figure is the Yoruba trickster god Ere Eshu,[9] which leads one to think that the Abeokutans were implicitly ridiculing the missionary in question. Or alternatively, the missionary figure could he interpreted as a metonym for the Christian church, which reinforces the idea that the African converts were not really committed to their newly adopted religious beliefs. These re-readings support the contention, that during the colonial period, in parts of Africa, indigenous artists often used their work 'as a vehicle for their real feelings' (Brett 1991: 116).

In 1867 a dispute between Yoruba chiefs and the British authorities on the coast eventually led to the expulsion of the missionaries, questionably 'not as Christians, but as Englishmen' (Townsend 1887: 111). Townsend returned to Lagos before eventually returning to Exeter to retire in 1876. Ten years later he died.

It is interesting to speculate as to why Townsend donated his collection of Yoruba artefacts to the RAMM, eighteen years before his death. Obviously, such a collection of souvenirs engenders a very personal narrative and according to Pearce 'no one is interested in other people's souvenirs' (1991: 141). In my opinion, Townsend's collection was of interest to other people, especially the people of Exeter. Exonians were evidently aware of Townsend's activities in Abeokuta. In 1859, they funded the building of the Exeter Church, the first of its kind, in Abeokuta. One of the key financial donors was Sir Thomas Acland, who was said to be 'a firm friend of Mr Townsend and his missionary work' (Townsend 1887: 103). Notably, Acland had been a leading member of the 1862 committee and, when the Museum was founded, he was appointed as one of the trustees

(Donisthorpe 1868: 10-11). Therefore, Townsend's donation can be interpreted as a kind of counter-gift, a reciprocal gesture to his fellow townsfolk and to his friend, Sir Thomas Acland.

Richard Dennett: trader and collector

Richard Edward Dennett (1857-1921), the son of Rev. R. Dennett, was born in Valparaiso, Chile. Although the Dennett family was working in Chile, it maintained a close relationship with the south-west of England. Dennett was sent back to Britain to be educated at Marlborough College, in Wiltshire (1869 - 1874)[10] and later, his parents returned to their home in Ashton, near Exeter. In 1879, at the age of twenty-two, Dennett left Britain for the south west coast of Africa, in the employ of the 'British African Merchants' Hatton and Cookson (Dennett 1906: 2). It was during his early years, as a trader in Luango, Congo Français (now Democratic Republic of Congo), that Dennett assembled his ethnographic collection and 'commenced studying the natives' habits and customs' (Dennett 1906: 8).

In the RAMM's twentieth annual report it was stated that:

> *Mr R. E. Dennett has presented a most valuable and interesting series of Ethnological specimens from Cacongo, on the west coast of Africa* (RAMM 1890: 3).

This is a truism: Dennett's collection predominantly comprised of a 'series' of power figures (*minkisi*) and other objects relating to 'fetishism' (Withers-Gill 1931). In contrast to Townsend's collection of souvenirs, Dennett's is, what Pearce terms, a 'systematic' collection, as she explains: 'systematics draw a viewer into their frame, they presuppose a two-way relationship between the collection which has something public (not private), to say, and the audience who may have something to learn, or something to disagree with' (1991: 149). Dennett was convinced that his collection did have something public to say; not only did he donate it to the RAMM for public consumption, he also produced eight ethnographic books oriented to the same subject, West African culture.[11]

According to one theory, when objects are grouped together in a series because they are 'the same', it then becomes necessary for the collector to signify their differences (Stewart 1984: 155). To some extent, Dennett's publications provided the means for him to differentiate between the *minkisi* in his collection. In particular, in his book, *At The Back of the Black Man's Mind* (1906), he went into great detail explaining the different classes of *minkisi*, how they are made and how life force is put into them. He also included photographs to supplement the narrative and specific references to indicate which figures were at Exeter Museum (Dennett 1906: 85-95). Furthermore, because of the public nature of the systematic collection, it tends to require an 'organised space in which to demonstrate its serial relationships' (Stewart 1984: 149). Even prior to giving his collection to the RAMM, Dennett displayed his 'Feteiches and curios' on a make-shift shelving system. The fact that he publicly arranged, displayed, photographed and published his collection reinforces its categorisation as a systematic collection of examples, guided by an intellectual rationale, rather than a 'fetishistic collection', which tends to be a private accumulation of similar objects.

In order to surmise the motives that inspired Dennett to collect *minkisi*, it is necessary to understand the nature of a 'serial' collection. 'Baudrillard... concludes that because of a collection's seriality a 'formal' interest always replaces a 'real' interest in collected objects' (Stewart 1984: 154). From this perspective, when Dennett acquired the *minkisi*, they no longer retained their original use value, rather, they entered a new system of value, based on their 'scientific' and academic worth. But this was not just the collector's idiosyncratic system of value, it was part of the wider cultural and economic value-systems of the Victorian age. Hence, in order to locate Dennett's collecting practices, it is necessary to scrutinise the nineteenth century discourses and structures of knowledge, that gave rise to these new spheres of value.

Figure 5: Dennett's Collection of 'Feitiches and Curios'. (Photograph: H.J.L Bennett).

An influential figure in Dennett's life was the Victorian travel writer Mary Kingsley (1862-1900). During her first visit to Africa (1893-4), Kingsley came into contact with the Fjort peoples (from the Luango and Congo provinces) and 'learnt much from Mr Dennett personally regarding their beliefs and customs' (Kingsley 1897: xviii). As well as staying with Dennett, she forged a special arrangement with his employers, Hatton and Cookson, who were one of the principal trading companies on the West African coast. This informal contract enabled her to use company 'cheques' to 'buy' goods from the Congolese villagers, who were then able to exchange these promissory notes for commodities on sale in the company's trading posts. In addition to obtaining valuable zoological collections for the British Museum, Kingsley acquired a small collection of ethnographic specimens and made comprehensive notes on West African ideas, which she 'subsequently utilised in published works and lectures' (DNB 1992: 1677). Before her untimely death in 1900, she had become a leading authority on African belief systems, which Dennett acknowledged, by remarking that 'by far the most comprehensive picture of fetishism ... [is] in Miss Kingsley's West African Studies' (Dennett 1906: 92).

It seems probable that Kingsley's writings on West African culture may have motivated Dennett to adopt a more systematic approach to collecting and studying *minkisi.* Whilst travelling in West Africa, she actively endeavoured to persuade traders and the like, men who were resident in Africa, 'to publish their information for the benefit of students of ethnology' in Britain (Kingsley 1897: iii). In-line with this advice, Dennett sent his manuscripts to the Folklore Society of Great Britain for publication, and in fact it was Kingsley who wrote the preface to his book *Notes on the Folklore of the Fjort* (1897). Being a member of the Folk-Lore Society, which had been established in 1878, for 'the purpose of collecting and preserving the fast-perishing relics of folklore' (Milne 1897: 2), Dennett would have received the Society's handbook, which provided instructions on how to collect desirable material. It explained that scientifically studying folklore, which was described as 'pre-scientific mental activity', facilitated the compilation of the 'unrecorded past in man's mental and social history' (Milne 1897: 3), as such its intellectual rationale indubitably echoed the ethnocentric, social evolutionary theories that were popular with the Victorian academics. This is not entirely surprising because two leading proponents of social evolutionary theory, General Augustus Pitt Rivers (1827-1900) and Edward Tylor (1832-1917), were vice-presidents of the Folk-Lore Society. Moreover, these two eminent Victorians, were also involved in the growth of museums and the 'scientific' value and institutionalisation of anthropology, therefore one would assume that they indirectly influenced Dennett's approach to the study and collection of West African folklore and material culture.[12]

Another distinguishing feature of the modern *epistème* was the emergence of the human sciences (Foucault 1970: 359). During this period, anthropology was just one of the human sciences that was institutionalised in the universities. In Britain, Tylor was appointed as the first professor of anthropology at Oxford University in 1896. Twenty-five years before becoming chair of anthropology, Tylor had outlined his theory of social evolution in his seminal text, *Primitive Culture* (1871). In brief, he posited that societies pass through three distinct stages – animism, polytheism, and monotheism – which served as indicators of their position on the evolutionary scale, that ranged from the most 'primitive' to the most 'civilised' states. Dennett was not totally convinced by this theory, he wanted to illustrate (*pace* Tylor and Kingsley (1906: 92)) how the 'primitive and degenerate' African people had, in addition to 'fetishism', 'a religion giving a much higher conception of God than is generally acknowledged...and...to make clear the vital importance of the kingly office to the African communities' (Dennett 1906: v). Basically, he wanted to dispel the widespread, ethnocentric view, which regarded 'fetishism' as the sole component of the African's religious beliefs. In addition to clarifying the African's religious beliefs, Dennett's monographs also served to convey a political, moral judgement on colonialism. He felt that the colonial governments had contributed to the regression of the African states by not taking into consideration the role of the omnipotent kingly office and in his words:

> *nothing could have been more disastrous to the welfare of the people and the country than the insane way this country was cut up between the French, the Portuguese, and the independent State of the Congo* (1906: 32).

Dennett even inferred that, 'fetishism' (or *Ndongoism*), notably the 'evil counterpart' of the higher religion (*Nkicism*) had burgeoned due to colonialism (1906: 168). To support this hypothesis, he indicated that this ritual practice particularly flourished in areas of the Congo, which had been targeted by the original Portuguese missionaries.

In keeping with his moral appraisal of colonialism, Dennett became actively involved in the politics of the Congo. He wrote a series of letters to *The African Mail* about the 'injustice of the French rule and the concessionaire system in Congo Français', the Lower Congo (Who Was Who 1929: 1063). In 1886, he edited a newspaper called the *Congo Mirror* and drew attention to irregularities in the Congo Free State, which was effectively the fiefdom of King Leopold II of Belgium (Schildkrout 1988: 155). In particular, he accused 'Congo officials of murders and atrocities' (Who Was Who 1929: 1063), and he continued to campaign for fairer treatment of the indigenous population, until the Congo Reform Association was founded.

In the late nineteenth century, the plight of the Congo Free State's colonial subjects had become an international affair; public opinion was divided between left and right factions. When Frederick Starr, the American anthropologist, returned to America, after collecting in the Congo during the 1890s, he 'created a public stir…by publishing a series of newspaper articles defending the Congo Free State' (Schildkrout 1988: 156). At the same time, he negotiated the sale of his Congolese collection to the American Museum of Natural History (AMNH). This latter institution serves as a prime example of the complex and intimate connections between nineteenth century museums and European colonial regimes. In the last decade of the nineteenth century, the AMNH had instigated its own Congo Expedition with the aim of acquiring 'complete', representative collections of ethnographic material from this cultural region. To facilitate such an objective, it entered into extensive negotiations with King Leopold's representatives and was ultimately 'offered a large collection of ethnological artefacts from the Congo' (Schildkrout 1988: 155).

It is interesting to speculate as to why Dennett assembled a serial collection of *minkisi* rather than a more representative collection of Congolese cultural artefacts like the one that had been sought by the AMNH. Being a member of the Royal Anthropological Institute, he would have realised that his collection constituted a useful research asset for this growing discipline. In fact, by the turn of the century, it seems that he was recognised as an authority on *minkisi* in anthropological circles. In 1901, he provided the Pitt Rivers Museum with detailed information about a *Mavungu* figure (part of the Kingsley collection), which was used for an extended object label. Possibly another reason for Dennett's focus on *minkisi* can be extrapolated from his observation that the objects in this class were 'apparently the bitter enemies of European Governments, who [seemed] to take a delight in clearing the country of them' (1906: 94). Therefore, it is feasible to assume that he felt the need or compulsion to preserve these much maligned figures for posterity and to make them available for public consumption in Europe's new, purpose-built institutions. In writing about the fate of Benin Bronzes, Dennett made his views about Europe's future role as the preserver of World heritage, explicit:

> *It is hoped that private collectors of these bronzes may some day bequeath their collections to the British Museum, and that photographs ... of those collections in the Hamburg and Berlin Museums may be obtained and made accessible to the public. The Future educated Bini as a British subject has a right to find as full a collection as possible ... in this Imperial Museum* (1906: 189).

Evidently, although Dennett did not condone the barbarity meted out by some European powers, he was nevertheless still a product and a party to the symbolic violence that was being perpetrated by the dominant, 'more civilised', western nations, in the Victorian period.

Rearticulations

> *An effective history recognises that the social is open, only partially fixed, and therefore...any site of the production of knowledge, is equally only partially fixed and thus external/internal relations are subject to movement and change* (Hooper-Greenhill 1992: 193).

At the RAMM, when internal relations changed, collections were often reorganised and redisplayed in order to produce new truths. These curatorial practices are contingent on the malleable nature of the ethnographic object: its lack of an innate, fixed identity. In semiotic terms, the object functions as a signifier, its meaning 'at any given moment depends on the discursive relations within which it is located. Its meaning is open to constant re-reading and reinterpretation' (Porter 1991: 105). To explore these shifts and discontinuities, necessitates locating Exeter's ethnographic displays in their historical contexts, which, in turn, entails looking at the wider discursive practices that generated and rationalised each respective paradigmatic rearticulation.

The evolutionary paradigm

The RAMM was a materialisation of Victorian ideology. It developed during a period when a whole new range of practices - Darwin's evolutionary theory, archaeology, anthropology, and colonialism - were being synthesised to constitute a new regime of truth. These new structures of knowledge interconnected to form a totalising order, which was geared to the reconstruction of the history of life, 'man', and civilisation. Enmeshed in this new totality of knowing were ethnographic objects.

A critical synopsis of Pitt Rivers' life, provides an illuminating insight into the way in which these new modalities of knowing affected the Victorian intelligentsia and the museum fraternity in general. A significant event during this period was the Great Exhibition of 1851: it was not only a precursor to the RAMM, but it also inspired Pitt Rivers, a young military officer, 'to collect objects of a broadly ethnographic kind' (Chapman 1985: 16). He was particularly interested in weapons, as such he began to assemble a collection that charted the technical development of weapons over time.

One important event, which influenced Pitt Rivers and his peers' approach to classifying material culture, was 'the revolution in archaeology' (Chapman 1985: 20); in particular, the accomplishment of the French archaeologist Boucher de Perthes:

> *although De Perthes' work in the Somme Valley went back to the 1840s, it was only after 1858, after the discoveries in Brixham Cave in Devon and the findings of the British delegation to Abbeville, that it was given general credibility* (Chapman 1985: 20).

Obviously such a breakthrough represented a significant rupture in the existing structures of knowledge because here was the realisation that the history of humankind's life on earth could not be reconciled with biblical chronology and as such knowledge and truth had to be repositioned on other structures of rationality.

The rich archaeological findings in Brixham Cave doubtless had a significant impact on the Devonshire intelligentsia. In fact, the RAMM received 'a great deal of the material from the British Association cave excavations in South Devon in the 1870s' (RAMM 1879: 16).

Another event, which had an 'immediate impact' (Chapman 1985: 20) on Pitt Rivers and certainly influenced the work of the British social theorist, Herbert Spencer - one of Pitt Rivers' personal acquaintances - was the publication of Darwin's *The Origin of the Species,* which delineated the author's theory of evolution by natural selection. In *Principles of Sociology* (1876-1896), Spencer adapted Darwin's biological theory of organic evolution to account for social evolution. Consequently, Pitt Rivers applied this new social evolutionary concept to his collection. In keeping with the Victorian ideology of education for the masses, Pitt Rivers stressed the need for a public ethnographic museum for education and research. In 1883, seven years before his death, he gave his collection of material culture to Oxford University for permanent display, on the understanding that the collection would retain its typological system of arrangement, during his lifetime.

It seems that from the outset, RAMM was aware of the Victorian museological trends. In 1869 when the temporary depot opened its doors to the public, Mr D'Urban had arranged the ethnographic objects so that they were 'geographically and ethnologically sequent' (RAMM 1887: 4). In particular, 'the weapons and other objects [were] assembled in groups on the walls or on screens fastened against them' (RAMM 1879: 16) and were regarded as 'specimens illustrative of the progress of Man' (Donisthorpe 1868: 29). Ironically, colonialism had provided the means to furnish the ethnographic gallery and the ethnographic display, in turn, served to legitimise colonialism: in effect, all discourses merged and mutually reinforced one another. In 1895, under the direction of the curator James Dallas the 'ethnological specimens' were removed from the depot and reclassified and redisplayed in the purpose-built 'Ethnological Room' in the Museum. This was another significant break from the past because the collections were:

> *entirely re-arranged, in order to make them Geographically and Ethnologically sequent, and...re-numbered throughout by a new method. A catalogue...[was] in course of preparation...together with a general guide to the Museum* (RAMM 1897: 4).

The exhibits were placed in 'wall cases adapted to the purpose, and labelled' (RAMM 1898: 4). Effectively, the surveillance apparatus was being overhauled and fine-tuned. However, during this period the curator, Dallas, was not totally committed and 'the development of the Museum was not maintained' (Express and Echo 1927).

In 1902, the appointment of a new curator: Mr F R Rowley 'wrought a remarkable *change* in the atmosphere of the RAMM' (Express and Echo 1927, author's emphasis). It is important to note that this 'change' coincided with a series of debates at the Museum Association, which were orientated to the ideal classificatory system for ethnographic material. The general consensus was that national collections should adopt the geographical arrangement and local museums should employ the typological schema (Coombes 1991: 195). Basically, the geographical display grouped together ethnographic objects from the same region, in order to reinforce the idea that specific races and cultures had evolved at different rates due to biological and environmental factors. In contrast, the typological display, arranged objects of the same type, from different places, in sequential order 'by placing forms classified as more 'natural' and organic at the beginning of a series culminating in more 'complex' and specialised forms' (Coombes 1991: 196) thereby suggesting an evolutionary progression of material culture.

At the same time, a greater effort was being made to stress the educational importance of material culture. The Education Act of 1902 reiterated the governmental prerogative of 'Education for All', in addition to which, it stipulated that school children, who were chaperoned by their teachers, could count visits to museums, as a component part of their curriculum (Coombes 1991: 191). In the same year, both contending parliamentary parties renewed their strategies and restated their objectives: 'to promote the concept of a homogeneous national identity and unity within Britain... [and] imperialism was one of the dominant ideologies mobilised to this end' (Coombes 1991: 190). Ethnographic collections were also enmeshed in these ideologies; they were classified and displayed to construct difference between self and other, between the progressive, autodidactic western subject and the 'primitive' non-western other. Thus the rhetoric of progress underscoring the displays not only served to validate the tutelary relations between the colonial power and its dependencies, it simultaneously and indirectly provided a cohesive, collective identity for western citizens. Two years later, in 1904, the League of Empire further promoted the necessity of the 'orderly arrangement and the transformation of mere curios into objects of scientific interest by appropriate classification' (cited in Coombes 1991: 194). It seems that Rowley was well aware of the wider discursive practices of the day and 'brought with him definite ideas of the place which a Museum...should fill in the scheme of social economy' (Express and Echo 1927). Moreover, he was actively involved in museological debates.: when the Museum Association held its thirty-sixth annual conference in Exeter in 1925, Rowley was inaugurated as 'President of the year' (Express and Echo 1925). In keeping with the Museum Association's directive, the RAMM's ethnographic gallery was rearranged in accordance with the 'scientific' rationale of the era. The ethnographic objects were rearticulated in order to 'tell a story' (Express and Echo 1927), in sum, the story of 'Man's' evolution. During this period, the Museum came to be regarded as 'a very important factor in the educational equipment of the City, and of the County' (Express and Echo 1927).

Figure 6: F.R. Rowley, RAMM Curator 1902 - 1934). (Photograph: Exeter City Museums and Art Gallery).

Although the ethnographic gallery went under the guise of the 'Ethnological Room', the displays combined both archaeological and ethnographic objects. Rowley's intention was to 'co-relate types' in order to show 'the process of evolution' (Express and Echo 1925), as such, it has been suggested that during this period the RAMM's Ethnological Room was 'broadly Pitt Rivers style'.[13] In a number of sections the objects were arranged geographically, however, in other areas there were displays adhering to the comparative, typological classificatory schema developed by Pitt Rivers. For example, British pre-history was juxtaposed with material culture from the colonies. According to an old guide book:

> *[the] cases ... contain specimens arranged to illustrate the use of stone in the formation of implements and weapons both in prehistoric times and amongst savage races at the present day* (Rowley 1932: 11).

The visual presentation also reinforced the racial hierarchisation of cultures, by displaying ethnographic objects alongside model samples of 'highly developed civilisation', for example, Inuit [Eskimo] kayaks were suspended from the ceiling and in cases devoted to 'ship-models', there was 'a beautiful contemporary model of a 46 gun French Frigate of the latter part of the 18th century, models of Devon fishing craft, also a series of models intended to illustrate important phases in the development of ships' (Rowley 1932: 12). The guide books, written by the knowing subjects, further reiterated the visual, evolutionary narrative, by informing the consuming subjects that the ethnographic objects 'no doubt seem strange, barbaric, and often grotesque to us who view them from the level of a highly developed civilisation' (RAMM 1964: 8).

Initially the RAMM developed in conjunction with the other modalities of knowing; for a time ethnographic collections and displays developed in symbiosis with anthropology, its new methodology and epistemology. According to Sturtevant the 'museum period of anthropology' lasted from about 1840 until 1890 (1969: 623), during a period when there was no formal teaching of anthropology in the universities. At the RAMM, the ethnographic gallery kept the evolutionary articulation for one hundred years, however, this was not an exception. It was, as Coombes argues, one of the most 'long-lived paradigms for the organisation of displays of material culture from non-western societies' (1991: 199). In Exeter, the evolutionary paradigm endured partially due to lack of funds but, more importantly, because of curatorial predilections. Up until the late 1960s, the curator was solely responsible for managing all the collections in the Museum, initially with the help of technicians and later aided by assistant curators; this personnel structure was reflected in the public spaces. None of the four curators, whose tenures spanned 104 years, were anthropologists.[14] Their interests and specialisations often lay elsewhere. For example, Rowley was an active geologist (Boylan 1969: 4), who added to the RAMM's geology collection, whereas Churchill-Blackie was predominantly interested in fine arts and silverware and during his tenure, he concentrated his energies on developing these areas of the Museum's collections.[15] Consequently, the ethnographic displays did not keep abreast with anthropological theories. So although such displays can be seen to reflect the epistemological developments in anthropology, these 'responses might not always be found in step with the modalities of knowing' (Hooper-Greenhill 1992:199).

Figure 7: Ethnological Room, pre. 1920's (Photograph: Exeter City Museums and Art Gallery).

The structural functionalist paradigm

In 1969 there was a major reorganisation of the RAMM's internal subject positions. Patrick Boylan was appointed to the newly created post of Director. At the beginning of his directorship, he implemented an organisational restructuring, creating four specialised curatorial posts. The four departmental curators were: Pam Inder, Curator of Fine Art; C. V. Adams, Curator of Natural History; Jane Baker, Curator of Applied Art; and Susan Pearce, Curator of Antiquities.[16] Again, this internal change was made visible in the public spaces: the ethnographic displays were dismantled and redisplayed to produce a 'new' truth, based on different structures of knowledge. Obviously, the imperial ideology that had informed the evolutionary paradigm was no longer appropriate, tenable or acceptable. There had been public debate and contestation 'since the 1950s of colonialism and Eurocentrism' (Clifford 1988: 235), and, in fact, by the late 1950s and early '60s, the majority of the British colonies had achieved independence. By 1969, the older rationalities that had guided the evolutionary paradigm were deemed erroneous and consequently rejected, which illustrates how 'our familiar common sense practices, brought about and sustained by our own social, cultural, and epistemological contexts, are tomorrow's quaint and misguided errors, explained by our lack of knowledge and sophistication' (Hooper-Greenhill 1992: 10).

Susan Pearce had been appointed in 1965 to set up the archaeology collection in Rougemont House, which is affiliated to the RAMM. Four years later, under Boylan's directorship, having effectively completed her original assignment, she took over responsibility for the ethnographic gallery. In doing so, she removed the British archaeological items from the Gallery and rearranged the ethnographic exhibits following a broadly geographical layout. She also initiated a programme of temporary exhibitions.[17] Each exhibition explored a specific geographical region through aspects of the ethnographic collection and was supplemented by a run of posters and catalogues.

The third temporary exhibition Pearce arranged was entitled *Masks of Africa.* To a degree, this took the form of a redisplay, inasmuch as it was installed in the main ethnographic gallery (unlike the other four temporary exhibitions) for four months after which, Susan Pearce retained certain elements of the exhibition for the permanent display. The catalogue accompanying this temporary exhibition, provided contextualised information about African society and the history of the ethnographic collection. In particular, it described the function of the mask in African culture, the role of missionaries, in particular Townsend, as well as other collectors, like colonial officials, who assembled material during this period (Pearce 1974: iv). On the one hand, this attempt by museums, over the last thirty years, to 'contextualise' ethnographic displays is very partial inasmuch as 'they tend to stress the complexity and integration, and (at most) the regional affiliations of cultures, rather than their susceptibility to change' (Durrans 1988: 163). Although such a critique does not take into account the historical specificity of an institution's restricted holdings, it certainly highlights the inescapable incompleteness of collections, which arguably needs to be addressed or mentioned in exhibition literature. Pearce's catalogue did not mention contemporary African art or the way in which contact with other cultures had influenced African artistic expression. Accordingly, the permanent display that took shape in the ethnographic gallery and the accompanying text, reiterated an ahistorical, structural functionalist narrative.

In British anthropology, structural functionalist theories had promulgated the notion that societies are self-regulating wholes, composed of networks of social relations and institutions which all operate in a complementary fashion. Such a unified, reductive view of society does not have the capacity to accommodate cultural inter-change and transformation. In the late 1960s, and 1970s a number of museums rearranged their ethnographic displays to bear out this structural functionalist proposition.[18] Collections were arranged geographically, by country or continent, and material culture was used to differentiate between different societies. Because fixed types and styles of material culture were displayed to represent specific societies, there was little or no scope to incorporate stylistic and material innovations and transformations.

In Exeter, the exhibition space was divided into six main 'sections'. Section one was reserved for displaying western firearms, section two for Asian material, section three for African material, section four for Pacific material, section five for foreign archaeology and a central area for the Native American display (Pearce 1970a: 1-13). In sum, the gallery space was predominantly classified and organised along geographical lines. Furthermore, whereas certain parts of the African section were sub-classified by tribe or region - there were cases devoted to 'Yoruba Wood-Carving', 'Masks from Yorubaland', 'Magical carvings from the Bakongo' - the other geographical sections were only classified by country or continent. For example, the Asian section comprised of 'Japan' and 'Southern India, Burma and the Andaman Islands'. This classificatory system further endorsed the ethnocentric notion that 'societies can be divided between African and American tribal culture and Asian national cultures with the implication that one is superior to the other' (Shelton 1992: 14).

Figure 8: 'African Masks' and 'Masks of the Yoruba People of Nigeria', RAMM Ethnography Gallery, 1995. (Photograph: Guy Levell).

The functionalist display also engendered other ideological implications. Like other provincial museums, the RAMM's ethnographic collection did not have the scope to comprehensively represent the non-western other. Consequently, when the collection was rearticulated in the early 1970s, each cultural group tended to be represented by certain types and classes of objects. For example, the peoples of the Congo were epitomised by Dennett's collection of *minkisi*, which, in effect, encouraged 'the notion that material specialisation corresponds to specific psychological dispositions' (Shelton 1992: 14). In addition, arranging ethnographic objects in categories, such as 'Masks from Yorubaland', served to entrench the reductive idea that certain art styles readily equate with particular ethnic identities. In this respect, because a Yoruba mask functions as a metonym for Yoruba culture (Clifford 1988: 220). Its distinct artistic style enables the West to construct difference and superficially discriminate Yoruba peoples from, for example, Igbos. Accordingly, this interpretation of material culture depends upon eurocentric concepts of what constitutes 'traditional', culturally-specific art styles:

> *western culture seems to have attained its official identity not only by defining itself against its own version of other peoples, but also by suppressing certain cultural strata at home (popular culture and history, for example)* (Brett 1991: 114).

The producing subjects were once again constructing the official version of 'history' for public consumption in and for the West. Non-western societies were placed in an ahistorical, 'traditional', context, which effectively ignored other histories, colonialism, globalisation and change. Whereas in the past the visual and textual narrative told of the story of the 'progress of man', when the ethnographic objects were rearticulated within the functionalist paradigm, an alternative narrative was generated. The consuming subject was proffered the 'edited' western version of the history of primitive, 'traditional' tribal cultures, reaffirming the assertion that even 'if exhibitions and catalogues can hardly avoid mentioning imperial dominance, this is discreetly done so as to close its history at the end of the colonial era itself, at political independence' (Durrans 1988: 150).

In 1983, David Rogers, an art historian, replaced Susan Pearce, as Curator of Antiquities. David Rogers only stayed at RAMM for two years and during this time, the ethnographic gallery retained Pearce's geographical layout. Due to David Roger's decorative arts bias, domestic clothing and household artefacts were replaced with sculptures. This shift, within the structural functionalist paradigm, generated a new 'truth': African societies were predominantly represented by the plastic arts, which confirmed the western stereotype, namely African art is synonymous with sculpture. According to Roger's successor, these displays embodied a 'heavy male bias', by principally focusing on ritual and power practices, they fuelled the stereotypical notion that African peoples are ritual-oriented, rather than practically minded.

In 1984 John Allan, the present curator of Antiquities, took over from David Rogers. Although John Allan added to the articles on display, in general, the organisation and classification of space was not significantly altered. Although he endeavoured to contextualise some of the exhibits, by placing photographs and maps inside the display cases, the exhibition remained decontextualised and just as ideologically impregnated as the earlier evolutionary paradigm. Until the displays were dismantled in 1996, the exhibition space was divided into geographical units, with parts of Africa sub-divided into tribal groupings. The African tribal groups were represented by plastic arts and ceremonial paraphernalia, in contrast to which Australasia was illustrated predominantly by weaponry. The text panels tended not to provide any historical context, notably there was no mention of Townsend or Dennett and, therefore, no possibility for the consuming subject to follow a different reading code. Basically, the visual presentation coupled with the functionalist narrative constituted the dominant reading code, dictated by the 'knowing' subject.

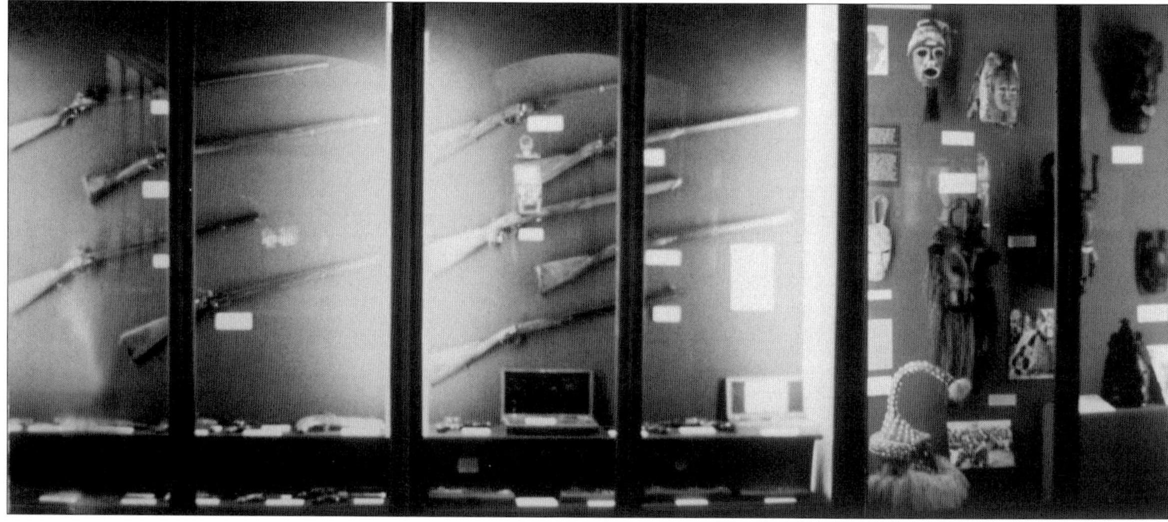

Figure 9: 'Western Firearms' and 'Masks of Africa', RAMM Ethnography Gallery, 1995. (Photograph: Guy Levell).

The exhibition space also subtly reinforced the primitivist, functionionalist narrative: the gallery was dimly-lit, with all the objects displayed in dark wooden-framed display cases, which had been installed in the 1930s. On entering the gallery, the first case the visitor encountered contained a display of western firearms (pistols and rifles) which implicitly conjured up ideas of imperialism and set the scene for a subtle ranking of cultures. The display cases had different coloured backdrops, depending on the geographical region, for example Africa was depicted by a deep red baize, Oceania by pale blue and Australasia by bright yellow. These colours evoked connotations of imperialism, oceans, and deserts, respectively, thereby proffering a sub-text that subtly reinforced the narrative classification of peoples.

Four years before the end of the twentieth century, the RAMM's ethnographic gallery housed a decontextualised, structural functionalist display, based on an out-dated academic paradigm, which, in retrospect, illustrates 'how marginal museum ethnography has been to mainstream anthropological thinking' (Durrans 1988: 163), to the prevailing modalities of knowing.

Conclusion

An effective history of the RAMM provides an illuminating insight into the way in which a provincial museum, which, in the past, promoted the image of being a neutral body and, even today, 'still perceives itself as both a purveyor of 'objective' scientific knowledge and as a potential resource centre for a broad-based multicultural education' (Coombes 1991: 210) is nonetheless a key player in the production of ideologically-informed knowledge. This role is facilitated by the curator, the knowing subject, who has often played an invisible yet significant part in the production of new and often partial truths. This practice, in turn, relies upon 'the target of the rearticulations of subject, object, space, and power [which] have no essential 'nature'' (Hooper-Greenhill 1992: 172) and therefore adopt contingent identities, according to the discursive practices in which they are located. This paper highlights the way in which the RAMM's ethnographic collection is an historical product, which should not only be displayed to yield knowledge about the histories of other cultures but should also he exhibited to illustrate Exeter's history, the local people's encounter with the wider world.

Notes

1. Originally the museum was named the 'Albert Memorial Museum' but in 1889 the Duke and Duchess of York (later King George and Queen Mary) officially opened a new wing and the institution was granted the title of the 'Royal Albert Memorial Museum'. For the sake of consistency, throughout this paper, I will refer to the museum as the Royal Albert Memorial Museum, hereafter abbreviated to RAMM.

2. This paper is based on a period of archival research undertaken at the RAMM and Local Studies Library Exeter (LSLE), in 1995. There are a number of people that I would like to acknowledge and thank: Anthony Shelton for providing intellectual stimulation, encouragement and support; staff at the RAMM, especially John Allan and Len Pole, who both gave so freely of their time, energies and knowledge, and Julia Simpson; staff at the LSLE, , especially Ian Maxted; Professor Susan Pearce and Dr. William Rea for finding time to discuss specifics; and last but not least Angela Levell for constantly supplying practical and emotional sustenance.

3. The dismantling of the ethnographic displays began in September 1996 and was completed by the end of April 1997. Personal communication, Len Pole, Curator of Ethnography, April 1997.

4. Personal correspondence with John Allan, Curator of Antiquities, March 1995.

5. See copy of page from RAMM's Register Ethnography 1868 - 1872 (1868: 1).

6. Throughout the literature, I have come encountered spellings of Yoruban words, for example: Dahomians/Dahomeyans and Chief Ogubonna/Ogubona/Okabunna, as such I have decided to adhere to the spellings used by G. Townsend in his book *Memoir of the Rev. Henry Townsend* (Exeter: James Townsend 1887).

7. Quoted from an old label c. 1930s. RAMM archive.

8. Information taken from an old label c. 1930s. RAMM archive.

9. Dr. Rea, personal communication, January 2000.

10. Personal communication with the Secretary of the Old Marlborians Club, April 1995.

11. Dennett's publications were *Seven Years Among the Fjort, Notes on the Folk-lore of the Fjort, At the Back of the Black Man's Mind, Nigerian Studies, West African Categories, British and German Trade in Nigeria, My Yoruba Alphabet,* and *The African Table of Periodic Law.* (Who was Who 1916-1928: 280).

12. Dennett was aware of Tylor's and Pitt Rivers' anthropological works. In *At the Back of the Black Man's Mind*, Dennett refers to Tylor's definition of fetishism (1906: 92) and suggests that interested scholars should read *Antiquities of Benin* by Pitt Rivers (Dennett 1906: 172).

13. Personal communication with Professor Susan Pearce, April 1995.

14. There were only four curators, namely: W. D'Urban (1865 - 1884); J. Dallas (1884 - 1900); F. R. Rowley (1902 - 1932), and Dr R. Churchill-Blackie (1932 - 1969).

15. Personal communication with John Allan, March 1995.

16. Personal communication with Professor Susan Pearce, April 1995.

17. The temporary exhibitions were: (1970) 'Yoruba Art and Archaeology', (1973) 'Arts of Polynesia', (1974) 'Masks of Africa', (1974) 'Redmen of North America', (1976) 'Towards the Pole' (Schumann 1986: 180).

18. Museums, such as: Brighton, Glasgow, Ipswich and Manchester organised their ethnographic displays according to cultural-cum-geographical regions without providing any substantial historical contextualisation (Shelton 1992: 14).

Bibliography

ALLAN, J. 1993. *Notes and diagram for the 1996-97 redisplay of the Ethnography gallery.* RAMM archive.

BAL, M. 1994. Telling Objects: A Narrative Perspective on Collecting. In Elsner, J. and Cardinal, R. (eds), *The Cultures of Collecting.* London: Reaktion Books.

BOYLAN, P. 1969. *Royal Albert Memorial Museum Centenary. Treasures of the Exeter Museums.* Exeter: Exeter City Council.

BRETT, G. 1991. Unofficial Versions. In Hiller, S. (ed), *The Myth of Primitivism: Perspectives on Art.* London: Routledge.

CHAPMAN, W. 1985. Rearranging Ethnology: A.H.L.F. Pitt Rivers and the Typological Tradition. In Stocking, G. (ed), *Objects and Others: Essays on Museums and Material Culture.* Madison and London: University of Wisconsin Press.

CHAPPEL, T. 1981. A Woodcarving from Abeokuta. *African Arts,* Vol.XV, No.1:38-43.

CLIFFORD, J. 1988. The Predicament of Culture. *Twentieth Century Ethnography, Literature and Art.* Cambridge, Mass.: Harvard University Press.

COOMBES, A. 1991. Ethnography and the Formation of National and Cultural Identities. In Hiller, S. (ed),

The Myth of Primitivism: Perspectives on Art. London: Routledge.

DENNETT, R. 1906. *At the Back of the Black Man's Mind.* London: MacMillan and Co. Ltd.

DNB. 1992. *The Concise Dictionary of National Biography,* Vol. II G-M. 1992. Oxford: Oxford University Press.

DONISTHORPE G.. 1868. *An Account of the Origin and Progress of the Devon and Exeter* Albert Memorial Museum, Exeter: Exeter and Plymouth Gazette. RAMM archive.

DURRANS, B. 1988. The Future of the Other: Changing Cultures of Display in Ethnographic Museums. In Lumley, R. (ed.) *The Museum Time-Machine. Putting Cultures on Display.* London: Routledge.

EXPRESS AND ECHO, 11 July 1925, nn. RAMM archive.

EXPRESS AND ECHO, 26 February 1927, nn. RAMM archive.

EXPRESS AND ECHO, 2 June 1934. 'Something to be seen in Exeter Museum'. nn. RAMM archive.

FOUCAULT, M. 1970. *The Order of Things. An Archaeology of the Human Sciences.* London: Tavistock Publications Ltd.

FOUCAULT, M. 1974. *The Archaeology of Knowledge.* Translated by Sheridan Smith, A.M. London: Tavistock Publications Ltd.

FOUCAULT, M. 1977. *Discipline and Punish: The Birth of the Prison.* Translated by Sheridan Smith, A.M. London: Allen Lane.

GREENWOOD, T. 1888. *Museums and Art Galleries.* London: Simpkin Marshall and Co.

HOOPER-GREENHILL, E. 1992. *Museums and the Shaping of Knowledge.* London: Routledge.

KINGSLEY, M. 1897. Introduction. In Dennett, R. *Folklore of the Fjort.* London: David Nutt.

LEVELL, N. 1996. On Keepers. In Hallam, E. and Levell, N. *Communicating Otherness: Cultural Encounters.* Brighton: The Graduate Research Centre in Culture and Communication at the University of Sussex.

MILNE, F. 1897. The Folklore Society. In Dennett, R. *Folklore of the Fjort.* London: David Nutt.

O'FARRELL, C. 1989. Foucault – *Historian or Philosopher*? London: MacMillan.

PEARCE, S. 1970a. *Notes and diagram for the 1970 redisplay of the ethnography gallery.* RAMM archive.

PEARCE, S. 1970b. *Yoruba Art and Archaeology.* Exeter: Exeter City Council.

PEARCE, S. 1974. *Masks of Africa.* Exeter: Exeter City Council.

PEARCE, S. 1989. Museum Studies in Material Culture. In Pearce, S. (ed), *Museum Studies in Material Culture.* Leicester: Leicester University Press.

PEARCE, S. 1991. Collecting Reconsidered. In Kavanagh, G. (ed), *Museum Languages: Objects and Texts.* Leicester: Leicester University Press.

POLE, L.M. 1994. *Ethnography in Devon*: Interim Report. RAMM archive.

PORTER, G. 1991. 'Partial Truths. In Kavanagh, G. (ed), *Museum Languages: Objects and Texts.* Leicester: Leicester University Press.

RAMM. 1879. *The Museum History and Description of the Devon and Exeter Albert Memorial Museum.* RAMM archive.

RAMM. 1887. *Annual Report of the Devon and Exeter Albert Memorial Museum 1886/7.* RAMM archive.

RAMM. 1890. *Twentieth Report of the Committee of the Devon and Exeter Albert Memorial Museum to the Town Council of the City of Exeter.* Exeter: Town Council of the City of Exeter. RAMM archive.

RAMM. 1897. *Twenty-seventh Annual Report of the Museum and Free Library Sub-Committee 1896-97.* RAMM archive.

RAMM. 1898. *Twenty-eighth Annual Report of the Museum and Free Library Sub-Committee 1897-98.* RAMM archive.

RAMM. 1964. *Royal Albert Memorial Museum. A Brief Description of its History and Collections.* Exeter: Exeter City Council. RAMM archive.

RAMM. 1995a. Royal Albert Memorial Museum Development Appeal. leaflet. RAMM archive.

RAMM. 1995b. Royal Albert Memorial Museum. leaflet. RAMM archive.

RAMM. 1998. Exeter Museums and Art Gallery. visitors' guide. RAMM archive.

RAMM. n.p.: Excert from *History of Abeokuta.* RAMM Archive.

ROWLEY, F.R .1932. *What to See in the Exeter Museum.* Exeter: Exeter City Council.

SCHILDKROUT, E. 1988. Art as Evidence: A Brief History of the American Museum of Natural History African Collection. In Vogel, S. (ed), *Art/Artifact.* New York: The Center for African Art.

SCHUMANN, Y. (ed). 1986. Interim Report. *Museum Ethnographers' Group Survey of Ethnographic Collections in the U.K., Eire, and the Channel Islands.* Vol.**1**, no.2.

SEYMOUR-SMITH, C. 1986. *Dictionary of Anthropology.* London: MacMillan Press Ltd.

SHELTON, A. 1992. The Recontextualisation of Culture in United Kingdom Museums. *Anthropology Today,* Vol. **8**, No.5: .11-16.

STEWART, S. 1984. *On Longing: Narratives of the Miniature, the Gigantic the Souvenir, the Collection.* Durham and London: Duke University Press.

STURTEVANT, W. 1969. Does Anthropology Need Museums? *Proceedings of the Biological Society of Washington.* Vol. **82**, 619-650.

TOWNSEND, G. 1887. *Memoir of the Rev. Henry Townsend.* Exeter: James Townsend.

WESTERN TIMES, 1 March 1886. The Late Rev. Henry Townsend. nn. RAMM archive.

WHO WAS WHO 1916 – 1928. 1929. London: Adam & Charles Black.

WITHERS GILL, J. 1931. *Notes on Dennett's Collection of Fetish Figures.* RAMM archive.

ZWERNEMAN, J. 1985. *Aus Afrika: Ahnen-Geister-Götter.* Hamburg: Druckerei Christians.

Rational Passions: Frederick John Horniman and Institutional Collectors

11

Anthony Shelton

There are few better documented examples of how a private collector and a succession of principal curators (later directors and keepers), stamped their individual predilections, tastes and styles of collecting on an ethnographic collection than that afforded by the Horniman Museum. Nicklin was able to distinguish four phases in the Museum's development based on the succession of collectors/curators/directors.[1] Successive work by Levell has vindicated such a chronological classification and demonstrated more clearly the distinctive character of each period. Despite large variations in the size of each of the Museum's regional collections, responsibility for the Ethnography Department (since 1995, anthropology) has been exercised by students of four of the five continental areas; Asianists include Frederick John Horniman (1860s-1901),[2] Richard Quick (181-1904), Otto Samson (1947-1965) and Ken Teague (1976 -present) shared an interest in Asia; Alfred Cort Haddon (1902-1915); Americanists include David Boston (1965-1993) and Anthony Shelton (1995-present); while Valerie Vowles (1976-1982) and Keith Nicklin (1982-1994), promoted an active Africanist focus. Nevertheless, not all the geographical areas represented in the collections grew at a similar rate.

This survey identifies four distinct periods in the Collection's history:

1. 1860-1901 when Frederick John Horniman (later assisted by R. Quick) exerted his personal authority over the formation of a collection consisting of antiquities, Oriental and European arts and crafts, curiosities, weapons and armour, instruments, books, and natural history specimens.

2. 1901-1946, the period when the collection and the new purpose-built museum building were presented to the London County Council and were presided over and developed by Alfred Cort Haddon, and Herbert

Spencer Harrison, later followed by L.W.G. Malcolm, Haddon's former student.

3. 1947-1965, the period of consolidation under Otto Samson, when ethnography and musical instruments became independent departments, and attempts were made to relinquish the natural history collections.

4. 1965-1998, the Boston and Houlihan directorships associated with the development of modern ethnographic field collecting, the rise of a temporary exhibition programme, and the increased professionalisation of all three curatorial departments.[3]

"A Veritable Cabinet of Curiosities of Arts and Industries of Different Nationalities." Frederick John Horniman's Founding Collection 1860-1901

Frederick Horniman harboured a fascination for things Oriental, antiquities, bygones, curiosities, and natural history specimens. Early newspaper accounts, including serialised descriptions of the collections Horniman displayed in his home, Surrey House, 100 London Road, Forest Hill, read almost like a guide to his personal tastes and interests. Although Horniman only catalogued his collection retrospectively, its early profile can be gauged from the guides to his Museum,[4] the predecessor of the present museum, and an analysis of the register entries made in March 1898 by Horniman's curator, Richard Quick (1891-1904), prior to the transfer of the material to the London County Council. In 1898, 7,920 ethnographic objects were entered into the registers. Of these 42% were Asian (16% from India); 18% were European (16.5% from the United Kingdom); 13% were African (including ancient Egypt); 5% Pacific; and 4% American.[5]

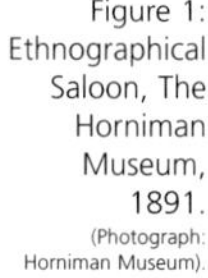

Figure 1: Ethnographical Saloon, The Horniman Museum, 1891. (Photograph: Horniman Museum).

The majority of Horniman's ethnographic collection presented to the County of London was derived from Asia and the United Kingdom. This suggests that he shared not only the Victorian fascination with the Orient, but the 19th century concern over the disappearance of rural life styles and skills under the advent of industrialisation and urbanisation. Such concerns were not uncommon in late 19th century Britain and confirm Horniman as 'a man of his times'. Despite the steep decline of the English peasantry, there was a strong movement to preserve or revive what were seen as important rural industries and crafts. The movement countered some influential members including Alexandra Princess of Wales, Maria de Rothschild and the Countess of Warwick,who established their own classes and schools to promote peasant crafts, partly as a means to improve the moral and economic condition of the population (Harrod 2000: 16). According to one advocate, craft classes "'exercised good influence' and resulted in 'happier lives and lighter hearts, tidier children, cleaner cottages, and a better moral tone all round'" (Harrod 2000: 17). Though highly idealistic, peasant art was acclaimed as a manufacture made for love, not money (Harrod 2000: 13). The movement also assembled collections, notably those now at the Charterhouse School Museum and Haslemere Museum (later Haslemere Education Museum) to help stimulate craftsmen (Shepley 2000: 7).

The promotion of folk life studies also interested the Museums Association. In 1891, Hazelius (1833-1901), an enthusiastic exponent of folk life studies in Sweden met with Bather, the then President of the Museums Association, who later fermented the growth of the folk life movement in Britain; trying in 1912, though unsuccessfully, to open a folk park in the grounds of the Crystal Palace, just a few kilometres from the Horniman Museum (Teague pers. comm.). While Horniman's own voice is conspicuously missing from records and publications about his collection, there are occasional references to the fine quality and

Figure 2: The Elizabethan Bed Room, The Horniman Museum c. 1890. (Photograph: Horniman Museum).

craftsmanship of the Oriental material that he exhibited. An interest in craftsmanship is also evidenced by his visit in 1894 to the Jeypore (Jaipur) School of Art, the Art Pottery Works in Bombay and, the Kandyan Art Association,[6] where he made significant purchases for his Museum. This interest in craftsmanship may also illuminate the reasons behind his collection of European arts and crafts; massive carved bedstead, tapestries, spinning wheels, leather bottles, watches, clocks, spring guns, old swords, etc.[7] It must be more than a little noteworthy that most of the items in his small African collection, with the exception of some beadwork from Natal purchased at the 1886 Colonial and Indian Exhibition, were derived from areas which were considered to have a higher level of craftsmanship – Benin and ancient Egypt – than was commonly believed to exist elsewhere on the continent. Other areas, like the Pacific and the Americas, not usually associated with significant technological achievements, were all but ignored, strengthening the supposition that the illustration of technique and fine craftsmanship provided a significant motivation underlying his collecting activities.

At the same time, Horniman was attracted by curiosities, lured by objects associated with singular events or personalities, and fascinated by the macabre and the absurd. Like his curator, Richard Quick, Horniman appeared in public a genial, informal, knowledgeable, and curious collector, not adverse to researching objects himself.[8] In the press he was often referred to as a collector of curios and specimens, perhaps situating him at a paradoxical juncture between romanticism and scientific positivism. Like all such collectors, he possessed his fair share of metonymic objects; the pistol supposedly used by Booth to assassinate Abraham Lincoln, a comb that once belonged to Elizabeth I; 'a chip of wood cleft by the axe of Mr. Gladstone ...'. In the Long Saloon he contrasted the large with the small '... a very fine specimen of an African lion, nine feet in length, supposed to be the largest, or one of the (largest), known to exist in this country .... As a striking contrast to this, ... an embryo elephant, preserved in spirits, measuring less than a foot from trunk to tail' was exhibited.[9] Most 19th century journalists concurred that:

> *The Horniman Free Museum ... is a Treasure of priceless value to the district. Some forty years ago Mr. Fredk. John Horniman, M.P., commenced collecting curios from all parts of the world. As year followed year, his ardour in this direction increased, and when in 1890 it was dedicated to the free use of the public it was found to be a veritable cabinet of curiosities, of Arts and Industries of different Nationalities, and a Natural History Gallery on a most extensive and magnificent scale. Since it first became an open Institution the exhibits have been vastly increased, and today, it is, without the shadow of a doubt, the most attractive museum of its kind, for every room abounds with richness.*[10]

Other contemporary accounts enhanced this summary description, by either focusing on the play of contrasts in the displays, or concentrating their description on particular noteworthy galleries.

> *On my first (visit) I was surrounded by everything that was beautiful and pleasing to the eye, and which had been brought from interesting Japan, but on Monday I found myself in the midst of all that was horrible, and which carried the mind back to the 15th century when*

living, one would imagine, was not quite so pleasant as in the present age. What a dreadful sensation took possession of me when I beheld the Spanish Torture Chair and reflected for a moment on the great sufferings it had probably inflicted upon hundreds of persons in times long gone by. ... I suddenly glanced around, but only to behold a creature in full armour which at first sight, I imagined, owing no doubt to the extreme torture my nerves had suffered, was to be my executioner. ... No matter were you turn in this room you behold figures in armour, and you cannot prevent a feeling of horror creeping over you, for in every corner are deadly weapons in endless variety. The whole of one side of the room is occupied by a large wall case, and this contains hundreds of guns, swords, pistols, bills, halberds, daggers, cutlasses, guisarmes, etc. ... There is also on view an old cannon that was dredged up at Spithead. In another case are modern cuirasses, dragoon helmets, and naval swords.[11]

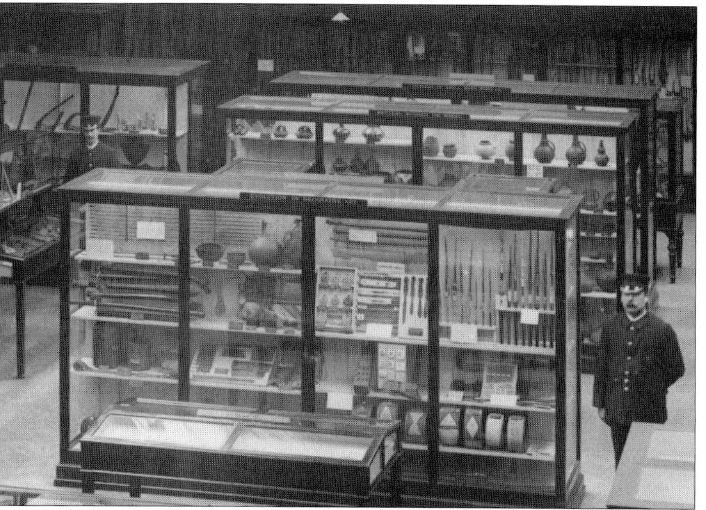

Figure 3: Evolution of Decorative Art case, South Hall, Horniman Museum 1904. (Photograph: Horniman Museum).

Another visitor complained of the gloomy surroundings conjured-up by the old English chambers: 'Visions of the Star Chamber, the Tower of London, and kindred horrors of bygone times would be recalled in an instant !'[12]

A similar bias towards mixing curios with specimens, was endemic to the multifarious sources that Horniman used to augment his collection: auction houses, dealers, trade and international exhibitions; the offices of friends, like Sir Somers Vine, one of the architects of the complex of museums and exhibition buildings that developed in South Kensington; antiquarians, like J. Corbet Anderson, Edward Lovett and Henry Willett; military men like W.J. Hider, Colonel Cochrane, and Captain Rooney who brought back pieces from campaigns in Benin (1897), Afghanistan (1898), and China; missionaries like the Rev. R. Davidson (1895), who worked in west China, and others who proved invaluable in sourcing material for Horniman's ever burgeoning collections that straddled the fast disappearing world of wonderment and the rapidly emerging and developing realms of the sciences.

Illustrating evolution; Haddon, Harrison and Malcolm 1901-1946

After 1901, with the Horniman under public administration and the appointment of the eminent Cambridge anthropologist Alfred Cort Haddon as advisory curator (1902-15), the motives underlying the

Figure 4: South Hall, Horniman Museum, 1901. (Photograph: Horniman Museum).

development of the collection changed radically. In 1904, Richard Quick left the Horniman to take up a post at Bristol Museum and Art Gallery. He was succeeded by Herbert Spencer Harrison who, like his mentor, Haddon, had been trained as a natural scientist, and shared his interest in applying the insights of evolutionary theory to the history of art and technology. In 1937, on his retirement Harrison was replaced by L.W.G. Malcolm, the former curator of the Wellcome Historical Medical Museum and a one-time student of Haddon, thus marking a forty-four year period, during which, the Horniman fell under the influence of Cambridge evolutionary anthropology.

During this period, the Horniman Museum mobilised an alternative source of pedagogic authority to transform itself into an educational institution: it acquired specimens to provide a practical illustration of the working of evolution, not only in the animal and plant kingdoms, but among the different human races that early anthropological theory had distinguished.[13] Through its incorporation into local government, the Museum became aligned with the state, and assumed an agency in the cultural reproduction of the ideological relations pertaining between national and foreign polities as well as the regional and social relations internal to the country itself. Collecting was re-focused on Africa - encouraged by two decades of exploration, pacification and settlement; the Americas and the Pacific, with the objective of acquiring material to 'fill the gaps' in the evolutionary series that Haddon and Harrison sought to mount. International exhibitions, such as the Alaska-Yukon-Pacific Exhibition (1909), and the Anglo-Japanese Exhibition (1910), were fruitful sources of acquisition. However, the personal contacts that Horniman had relied on to build his collection, were replaced by an emerging cadre of graduates, who had usually taken some formal training in anthropology, often at Cambridge and not unusually under Haddon's tutorship. The Museum also used a corps of professional fieldworkers including Haddon's son, Ernest, as well as friends and colleagues, some of whom had been members of the important 1898 Torres Strait Expedition. Donors included Charles Hose,Charles Seligman, Cooke Daniels, Stanley Gardiner and Emil Torday, as well as students, like A.R. Radcliffe-Brown, who were completing their anthropological training at Cambridge. Nevertheless, collecting was tightly constrained and appears to have been strictly subordinated to illustrating aspects of evolutionary theory. New collections were acquired like those assembled by M. Protheroe (1908), and Radcliffe-Brown (1910) in the Andaman Islands, for example, to provide a comprehensive illustration of what was then considered one of the most primitive technologies in existence. Haddon donated some of his own Torres Strait material for use in a case intended to illustrate the evolution of decorative art, and in 1909, while on a lecture tour in the United States, he purchased Inuit and Northwest Coast artefacts, some of which were exhibited to exemplify their similarities with Palaeolithic carvings and cave painting.

Oceanic material was acquired from James Edge Partington (32 objects in 1913); Sir Everard Im Thurn (1918-20); J.K. Hutchin (1903); W.H. Abbot (1903); L.P. Robbins (1932); and Lord Moyne (1936), among others. Unlike Balfour at the Pitt Rivers Museum, Haddon sought not to illustrate the global workings of the process of cultural evolution within specific typological categories, but to concentrate instead on particular regions. This may account both for Haddon encouraging the development of new collection areas - Oceania, for example, to furnish the series necessary for his decorative art displays - as well as his stringent and discriminatory acquisitions policy.

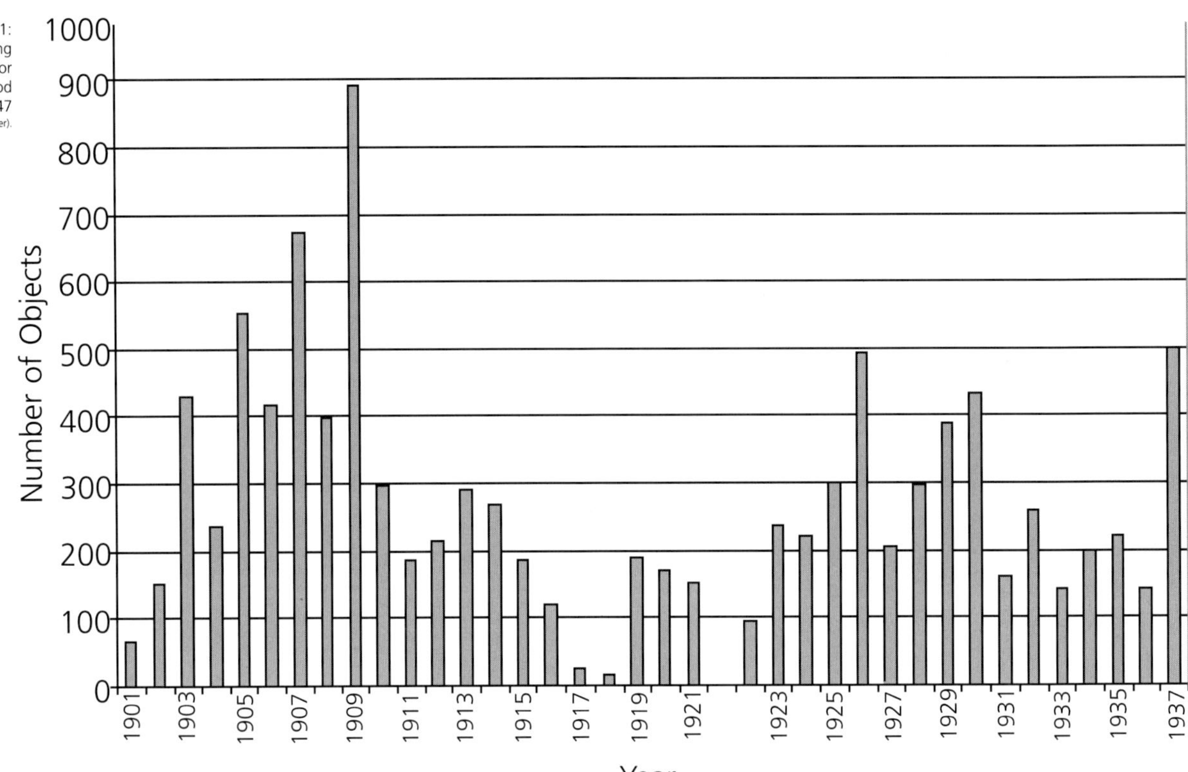

Graph 1: plotting acquisition for the period 1901-1947 (Graph: Esther Filer).

Between 1901-1947, 10,231 ethnographic items were added to the collection.[14] The period can be subdivided into 1901-1937 and 1937-1947. During the first 36 years the growth of the collection was sporadic and seldom exceeded 500 items per year; far less in most years. Only in 1907, which had seen unusually high activity in the salesrooms, and in 1909, when the Museum received the Morten Bequest of 315 ivories and related works,[15] as well as Haddon's collection of 110 Arctic and Northwest Coast objects, did the annual purchases exceed 500.

As the First World War dramatically affected the growth of the collection during the first half of the period, the Second World War had a similar impact on the second part. Yearly registers were not kept for the period 1938-1947, which corresponds to the curatorship of L.W.G. Malcolm. However, the 1968 survey of the collections estimated that no more than a total of 500 objects came into the Museum in those nine years. Furthermore, it is unclear whether these were new acquisitions or previously acquired objects that until then had not been registered. Taking these two periods together, 1901-47, the collection grew at a yearly average of 270 items, perhaps suggestive of the subordination of passion to the requirement of scientific illustration in this phase of the collection's history, but also, no doubt, to the financial limitations that the London County Council imposed on its activites.

The Second World War not only disrupted travel abroad and the art market, but also the Museum's work at home. Surrey Mount, Horniman's former residence, which stood in the gardens in close proximity to the purpose-built iron framed Museum and was used as a store, was bombed, forcing the Museum to temporarily close. It was not until the following period that any concerted, systematic collections policy was again pursued.

Otto William Samson 1947-1965. The period of consolidation.

No detailed research has been done on the Samson period, although it was perhaps one of the most important and fruitful phases in the Museum's history which witnessed the consolidation and diversification of the collections. It was also the period when the collections moved away from being a simple reflection of those cultures that fell within regions of British geo-political interests, like so many of the country's other ethnographic collections, and became more representative of the world at large.

Otto William Samson was one of a number of central European scholars - Ladislav Holy, Leonhard Adam and Ernst Gombrich were others - who fleeing the rise and spread of Nazism, took refuge in Britain where they re-invigorated the study of non-western art and material culture.[16] Prior to Hitler's political rise, Samson had been assistant keeper (1928-30), and then Keeper (1930-33) of the Far Eastern Department at the Hamburg ethnographic museum. In Britain, he held various appointments at: the Galton Laboratory of London University (1933 and 1937-9); The University of Edinburgh (1935-7); The British Museum (1939 and 1942-7), and as Curator of the Horniman Museum (1947-1965). His influence on the Horniman, despite sometimes terse relations with its governing body, was enormous; again re-orienting and re-vitalising its established networks and its sources of acquisition, to say nothing of its focus, which now turned away from evolution to material culture studies and art. He was also responsible for establishing the education centre and a handling collection for school use although at the same time, according to the recollections of some of his colleagues, he harboured a distaste for natural history and may have been responsible for deaccessioning part of its collections. According to one assessment made by W.G. Archer, the respected Indologist and keeper at the Victoria and Albert Museum:

Figure 5: Dr. Otto William Samson, (1900 - 1976) (Photograph: Horniman Museum).

> *In spite of its sparse financial resources, he (Samson) changed an old-fashioned institution into one of the best ethnographic museums in Europe and in particular built up its famous collection of musical instruments* (1976: 93).

Samson established close links with other European museums that facilitated the opening up of new collection areas. He worked with the National Folk Art Museum of Romania to assemble a large and important collection of the country's rural crafts. He obtained examples of Swiss costumes and Carnival masquerades through contacts at the Museum für Völkerkunde, Basle (1953), and the Ethnography

Department of the University of Zürich (1951); and Polish material from the Polish Cultural Institute in London (1956). He instigated an exchange with the Musée de l'Homme in Paris which, in 1958, resulted in another 36 articles from all over the European continent. Zambian material was acquired from the Rhodes Livingstone Museum (1959 and 1962), and he started to gather important photographic archives on such diverse regions as Bali and Romania. He also maintained an astute eye on museums and other organisations with ethnographic holdings in the United Kingdom which, he suspected might want to relinquish their collections in response to calls for rationalisation. In this way, he acquired collections from the Wellcome Historical Medical Museum (1949); the Imperial Institute (1950); Reading Museum (1952); Leicester Museum and Art Gallery (1953); the Whitechapel Museum (1954); the Victoria and Albert Museum (1956 and later); the Woodlands Museum, Gillingham, Kent (1957); the Royal Botanic Gardens (1958 and 1961); the Royal Museum, Canterbury (1961); the Church Missionary Society (1961 and 1965); the London Missionary Society (1962); the Commonwealth Institute (1962); and the Bethnal Green Museum (1963). Despite his restricted budget, he further augmented these collections with purchases from the Berkeley Gallery and H.F. Reiser, both London-based dealers, as well as Sotheby's.

Samson himself had done fieldwork in China (1931-2), and made field collections in the Shan area of Burma and Orissa for the Cambridge Museum of Anthropology and Archaeology (1935-7). It is not surprising that given his German background, he saw material culture as providing evidence for the diffusion of ideas and cultural complexes from one region of the globe to another. His own collecting trips to Orissa, Kashmir and Tibet had been made to increase his understanding of the cultural and historical relationships between India and China. Describing Samson's passion for Oriental art, Archer noted:

> *Although he valued their aesthetic qualities, it was their roots in popular fancy that excited him. He could see similarities of thought, feeling, symbolism, and style stretching all over Asia and with the eagerness of the born explorer, adventurer, and "big-game hunter", he included them all in his fabulous "bag"* (1976: 94).

At the Horniman, Samson established the tradition of curatorial fieldwork which has become one of the hall marks of the Museum's distinct identity. Not only did he himself make collecting trips to different regions of Europe, as well as Kashmir and Tibet (1948),[17] but he encouraged others, like the ethnomusicologist Jean Jenkins, to undertake trips to Bulgaria (1958), Ethiopia (1965), and elsewhere.[18] In 1956, he acquired the first material culture archive from Colin Turnbull thus instigating the series of mono-cultural collections which over the following decades would add to the Museum's unique resources. Samson was also a generous benefactor to the Museum, inaugurating his directorship with the gift of 437 items and adding to these throughout his term of office. Seldom did Samson travel abroad without bringing items back both as gifts for the Museum, and for himself. His private collection was described as little short of spectacular:

> *Here, in stimulating juxtaposition, were objects from the entire eastern world - pots, textiles, paintings, sculptures, bronzes, masks. My eye was caught by two examples of medieval Orissan*

sculpture showing lovers in wild embraces, a tall wooden female, also Orissan, and fondly termed "Radha", a framed picture of Srinathji, a Kalighat painting of a top-hatted English judge presiding at a murder trial, a unique Nepalese tanka displaying with superlative elegance the miniature style of Pala painting on a grandly enlarged scale. There was seemingly no end to Otto's compulsive zest for salvaging and hoarding anything that had a whiff of the primitive, popular, or Oriental (Archer 1976: 93).

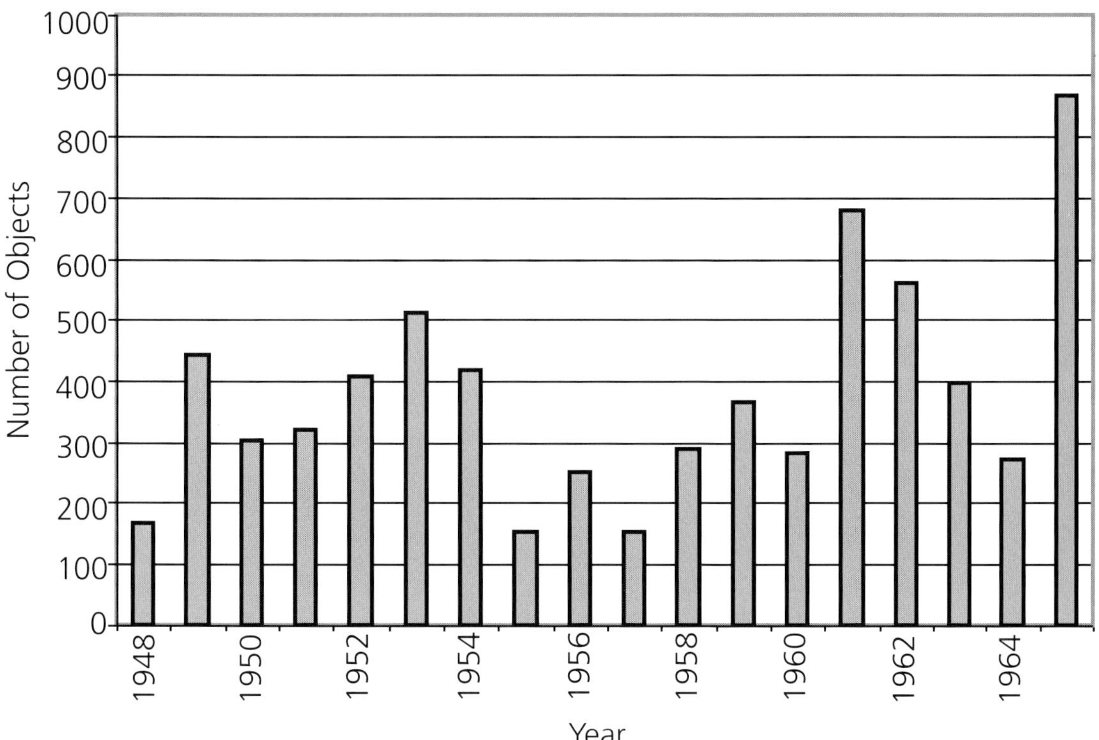

Graph 2: plotting the development of the collection, 1948-1965. (Graph: Esther Filer).

Samson retired from the Museum in 1965, and died on the 12th March 1976. On the death of his wife, Elizabeth, their collection, together with his "enormous library" and personal papers, appears to have disappeared without trace.[19] Otto Samson's relentless collecting over a period of seventeen years brought an estimated 10,000 ethnographic items into the Museum and established its international reputation.

For most of the years during this period, the growth of the collection rarely exceeded 500 items per annum. Nevertheless, the acquisition of a number of large collections; part of the collections of the Church Missionary Society and Canterbury's Royal Museum in 1961, followed by some of the London Missionary Society in the following year, and a further consignment from the Church Missionary Society at the end of his tenure in office in 1965, contributed towards the highest yearly average growth in acquisitions (588 items), that the Museum has experienced.

The Museum in the field. Boston and Houlihan 1965-1998

It was during the next period (1965-1998), with its unprecedented global political, market, and institutional changes, that witnessed the seeds of field ethnography and the consolidation and institutionalisation ideal of the Museum as an archive of material culture.

In this period, the number of institutional donations became fewer,[20] followed, from 1970, by an ever decreasing number of personal donations. The fall in personal donations may have resulted from the sharp contraction in the number of British personnel working in the former colonies and the closure of some sources of foreign items as a result of European de-colonisation and geo-global adjustments. It was further exacerbated by the dramatic increase in the market value of ethnographic and Oriental materials which gradually trickled into public awareness through popular television programmes and magazines. New sources of acquisitions and politically more sensitive collecting strategies needed to be formulated to compensate for these changes of circumstances,[21] as well as for the new situation of the Museum which first became subsumed under the London Residuary Body and then, after failed attempts to make it into a borough museum, finally came of age under central government.

Samson had already divided music from ethnography and instigated field collecting for both departments. His lead was greatly encouraged by David Boston who maintained the stable, systematic and consistent growth of the collections using similar strategies to those of his predecessor. Using outside researchers, to supplement the Museum's curators, to undertake fieldwork, and actively campaigning to encourage donations and transfers from other institutions, Boston imposed a new maturity on the institution's activities. It was his untiring commitment and that of his curators which brought the Museum no less than 13 mono-cultural collections. Boston adopted a strategy to use, when possible, some of the beneficiaries of the Emslie Horniman Scholarship Fund, administered by the Royal Anthropological Institute, to collect for the Museum. Together with the support of outside fieldworkers collecting material on behalf of the Museum, Boston and his successor, Mike Houlihan, were able to develop a highly effective and forward looking acquisitions policy, at a time of unprecedented change. Marilyn Strathern collected in the Mount Hagen district of Papua New Guinea (1966); James Woodburn collected among the Hadza of Tanzania (1966); Jean Jenkins in Ethiopia (1966); C.J. Edmonds among the Kurds and Lur of Iraq/Iran (1968); Valerie Vowles among the San of Botswana (1970-1); P. Andrews among the Shah Sevan of Iran (1971); Jeremy Keenan among the Tuareg, Algeria (1971); Erik Bigalke in Transkei, Transvaal and Lesotho (1972); Jean Brown and Cordelia Rose among the Samburu of Kenya (1972); A.G. van Beek among the Bedamuni, Papua New Guinea (1978-9); Marion Wood among the Navajo (1981); Anna Lewington in Ecuador (1987); Keith Nicklin in Kenya (1987), Nigeria and Cameroon (1980s), the Yoruba of Nigeria (1990), in the Republic of Benin (1998), and Jill Salmons, among the Ogoni of Nigeria (1992), and in northeast Brazil (1998); Ken Teague in Mongolia (1979) and Nepal (1984, 1986, 1987, 1992); Natalie Tobert in the southwest U.S.A (1993); Anthony Shelton in the Southwest U.S.A (1996 and 1998); Phil Cope in Haiti (1998); and Kathryn Chan in Trinidad (1998).

With the position of 'curator' re-titled 'director' and the consolidation of the professional organisational structure, management and curatorial functions became divorced. Samson had previously created three

Figure 6: African Worlds, South Hall, Horniman Museum, 1999.
(Photograph: Jasper Jacobs Associates).

curatorial departments, each under the direction of a Keeper. George Jarvis (1958-1976) became the first Keeper of Ethnography, followed by Valerie Vowles (1976-1982), Keith Nicklin (1982-1994) and Anthony Shelton (1995-present). Under Boston, the Ethnography Department was enlarged to include two further full-time curatorial positions to permit the geographical area specialisation necessary to develop and interpret the collections, as well as provide adequate curatorial services to the public at large (enquiries, lectures, consultancy work and exhibitions). Collections management responsibilities were transferred to a new department in 1994, under the supervision of Kirsten Walker.

The African collections assumed prominence from 1976 to 1999, during the keeperships of Vowles, Nicklin and Shelton. Vowles conducted fieldwork in south and east Africa. Nicklin continued his long term studies in Nigeria and Cameroon and built important contemporary collections from the Yoruba (1990), various southeast Nigerian groups (1980s), and the Ogoni (1992). In 1987, he collected among diverse groups in Kenya and, in 1998, as a freelance researcher, he collected shrine material from the Republic of Benin and Brazil to illustrate similarities in belief between the two areas. The work of Vowles, Nicklin and others in building this part of the collection was crucial in enabling the establishment of a new gallery dedicated to the visual cultures of Africa and the Caribbean which was opened by Sir David Attenborough on 22nd March, 1999.

Anthony Shelton continued his long term interest in the cultural similarities between Uto-Aztecan groups in central and North-west Mexico and the American South-west by focusing on the Hopi (1996 and 1998), and acquiring for the Museum a collection of katsinam and Pueblo musical instruments. His attendance at conferences also allowed for some opportunistic collecting of, for example, saint carvings from Puerto Rico, and masks from the Huasteca region of Mexico.

Mike Hitchcock (1984–1989), assistant keeper for the Americas and Europe carried out fieldwork in South China and Eastern Europe. His successor, Natalie Tobert (1990–1996) worked on pottery production in the the American South-west (1993), and India (1993), as well as on the religious practices of Hindu populations in London and Leicester (1993, 1994). Ken Teague, the Asian curator, has conducted intensive fieldwork in Nepal (1981, 1984, 1986, 1987, 1991, 1994), Mongolia (1979, 1990, 1992), Turkey (1989, 1990, 1993, 1994), and India (1995), and his current four year project in former Soviet Central Asia, is creating important collections which document the changes in material culture since the region's independence.

The number of outside fieldworkers contributing to the growth of the ethnographic collections in the last three years has increased significantly. Since 1995 the Anthropology Department has sought to build on Samson's legacy by focusing its acquisition policy on cultural areas not well represented in other museums in the United Kingdom. For Africa, important collections are being made of contemporary Dogon mask styles and musical instruments (Polly Richards 1998-2001); Bedu masquerades (Karel Arnaut 1997-1999), Lobi carvings and musical instruments (Michael Pennie 1997-2000). However, more traditional collection areas have also been developed, most notably through the work of Emmanuel Arinze who commissioned on the Museum's behalf, an Ijele masquerade, and display figures from the Nigerian Igbo (1997-1999).

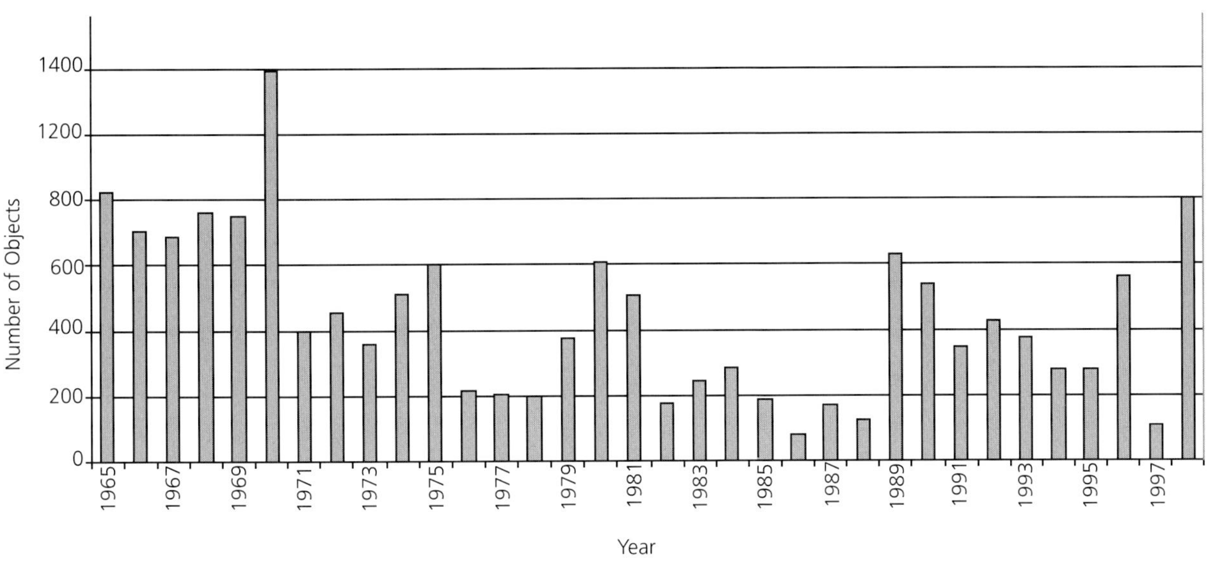

Graph 3: Plotting the Development of the Collection, 1965-1998. (Graph: Esther Filer).

For Asia, emphasis has been placed on plotting changes in the material culture and musical traditions associated with life cycle ceremonies in Uzbekistan and neighbouring countries since their independence from Soviet Russia (Ken Teague with Margaret Birley, 1998-2001). Taken together, these new emphases in the collecting policy, have effectively consolidated the course first taken by Samson, and affirmed the Horniman's as a field museum.

The Boston - Houlihan period was also distinguished by a emphasis on close collaboration with the Museums and antiquities departments of host countries. Valerie Vowles worked with the National Museum and Art Gallery, Gaborone, during her research on the San in Botswana; Jean Brown and Cordelia Rose were associated with the Institute of African Studies in Nairobi during their work on the Samburu; Keith Nicklin worked under the auspices of the National Commission for Museums and Monuments in Nigeria and in 1998, did joint fieldwork with the Musée Historique in Ouidah; Michael Pennie has nurtured close links with the National Museuma and Monuments Board in Ghana, who have directly helped the Horniman acquire Lobi material. The Ijele project and the Benin Historical and Educational Project have been sanctioned by Nigeria's National Commission on Museums and Monuments. An approach to collecting which has proven to be an extremely fruitful way of stimulating co-operation between the Horniman and the cultural institutions of other countries, as well as enhancing the documentation of the already existing collections in the Museum's holdings.

For the first six years of this fourth period (1966-1971), acquisitions remained consistently high both as a result of Boston's commitment to sponsoring field projects and to his acceptance of a series of significant private donations.[22] The peak year of 1971, however, is deceptive as it included large archaeological shard collections given to the Museum in the previous year and 118 items destined for the Museum's educational handling collections. Other years, 1976 and 1981, when the Museum acquired more than 500 ethnographic items per annum, were the result of transfers from outside institutions. With these exceptions noted, the rate of acquisition remained fairly stable throughout the period. It is estimated that in the 33 years encompassed by the Boston and Houlihan directorships, the collections grew by 14,573 items. This gives an average per annum growth of 441 items which although representing a considerable decrease from the previous period, nevertheless reflected a more systematic and coherent approach than had been attempted since the early years of Haddon.

Taking the rate of growth for the collection over the past 97 years - from 1901 when the Museum became a public institution to 1998 – at an average of 440 items per annum, the Horniman's collections show a clear and remarkably consistent and stable increase throughout the whole of its history as a public institution. Continued rationalisation in 1997, aimed at promoting interdisciplinarily, abolished curatorial departments: they were combined with Conservation and Collection Management sections in the newly established Horniman Centre for Interpretation and Research into Cultural and Natural History. Although the move met with mixed feelings, Houlihan's restructuring proved successful in promoting the organisation of seminars, annual conferences, collaborative ventures with other museums and universities, research and publications into the history of the collections as well as in more clearly defined programmes and management of research, some of which, under Janet Vitmayer, his successor, is at last assuming an interdisciplinary character.

Rational passions, curiosity and serendipity

The development of the Horniman collections discloses an undeniably strong correlation with shifts in the intellectual commitments and interests of specific institutional collectors (directors and curators); changes in their uses for research and exhibition; and differences in the focus and strategies underlying acquisition. Taken together, these have moulded the evolution of the collection away from an assemblage of Oriental crafts, curiosities, exotica, and European bygones, to an illustrative archive of artefacts that evidence the technology and expressive culture of particular societies at specific times and in determining geographies.[23]

Period	Date	No of Artefacts
Horniman's Founding Collection	1860 - 1901	7,920
The Haddon Circle	1901 - 1948	10,231
The Otto Samson Directorship	1948 - 1965	10,000
The Boston and Houlihan Directorships	1965 - 1998	14,573

The growth and character of the collections can be explained the result of specific changing narratives that different collectors, curators, and directors have tried to express at different points in the Museum's history. Contrary to the view that scientific paradigms establish a limiting rationality over collecting, the transformation of collections of curiosities, which by their very nature and rarity are limited, into scientific orders and illustrations, entail an irresistible tendency towards universalisation and inclusivity, which although endemic to science, has, so far, been resisted by the Horniman. Failure to achieve a clear illustration of a paradigm can, however, be seen as nothing less than a failure of a museum measured against the authority of science itself. Furthermore, scientific paradigms change, they become more or less comprehensive, sometimes they decline, or like cultural evolution, diffusionism, and functionalism, on which the idea of a material culture archive is partly predicated, they become discredited. These tendencies generate an incessant re-assertion and commitment to the renewal and redirection of the labour of collecting. Unlike art galleries, museums occupy a more invidious position which severely curtails their ability to de-accession collections, even when these have been made to illustrate non-current scientific paradigms. When a paradigm fails, the objects previously used in its elaboration or illustration revert to their past enigmatic status, becoming again sources for new research and evaluation in the continual and exhaustive games of knowledge creation. It would be no exaggeration to see such knowledge quests, whether informed by the rationalist or empirical motivations attributed to systematic collecting, as lacking none of the passion, furore and personal commitment, usually attributable only to private collectors.

Acknowledgement

This paper would not have been written without the encouragement and support of Nicky Levell, and her generosity in sharing the findings of her own research, including her survey of the Horniman's collections. I am particularly grateful to Esther Filer for her untiring work in making the bar charts that accompany this article. David Allen and Anne James, of the Horniman Library, helped track down various obscure or difficult references, and Ken Teague, Robbin Kenward (née Place), and Shelagh Weir, kindly shared their personal recollections of Otto Samson. I should also like to thank Nicky Levell and Ken Teague for their incisive readings of earlier drafts of this paper.

Notes

1. Nicklin ignored the period 1937-1947 and ended his survey in 1993 on the retirement of David Boston as director. Otherwise his chronology is similar to that I use here.

2. Dates refer to the period of active collecting for the Museum.

3. Boston and Houlihan have been bracketed together on the basis of their shared collection strategy. However, this ignores the tremendous institutional changes that occurred during their directorships as a result of the Horniman first being incorporated into the Inner London Education Authority, and later being subsumed with the large national museums under central government control. These changes inevitably had wide consequences on the operation of the Museum, its collections policy and research programmes.

4. In 1890, Surrey House was opened to the public and renamed the Horniman Museum.

5. These figures are based on the statistical survey of early register entries carried out by Nicky Levell in 1997. An earlier survey dated 9th October, 1968, notes 6,174 ethnographic items listed in the registers (Dept. of Anthropology Archive).

6. Nicky Levell, personal communication.

7. *Surrey House Museum* Guide 1890: 5.

8. Horniman also pursued his own research on his collection. In 1882, while visiting Regensburg, Horniman made investigations concerning Joseph Schweiger, an instrument maker who had made a lyre-guitar belonging to him.

9. L.W. 1887. *A Second Visit to Surrey House Museum.* Horniman Museum Archive.

10. Forest Hill's Popular Institution. *Forest Hill and Sydenham Examiner and Crystal Palace Intelligencer.* April. 1897: 3.

11. Through the Horniman Museum By a Visitor II. *Forest Hill and Sydenham Examiner and Crystal Palace Intelligencer.* Sept. 1896: 3.

12. L.W. 1887. *A Second Visit to Surrey House Museum.* Horniman Museum Archive.

13. Nicky Levell, Alfred Cort Haddon: *Illustrating Evolution at the Horniman Museum* (forthcoming).

14. Based on estimates from the 1968 survey.

15. The majority of which was later returned to the family who previously owned them..

16. Samson was a good friend of Arthur Waley who probably introduced him to Beryl de Zoete who donated her superb photographs of Bali to the Museum. Waley was also well acquainted with the Seligmans, who had been involved in helping fund an underground network to help scholars and artists, in danger of being persecuted by the Nazi's to flee to Germany. It has been suggested (Levell. personal communication), that the Seligman's may have helped Samson settle in Britain.

17. He later developed an interest in Mexico, possibly stimulated by Rodney Gallup, who in 1960, and again in 1967, donated a collection of 65 Mexican masks to the Museum. Samson applied to the General Purposes Sub-Committee of the London County Council's Education Committee to fund to the sum of £480 a collecting trip to Mexico. Unfortunately, because he proposed to make the trip after his official retirement, the application was deferred and later refused (Report of the General Purposes Sub-committee dated 24.11.1964). Given Samon's often frictious relations with the London's County Council it is difficult not to see their decision to withold funding as an expression of peevishness.

18. Later Jenkins made fieldtrips to Malaysia and Indonesia (1972, 1973), as well as returning to Ethiopia (see Birley, thi volume). Jean Jenkin's private collections were divided between the Horniman and the Royal Museums of Scotland.

19. After Samson's death, his wife's flat on Taymount Rise, almost opposite the Museum, was burgled several times and material stolen (Ken Teague personal communication).

20. Though a number of large collections from the National Museum of Wales; the Wellcome Museum, Bognor and the Cuming entered the Museum in the successive period.

21. Field collecting was first undertaken by individual curators during vacations, without the support of the Museum's management. Ken Teague, personal communication.

22. 1965 and 1966; Jean Jenkins Ethiopian fieldtrip resulted in 88 ethnographic objects; James Woodburn's work among the Hadza of Tanzania brought a further 74 items; and Nancy Stanfield's Yoruba research added 110 pieces to the collections. In 1967 the Museum acquired the Navajo textile collection of J.W.F Morton amounting to 86 items, and 165 European pieces belonging to Lady Vaughan- Morgan. In 1968, Boston obtained Leroux's central African collection numbering 188 pieces.

1969, saw the arrival of the Guppy collection consisting of 194 lowland South American articles; the Cooper collection of 124 pieces; the 113 items of the Radford's Ethiopian collection and Kiernan's 79 Naga objects. 1970, 110 items from the Congo donated by the Rev. L.G. West and 85 objects from Valerie Vowle's fieldtrip to Botswana and Swaziland.

23. The analysis of the growth of the Horniman's collections is based on a statistical model. All the collection figures have been obtained from the number of accessions recorded in the Museum's registers. Although we can be fairly certain that these are accurate for the first two periods, errors may have occurred after that. While we can assume a fairly close concordance between the year in which an object was entered and the year it was acquired, the two may not always have corresponded. Nevertheless this would create a minimum of error within each of the four periods that have been distinguished. Finally, it should be noted that this model finds a discrepancy between the estimated number of objects in the collection (60,000) and the number of objects recorded in the accession registers (42,724). All calculations are based on this latter figure. While it is conceivable that part of the collection was not entered into the registers (there is a no number series which has not been entered into the registers), the discrepancy between these two figures will only be resolved once the number of computerised entries has been matched with the actual number of objects in store.

A further margin of error can be expected from deaccessioning, which is not, in the main, noted in the registers. It has been ascertained that deaccessioning occurred at major junctures in the Museum's history; during its rationalisation in the early part of this century, in 1914, 1916 and 1919, when furniture and crafts were transferred to the Geffrye Museum. There is also a fairly strong local memory of a sale at the Horniman in the 1940s, when further specimens were disposed of. No accurate picture of these dispersals is presently available and further research is urgently needed, before a more realistic picture of the development of the collections can be obtained. Because of these factors the above statistical analysis of the growth of the collections should be regarded as having only provisional validity.

Bibliography

ARCHER, W. 1976. Obituary. Dr. Otto William Samson. *Journal of the Royal Asiatic Society.* 1: 93-4.

HARROD, T. 2000. For Love not for Money: Reviving 'Peasant Art' in Britain 1880 - 1930. In Crowley D. and Taylor L. (eds), *The Lost Arts of Europe. The Haslemere Museum Collection of European Peasant Art.* Haslemere: Haslemere Educational Museum.

LEVELL, N. Forthcoming. Illustrating Evolution: Alfred Cort Haddon and the Horniman Museum, 1901-1915. In Porto N. (ed), *Museums, Science, and Education.* London and Coimbra: Horniman Museum and University of Coimbra.

NICKLIN, K. 1995. Report on the Establishment and Growth of the Ethnography Collection and its Use at the Horniman Museum. Unpublished manuscript in the Horniman Museum Archive.

SHEPLEY, E. 2000. The Haslemere Context. In Crowley D. and Taylor L. (eds), *The Lost Arts of Europe. The Haslemere Museum Collection of European Peasant Art.* Haslemere: Haslemere Educational Museum.

The Arts of the Portuguese Empire: the Emergence of Cokwé art in the Province of Angola[1]

12

Nuno Porto

In his revised work on the historical formations of modern nationalism, Anderson has placed museums at the core of emerging power–knowledge relations between the metropolis and its colonies. The colonial state, acting as a guardian of collective memories and traditions, thereby deviates discourses of legitimacy to this role, dropping former claims based on 'rights of conquest' (Anderson 1991:181). In the substitution of former relationships based on trading corporations, museums were to play a central role in strengthening the bonds between the metropolis and the colonies which came to characterise modern colonialism (Ibid:180). Insofar as Anderson's approach stresses the dimensions of control and discipline, it might be glossed as state-centred. In Gramscian terms, it follows a 'political society' view, as opposed to a 'civil society' oriented approach where Karp locates the possibilities for the problematising of the very notion of community, pluralising its nature and enquiring into the fragmented social instances available for identity formation (Karp 1992: 3–5). This shift to a more processual approach to the museum is entailed in the midst of a renewed interest in museums as complex institutional sites: museums have recently tended to be seen as constitutive, rather than merely representative, of the objects they exhibit and the ideas they convey (Kirshenblatt-Gimblett 1991; Coombes 1994) as well as of the disciplines to which they refer (Latour 1989). Returning to Anderson's work, the questions we now need to pose are four: How have museums come to play the role he assigns them in the formation of modern colonialism? What sort of strategies have their curators and publics followed? What kind of museum objects have been produced by the museum culture? And even whether their purpose was previously explicitly envisaged as such, or if it was no more than the accumulated result of disparate practices geared to immediate intentions.

The purpose of this paper is to deal with such questions in the analysis of a museum developed during the Portuguese–Angolan colonial situation. This analysis contends that museological work produced in the colonial period bears a significant influence in contemporary Angolan cultural politics, namely in current debates about national culture, museology and patrimony. The aims of the present paper have, however, a more modest scope: that of disentangling the threads that led to the institutionalisation of Cokwé art during the 1950s at the Dundo Museum, in Angola. These threads articulate the museum within political, economic and scientific networks, through which diverse agencies, institutions and actors interacted, thus locating the museological constitution of Cokwé art in the processes of community imagining both at the Dundo and within the metropolis.

There are two elements involved in the outline of an ethnographic approach to the museum setting in this specific situation. On the one hand it adopts a contact perspective, though one that is different from Clifford's notion of museums as a 'contact zone' (1997), which was designed to envisage 'multicultural' social contexts. The contact perspective, formerly articulated by Pratt, was intended to treat ' . . . the relations among colonisers and colonised, or travellers and "travelees", not in terms of separateness or apartheid, but in terms of co-presence, interaction, interlocking understandings and practices, often within radically asymmetrical relations of power' (1992: 7). Clifford's application of this notion to museum analysis focuses on cultural relations within the same state, region or city, since the distances with which it deals are social and not geographical (Clifford 1997: 204). As contact zones, museums are very much a 'work in progress' rather than a finished product; they are seen as arenas for cultural and political contestation centred around the debate on group identity formation, epitomised through cultural heritage and repatriation issues (Ibid: 211). Used critically, divorced from its contemporary north-western coast contingencies, this notion proves to be remarkably fertile in analysing the position of the Dundo Museum. The binary bias the notion has so far carried (Western–other, museum–public, and so forth) does not, however, apply to the Dundo case. Furthermore, distancing itself from the notion of museums as closed, bounded places, such an approach relocates them as sites intersected by networks of diverse meaning and purpose, providing the materiality of a world to which both science and common sense relate (Latour 1990: 147). Museum work is, in this sense, a work of purification, that is of dividing, classifying, separating ideas and objects from their social constituencies, rendering them as totally isolated knowledge results (idem, 1991).

Looked at in these terms, Cokwé art is something other than the pre-colonial material culture of the Cokwé people of Angola; something other than a result of the colonial sciences practised at the Dundo Museum; something other than a vanity of the Diamang – the Diamonds Company of Angola – that was its owner; and something other than the objectified other of the Portuguese colonial community. Nevertheless, at the same time it bears in its meaning something of all of them.

The first section of the paper deals with an event. It is through this event, voiced by concrete agents, that the Dundo, a peripheral locality in a remote neighbourhood of the Portuguese Empire, becomes embroiled in the debate over the future of the Portuguese colonies. Cokwé art emerges next, as a response to this debate.

In Medias Res: A Museum in the Heart of Africa

Gilberto Freyre at the Dundo in 1951

I will begin this account of the Museum in medias res by quoting from one of its most distinguished guests, the Brazilian intellectual Gilberto Freyre. Freyre visited the Dundo Museum in 1951, when he travelled through Portugal and its Empire, at the invitation of the Ministry of the Colonies, in order to study the 'national character' and the Portuguese colonial culture. In the book he published reporting the impressions of his visit, *Adventure and Routine* (Aventura e Rotina 1952), he dedicates some ten pages to the Dundo, which he described as follows.

> *The headquarters of the Angola Diamonds Company at the Dundo welcomes us with lights that seem to be from some festive evening, but which belong to any and every evening. It is always evening feast at the Dundo, because of the contrast of its many lights with the darkness of the bush and the African villages. Its lights illuminate sophisticated gardens: civilised forms of tropical vegetation tamed by hands that we sense, from our first contacts, don't belong to the Portuguese but to other Europeans. They also illuminate red-brick houses which give me the impression of being in the United States: in California. I remember the days I spent as a professor at Stanford University: where I encountered several small towns which in the evening were almost like this one. The same tropical scenography. But only the scenography. In the air, in the environment, in the climate itself, something profoundly anti-tropical that would dominate nature, smashing its spontaneity, subjecting it to something puritanical and even to hygienic policing, profiting only from its superficial picturesqueness.*
>
> *In truth, one has here a prophylactic and almost clinical comfort, that northern Europeans, and especially North Americans, surround themselves with in the tropics; that enables them to live the life of strangers to tropical nature. Individuals who, in order not to contaminate themselves by tropical environments, live like rich patients in hospitals or clinics. An artificial life. This is my strongest feeling as I arrive at the Dundo, under this festive and, at the same time, clinical and policing lighting, with which the Diamonds Company of Angola welcomes us.*
>
> *Policing because the Dundo lives – and needs to live – in a state of permanent defence, not only against tropical diseases that might arm the technicians and other white employees that*

> *live here, an almost chemically pure life, but also against thieves that might profit from the shadows of the night, from the dark of tropical nights, to invest against the safes where hundreds and hundreds of diamonds are kept. One senses that no foreigner, no Company's employee, no white, no black is here a man at ease but is surveyed, spied on, and subtly checked by secret police . . . [The environment] is that of British novels or mystery movies. The novels and the movies I prefer. I have the feeling of being an accomplice in the making of one of those movies. The impression of being filmed. The impression that I play here some role. I'm just not sure on which side: on that of Al Capone or of Mr Holmes* (1952: 350–51).

As a guest at the Dundo, Gilberto Freyre had the opportunity to see the houses of the workers, the repair shops, the hospital and its radiology service; the nursing homes, for white and black women; the workers' meeting house, the cinema, the gambling rooms, the swimming pool and the open-air football stadium. He visited the local broadcasting station (with its fine discotheque), and praised the Diamang for its pioneering project of collecting musical folklore. Then he proceeds:

> *I also visit the Ethnographic museum kept by the company. Another remarkable achievement because of its cultural significance . . . At the Dundo Museum drawings and sculptures represent Cokwé art. A magnificent wealth of African sculpture: the kind which might be considered the dark or even black eminence behind the great experiments of European modern art. What would have become of Picasso without these dark eminences backing his Spanish genius? At the Dundo these sculptures let themselves be admired with rare exuberance. Some people consider it the most complete museum of Cokwé art . . .* (Ibid: 355).
>
> *Besides art, the museum also houses collections of . . . domestic artefacts, weapons, tools, that allow us to reconstruct indigenous life in all its purity. Our interest is caught by the good presentation that the curator has learned to give to such fine material. He chooses for exhibition purposes only the typical, the expressive, and the representative of Cokwé life and culture, leaving superfluous documentation to specialists. Once again, as I visit this museum, I am invaded by the sweet Lusitanian pride. For this is the work of the good and honest science of the Portuguese, sponsored by a company that must have some of the defects it is accused of which does not need to be attacked to fulfil its duties of a rich enterprise in relationship to the intellectual and artistic culture of the nation where it exercises its activities.*
>
> *The tendency of the Diamonds Company – and of the enterprises and companies of the kind that operate in Portuguese Africa in the same way as they do in the other Africas – perhaps reduce the natives to pure museum material. Living natives interest them almost exclusively as a labour force; and the more uprooted from their mother cultures and mechanised into technicians, workers and substitutes to cargo animals, the better they are . . .* (Ibid: 356).

I let myself be photographed, inside the museum, side by side with an old 'soba', dressed as in his glorious princely days. He is kept by the Company to give a tropical accent to the Dundo. A poor carnivalesque chief. His survival, almost as a museum figure, symbolises a whole policy of violent and quick extermination of indigenous cultures, to which the large capitalist enterprises in Africa are committed, more eager than ever to use what they call the 'living breath'. . . Natives are torn away from their tribes and are not given the opportunity to participate in new systems of sociality and culture. They are kept in a socially artificial environment – and not only artificial: humiliating – from which only their degradation might result'. (Ibid: 356).

The Angola Diamonds Company

Since its origin in 1917, the Diamang had always been considered a 'state within the state'. Its concession was constituted at the north-east of Angola, bordered in the north by the Belgian Congo, and in the east by northern Rhodesia. In addition to its geographical isolation, with the sole exception of Portuguese government agents or guests, all visitors required a Diamang permit to enter this highly policed area – it was clearly a no-go area, except for the Company's employees. Within this territory a self-sufficient, entrepreneurial culture emerged, which in the thirty-four years between the establishment of the Company and Gilberto Freyre's visit, had turned the ancient Lunda kingdom into a neighbourhood of the Portuguese Empire. Through the construction of a network of roads, the foundation of several colonial villages that spread the Portuguese toponymy over the map, and by providing schooling, training facilities and health care in the area, this part of Africa became transformed into a Portuguese neighbourhood. The Dundo was the social centre of this entrepreneurial complex, designed solely to extract and sell, at the lowest possible cost, diamonds.

I will argue that a tentatively complete understanding of Gilberto Freyre's impressions can only be acquired by looking at the relations between the centre and the periphery within the context of the world system. The same analytical prescription applies to the comprehension of the development process of the Dundo Museum. The Dundo Museum provides the means through which the cultural construction of the metropolis is mediated and channelled – a process that also shapes the identity and nature of the Museum itself. At the periphery of the Portuguese Empire, the very development of the Dundo Museum is engaged in the play of power between metropolitan nations. Gilberto Freyre's visit to the Dundo is an episode in such a play.

Although financed by transnational capital, the Company kept a Portuguese majority on the Administration Board. Its status linked it directly to the civilisational purposes of colonisation within the Portuguese dictatorial regime of the Estado Novo ('New State'). In the fifties, the Company controlled a territory of some 56,000 km^2 and employed a workforce divided between labourers concentrated in the Lunda district and white-collar functionaries distributed between Luanda, Lisbon, Paris, London, Brussels and Antwerp, which by the end of the decade exceeded more than 25,000 people. The Diamang was, since the thirties, the largest source of income for the revenues of the Angolan colonial government, which after the settler period adopted a discriminatory recruitment policy that privileged Portuguese over other nationals (Sá 1997). From its inception then, the Dundo had its existence defined by the world economic system in which it actively participated.

To make a long story short, after World War II international pressure against Portuguese colonial policy increased. Opposition was encouraged by two factors: together with Spain, Portugal was the only dictatorship remaining in Western Europe, and was therefore able to avoid (initially at least) participating in the Marshall Plan and succumbing to American, European, or other international pressure. Secondly, and most importantly, the Portuguese government had systematically refused to revise the 1930s Colonial Act, according to which a double status, based on race, was given to the population of the colonies. Whiteness was identified with citizenship; 'natives', on the other hand, according to the Indigenous Status law that regulated the premises of the Colonial Act, were obliged to fulfil every obligation towards the Colonial government, namely paying taxes, while compelled to channel any legal complaints to their traditional authorities and submit themselves to the customary judicial system. In other words those classified as natives were deprived of civil rights.

As everywhere else in colonial Africa, tax collecting ran in parallel with the institution of monetary economic practices. When natives were unable to pay taxes, they were legally forced to provide labour. This sort of practice fell under close international surveillance after World War II. In 1951, the Portuguese government undertook a constitutional revision that reframed colonial policy according to nationalist conceptions. Co-existent but separate development policies were substituted for assimilation, through which all peoples in colonial territories were made Portuguese subjects. The colonies were redefined no longer as part of the empire, but of the nation. Colonies became designated as 'overseas provinces', sharing an equivalent administrative status to the metropolitan provinces. This new conception was inspired by the 1930s doctrine of Luso-tropicalism, originally designed to explain Brazilian cultural 'reality'. According to this doctrine Portugal's relationship to its colonies was specific in that: a) it had always relied not on Eurocentric values, but on universal ones, such as Christianity, and b) the Portuguese had always mingled, both culturally and biologically, with other peoples in a quite free and voluntary way.

This is the direct link that explains why Gilberto Freyre, the author of Luso-tropicalism, was invited to visit Portugal and the colonies that year. It also explains why, when in Angola, he was taken to the Dundo. Metonymically the Diamang represented how the Angolan colonial way of life should be.

The Museal Complex

The history of the development of colonial Angola and the Diamang is reflected in the Dundo Museum, at least as far as the production of strategies for imagining communities is concerned.

Gilberto Freyre's impressions of the Dundo became, in this sense, a case in point. His rather ambiguous perception both of the Company and of the museological practices had a tremendous public impact, calling for a definitive public reply from those in charge. After the publication of the book in Lisbon, the Delegate-Administrator of the Company himself published a sequence of long front-page articles in a national newspaper pleading for his cause, the entrepreneurial side of the question (Vilhena 1954). He delegated the contest over the Museum's meaning to a writer who had already published some work on the Museum in quite sympathetic terms. José Osório de Oliveira formerly classified the Museum as a 'functional museum', as opposed to the notion of a graveyard.

> *The Diamonds Company of Angola has constituted, from 1936, an ethnographic collection that was to become the basis of a museum that is, I think, unique in the whole world: the Dundo Museum, created, in 1942, in the administrative centre of the Diamang in the Lunda district. A museum alive, functional, a museum of the Man of one region, founded in the centre of that region, to the Man of that region, and all this in the heart of Black Africa – I don't think that there is another like it nor so complete.*
>
> *Dedicated 'To the Lunda Peoples and their History', as the legend in its 'Honour Room' states, the Museum constitutes above all a tribute, unique in the world, from the white race to the African gentry of an African territory, which although occupied for economical purposes of material civilisation also maintains the intention of accomplishing a cultural work. Such work, to be effective, could not despise the culture that is specific to the natives. To have realised it is, in my view, the greatest honour of the men who run the Diamonds Company of Angola* (Ibid: 30–31).

Figure 1: General view of the entrance to the Dundo Museum, the Dundo Museum, the indigenous or Honour Room. c. 1954. (Photograph: Agosiniano de Oliveira. Museu Antropológico da Universidade de Coimbra. Arquivo Diamang negative number 13.713).

> *The original idea behind the Museum was to make it the tribal mansion of the Luanda Peoples, and so it is considered by the natives that visit it, whether they live in the Concession area of the Company, or whether they come from far away to work in the diamond mines. 'This is ours!' – such is the declaration of many native visitors, that by these words they sustain the pride (so necessary to cultivate their human dignity) of the civilisation that is theirs . . .*
>
> *Other facts demonstrate that the native of the Lunda has understood the purposes and meaning of the Dundo Museum. For instance, the spontaneous and symbolic offering of objects, such as the one that a Lunda Soba made when in conflict with his king. He took his insignia of authority that marked him as a subordinate to his king and gave them to the Museum. Or the case of a chief from the Congo, who remarking on the lack of objects from his people, offered some to the Museum . . .*

> *Let us not imagine that when they enter the Museum, objects used in animist cults lose, in the native's views, any of their significance. Workers from distant areas, when they arrive at the Dundo to accomplish their working contract, visit the Museum. When they enter the rooms devoted to their beliefs some of them run away with religious fear. There could be no better evidence that, instead of representing a cold exhibition of objects, deprived of their intrinsic meaning, the Dundo Museum is almost a temple for the peoples of the area.* (Ibid: 32–3).

José Osório de Oliveira had also written a short analysis of the Dundo Museum, to which he accords a specific value:

> *At the entrance of [the Dundo], so perfectly urbanised that I consider it a model-village in the tropics, stands the vast building of the Museum, as if the purpose had been to make it the guest room of the locality – and not only of it but of the Concession area of the Diamang . . .*
>
> *The Museum in itself is constituted by twelve large rooms: the Honour room, the Domestic Life room, Hunting and Fishing, Industries, the History of the Lunda and of Diamang, two rooms for Animistic Beliefs, Geology and Pre-History, the Room for the Reception of Natives, Fauna room, Musical Instruments and of Indigenous Art or, more specifically, of Sculpture* (Ibid: 4–42).

It is this enthusiast of the Museum who will be encouraged to reply to Gilberto Freyre. One should probably consider the publication of this reply in the form of a book within the context of a contest over the Museum's meaning and the attempt to reposition its official view. Hence Gilberto Freyre's views are dismissed as erroneous not on intellectual grounds, but because of the superficial contact he had had (only three days) with the Dundo and his obsession with the criticism of capitalist enterprises:

> *There is a very painful fact which is that, for the first time in my life, I cannot give my acceptance to a work of Gilberto Freyre. For doesn't he speak, with the lightness of a reporter, of the 'poor carnivalesque soba' of the Dundo Museum that the Diamonds Company of Angola would keep for the sake of the picturesque? This is a major injustice towards a Company that has created in the heart of Black Africa an ethnographic museum that orders the recollection of musical folklore not only to preserve, for scientific curiosity, the social culture and the arts of the people of the region, but to keep the natives faithful to their traditions, that is to their collective soul.*
>
> *What an injustice he did towards the Museum soba, the so worthy Sacamanda. If, instead of a short three days visit he had spent, as I did, twenty days at the Lunda; if instead of being concerned with diamond exploitation he had dedicated his attention to indigenous life, like I*

> *did; if he had assisted, as I did, in the circumcision mukanda and seen the respect that the old Sacamanda inspires in the natives, he would not, I am sure, have committed such conspicuous and double injustice: towards the Whites, and towards the Blacks* (Ibid: 23–4).

Despite dissent over whether the Museum is a tribute to a devastating colonial policy or, on the contrary, to the African peoples of the area, two issues seem to be beyond question: the first of them lies in the agreement over the Museum as the arena under dispute. Inasmuch as the Museum is thought of as a surrogate for the Company's practices, the dispute becomes a problem of interpretation. This, in turn, is not focused on the Museum as such, but rather on what its practices and its policies of representation reveal about the Company's purposes, and about Portuguese colonial identity. Hence any assertion over the nature of museological practices becomes a battleground. Do such practices provide the means of preventing native cultures from becoming extinct? – in which case the action of the Portuguese is in line with their Luso-tropical strategy; or are they means of turning indigenous peoples into museum objects? – in which case there is no distinction between Portuguese and other colonial cultures. Thus, the Museum, the corporation and Portuguese colonial identity are wrapped in the same discoursive formation, each of them forming the different sides of the same object, and each providing, reflectively, the means to understand the other. You want to understand the Company's role in the civilizing mission? Go to the Museum. You wonder whether this role is akin to other colonial policies or if it has a Portuguese specificity? Visit the Museum: there you can check the Company's activities, learn about its relationships with the 'natives', compare it with other African colonialisms and situate them alongside the history of the Portuguese in Angola. All the questions lead in one direction: the direction of the Museum.

The exchange of arguments is therefore akin to a backstage debate on museum culture (Sherman & Roggoff 1995), in which the representation of 'native cultures' becomes a resource to characterise colonial culture. Self becomes the other's other, the characterisation of which the Museum is called to define. The dialogue over such a definition circumscribes a second area of consensus around the notion of African art, which is made a valued issue in establishing the specificity of Portuguese colonial identity. In both discourses African art, rather than just a product of mere recollection, has a scientific status. To José Osório de Oliveira, art even fulfils an emancipatory role in the 'natives' ' lives, since it contributes to keeping the 'natives' 'faithful to their traditions'. In Gilberto Freyre's view, African art reconciles 'the good and honest science of the Portuguese' with their universalistic attitude, revealing to the world the roots of Western modernist fine arts. This consensual museum artefact, 'African art', is used to deploy a localising strategy depicting a Portuguese colonial identity as based either on the recognition of the other, mutual respect and even praise, for it which echoes concerns over the problem of 'native' detribalisation, or in Gilberto Freyre's theory, of the Luso-tropical universalistic, and the uniqueness of the Portuguese way of relating to other cultures.

In this sense the Museum becomes more than just a double-sided contact zone relating self and other as an unproblematic pair, but an arena in which the fragmentary and constructed nature of such categories becomes apparent. As this dispute demonstrates, from the contact between the Portuguese and the 'natives' a second sort of contact is produced in which one of the terms, the otherwise nonproblematic 'us', becomes strongly subjected to contestation. This contest over the definition of the 'us' that emerges in the contact process with a much more easily acceptable 'them' demands that the Museum – as the zone where the contact process is seen to originate – is situated within its field of influence. It demands that the Museum is apprehended as the articulating locus of diverse networking procedures, rather than being assumed to constitute a bounded, closed or self-contained entity. In other words, only a shift to a broader perspective might give a comprehensive account of the multiple layers that build up the field (or 'zone'), and only a shift in methods might recover the complexities of the contact as a multi-oriented process.

In so doing one has to acknowledge that the undisputed assumptions about 'the other' which accord it a fixed and stable temporality, which exclude it from any possible historical agency and frame its culture as a bounded, self-contained whole susceptible of being reconstructed through the accumulation and display of objects, result from the same modernist assumptions (in the sense of Latour 1991) that subordinate its future under Portuguese history. In the process of transforming the Lundas on the periphery of the Portuguese Empire, the Museum is given the role of a mediating device through which the divide between nature and culture, past and future, atavism and scientific knowledge is rendered into purified elements. The debate between Gilberto Freyre and José Osório de Oliveira is therefore nothing other than a discussion of the outcome of such an achievement.

In this sense the issue at stake presents the clash between two different tendencies in the cultural construction of the periphery (Hannerz 1991). On one side Freyre questions whether or not Portuguese colonialism is similar to any other forms of colonialism, concluding that its effects, at the periphery (albeit in an ambiguous form), are not dissimilar to other forms of European colonialism in Africa. Against this diagnosis, the result of which would be the establishment of homogenous cultural forms (idem 1991: 122), Oliveira advocates the specificity of its geographical and cultural setting, vindicating the whole process as one of maturation. Both positions are, nevertheless, determined by complex interwoven networks in comprising the interests of the Portuguese government and the Company regardless of the common or distinctive nature of their shared practices. The scale of this debate is not local, nor even national. In order to legitimise its positions vis-à-vis other states and international organisations, the Portuguese government mobilised the Portuguese-speaking world, making one of its leading mentors, Gilberto Freyre, into its spokesperson. The Company, in turn, mobilises its own communication networks to place its own delegates at scientific congresses, popular exhibitions and major newspapers. In the process a set of mediators is produced or enacted: texts are written and published in books or presented at congresses; exhibitions, based on museum collections, are organised and toured nationally and internationally; opinions from the elite visitors of the Dundo Museum are printed and circulated. It is these shifts in networks and agency roles, the extension in the scale of the issues brought to the foreground of the dispute, as well as the positions of the mediators produced in the course of the contest that have to be taken into account when dealing with the Museum as a contact zone.

The notion of 'African art', which brings both contestants onto a common ground, is one such mediation. It is spurious to establish a causal link between Gilberto Freyre's visit and the growth of African art collections at the Dundo Museum. Instead, its steady and articulated development during the fifties should be accepted as a matter of fact. Such development is reinforced by the self-proclaimed policy of developing colonial sciences in the Museum complex, a policy very much in agreement with the Portuguese state's encouragement of procuring scientific knowledge of its overseas territories. The Museum possessed a few hired scientists supervising the areas of ethnography, pre-history, zoology and botany, who established an effective lead in worldwide academic networks which made the Museum into a field laboratory. The resulting scientific investigations of the diverse areas of knowledge were circulated in printed form in the Diamang's Cultural Publications, a glossy journal distributed worldwide, and exchanged with other major scientific publications. Until 1952, it was Portugal's only serial scientific publication exclusively devoted to scientific knowledge of overseas territories. In the context of such practices, the collection and display of African arts became a strategic field to be developed at the Dundo Museum.

African Art at the Dundo Museum

The notion of 'African art' reveals sets of specific practices which, once again, place the Museum at the centre of disparate confluences of meanings which articulate local structures with broader networks, linking the Company with international markets, the scientific communities both in Angola and abroad, political concern regarding 'native' policy, and even with the international division of labour. At the Museum level these different issues are conflated in the making of 'African art' collections.

Three sort of objects can be classified as African art: first, ancient objects that were collected locally – resulting from the Museum's own activities since 1936, or from the work of visiting ethnographers, such as the German Hermann Baumann, or the Belgian Marie-Louise Bastin, respectively from the Berlin Museum and the Musée Royale d'Afrique Centrale of Tervuren. In addition, African 'art' works were acquired from other museums, 'primitive art' galleries and auctions in Europe (by Diamang agents in Lisbon, Brussels, Antwerp and London). These objects were displayed, mainly, in the African Art Room, except for the objects collected by Baumann, which were grouped and preserved as a distinct collection (The Hermann Baumann Collection) in their own room. Secondly, African 'art' also included part of the objects relating to Cokwé cultural life displayed for ethnographic purposes. The Honour Room, for instance, displayed a rich series of ancient chiefs' thrones locally collected and praised for their artistry. Finally, 'African arts' also applied to contemporary objects, the majority of which were produced at the Museum's Native Village. On the one hand, the village served as a memorial to the typical Cokwé villages that were doomed to disappear due to progress; on the other hand, it provided lodging for working artists, in order to avoid the extinction of traditional arts and crafts in the area. Additionally, the Native Village also housed the Museum *soba* (chief) and native visitors that came to cooperate in the Museum's research programmes, or simply to visit the Museum. Natives housed at the

Figure 2: The Museum Native Village. 1956. (Photograph: Agosiniano de Oliveira. Museu Antropológico da Universidade de Coimbra. Arquivo Diamang negative number 15.006/956).

Native Village were all Diamang employees assigned to the Museum services: 'smiths', 'painters', 'weavers', 'musicians', 'dancers', 'sculptors' were all hired artists living by the clock, working under the supervision of a white employee and producing objects for the Museum. These contemporary objects were signed. 'Artists' were, under the Company's division of labour, 'skilled workers', earning the salary accordant to their category.

Besides classifying objects and persons, the notion of 'African arts' was also extended to performances, disciplinised as folklore, that played a significant part of the Company's yearly celebrations as well as of the occasional ceremonies offered to 'distinguished guests'. The most important of these regular celebrations was the 'Yearly Indigenous Grand Feast', which was regularly held from the 1950s onwards. This celebration developed as a definitional ceremony (Myerhoff 1986): early in the morning the population would concentrate at the Dundo central square, named after the nineteenth-century Portuguese explorer Henrique de Carvalho, to participate in hoisting the national flag and singing the national hymn. An award of medals and Portuguese flags would be made to cooperative traditional chiefs, then everyone would attend an open-air mass after which they would visit the Museum. From here, they would go to the Native Village, where they would watch a 'native' show that would include music and dance. The music and dance at the Native Village's show ground alternated with speeches from the District Governor, the Company's Administrator at the Dundo, or some other high-ranking colonial officer or company agent. Medals or monetary prizes were then distributed to 'remarkable' or 'retiring' company workers.

The notion of African 'art' at the Dundo refers to these different objects and practices. In the first sense reported, the economic networks of the Company overlap with the cultural and scientific networks, at the core of which art serves as a means of retracing Cokwé cultural identity as well as a classificatory device of the social landscape, and an administrative category, which identifies the 'artist' as a type of 'native' worker. These, in turn, relate the Company's organisation of the labour force to its ascribed role, through the Museum, of salvaging local cultures by maintaining the production of certain kinds of objects that would otherwise be condemned to extinction. Through such a process, the Company's administration saw itself as fulfiling the social purpose of preventing detribalisation by providing the 'natives' the means of cultural reproduction.

Such a diversity of practices related to objects (regional collection, worldwide acquisition, museum production) was consistent with the new Portuguese colonial policy of assimilation, based on the Luso-tropical doctrine which took for granted the Hamitic theory, in which African peoples were descended from a common source, and their adaptation to different environments had given rise to the African's typical organisation, the tribe. Tribes, in this sense, were local variations on a common human adaptive response whose racial basis was historically justified allowing for an essentialist discourses on the African Man, spirit, or soul.[2] Thus, sculptures and other African art objects were sent to the Dundo as part of a repatriating operation, without having ever left the national territory. They were sent back to the African motherland, regardless of their cultural origin, which was only relevant inasmuch as it added another piece to the African puzzle. At the Dundo Museum this perception of 'African art' supported the salvaging process as a means of preserving local recollection, as well as sustaining local production to secure those cultural values threatened by colonial progress. The securing of such cultural values had less of a philanthropic basis than a social one, since the rapid extinction of local tradition would have entailed the danger of detribalisation, and of their unsuccessful assimilation into the coloniser's culture.

The purification of the category 'African art' began to take place only in the mid-fifties, through the work of Marie-Louise Bastin. Her work on artistic styles contributed to the beginning of serious speculation about pre-colonial cultural boundaries, and for the periodicisation and dissemination of technical skills. It also permitted the formulation of a hierarchy between cultural areas according to the refinement of their material expressions.

Marie-Louise Bastin's first works were published by the Diamang after her fieldwork at the Dundo in the fifties. Her research asserted, using aesthetic criteria, the courtly nature of Cokwé art. Her classification opposed the thesis that Cokwé art was 'merely tribal' (Bastin 1982: 46). The argument she set forth had implications that went far beyond strict aesthetic qualifications. Courtly art implied a more complex form of social organisation. As this form was not contemporary, it endowed the Cokwé with historical depth. The tracing of this history, anchored on the formal character of art objects, provided a broader context for the Cokwés' own existence and regional relevance. What was once local and accidental, confined to the parochial interests of a colonial district, became of regional and wider significance for the understanding of specific African peoples' territorial migrations, their social organisation, their political institutions and their historical development.[3] Conversely, objects that dialectically sustained this discourse had their documentary, historical and market values significantly increased. As the work progressed, the concomitant development of the African art rhetoric and market effected further displacement of material culture from Africa, by privileging its material testimony over its historical, cultural and aesthetic significance and relocating it in a Western network of museums, galleries and private collections, which appoint themselves as guardians of African knowledge. Once again, Bastin couldn't put it more clearly. Her later description of styles and sub-styles of Cokwé art is based on objects not only from the Dundo and the Tervuren museum, but also from the Museum für Völkerkunde (Berlin), the Museu Nacional de Etnologia (Lisbon), the Museu de Antropologia da Universidade do Porto (Porto), the Museu e Laboratório Antropológico (Coimbra), the Casa Museu Teixeira Lopes (Vila Nova de Gaia), the Pace Gallery (New York), as well as from the private collections of Lance Entwistle, Warren Robbins, Jeff and René Vander Straete, Jean-Claude Bellier, and the Ginzbergs. Concluding her study she remarks:

> *These 'contemporary' carvers sometimes display considerable technical skills. Though their productions are generally mediocre, this is probably because they have been caught between two civilisations. On the one hand, they cannot fall back on traditional values. On the other, they are awkward in assimilating what Europe has to offer. It seems that all African artists are faced with the same problem* (Ibid: 255).

In other words, African art related to past history, was rarely to be found in Africa, and was anyway not susceptible of being voiced by Africans.[4]

Last, but certainly not least, African art was becoming a promising global commodity, valued under the same empowering criteria as other arts, mixed with ethnographic varnish, and polished by the rhetoric of antiquities. A good object should have a specific style, it should have been used in some sort of local ceremony, and preferably should no longer be actively produced. In other words, it was the western global discourse on African arts that set the stage for the validation of Cokwé artefacts as a distinct feature within the global inventory of African objects. The Dundo Museum, its collections, its workers, its owners and the nation that hosted them disseminated the consequences such a novel condition implied.

Objects produced locally, by contemporary artists experiencing the difficulty of 'fall[ing] back on traditional values' and the awkwardness in 'assimilating what Europe ha[d] to offer', progressively became disassociated from the 'art' label and re-evaluated as handicrafts. As such, circulating side by side with the originals in exhibitions, photographed in catalogues and described in texts, new sculptures became the tokens of the assimilation process, objectifying Portuguese colonial domination. Unlike displaced art objects, these museum-made, contact artefacts conveyed the exploitative material system of their production, circulation and consumption, as well as the diverse investments of meaning they were (inter)subjected to in those processes. Being initially engendered within the networks of scientific knowledge, they then shifted to the subordinated practices of a form of life which situated the Cokwé in the world system. By the sixties, objects such as those sculpted at the Museum workshop by the Company's specialised employees labelled as sculptors were offered to distinguished guests of the Dundo Museum. Later classified as fakes, they were the white man's trophies of his civilizing mission.

Thus the 'Other Nations', the Lunda peoples, the Cokwé, the colons, as well as the Portuguese were all established as social categories through museum practices. These did not, however, become stable cultural forms. They were rather relational, mutually interactive and, internally among themselves and externally against each other, open to contest. It was in the midst of such contest that objects such as these were commonalised. Meeting a colonial one-sided view of the situation, they also met what had by then been established as valued native identity, 'the artist', and a current basis of social interaction: the production of traditional 'art' objects according to formal criteria that had been formerly tamed and displaced.

As a product of contact, African art became as dynamic a category as the contact itself. The idealisation and purification of this category reveals itself to be a process, rather than an achievement accomplished and taken for granted. Alongside the process different networks of interests, operating at different levels, shape the Museum as the locus of contact, highlighting the fluidity of its boundaries and the articulation it promotes between operative instances and agencies mobilised by distinct ideas and objectives. These sometimes ignored one another, sometimes conflicted and at other times worked towards mutually negotiated purposes. Therefore, the ongoing contact is a feature of the Museum itself in part because as a peripheral zone within the modern world system it was built at the crossroads of diverse paths of cultural, political and economical meanings, distributed through diverse interlinked and sometimes superimposed networks of dissemination. Objects were tokens of those dynamics: for the sculptor they were part of his subordinated way of life; for the Museum and the Company they were as much a material proof of their success in salvaging the very cultures they afflicted, as a statement of their identity as the agents of that process; for the visitor who received them they were tokens of their participation in the endeavour.

Consequently, the redistribution issue raised by the debate between J. O. Oliveira and Gilberto Freyre became resolved through these museum dynamics. Not because there is only one possible answer in this debate, but rather because the process of purification of the category of 'African art' engenders its own impure other. Thus depending on the threads each disputant followed in the search for an answer, both were right and wrong. The role of Cokwé agents engaged in this process largely remains still to be explored. It is quite obvious though that for a generation born in the twenties in the Lunda district, the Company and Portuguese sovereignty were experienced early in their lives. The particular socio-economic conditions they created constituted a naturalised social instance endowed with specific agencies with which they interacted. That the Museum became one of such agencies is also obvious, and in a context of the progressive repression of pre-colonial habits it provided some sanctuary as well as functioning as a source of that repression. The establishment of colonial hegemony makes its existence desirable and praiseworthy, because when the use of specific artefacts was prohibited, after being offered to the Museum they could again be used and their narratives handed down to future generations. When, on the 'natives' ' side, traditional oppression became untenable, subordinates could shift to another oppressor (the colonial one). Since the Portuguese administration nominated most of the 'traditional' *sobas* according to innumerable factors it might very well have happened that a chief's offer of his status signs to the Museum was meant as an ironic gesture. Finally, it might not hurt to speculate that the Museum's attribution of value to certain objects, namely ceremonial ones, is not completely at odds with the gerontocratical values of Cokwé culture, and their own notion of *Mutenje* (the place where spiritually powered objects are kept).

With these and many other speculations in mind (after two previous refusals due to warfare in the area), in November 1997 I was allowed to visit the Dundo Museum. What is now called the North Lunda district is one of those Angolan regions where war has been raging for more than thirty years; beginning with the nationalist movements against the Portuguese, and followed from 1975 onwards by conflicts between the government party, MPLA (Popular Movement for the Liberation of Angola), and UNITA (National Union for the Total Independence of Angola), each previously backed by Eastern or Western blocs during the Cold War. What follows is largely based on a two-week period in Angola, of which five days were spent at the Dundo.

What I've been saying so far, however, is linked to my glimpses of the contemporary debate on Angolan national culture (and from other post-colonial situations). My view is that the national culture strives against one central problem in dealing with museum collections: since colonial collections, such as those housed in the Dundo Museum, were largely means of appropriating 'native culture', the question is how to appropriate an appropriation.

The National Museum of Anthropology

The location of the major shifts in scale and the nature of the centre–periphery relations that envelop contemporary museological scenarios are firmly situated in the process that led to the formation of the Popular Republic of Angola on 11 November 1975.

After the nationalist movement led by the MPLA took power, the whole territorial grounding of the state was reshaped, in line with attributed pre-colonial regional identities. As elsewhere, the former metropolis and its institutions and practices became the other to be expunged, as Angola repositioned itself within the Eastern Cold War bloc, and emerged as a regional potency. Within the first decade of independence Angola replaced all Portuguese topographical designations with pre-colonial ones. All museums were nationalised under the 1976 constitution and placed under the National Direction of Museums and Monuments, which was intended to return to the people what had been taken from them by the colonialists.

This, together with the ideological claim that the state embodied a popular movement, in fact became a distinctive feature of post-colonial Angolan museology. The official *Manual de Museologia* described the situation in the following terms:

Figure 3: The Indigenous or Honour Room. (Note the portrait of Agosthino Neto the first President of Angola, top left, and the portrait of Eduardo dos Santos, the current President of Angola). (Photograph: Nuno Porto)

> *Under colonial dominion, the people, ever and ever more engaged in the consumer society created by colonialism, were not interested in cooperating with museums. We still do not know what the popular reaction will be to a request for objects for the Museums. We are sure that it will make this Museological Movement grow. That such a movement will lead the people to make voluntary deliveries each time bigger, though we should not forget that each fabricated artefact implies a certain amount of work and that work is the people's capital. It will be necessary to conscientise the people to help the Museums. It will be necessary to lead them to be co-author of museums (together with museum workers), to provide objects neither refusing them nor trying to sell them.*
>
> *The main task of contemporary museology, even before that of the collection of patrimony, is to make an inventory and provide for secure conditions.* (Manual de Museologia 1979: 24–5).

Such a need sprang from the fact that parts of the collections housed in what are now national museums previously belonged to individual colonialists, and were not fully inventoried. The execution of the movement itself relied on a programme of Experimental Museums, divided between Urban and Rural Museums, each with its own public orientations. Its common ground consisted of five objectives:

a - To lead the People to make museums themselves.
b - To bring to light dispersed, and sometimes hidden, patrimonial properties.
c - To discover the interests of each layer of the population.
d - To progressively identify errors, or incorrect ideas, concerning the objects.
e - To gather information (Ibid: 25).

Such a project would be accomplished, at the Urban Experimental Museum, by leaving its rooms empty and available to public curatorship. The *Manual* then proceeded to suggest that 'In these exhibitions, some rare or highly valuable objects will eventually appear. These will be immediately classified or acquired' (Ibid: 26). In contrast the Rural Experimental Museum is

> *even simpler. It is constituted by one or two pieces from each Regional Culture. Or two fine-arts pieces, one or two from the Nature Museum. With this material, a dynamisor (this may be done during campaigns) tries to conscientise the people from a Sanzala, especially elders and sobas, doing a brief presentation and colloquia. She will then invite the people to offer a large house where they can display what she thinks to be expressive of their culture. The People should also nominate, from among honoured persons of the village, those responsible for the Museum . . . This process can be started by a visit of a soba, of the Elders, or of a specific group of villagers to the closer Regional or National museum* (Ibid: 27).

The Experimental Museum, be it Urban or Rural, is meant to be a nodal point in a national network of museums that is organised by political administrative agencies. According to the *Manual* there should be a planned museological development that would encompass the creation of Agencies for the National and Special Museums; Regional Museums, Provincial Museums, Municipal Museums, Communal Museums, School Museums, Units of Production Museums, and so on (Ibid: 33). The purpose of such a network would be:

a – To influence the ideological formation of the masses, especially working, peasant and student masses, in the direction of the acquisition and consolidation of materialist thoughts, scientific knowledges and realistic vision of the national problematic.
b – To combat through scientific explanation the alienations of the past that colonialism has tried to instil in our people.
c – To develop the creative activity of our people, of their artists and intellectuals in particular, within the Cultural Revolution defined by the competent organisms of the

MPLA and of the government.

d – To preserve for future generations the creations of past men and explain scientifically the true nature of the transformations of historical, social, political, natural and other phenomena.

e – To research, improve and systematise human knowledge, especially of Angolans, through the diverse Museological Disciplines.

f – To create an ever greater identity amidst the working staff of the Museum and the worker or student public of the Museum, in a way that both groups may feel equally concerned by the Museological Collection and the civilisation it represents (Ibid: 31–2).

If this project still holds, the real politics of contemporary Angola has, in the face of warfare, an unstable economic system, widespread poverty and consequent restrictions on state cultural policy, suffered serious compromise. The National Museum of Anthropology has become, in this process, one of the objects of state interest.

The history of this museum in relation to the shift from colonial to contemporary museology in Angola is telling. In 1979 the collections of the National Museum of Anthropology were estimated at about 60,000 objects. From these, about 3,000 were first-choice artefacts that had been sent from the Dundo Museum in 1974, to be housed in the headquarters of the Diamang in Luanda, as part of an operation established to reverse the secretive policy followed, until then, by the Company. Despite the War of Independence, the sixties were the most prosperous years of the province, and faced with international pressure it was thought that secrecy no longer served the Company's interests. In effect, the Diamang brought to Luanda objects from the Dundo to give its enterprise more visibility, especially its social programmes.

At the National Museum of Anthropology, located at the former Diamang Luanda headquarters building, a significant number of objects from the African Art Room of the Dundo Museum, as well as ancient Cokwé sculptures, are displayed to give an overview of the cultural diversity of Angola. Objects of this sort become identified with the notion of patrimony, in the sense of constituting a common national heritage, a political category operationalised to oppose discourses on individual identity that incorporated race, ethnicity, religion, class, education or urbanisation, to name just a few. The point was that, as Angolans, all nationals should be able to identify themselves with these objects, which were destined to become part of everyday visual culture, and become identified as the 'Angolan thing'. The dissemination of these objects as the common patrimony became so focused that it provided a source of ironic comments. In a footnote to a text dealing with the problem of motivating the authorities to acknowledge, in a broader sense, cultural patrimony, Henrique Abranches, one of the leading intellectuals in the Museum-oriented debate in Angola remarked that the ignorance of those responsible for the collections makes it impossible to demand the return of several objects. He laments

> *the secrecy, the total absence of any reference in the national or foreign press of [what he calls the] 'catastrophic theft' of several paintings from the Luanda Central Depots. These paintings, it is assumed, didn't count much to the 'mediocre' authorities because they were foreign: Dufy, Lautrec, Matisse . . .* (Abranches 1989: 16, note 1).

At the national policy level what is being defined as national patrimony are those artefacts easily classifiable as African art, which in the specific case of Angola had been directly linked with the long duration of Portuguese colonial domination. What colonialists had valued for artistic and aesthetic qualities, now, under the nationalist state, became valued as pristine, pre-colonial, and historically formative of the present cultural diversity of the country. Such is the source of their artistry, and for this reason they must be seen as constitutive of the common legacy. This political view of these objects, furthermore, defends the survival of colonial objectifications and social practices, which had been made popular from the end of the fifties, through the establishment of handicraft centres.

From the contemporary perspective, handicraft centres were devices to control a proletariat that would otherwise rebel against colonial oppression. Artefacts produced there, like those of the Dundo Native Village, lacked any spontaneity as well as traditional inspiration. They were, however, classified as African art in order to cover up the exportation to Europe of valuable objects. The colonial project of deprivation, both material and conceptual, was what had given rise to this 'degenerated art' (Abranches' expression). With the destruction of the colonial system such products must be erased. One way to achieve this was to promote true objects (Ibid 1980: 35–42). But this could only be accomplished with the development of an art history that participated in Angolan cultural life (Ibid 1989: 16).

By the end of the eighties it was thought Angola would be militarily pacified and, as a result of the fall of the Eastern Bloc, would adopt a more flexible policy towards capitalist enterprises. At the beginning of the nineties the MPLA and UNITA signed another peace treaty that led to elections. Transnational companies invaded the country with services that ranged from civil construction to nearly anything else (which includes all kinds and scales of security services), but especially those geared towards oil and the eternal diamond. After the Portuguese, and then the Cubans and Russians, Luanda became more variegated and cosmopolitan. Nationals from virtually any country, NGOs of every sort, all kinds of UNO agencies, made themselves present everywhere. In spite of the fact that the nineties have seen a dramatic and unprecedented escalation of warfare, after the 1992 elections everyone attempted to do business as usual. The sponsorship of cultural events, which are not expensive, formed an easy way to build a public corporation's image, and became part of the normalisation of business life.

Two Remarks on a Book

Odebrechts is a corporation engaged in this process of cultural and economic normalisation. In 1991 it sponsored the publication of a book by the then Director of the National Museum of Anthropology, Ana Maria Oliveira, until 1999 the Minister of Culture, and herself an anthropologist. Her book has several characteristics that are ethnographical about the politics of culture in the early nineties. Four or five years before 1991, the idea of having a major transnational company fund anything related to national culture would have appeared as treason. The book is a festival of wealth and prestige: it is signed by the President of the Odebrecht Foundation in Luanda, who praises both the book and the Company's own activities in the country. The Brazilian Ambassador reaffirms the pride of Brazilian African origins in his preface. A top Brazilian photographer, Mário Cravo Neto (whose inclusion expresses that it was produced without regard for expenses), did the full-page colour photographs for the book. With its high-quality printing and cloth binding, the book, which is supposed to portray Angolan cultural diversity through a presentation of the most significant objects from the NMA (National Museum of Anthropology), is not for general sale: the 3,000 copies of the first edition and the 3,000 copies of the second edition, the latter sponsored by the Bank of Angola after the author had become Vice-Minister of Culture, were intended to be given to distinguished guests.

Figure 4: 'Angola and the Expression of its Material Cultures'. (Photograph: Mário Cravo Neto).

Two comments of the author on the purposes of the book are, I think, extremely relevant. The first is that national patrimony had become subject to international robbery and smuggling and the book's publication provided a means of making Angolan art known worldwide, to prevent the easy trade of stolen objects in the African arts market. The most painful example of such illegal activity was the first object presented in the book, the Cokwé sculpture known as *The Thinker*, which became a national symbol after independence. The original was said to have dated from the nineteenth century, and was stolen in the 1980s. The photograph depicts a copy, based on the original. The objective of securing treasures that still existed is then immediately set forward, on the first pages. (At the same time, I for one find this hard to square with the fact that all copyright is owned by the Odebrechts Foundation, who solely decided on the circulation of the countrys images).

The second comment concerns the way the jacket of the book was explained to me. According to the author the jacket presents a survey of Angola, through national symbols to material objects representing each of its main socio-cultural areas. The author had worked on the jacket closely with the photographer and had relied on her experience as an exhibition curator, in order to create an image that would be immediately perceived as a synthesis of Angola. In other words, the visualisation of national culture was equated with a conceptual installation of artefacts.

Alongside this process, one should note that in contemporary visual culture such imaging activity is pursued with different intentions and results. On the one hand, Cokwé objects which were elected national symbols since the inception of the independent state are now presented as Cokwé again, even though still inscribed in the national iconography. On the other hand, by placing other objects near them the design of the jacket extends the status of national objects to other cultural items. This balancing process is not unaccompanied by other state-oriented practices in Angola, nor by everyday indeterminacy like the theft of national objects, which happen to be, more often than not, Cokwé artefacts.

Hence the reliance of local administrations on traditional authorities, the acknowledgement of different cultural identities within the nation (which provides for regional TV broadcasts in six different languages) and the already referred to process of cosmopolitanisation of Luanda, supported by an incipient democratic process that has provided for the existence of political parties other than that of the government, are significant factors in analysing the contemporary discussion of national identities.[5]

The above probably determines the arena that frames the recent demand for the repatriation of objects housed in the NMA to their Cokwé homeland, or more specifically to the Dundo National Museum, made by the Deputy of the Democratic Renovation Party in November 1997. Although the Angolan Constitution prohibits parties with an ethnic basis, the DRP (Democratic Renovation Party) is known as the Cokwé Party. The leader bears the traditional title of Supreme Chief or *Muatxissengue Ua Tembo,* and in public demonstrations is accompanied by the traditional authorities of the Lunda area. The claim for the return of objects was voiced at a national meeting in the context of the 'Culture in November' activities, and it expressed the feeling of abandonment experienced by both the Lundas and the Dundo Museum.

The central complaint regards the unfulfilled promise of the ENDIAMA (the national successor of the Diamang) to restore the Museum building. Their argument is that the Cokwé are, for a second time in their recent history, being dispossessed of their identity, an argument that is better understood if it is acknowledged that the Dundo was subjected to major changes during the last decade. From a population of 5,000 persons at the beginning of the 1980s the Dundo now supports between 60,000 to 80,000 persons. Such population growth is the result of creeping urbanisation, the joining of the villages in the area to the outskirts of the town, augmented by warfare, the immigration of Congo nationals, and to the arrival of diverse migrant diamond traders. These trends have been encouraged by legalised companies, international smuggling networks and by those followers of that romanticised tradition of gentlemen of fortune. The increase of population also relates to the growth of community-making processes, with seven or eight international local and sectarian religions having spread into the area. It is lso an effect on the unofficial diamond economy, which accounts for the large amounts of money circulating as well as for the loss of traditional authority and power in favour of what is commonly phrased as 'immorality and dissolution', or the power of dollars.

This contest over the property rights vested in material objects expressed by Cokwé representatives, which is just beginning, brings the Dundo Museum to the foreground of this debate.

Notes

1. An oral version of this text was first presented in February 1998 in the Seminar on 'Colonialisms, responses in the Longe Durée, held at the Department of Anthropology, University College, London, UK. I would like to acknowledge the organiser of the seminar, Prof. Mukulika Banerjee, and the author of the paper Prof. Mike Rowlands, for his precious remarks, as well s the participants in the seminar for the helpful discussion they provided. The paper was written as part of my doctoral research at the University of Coimbra, Portugal, under the supervision of Prof. Nélia Dias and Prof. Manuel Laranjeira, whom I also

acknowledge. The research was funded by the Ministry of Science and Technology, under the title *Science as Culture in the Portuguese-Angolan colonial Situation: the case of the Dundo Museum 1940- 1974*, and the code name of Praxis XXI PCSH/P/ANT/41/96.

2. See Appia (1992) for a critical account of this theory. Ravenhill (1996) shows how the tribe became an organising device in French colonial museography, thereby providing materiality to the concept.

3. In this sense, such discourse engages in an anti-conquest type of narrative in Prat's (1992) terms. Such a fact may account for the contemporary difficulty in distancing from it (see below).

4. Although I think these are immediate effects of Bastin's work I am not implying that they were intended to have led to such unpredictable results, nor do I imply any devaluation of its merits. I picture this as a common situation of non-scientific results of scientific practice.

5. A process which relates to the complex settings of identity discussion, such as those referred to by Karp (1992).

Bibliography

ABRANCHES, H. 1980. *Reflexões sobre Cultura Nacional.* 7**0**, Lisbon: Edições,

ABRANCHES, H. 1989. *Identidade e Património Cultural.* 7**0**, Lisbon: Edições.

ANDERSON, B. 1991 (1983). *Imagined Communities, Reflections on the Origin and Spread of Nationalism.* London and New York: Verso.

APPIA, K. 1997 (1992). *Na Casa de Meu Pai, África na Filosofia da Cultura.* Rio de Janeiro: Contraponto.

BASTIN, M. 1961. *Art Décoratif Tshokwe.* Lisbon: Publicações Culturais da Companhia de Diamantes de Angola.

BASTIN, M. 1982. *La Sculpture Tshokwe.* France: Alain et Françoise Chaffin.

CLIFFFORD, J. 1997, Museums as Contact Zones. In *Routes, Travel and Translation in the Late Twentieth Century.* Cambridge (Mass.) and London: Harvard University Press.

COOMBES, A. 1994, *Reinventing Africa. Museums, Material Culture and Popular Imagination in Victorian England.* New Haven: Yale University Press.

FREYRE, G. 1952. *Aventura e Rotina.* Lisbon: Livros do Brasil.

HANNERZ, U. 1991. Scenarios for Peripheral Cultures. In King, A. (ed), *Culture, Globalization and the World System.* New York and London: Macmillan Press.

KARP, I. 1992, Introduction: Museums and Communities: The Politics of Public Culture. In Karp, Kramer & Lavine (eds), *Museums and Communities, The Politics of Public Culture.* Washington: Smithsonian Institution Press.

KIRSHENBLATT-GIMBLETT, B. 1991. Objects of Ethnography. In Karp, Ivan & Lavine, Steven (eds), *Exhibiting Cultures, The Politics and Poetics of Museum Display.* Washington: Smithsonian Institution Press.

LATOUR, B. 1989 (1990). Joliot: a história e a física misturadas. In Serres, Michel (ed), *História das Ciências, vol. III: De Pasteur ao Computador.* Lisbon: Terramar. 131–55.

LATOUR, B. 1991 (1993). *We Have Never been Modern.* Harvester Wheatsheaf.

OLIVEIRA, A. 1994 (1991). *Angola e a Expressão da sua Cultura Material,* (ed.), Fundação Odebrechts. Luanda: Banco Nacional de Angola.

OLIVEIRA, J. 1954. *Uma Acção Cultural em África,* (2nd ed.). Lisbon.

MYERHOFF, B. 1986. Life is not Death in Venice: Its Second Life. In Tuner, V. & Bruner, E. (eds), *The Anthropology of Experience.* Urbana and Chicago: University of Illinois Press.

PRATT, M. 1992. *Imperial Eyes, Travel Writing and Transculturation.* London: Routledge.

RAVENHILL, P. 1996. The Passive Object and the Tribal Paradigm: Colonial Museography in French West Africa. In Arnoldi, Geary and Hardin (eds), *African Material Culture.* Bloomington and Indianapolis: Indiana University Press.

SÁ, V. de. 1997. *A Lunda, os Diamantes, A Endiama.* Luanda: Coedição Elo e Endiama.

VILHENA, E. de, 1955. *Aventura e Rotina (Crítica de uma crítica).* Lisbon.

Notes on Contributors

Margaret Birley is Acting Keeper of Musical Instruments at the Horniman Museum. She studied music at Oxford University and ethnomusicology at Goldsmiths College, University of London. She has undertaken fieldwork in the republic of the former Soviet Union and has published various articles on the history of the Horniman Museum's instrument collection. She has also contributed as an editor to the work of the International Committee for Musical Instrument Collections (CIMCIM) of the International Council of Museums.

Roger Cardinal is Professor of Literary and Visual Studies, Rutherford College, University of Kent. He is the joint editor of *The Cultures of Collecting* (1994), and *'The Artist Outsider: Creativity and the Boundaries of Culture* (1994). as well as the author of *Raw Creation: Outsider Art and Beyond* (1996).

Sarah Cheang is a D.Phil candidate in Art history at the University of Sussex. She is editor of the online publication *Sussex History of Art Research Publication (SHARP)*, in which she published the article *Memorials to the Missing: Commemorating the Indian Dead of World War One in Bodies, Texts, Arcives and Architectures* (2000).

Celina Jeffery studied Critical Museology at the University of Sussex, before becoming a doctoral candidate in Art History at the University of Essex. She is the author of *Leon Underwood's Collection of African Art* (2000).

Nicky Levell holds an MA in Critical Museology from the University of Sussex. She has been Acting Keeper of Anthropology and Non-Western Art, Brighton Museum and Art Gallery (1995-6), and is currently Curator of Collection History at the Horniman Museum (1996-). She is the author of *Oriental Visions: Exhibitions, Travel and Collecting in the Victorian Age* (2000) as well as various articles on the history of collecting, museology and European popular culture. She has curated *Cultural Encounter: Communicating Otherness* (Brighton 1996), and is currently curating a permenant gallery on the history of collecting at the Horniman Museum.

Keith Nicklin has been ethnographer in charge of Cross River State for the Nigerian National Commission for Museums and Monuments (1970-1978); Curator of the Powell-Cotton Museum (1980-1982); and Keeper of Ethnography at the Horniman Museum (1982-1995). He is currently

Visiting Curator of the Horniman Museum and Fellow of Eliot College, University of Kent. The most recent of his numerous publications is *Ekpu. The Oron Anscestor Figures of South Eastern Nigeria* (2000).

Nuno Porto is lecturer in Anthropology at the Museu Antropólogico, Universidade de Coimbra, Portugal. He is the author of *Angola a preto e branco* (1998), and curator of the exhibition by the same name. He has published various articles on the ethnography of the Dundo Museum, Angola and European Colonial Museology.

Anthony Shelton taught Critical Museology at the University of Sussex (1991-1998). He is currently Head of Collections (Research and Development), at the Horniman Museum, and Honorary Research Fellow in Anthropology, University College, London.

Ken Teague is Deputy Keeper and Curator of Asian Collections at the Horniman Museum. He has done extensive fieldwork in Nepal, Mongolia, Turkey and Uzbekistan. Apart from numerous articles his publications include *Mr Horniman and the Tea Trade* (1993), *Central Asian Metal Work* (1990); and *Nomads. Nomadic Material Culture in the Asian Collections of the Horniman Museum.* (2000). He is co-editor of *Souvenirs: The Material Culture of Tourism* (2000).

Louise Tythacott taught Critical Museology at the University of Sussex (1996). She is currently Head of the Asian, African, American and Oceanic Section of Liverpool Museum. She has written various papers on Asian and African art, and is presently completing a work on the ethnographic collections assembled by the French surrealists, *Surrealism and the Exotic.*

Andy West has held curatorial position at Liverpool Museum and has lectured at the University of Humberside, Hull. He currently works for Save the Children in Kunming, China. His publications include *The History of the Ethnography Collections of W.H. Lever* (1992), *The Ethnography of Curiosities: Being the Problem of Describing Lord Lever's 'Ethnographic' Collection* (1996), *The Business of Ethnography: W.H. Lever, Collecting and Colonialism* (1997), and *Transformations of the Tourist and Souvenir: The Travels and Collections of Philla Davis* (2000).